The Complete Book of
Self-Sufficiency

John Seymour

A DORLING KINDERSLEY BOOK

First published in Great Britain in 1975
This edition published 1996 by Dorling Kindersley Limited
9 Henrietta Street
London WC2E 8PS

Editorial Director Christopher Davis
Art Director Roger Bristow
Managing Editor Jackie Douglas
Text Editor David Reynolds
Designer Sheilagh Noble
Assistant Editor Sybil de Strother
Assistant Designer Christopher Meehan

Visit us on the World Wide Web at
http://www.dk.com

A CIP catalogue record for this book is available from the
British Library

ISBN 0–7513–0426–3

Typesetting by Diagraphic Typesetters Limited, London and
TJB Photosetting, London
Reproduction by Photoprint Plates Limited, Rayleigh
Printed and bound in Italy by Mondadori Editore, Verona

Contents

FOREWORD

This book first came out exactly twenty years ago, created by Dorling Kindersley, with a little help from me, but published by Faber and Faber. It is now being published for the first time by Dorling Kindersley.

The book has been translated into some eight or nine languages including, I was once told, Serbo-Croat and Japanese. Certainly the book has got about. I have travelled in at least a dozen countries since I wrote it (to say nothing of four continents) and in every one of them people have come up to me with their copy for me to sign. I have been delighted to find wine stains on the wine-making pages, fruit stains on the fruit bottling pages, blood on the butchering pages, milk stains on the cheese-making pages, and good honest dirt on the gardening pages. It is certainly a book that has been *used*.

I have read through the book carefully in the last couple of weeks to see where it could be improved, but I have not seen fit to turn it into the "*Even More Complete Book of Self-Sufficiency*". It is still complete enough for me. Of course I have learned a lot since I wrote it (when you cease learning things they take you away in a box), and I have changed the odd recipe here and there. I have never been much of a recipe man myself – I like to know how the process *works* and then leave little details like the exact quantities of this and that to common sense. (Which may explain a lot to people who have sampled the results of my very occasional forays into the culinary art.)

I still live a pretty self-sufficient life. I no longer grow my own wheat, not having enough land now, but Polly, my cow, provides me and the other people who live here, with all our milk, butter, cheese and yoghurt, to say nothing of a quarter of a ton of magnificent beef every year and enough glorious muck to keep a very large vegetable garden at the peak of fertility. The milk by-products provide most of the nourishment required for pigs, poultry, cats, and a dog – in fact Polly is the fountain of health and happiness in our little multi-species community. Would I have more time to write books if I did not have to milk a cow? Well, there are already too many books in this world, and I learn a lot from Polly who has a philosophy far sounder than that of many a PhD of my acquaintance.

There are very few processes described in this book that I have not performed myself: albeit, perhaps, some of them ineptly. Does this make me a Jack-of-all-trades and master of none? Well I'd rather be that than a person who can only do one thing. To me that would be Hell. I have embarked on many an enterprise without the faintest idea of how to do it – but I have always ended up with the thing done and with a great deal more knowledge than I had when I started.

Would I advise other people to follow this lifestyle? I wouldn't advise anybody to do anything. The purpose of this book is not to shape other people's lives but simply to help people to do things if they decide to. This way of life suits me – it has kept me fighting fit and at least partly sane into my eighty-second year, and it has prevented me from doing too much harm to our poor old planet.

I would like to acknowledge here the unfailing help I have had during the last two decades from Ms Angela Ashe, who has shared the trials and labours as well as the joys of this way of life, and also Mr Will Sutherland, who has come into partnership with us to start a school of self-sufficiency here in Ireland, to which all honest men, women and children are welcome, provided they can find the fees!

To people lucky enough to get their fair share of our planet, and who wish to follow something of the lifestyle described in this book, I would offer this advice: do not try to do everything at once. This is an organic way of life and organic processes tend to be slow and steady. Rome was not built in a day and Rome was probably not worth building. A sound self-sufficient smallholding certainly is.

I would also like to offer this motto: "I am only one. I can only do what one can do. But what one can do, I will do!"

Happy grub-grubbing! (Better than money-grubbing any day!)

John Seymour, May 1996

Killowen
New Ross
Co. Wexford
Ireland

The Way to Self-Sufficiency

The first questions we must answer are: What is this book about? What is self-sufficiency, and why do it?

Now self-sufficiency is not "going back" to some idealized past in which people grubbed for their food with primitive implements and burned each other for witchcraft. It is going *forward* to a new and better sort of life, a life which is more fun than the over-specialized round of office or factory, a life that brings challenge and the use of daily initiative back to work, and variety, and occasional great success and occasional abysmal failure. It means the acceptance of complete responsibility for what you do or what you do not do, and one of its greatest rewards is the joy that comes from seeing each job right through – from sowing your own wheat to eating your own bread, from planting a field of pig food to slicing a side of bacon.

Self-sufficiency does not mean "going back" to the acceptance of a lower standard of living. On the contrary, it is the striving for a higher standard of living, for food which is fresh and organically-grown and good, for the good life in pleasant surroundings, for the health of body and peace of mind which come with hard varied work in the open air, and for the satisfaction that comes from doing difficult and intricate jobs well and successfully.

A further preoccupation of the self-sufficient person should be the correct attitude to the land. If it ever comes to pass that we have used up all, or most of, the oil on this planet, we will have to reconsider our attitude to our only real and abiding asset – the land itself. We will one day have to derive our sustenance from what the land, unaided by oil-derived chemicals, can produce. We may not wish in the future to maintain a standard of living that depends entirely on elaborate and expensive equipment and machinery, but we will always want to maintain a high standard of living in the things that really matter – good food, clothing, shelter, health, happiness, and fun with other people. The land *can* support us, and it can do it without huge applications of artificial chemicals and manures and the use of expensive machinery. But everyone who owns a piece of land should husband that land as wisely, knowledgeably, and intensively as possible. The so-called "self-supporter" sitting among a riot of docks and thistles talking philosophy ought to go back to town. He is not doing any good at all, and is occupying land which should be occupied by somebody who can really use it.

Other forms of life, too, besides our own, should merit our consideration. Man should be a husbandman, not an exploiter. This planet is not exclusively for our own use. To destroy every form of life except such forms as are obviously directly of use to us is immoral, and ultimately, quite possibly, will contribute to our own destruction. The kind of varied, carefully thought-out, husbandry of the self-supporting holding fosters a great variety of life forms, and every self-supporter will wish to leave some areas of true wilderness on his holding, where wild forms of life can continue to flourish undisturbed and in peace.

And then there is the question of our relations with other people. Many people move from the cities back to the land precisely because they find city life, surrounded by people, too lonely. A self-supporter, living alone surrounded by giant commercial farms, may be lonely too; but if he has other self-supporters near him he will be forced into cooperation with them and find himself, very quickly, part of a living and warm community. There will be shared work in the fields, there will be relief milking and animal feeding duties when other people go on holiday, the sharing of child minding duties, there will be barn-raisings and corn-shuckings and celebrations of all kinds. This kind of social life is already beginning in those parts of Europe and North America where self-supporting individuals, or communities, are becoming common.

Good relations with the old indigenous population of the countryside are important too. In my area, the old country people are very sympathetic to the new "drop-ins." They rejoice to see us reviving and preserving the old skills they practised in their youth and they take pleasure in imparting them to us. They wax eloquent when they see the hams and flitches of bacon hung up in my chimney. "That's *real* bacon!" they say. "Better than the stuff we get in the shops. My mother used to make that when I was a boy – we grew all our own food then." "Why don't you grow it now?" I ask. "Ah – times have changed." Well, they are changing again.

Self-sufficiency is not only for those who have five acres of their own country. The man in a city apartment who learns how to mend his own shoes is becoming, to some extent, self-sufficient. Not only does he save money, he increases his own satisfaction and self-respect too. Man was not *meant* to be a one-job animal. We do not thrive as parts of a machine. We are intended by nature to be diverse, to do diverse things, to have many skills. The city person who buys a sack of wheat from a farmer on a visit to the countryside and grinds his own flour to make his own bread cuts out a lot of middle men and furthermore gets better bread. He gets good exercise turning the handle of the grinding machine too. And any suburban gardener can dig up some of that useless lawn and put some of those dreary hardy perennials on the compost heap and grow his own cabbages. A good sized suburban garden can practically keep a family. I knew a woman who grew the finest outdoor tomatoes I ever saw in a window-box twelve storeys up in a tower-block. They were too high up to get the blight.

So good luck and long life to all self supporters! And if every reader of this book learns something useful to him that he did not know before, and could not very easily find out, then I shall be happy and feel that the hard work that not only I as author have put into it, but also the hard-working and dedicated people who have done the very arduous and difficult work of putting it together, and illustrating it, have not worked in vain.

Man & his Environment

The true homesteader will seek to husband his land, not exploit it. He will wish to improve and maintain the "heart" of his land, its fertility. He will learn by observing nature that growing one crop only, or keeping one species of animal only, on the same piece of land is not in the natural order of things. He will therefore wish to nurture the animals and plants on his land to ensure the survival of the widest possible variety of natural forms. He will understand and encourage the interaction between them. He will even leave some areas of wilderness on his land, where wild forms of life can flourish. Where he cultivates he will always keep in mind the needs of his soil, considering each animal and each plant for what beneficial effect it might have on the land. Above all, he will realize that if he interferes with the chain of life (of which he is a part) he does so at his peril, for he cannot avoid disturbing a natural balance.

The Way to Self-Sufficiency

THE FIRST PRINCIPLES OF SELF-SUFFICIENCY

The only way that the homesteader can farm his piece of land as well and intensively as possible is to institute some variant of what was called "High Farming" in Europe in the last century. This was a carefully worked out balance between animals and plants, so that each fed the other: the plants feeding the animals directly, the animals feeding the soil with their manure and the land feeding the plants. A variety of both animals and plants were rotated about the same land so that each species took what it needed out and put what it had to contribute back, and the needs of the soil were kept uppermost always in the husbandman's mind. Each animal and crop was considered for what beneficial effect it might have on the soil.

If the same crop is grown on a piece of land year after year the disease organisms that attack that crop will build up in the area until they become uncontrollable. Nature abhors monoculture: any cursory inspection of a natural plant and animal environment will reveal a great variety of species. If one species becomes too predominant some pest or disease is sure to develop to strike it down. Man has managed to defy this law, to date, by the application of stronger and stronger chemical controls, but the pests (particularly the fast-evolving viruses) adapt very quickly to withstand each new chemical and to date the chemist has managed to keep only a short jump ahead of the disease.

The new homesteader will wish to husband his land in accordance with the principles of High Farming. He will have to substitute the labour of his hands for imported chemicals and sophisticated machinery. He will have to use his brain and his cunning to save the work of his hands. For instance, if he can get his animals to go out into his fields and consume their share of his crops there, then he will save himself the work of harvesting the crops for them and carrying them in. In other words, take the animals to the crops, not the crops to the animals. So also, if he can get the animals to deposit their dung on his land, then this will save him the labour of carrying the dung out himself. Thus the keeping of animals on limited free range will appeal to him: sheep can be "folded" on arable land (folding means penning animals on a small area of some fodder crop and moving the pen from time to time), chickens can be housed in arks that can be moved over the land so as to distribute the hens' manure while allowing the hens to graze fresh grass, and pigs can be kept behind electric fences which can also be easily moved. Thus the pigs harvest their food for themselves and also distribute their own manure. (To say nothing of the fact that pigs are the finest free cultivators that were ever invented! They will clear your land, and plough it, and dung it, and harrow it, and leave it nearly ready for you to put your seed in, with no more labour to you than the occasional shifting of an electric fence.)

Now the true husbandman will not keep the same species of animal on a piece of land too long, just as he will not grow the same crop year after year in the same place. He will follow his young calves with his older cattle, his cattle with sheep, his sheep with horses, while geese and other poultry either run free or are progressively moved over his grassland and arable (arable means land that gets ploughed and planted with crops as opposed to land that is grass all the time). All animals suffer from parasites and if you keep one species on one piece of land for too long there will be a build-up of parasites and disease organisms. As a rule the parasites of one animal do not affect another and therefore following one species with another over the land will eliminate parasites.

Also, the true husbandman will find that every enterprise on his holding, if it is correctly planned, will interact beneficially with every other. If he keeps cows their dung will manure the land which will provide food, not only for the cows, but for the humans and pigs also. The by-products of the milk of the cows (skimmed milk from butter making and whey from cheese making) are a marvellous whole food for pigs and poultry. The dung from the pigs and poultry helps grow the food for the cows. Chickens will scratch about in the dung of other animals and will salvage any undigested grain.

All crop residues help to feed the appropriate animals – and such residues as not even the pigs can eat they will tread into the ground, and activate with their manure, and turn into the finest *in situ* compost without the husbandman lifting a spade. All residues from slaughtered birds or animals go either to feed the pigs, or the sheep dogs, or to activate the compost heap. Nothing is wasted. Nothing is an expensive embarrassment to be taken away to pollute the environment. There should be no need of a dustman on the self-sufficient holding. Even old newspapers can make litter for pigs, or be composted. Anything that has to be burnt makes good potash for the land. Nothing is wasted – there is no "rubbish."

But before the potential self-supporter embarks on the pursuit of "true husbandry" he should acquaint himself with some of the basic laws of nature, so that he can better understand why certain things will happen on his holding and why other things will not.

THE FOOD CHAIN

Life on this planet has been likened to a pyramid: a pyramid with an unbelievably wide base and a small apex.

All life needs nitrogen, for it is one of the most essential constituents of living matter, but most creatures cannot use the free, uncombined, nitrogen which makes up a great part of our atmosphere. The base of our biotic pyramid, therefore, is made up of the bacteria that live in the soil, sometimes in symbiosis with higher plants, and have the power of fixing nitrogen from the air. The number of these organisms in the soil is unimaginably great: suffice it to say that there are millions in a speck of soil as big as a pin-head.

On these, the basic and most essential of all forms of life, lives a vast host of microscopic animals. As we work up the pyramid, or the food chain whichever way we like to consider it, we find that each superimposed layer is far less in number than the layer it preys upon. On the higher plants graze the herbivores. Every antelope, for example, must have millions of grass plants to support him. On the herbivores "graze" the carnivores. And every lion must have hundreds of antelopes to support him. The true carnivores are right at the apex of the biotic pyramid. Man is somewhere near the top but not at the top because he is an omnivore. He is one of those lucky animals that can subsist on a wide range of food: vegetable and animal.

Up and down the chain, or up and down between the layers of the pyramid, there is a vast complexity of inter-relationships. There are, for example, purely carnivorous micro-organisms. There are all kinds of parasitic and saprophitic organisms: the former live on their hosts and sap their strength, the latter live in symbiosis, or in friendly cooperation, with other organisms, animal or vegetable. We have said that the carnivores are at the apex of the food chain. Where in it stands a flea on a lion's back? Or a parasite in a lion's gut?

And what about the bacterium that is specialised (and you can bet there is one) to live inside the body of the lion flea? A system of such gargantuan complexity can best, perhaps, be understood by the utter simplification of the famous verse:

Little bugs have lesser bugs upon their backs to bite 'em,
And lesser bugs have lesser bugs and so ad infinitum!

This refers to parasitism alone of course, but it is note-worthy that all up and down the pyramid *everything* is consumed, eventually, by something else. And that includes us, unless we break the chain of life by the purely destructive process of cremation.

Now Man, the thinking monkey, has to interfere with this system (of which he should never forget that he is a part) but he does so at his peril. If we eliminate many carnivores among the larger mammals, the herbivores on which these carnivores preyed become overcrowded, overgraze, and create deserts. If, on the other hand, we eliminate too many herbivores the herbage grows rank and out of control and good pasture goes back to scrub and cannot, unless it is cleared, support many herbivores. If we eliminate every species of herbivore except one the grazing is less efficiently grazed. Thus sheep graze very close to the ground (they bite the grass off with their front teeth) while cows, which rip grass up by wrapping their tongues round it, like long grass. The hills produce more and better sheep if cattle graze on them too. It is up to Man the Husbandman to consider very carefully, and act very wisely, before he uses his powers to interfere with the rest of the biotic pyramid.

Plants, too, exist in great variety in natural environments and for very good reasons. Different plants take different things out of the soil, and put different things back. Members of the pea-bean-and-clover family, for example, have nitro-gen-fixing bacteria in nodules on their roots. Thus they can fix their own nitrogen. But you can wipe the clovers out of a pasture by applying artificial nitrogen. It is not that the clovers do not like the artificial nitrogen, but that you remove the "unfair advantage" that they had over the grasses (which are *not* nitrogen-fixing) by supplying the latter with plenty of free nitrogen and, being naturally more vigorous than the clovers, they smother them out.

It is obvious from observing nature that monoculture is not in the natural order of things. We can only sustain a one-crop-only system by adding the elements that the crop needs from the fertilizer bag and destroying all the crop's rivals and enemies with chemicals. If we wish to farm more in accordance with the laws and customs of nature we must diversify as much as we can, both with plants and animals.

THE SOIL

The basis of all life on Earth is, of course, the soil. But the soil that we terrestrial animals have to draw our subsistence from is the powdered rock that covers, fortunately for us, much of the land surface of the Earth. Some of this powder, or earth, was derived from the rock directly below it, some has been carried down by water from rock somewhere above it, some (such as the famous loess soil of North America and China) has been blown there by wind, and some dragged into its present position by glaciers in one or other of the ice ages. But however the soil got to where it is now, it was originally pulverized from the rock by agencies of weather. Frost splits rock, so does alternate intense heat and cold, water wears it, wind erodes it, and it is now known that bacteria and certain algae actually eat it; the hardest rock in the world will be ground down and eroded in time if it comes to the surface.

Newly-formed soil will have all the plant foods that were in the original rock, but it will completely lack one essential element – *humus*. It will not contain humus until life itself – that is, things that were living and have died and are in decay – puts it there. Only then does it become real complete soil, fit to grow the vegetation that sustains all animal life on land.

Because soil derives from many kinds of rock there are many varieties of soil. As we cannot always get exactly the kind of soil that we require, the husbandman must learn to make the best of the soil that he has. Depending on the size of their particles soils are classified as *light* or *heavy*, with an infinite range of gradations in between. Light means composed of large particles. Heavy means composed of small particles. Gravel can hardly be called soil but sand can, and pure sand is the lightest soil you can get. The kind of clay which is made of the very smallest particles is the

The Natural Cycle

Wild crops   Fruit and nuts   Grass   Wheat   Oats   Barley

Bees   Cows   Pigs   Sheep   Chickens

Manure/compost

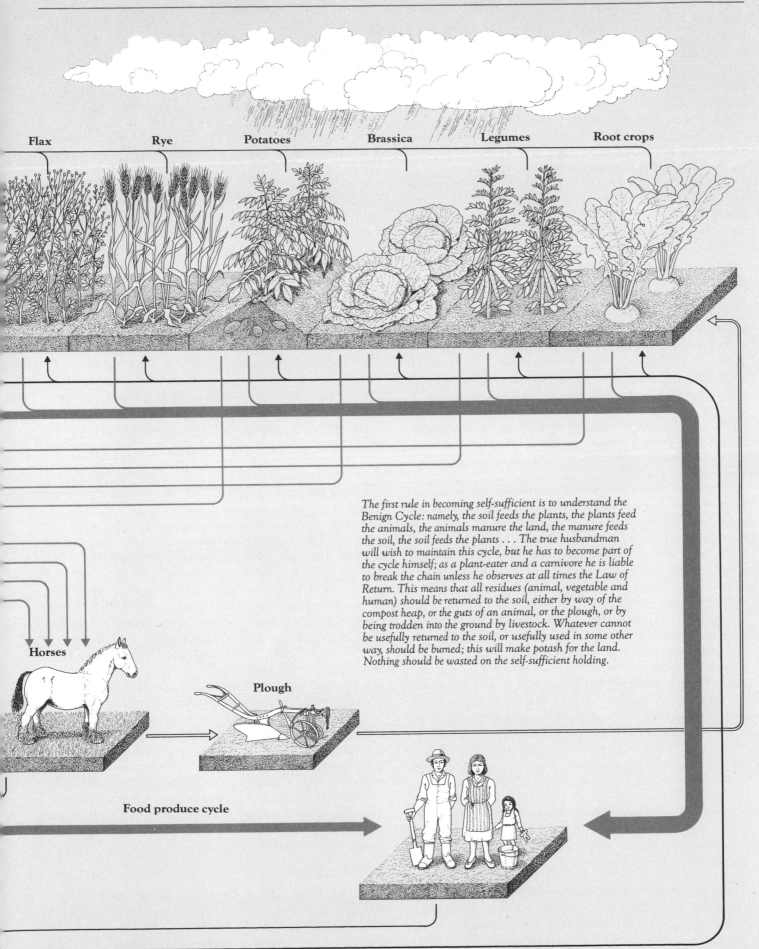

Flax   Rye   Potatoes   Brassica   Legumes   Root crops

The first rule in becoming self-sufficient is to understand the Benign Cycle: namely, the soil feeds the plants, the plants feed the animals, the animals manure the land, the manure feeds the soil, the soil feeds the plants . . . The true husbandman will wish to maintain this cycle, but he has to become part of the cycle himself; as a plant-eater and a carnivore he is liable to break the chain unless he observes at all times the Law of Return. This means that all residues (animal, vegetable and human) should be returned to the soil, either by way of the compost heap, or the guts of an animal, or the plough, or by being trodden into the ground by livestock. Whatever cannot be usefully returned to the soil, or usefully used in some other way, should be burned; this will make potash for the land. Nothing should be wasted on the self-sufficient holding.

Horses

Plough

Food produce cycle

Residue cycle

heaviest. The terms "light" and "heavy" in this context have nothing to do with weight but with the ease of working of the soil. You can dig sand, or otherwise work with it, no matter how wet it is, and do it no harm. Heavy clay is very hard to dig or plough, gets very puddingy and sticky, and is easily damaged by working it when it is wet.

What we call soil generally has a thickness to be measured in inches rather than feet. It merges below with the subsoil which is generally pretty humus-free but may be rich in mineral foods needed by plants. Deep-rooting plants such as some trees, lucerne or alfalfa, comfrey, and many herbs, send their roots right down into the subsoil, and extract these nutriments from it. The nature of the subsoil is very important because of its influence on drainage. If it is heavy clay, for example, then the drainage will be bad and the field will be wet. If it is sand, gravel, decayed chalk or limestone, then the field will probably be dry. Below the subsoil lies rock, and rock goes on down to the centre of the Earth. The rock, too, can affect drainage: chalk, limestone, sandstone and other pervious rocks make for good drainage: clay (geologists consider this a rock too), slate, mudstone, some shales, granite and other igneous rocks generally make for poor drainage. Badly-drained soils can always be drained – provided enough expenditure of labour and capital is put to doing it.

Let us now consider various types of soil:

Heavy clay This, if it can be drained and if it is worked with great care and knowledge, can be very fertile soil, at least for many crops. Wheat, oak trees, field beans, potatoes, and many other crops, do superbly on well-farmed clay. Farmers often refer to it as *strong* land. But great experience is needed to farm it effectively. This is because of the propensity of clay to "flocculate" – that is, the microscopic particles which make up clay gather together in larger particles. When this happens the clay is more easily worked, drains better, allows air to get down into it (an essential condition for plant growth), and allows the roots of plants to penetrate it more easily. In other words it becomes good soil. When it does the opposite of flocculate it "puddles" – that is, it forms a sticky mass, such as the potter uses to make his pots, becomes almost impossible to cultivate, and gets as hard as brick when it dries out. When it is in this condition the land forms big cracks and is useless.

Factors which cause clay to flocculate are alkalinity rather than acidity, exposure to air and frost, incorporation of humus, and good drainage. Acidity causes it to puddle, so does working it while wet. Heavy machines tend to puddle it. Clay must be ploughed or dug when in exactly the right condition of humidity, and left strictly alone when wet.

Clay can always be improved by the addition of humus (compost, "muck" or farmyard manure, leaf-mould, green manuring: any vegetable or animal residue), by drainage, by ploughing it up at the right time and letting the air and frost get to it (frost separates the particles by forcing them

apart), by liming if acid, even, in extreme cases, by incorporating sand with the clay. Clay soil is "late" soil, which means it will not produce crops early in the year. It is difficult soil. It is not "hungry" soil – that is, if you put humus in it the humus will last a long time. It tends to be rich in potash and is often naturally alkaline in which case it does not need liming.

Loam Loam is intermediate between clay and sand, and has many gradations of heaviness or lightness. You can have a very heavy loam and a very light loam. A medium loam is perhaps the perfect soil for most kinds of farming. Most loam is a mixture of clay and sand, although some loams probably have particles all of the same size. If loam (or any other soil) lies on a limestone or chalk rock it will probably be alkaline and will not need liming, although this is not always the case: there are limestone soils which, surprisingly, do need liming. Loam, like every other kind of soil, will always benefit by humus addition.

Sand Sandy soil, or the lighter end of the spectrum of heavy-light soils, is generally well-drained, often acid (in which case it will need liming) and often deficient in potash and phosphates. It is "early" soil – that is, it warms up very quickly after the winter and produces crops early in the year. It is also "hungry" soil; when you put humus into it the humus does not last long. In fact, to make sandy soil productive you must put large quantities of organic manure into it and inorganic manure gets quickly washed away from it. Sandy soils are favoured for market gardening, being early and easy to work and very responsive to heavy dressings of manure. They are good soils for such techniques as folding sheep or pigs or other animals on the land. They are good for wintering cattle on because they do not "poach" like heavy soils do (i.e. turn into a quagmire when trodden). They recover quickly from treading when under grass. But they won't grow as heavy crops of grass or other crops as heavier land. They dry out very quickly and suffer from drought more than clay soils do.

Peat Peat soils are in a class of their own but unfortunately are fairly rare. Peat is formed of vegetable matter which has been compressed in unaerobic conditions (i.e. under water) and has not rotted away. Sour wet peatland is not much good for farming, although such soil, if drained, will grow potatoes, oats, celery and certain other crops. But naturally drained peatlands are, quite simply, the best soils in the world. They will grow *anything,* and grow it better than any other soil. They don't need manure, they *are* manure. Happy is the self-supporter who can get hold of such land for his crops are most unlikely to fail.

MANURING

Plants require traces of almost all the elements, but the elements that they need in large quantities are: nitrogen, phosphorus, potassium and calcium.

Nitrogen, as we have seen, can be fixed from the

atmosphere by nitrogen-fixing bacteria, and the organic grower is most apt to rely on this source. However, to ensure a really good supply, animal dung should be added to the soil and this will release nitrogen as it decays.

Phosphorus is probably present in the soil, but perhaps it is not being released in sufficient quantities. If analysis shows a serious phosphate deficiency then phosphorus should be added. Phosphorus deficiency may be seen sometimes by a purplish discoloration in seedlings, followed by yellowing as the plant gets older, stunted growth and lateness in coming to maturity. "Basic slag" is a common phosphatic fertilizer: it is the ground-up limestone lining of blast-furnaces and is thus a by-product of the steel industry. The word "basic" here means alkaline – it helps to correct acidity as lime does. Unfortunately new methods of steel making are reducing the supply. Ground rock phosphate is slower acting than slag, but it is longer lasting, and many organic growers think better. Superphosphate is rock phosphate (or bones) that have been dissolved in sulphuric acid; it is quick-acting but expensive and it may harm the soil organisms.

Potassium deficiency may show itself by yellowing of leaf-tips, and by a weakness in the stems of cereals – they fall down in wind or rain. There are huge rock-potash deposits in many parts of the world and until these are exhausted we can correct potassium deficiency by applying this material. Clay soil is seldom deficient in potassium.

Calcium deficiency causes acid soil and can lead to malformation of plants. In any case lime in some form or another will probably be added by the husbandman to soils which are acid, and calcium deficiency will then not occur. Lime can be added as lumps of lime or chalk (very slow acting), as ground lime or chalk (fairly slow acting), as quick lime or chalk (quick acting), and as slaked lime or chalk (quick acting). Quick lime, however, will burn plants and soil organisms; slaked lime is benign.

There are other elements in which your soil may be deficient. If, despite the addition of the elements listed above, you find that plants or animals are still sickly then you may suspect such things as boron deficiency, or deficiencies of other of these so-called "trace elements," and you should call in expert advice.

But if your land has had proper additions of compost, or farmyard manure or the dung of animals added direct, or seaweed (which has in it *every* element), it is most unlikely to be deficient in anything. By getting your soil analysed when you take it over, and adding once and for all whatever element the analysis shows the soil to be deficient in, and thereafter farming in a sound organic way, the "heart" (fertility) of your land should increase continually until it is at a very high level. There should be no need to spend any further money at all on "fertilizers". And, very often, if land is virgin, or if it has been properly farmed in the past, you may not even need to get it analysed.

THE ECOLOGICALLY SOUND HOLDING

One of the chief features of the High Farming era of eighteenth-century England was the famous "Norfolk Four Course Rotation." It was an ecologically sound system of husbandry, and it still remains a model for the productive growing of a variety of crops in both large and small-scale farming. The Norfolk Four Course Rotation worked like this:

1 One-year Ley A Ley is grass-and-clover sown for a temporary period. The grass-and-clover was grazed off by stock and the purpose of it was to increase the fertility of the land by the nitrogen fixed in the root nodules of the clover, by the dung of the grazing animals, and ultimately by the mass of vegetation ploughed into the land when the Ley was ploughed up.

2 Root Break The crops in the Root Break might have been turnips or swedes to be fed to cattle, sheep or pigs, potatoes to be fed mostly to humans, mangolds for cattle, and various kinds of kale – the latter not actually "roots" of course but taking the same place in the Root Break. The effect of the Root Break was to increase the fertility of the soil, because nearly all the farmyard manure produced on the farm was applied to the root crop, and to "clean" (make weed-free) the land. Root crops are "cleaning-crops" because, by being planted in rows, they have to be hoed several times. The third effect of the Root Break was to produce crops which stored the summer's growth for winter feeding.

3 Winter Cereal Break This was wheat, beans, barley, oats or rye sown in the autumn. It "cashed" the fertility put into the land by the Ley and the Roots, benefited from the cleanliness of the land after Roots, and was the farmer's chief "cash crop" – the crop from which he made his money. The beans, however, were for feeding to horses and cattle.

4 Spring Cereal Break This was possibly spring-sown wheat but it was more likely to be barley. After the barley had been drilled, grass-and-clover seed was *undersown* – that is, broadcast on the ground along with the cereal seed. As the barley grew, the grass-and-clover grew and when the barley was harvested a good growth of grass-and-clover was left to be grazed off next spring and summer, or to be cut for hay and grazed the following winter too. The barley went principally to feed stock but the best of it went to be malted for beer. The oats and barley straw was fed to the cattle, the wheat straw went under their feet to provide all that vast tonnage of farmyard manure (the best compost that ever was invented), rye straw was used for thatching, the roots were mostly fed to the cattle or to the sheep, and wheat, malting barley, beef, and wool went off to be sold to the city man. In the late eighteenth and nineteenth centuries, land properly managed in this way often grew two tons of wheat to the acre and this with *no* input of oil-derived chemicals whatever. There weren't any.

Now we can emulate this ecologically sound system, changing it to suit our different needs. We may not wish to live primarily on the bread, beef and beer of the eighteenth-

The Seasons

Early spring

Plough your land when the winter's frosts have broken up the soil. Prepare the fields to be sown with spring crops by harrowing with discs and spikes, and add lime or phosphate if your soil needs it. Make the most of shooting game before the close seasons begin. Be ready for lambing to begin; early spring is the ideal time for then the lambs can grow with the grass.

Late spring

Broadcast your seed or drill it into the earth, and be ready to combat the weeds that will race the young shoots to meet the sun. Plant your early potatoes under glass to force them on, and use cloches to protect melons and other squashes from late frosts. This is a good time for brewing beer in preparation for such thirsty jobs as shearing and haymaking later on. Mill some grain every month of the year so that you always have fresh flour.

Early summer

In early summer you have the delightful job of shearing your sheep. Wool from five of them will clothe a large family. With the summer flush of grass your cows will pour out milk and you should make butter nearly every day. Store some of your milk for the winter by making plenty of cheese. In midsummer comes the back-breaking, but satisfying, business of haymaking. You will need help from your friends and neighbours and you will all need plenty of home brew.

Late summer

The wheat harvest in late summer is the crown of the year. Again you will need help from your friends, and again you will deserve to celebrate for you should have earned yourself a year's supply of bread. Orchard fruit, soft fruit, nuts, mushrooms and wild berries are gathered, and go into pots or pickle jars to be stored against winter scarcity. Wine-making continues through this time, and the last of the green tomatoes go for chutney.

Autumn

Autumn is the time to harvest root crops, and clamp them or store them in root cellars. Plant winter wheat, broad and field beans. The sap is down in the trees which makes this an ideal time to fell those which have reached maturity. At the same time haul out wood which has fallen before it gets wet and use it for firewood. In the late autumn your barley is ready for malting, and you should have time to spin wool and the year's harvest of flax as well.

Winter

In midwinter, when the leaves are off the trees, you can build new hedges and rebuild old ones, make and repair fences, gates and hurdles, sharpen and restore the implements on your holding. The weather will be cold enough for killing and hanging beef and mutton, and early in the New Year is the best time for slaughtering your baconers. Bacon and ham can be salt-pickled in brine, sweet-pickled, or dry salted and carried to the smokehouse. Above all, this is the time of year for you to enjoy the fruits of your labours.

century Englishman. We may need more dairy products: butter, cheese and milk, more vegetables, a greater variety of food altogether. Also we have new techniques: new crops such as Jerusalem artichokes, fodder radish, fodder beet, maize in nothern climates, and devices such as the electric fence, which widen our possible courses of action.

Now whether our would-be self-supporter has nothing more than a back garden, or perhaps a city allotment, or whether he has say a hundred acre farm, or whether he is part of a community owning a thousand acres, the principles he should follow are the same. He should try to work with Nature, not against her, and he should, as far as he can while still serving his own ends, emulate Nature in his methods. Thus if he is to improve and maintain the heart of his land he should remember:

1 Monoculture, or the growing of the same crop on land year after year should be avoided. Disease organisms which attack any particular crop always build up in land on which that crop is grown year after year. Also each crop has different requirements from the soil and its residues return different materials to the soil.

2 The keeping of one species of animal on the soil and one only should be avoided, for much the same reasons as the reasons against crop monoculture. The old High Farming practitioners in England used to say:"A full bullock yard makes a full stack yard." In other words, the dung from the animals is good for the soil. Mixed stocking is always better than mono-stocking, and rotational grazing is the best of all: the penning or folding of a species of animal over the land so that the animals leave their droppings (and the inevitable eggs of parasites) behind and so break the lifecycle of the parasites. Following one species with another in such a rotation should be practised wherever possible.

3 To grow "leys," graze them, and ultimately plough them in.

4 To practise "green manuring." That is, if you don't want to grow some crop to graze off or feed off to animals, grow the crop anyway and then plough it in, or, better still, work it in with discs or other instruments.

5 To avoid ploughing too much or too deep. To bury the topsoil and bring the subsoil to the surface is not good. On the other hand, chisel ploughing – the cutting of furrows in the soil by dragging knives through it – does not invert the soil, helps drainage, breaks "pans" (hard layers under the surface) and can only do good.

6 To suffer not his land to remain bare and exposed to the weather more than absolutely necessary. When it is covered with vegetation, even with "weeds," it will not erode or deteriorate. If left bare, it will. A growing crop will take up and store the nitrogen and other elements of the soil and release them when it rots down. In bare soil many soluble plant-foods are "leached-out," or washed away.

7 To attend to drainage. Waterlogged soil is no-good soil and will deteriorate unless, of course, you are growing rice, or keeping water-buffalo.

8 To observe, at all times, the Law of Return. All crop and animal residues should be returned to the soil. If you sell anything off the holding then you should import something of equal manurial value back on to it. The Law of Return should apply to human excrement too.

Now if the Law of Return is properly observed it is theoretically possible to maintain, if not increase, the fertility of a piece of land without animals at all. Careful composting of vegetable residue is necessary, but it is noteworthy that on holdings where no animals are kept, but a high standard of fertility is maintained, almost always vegetable matter is brought in from outside the holding, and very often other high-energy substances, such as compost-activator, too. Seaweed, leaf-mould from woods, dead leaves from city street cleaning services, waste vegetables from greengrocers, straw or spoiled hay, nettles or bracken mown on common ground or waste ground or neighbours' land: all such inputs of vegetable residues are possible, and will keep up the fertility of land which has no animals. It is difficult to see *why* putting vegetable matter into animals and then returning it to the land as shit should be better than putting it direct on to the land, but it is demonstrably so. There is no doubt about it, as any husbandman with any experience knows, but there is some potent magic that transmutes vegetable residues into manure of extraordinary value by putting it through the guts of an animal. But when it is realized that animals and plants have evolved *together* on this planet perhaps this is not surprising. Nature does not seem to show any examples of an animal-free vegetable environment. Even the gases inhaled and exhaled by these two different orders of life seem to be complementary: plants inhale carbon-dioxide and exhale oxygen, animals do the opposite.

VEGETARIAN OR NON-VEGETARIAN

To be or not to be vegetarian: this is the argument that could (but mustn't) split the Organic Movement. Now there is not the slightest reason why vegetarians and non-vegetarians should not live perfectly happily side by side. The vegetarians say, on their side, that it takes so many units of vegetable protein fed to an animal to produce one unit of protein in the form of meat. Therefore it would be better for humans to eliminate animals and eat the vegetable protein direct. The non-vegetarians point out that the units of protein that are not directly turned into meat are not wasted: they are returned to the soil again in a transmuted form to improve its fertility and grow more crops. The vegetarians point out that it is cruel to kill animals. The non-vegetarians point out that *some* factor has got to control the population-increase rate of every species: either predators (such as non-vegetarians!), disease, or famine, and of these, predators are possibly the most humane. Vegetarianism seems to be almost wholly an urban, or big-city, phenomenon, and is possibly due to people having been cut off from animals for so long that they tend to anthropomorphism. The humane non-vegetarian says (and I am one) that animals should be kept in the conditions most nearly approaching those for which they were evolved as possible, treated humanely and subjected to no cruelties and indignities, and, when their time comes, killed instantly and with no long journeys to far-away markets or abattoirs. This is perfectly possible on the self-supporting holding, and the animal need have no inkling that anything is going to happen to it.

Having said all this I will now say that it is perfectly possible to live a self-sufficient existence on an animal-free holding, and that it is perfectly possible to live healthily on a meat-free diet. It is also possible to do the opposite.

THE ONE ACRE HOLDING

Everyone will have an entirely different approach to husbanding his land, and it is unlikely that any two small-holders with one acre each will adopt the same plan or methods. Some people like cows, other people are afraid of them. Some people like goats, other people cannot keep them out of the garden (I never could and I don't know many people who can). Some people will not kill animals and have to sell their surplus stock off to people who will kill them, others will not sell surplus stock off at all because they know that the animals will be killed. Some people are happy to keep more stock than their land can support and to buy in fodder from outside, while other people regard this as contrary to the principles of self-sufficiency.

Myself, if I had an acre of good well-drained land I think I would keep a cow and a goat, a few pigs and maybe a dozen hens. The goat would provide me with milk when the cow was dry. I might keep two or more goats in fact. I would have the cow (a Jersey) to provide me and the pigs with milk, but more important I would keep her to provide me with heaps and heaps of lovely manure. For if I was to derive any sort of living from that one acre, without the application of a lot of artificial fertilizer, it would have to be heavily manured.

Now the acre would only just support the cow and do nothing else, so I would, quite shamelessly, buy in most of my food for the cow from outside. I would buy all my hay, plenty of straw (unless I could cut bracken on a nearby common), all my barley meal and some wheat meal, and maybe some high protein in the form of bean meal or fish meal (although I would aim to grow beans).

It will be argued that it is ridiculous to say you are self-supporting when you have to buy in all this food. True, you would grow much of the food for cows, pigs, and poultry: fodder beet, mangolds, kale, "chat" (small) potatoes, comfrey, lucerne or alfalfa, and all garden produce not actually eaten by people. But you would still have to buy say a ton or a ton and a half of hay a year and say a ton a year of grain of different sorts including your own bread

wheat, and a ton or two of straw. For I would not envisage growing wheat or barley on such a small area as an acre, preferring to concentrate on dearer things than cereals, and things that it was more important to have fresh. Also the growing of cereals on very small acreages is often impossible because of excessive bird damage, although I have grown wheat successfully on a garden scale.

The big question here is – a cow or no cow? The pros and cons are many and various. In favour of having a cow is the fact that nothing keeps the health of a family – and a holding – at a high level better than a cow. If you and your children have ample good, fresh, unpasteurized, unadulterated milk, butter, butter-milk, soft cheese, hard cheese, yoghourt, sour milk and whey, you will simply be a healthy family and that is an end to it. A cow will give you the complete basis of good health. If your pigs and poultry, also, get their share of the milk by-products, they too will be healthy and will thrive. If your garden gets plenty of cow manure, that too will be healthy and thrive. This cow will be the mainspring of all your health and well-being.

On the other hand, the food that you buy in for this cow will cost you perhaps two hundred pounds a year. Against this you can set whatever money you would pay for dairy produce in that year for yourself and your family (and if you work that out you will find it to be quite substantial), plus the increased value of the eggs, poultry-meat and pig-meat that you will get (you can probably say that, in value, a quarter of your pig meat will be creditable to the cow), plus the ever-growing fertility of your land. But a serious *contra* consideration is that you will have to milk the cow. Twice a day for at least ten months of the year you will have to milk the cow. It doesn't take very *long* to milk a cow (perhaps eight minutes), it is very pleasant when you really know how to do it and if she is a quiet nice cow, but you will have to *do* it. So the buying of a cow is a very important step, and you shouldn't do it unless you do not intend to go away very much, or you can make arrangements for somebody else to relieve you with milking. Of course, if you only have a budgerigar somebody has got to feed it.

So let us plan our one acre holding on the assumption that we are going to keep a cow.

One acre holding with a cow

Half the land will be put down to grass, leaving half an acre arable (I am not allowing for the land on which the house and buildings stand). Now the grass half could remain permanent pasture and never be ploughed up at all, or it could be rotated by ploughing it up say every four years. If the latter is done it were better done in strips of a quarter of the half acre each, so each year you grass down an eighth of an acre of your land. Thus there is some freshly-sown pasture every year, some two year-old ley, some three-year-old ley and some four-year-old ley. The holding will be more productive if you rotate your pasture thus every four years.

The One Acre Holding

If you had one acre of good well-drained land, you might choose to use all of it to grow fruit and vegetables. Myself, I would divide it in half and put half an acre down to grass on which I would graze a cow, and perhaps a goat to give milk during the short periods when the cow would be dry, a sow for breeding and a dozen chickens. I would admittedly have to buy in food from outside to feed these animals through the winter, but this is preferable to buying in dairy products and meat, which would be the alternative. My remaining half-acre I would divide into four plots for intensive vegetable production, devoting a plot each to potatoes, pulses (peas and beans), brassica (cabbage family) and roots. I would divide the grass half-acre into four plots as well and rotate the whole holding every year. This means I would be planting a grass plot every year and it would stay grass until I ploughed it up four years later. I would build a cowshed for the cow, because I would not have enough grass to keep her outdoors all year. I would have a greenhouse for tomatoes and hives for bees and I would plant a vegetable patch with extra household vegetables, herbs and soft fruit.

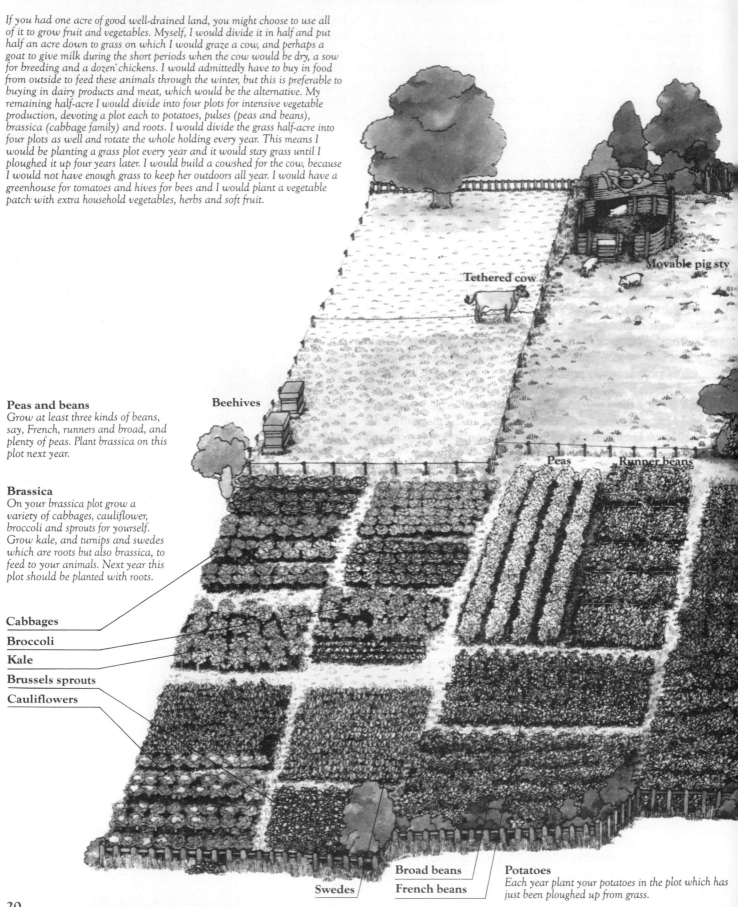

Movable pig sty

Tethered cow

Beehives

Peas

Runner beans

Peas and beans
Grow at least three kinds of beans, say, French, runners and broad, and plenty of peas. Plant brassica on this plot next year.

Brassica
On your brassica plot grow a variety of cabbages, cauliflower, broccoli and sprouts for yourself. Grow kale, and turnips and swedes which are roots but also brassica, to feed to your animals. Next year this plot should be planted with roots.

Cabbages

Broccoli

Kale

Brussels sprouts

Cauliflowers

Swedes

Broad beans

French beans

Potatoes
Each year plant your potatoes in the plot which has just been ploughed up from grass.

A half-acre of grass
Your half-acre of grass will feed your cow all through the summer. Let your hens run on it and give them a movable chicken ark. When you want to plough up your annual eighth of an acre, put the pigs on it and let them do the work for you.

Vegetable patch
In your home vegetable patch plant extra vegetables for your own consumption. Spinach, carrots, lettuce, celery, leeks and onions, when added to your brassica, pulses and potatoes should give you a varied diet. Plant a herb garden near the kitchen and sunflowers so you can press your own oil.

Movable chicken ark

Greenhouse
Tool shed
Cold frames
Cowshed

Compost heap

Fruit trees

Potatoes

Carrots

Sunflowers
Herbs
Strawberries
Currants

Leeks   Onions

Beetroot

Roots
Grow roots to feed your animals in winter, especially mangolds and fodder beet, where the brassica were last year. Next year this plot will be grassed.

Fodder beet

Rhubarb   Raspberries

The Way to Self-Sufficiency

The holding may break naturally into half: for example, an easily-worked half acre of garden, and a half acre of roughish pasture. You will begin then by ploughing up or pigging (allowing pigs to root it up behind an electric fence) or rotovating half of your holding. This land you will put down to a grass-and-clover-and-herb mixture. If you sow the seed in the autumn you can winter your cow indoors on bought hay and hope for grazing next spring. If your timetable favours your sowing in the spring, and if you live in a moist enough climate to do so, then you will be able to do a little light grazing that summer. It is better *not* to cut hay the first summer after spring-sowing of grass, so just graze it lightly with your little cow; at the first sign of "poaching" (destruction of grass by treading) take her away. Better still, tether your cow, or strip-graze behind an electric fence. Just allow the cow to have, say, a sixth part of the grass at one time, leave her on that for perhaps a week, then move her to the next strip. The length of time she stays on one strip must be left to your common sense (which you must develop if you are to become a self-supporter). The point about strip-grazing is that grass grows better and produces more if it is allowed to grow for as long as possible before being grazed or cut, then grazed or cut right down, then rested again. If it is grazed down all the time it never really has a chance to develop its root system. In such super-intensive husbandry as we are envisaging now it is essential to graze as carefully as possible.

Tether-grazing, on such a small area, might well be better than electric fencing. A little Jersey quickly gets used to being tethered and this was, indeed, the system that they were developed for on the island of Jersey, where they were first bred. I so unequivocably recommend a Jersey to the one acre man, incidentally, because I am convinced that for this sort of purpose she is without any peer. I have tried Dexters, with complete lack of success, but if you *really* know of a Dexter that gives anything like a decent amount of milk (my two gave less than a goat), is quiet and amenable, then go ahead and get a Dexter and good luck to you. But remember, a well-bred-Jersey gives plenty of milk which is quite simply the richest in butter-fat of any milk in the world, she is small, so docile that you will have trouble resisting taking her into the house with you, moderate in her eating demands, pretty, lovable, healthy, and very hardy.

Now your half acre of grass, once established, should provide your cow with nearly all the food she needs for the summer months. You are unlikely to get any hay off it as well, but if you *did* find that the grass grew away from the cow then you could cut some of it for hay.

The remaining half of your holding – the arable half – will then be farmed as a highly intensive garden. It will be divided, ideally, into four plots, around which all the annual crops that you want to grow, will follow each other in strict rotation. (I will discuss this rotation in detail in the section Food from the Garden, pp 160-171). The only difference that you will have to make in this rotation is that every year you will have to grass a quarter down, and every year plough a quarter of your grassland up. I suggest that your potatoes come after the newly-ploughed bit. The rotation will thus be: *grass (for four years) – potatoes – pea-and-bean family – brassica (cabbage family) – roots – grass again (for four years)*.

To sow autumn-sown grass after your roots, you will have to lift them early. In a temperate climate it would be quite practicable to do this; in countries with more severe winters it might be necessary to wait until the following spring. In areas with dry summers, unless you have irrigation, it would probably be better to sow in the autumn. In some climates (dry summers and cold winters) it might be found best to sow your grass in the late summer after the pea- and-bean break instead of after the root break, for the peas-and-beans are off the ground earlier than the roots. It might then pay you to follow the grass with potatoes, and your succession could be like this: *grass (for four years) – potatoes – brassica (cabbage family) – roots – pea-and-bean family – grass (for four years)*.

A disadvantage of this might be that the brassica, following main-crop potatoes, might have to wait until the summer following the autumn in which the potatoes were lifted before they could be planted. When brassica are planted after pea-and-bean family they can go in immediately, because the brassica plants have been reared in a nursery-bed and it is not too late in the summer to transplant them after the peas and beans have been cleared. But potatoes cannot be lifted (main crop can't anyway) until the autumn, when it is too late to plant brassica. Actually, with this regime you will be able to plant some of your brassica that first summer, after early potatoes. Or if you grow only earlies, you may get the lot in. One possibility would be to follow the potatoes immediately with brassica (thus saving a year) by lifting some earlies very early and planting immediately with the earliest brassica, then following each lifting of potatoes with more brassica, ending with spring cabbages after the main crop have come out. This would only be possible in fairly temperate climates though.

All this sounds complicated, but it is easier to understand when you *do* it than when you talk about it. And consider the advantages of this sort of rotation. It means that a quarter of your arable land is newly-ploughed-up four-year-ley every year: intensely fertile because of the stored-up fertility of all that grass, clover, and herbs that have just been ploughed in to rot, plus the dung of your cow for four summers. It means that because your cow is inwintered, on bought-in hay, and treading and dunging on bought-in straw, you will have an enormous quantity of marvellous *muck* to put on your arable land. It means that all the crop residues that you cannot consume go to help feed the cow, or the pigs or poultry, and I would be very surprised if, after following this regime for a few years, you did not find that your acre of land increased enormously in fertility, and that it was producing more *food*, for humans, than many a ten acres farmed on ordinary commercial lines.

You may complain that by having half your acre down to grass you thus confine your gardening activities to a mere half acre. But actually half an acre is quite a lot, and if you garden it really well it will grow more food for you than if you "scratch" over a whole acre. And the effect of being under grass, and grazed and dunged, for half its life, will enormously increase the fertility of it. I believe you will grow more actual vegetables than you would on the whole acre if you had no cow, or grass break.

We will discuss the treatment of the various kinds of stock, and of the crops, in the appropriate sections of this book, but there are a few general remarks to make about this particular situation. First, the cow will not be able to be out of doors all the year. On such a small acreage she would poach it horribly. She should spend most of the winter indoors, only being turned out during the daytime in dry weather to get a little exercise and fresh air. Cows do not really benefit by being out in all weathers in the winter time, although they put up with it. They are better for the most part kept in, where they make lovely manure for you, and your cow will have plenty of greenstuffs and roots that you will grow for her in the garden. In the summer you will let her out, night and day, for as long as you find the pasture stands up to it. You could keep the cow on "deep litter": that is, straw which she would dung on and turn into good manure, and you would put more clean straw on it every day. I have milked a cow for years like this and the milk was perfect, made good butter and cheese, and kept well.

Or you could keep the cow on a concrete floor (insulated if possible), giving her a good bed of straw every day and removing the soiled straw, and putting it carefully on the muck-heap – that fount of fertility for everything on your acre – every day. You would probably find that your cow did not need hay at all during the summer, but she would be entirely dependent on it right throughout the winter, and you could reckon on having to buy her at least a ton. If you wished to rear her yearly calf until he reached some value you would need perhaps half a ton more hay too.

Pigs you would have to be prepared to confine in a house for at least part of the year (and you would need straw for them). This is because on a one acre holding you are unlikely to have enough fresh land to keep them healthy. The best thing you could have for them would be a movable house with a strong movable fence outside it, or you could have a permanent pig-sty as well. But the pigs would have a lot of outdoor work to do: they would spend part of their time ploughing up your eighth of an acre of grassland; they could run over your potato land after you had lifted the crop; they could clear up after you had lifted your roots, or after you had lifted any crop. But they could only do this if you had time to let them do it. Sometimes you would be in too much of a hurry to get the next crop in. As for their food, you would have to buy in some corn, barley, or maize. This, supplemented with the skimmed milk and whey you would have from your cow, plus a share of the garden produce and such specially grown fodder crops as you could spare the land for, would keep them excellently. If you could find a neighbour who would let you use his boar I would recommend that you kept a sow and bred from her. She might well give you twenty piglets a year. Two or three of these you would keep to fatten for your bacon and ham supply, the rest you would sell as "weaners" (piglets from eight to twelve weeks old, depending on the requirements of your particular market), and they would probably fetch enough money to pay for every scrap of food you had to buy for them, the poultry, and the cow too. If you could not get the service of a boar you would probably buy weaners yourself – just enough for your own use – and fatten them.

Poultry could be kept on the Balfour method (described on p. 126), in which case they would stay for years in the same corner of your garden. Or better in my opinion, they could be kept in movable arks on the land. They could then be moved over the grassland, where by their scratching and dunging they would do it good. I would not recommend keeping very many. A dozen hens should give you enough eggs for a small family, with a few occasionally to sell or give away in the summer time. You would have to buy a little corn for them, and in the winter some protein supplement unless you could grow enough beans. You might try growing sunflowers, buck-wheat, or other food specially for them. You might consider confining them in a small permanent house, with two outdoor runs à la Balfour system, during the worst months of the winter, with electric light on in the evenings to fool them that it was the time of the year to lay and thus get enough winter eggs.

Crops would be all the ordinary garden crops, plus as much land as you could spare for fodder crops for the animals. But you would bear in mind that practically *any* garden crop that you grew for yourself would be good for the animals too, so everything surplus to your requirements would go to them. You would not have a "compost heap." Your animals would be your compost heap.

If you decided to keep goats instead of a cow (and who am I to say this would not be a sensible decision?) you could manage things in much the same way. You would only get a small fraction of the manure from goats, but on the other hand you would not have to buy anything like so much hay and straw, indeed perhaps not any. You would have nothing like so much whey and skimmed milk to rear pigs and poultry on, and you would not build up the fertility of your land as quickly as you would with a cow.

If you kept no animals at all, or maybe only some poultry, you might well try farming half an acre as garden and growing wheat in the other half acre. You would then rotate your land as we described above but substituting wheat for the

The Five Acre Holding

If you had five acres of good well-drained land, you could support a family of, say, six people and have occasional surpluses to sell. Of course, no two five acre plots are ever the same, but in an ideal situation I would set aside one of my acres for the house, farm buildings, kitchen garden and orchard, and the other four acres I would divide into eight half-acre plots. Three of them I would put down to grass every year, and there I would run: two cows for dairy produce; four sows, a boar, some sheep and some geese for meat; and some chickens for eggs. As well as these animals I would keep ducks, rabbits, pigeons and bees wherever I could fit them in. Now, on the five remaining plots I would sow: wheat; roots; Jerusalem artichokes or potatoes; peas and beans; oats, and barley undersown with grass and clover. I would rotate all eight plots every year so no plot ever grew the same crop two years running, unless it was grass. A grass plot would stay grass for three years before being ploughed.

Pasture
Your pasture can cover one and a half acres. Here you can graze cows, sheep, geese and chickens, and when you want to plough up some of your grassland, you can bring your pigs back from the woods and fold them on small areas at a time. The top end of the field has not yet been cut for hay.

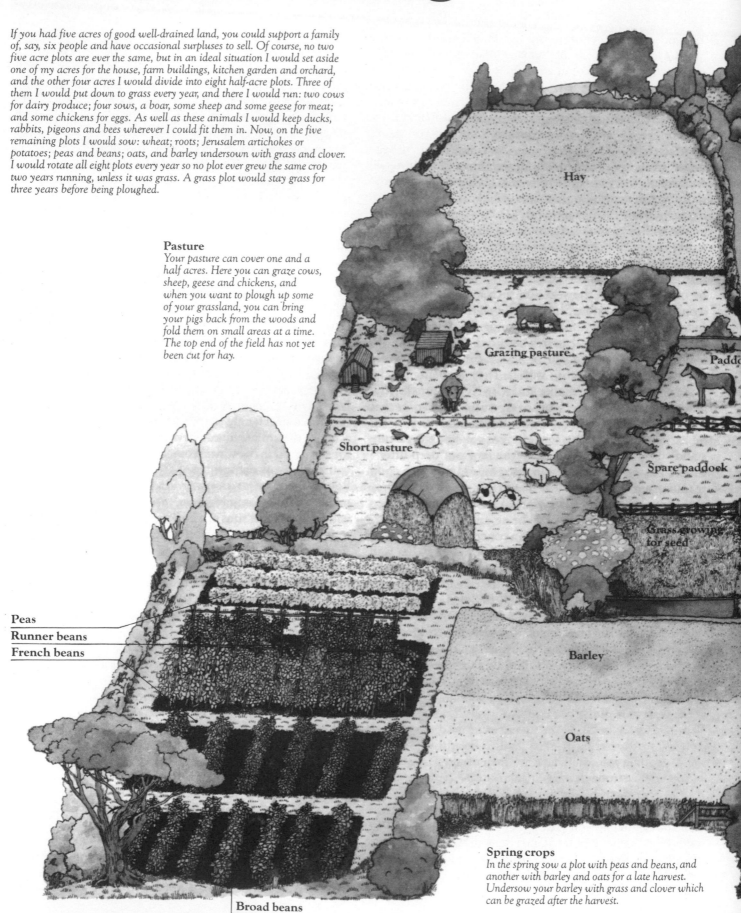

Hay

Grazing pasture

Paddo[ck]

Short pasture

Spare paddock

Grass growing for seed

Peas
Runner beans
French beans

Barley

Oats

Broad beans

Spring crops
In the spring sow a plot with peas and beans, and another with barley and oats for a late harvest. Undersow your barley with grass and clover which can be grazed after the harvest.

Root break
Divide your half-acre for roots into several small plots and grow a selection of roots for feeding your animals in winter. When you have dug your roots and stored them in a clamp or root cellar, put your pigs on the land.

Woodland
If you have some woodland, farm it for timber and firewood just as you would farm the rest of your holding. Each year fell the old, mature trees and clear the undergrowth with your pigs. Plant new trees like ash, larch, sweet chestnut and spruce.

Young spruce plantation

Greenhouse

Water wheel and mill

The home acre
This is the hub of your holding. Round the farmyard are your house, barn, cowsheds and dairy. Keep a horse in the paddock, ducks in the pond and bees in the orchard, but be sure to allow plenty of space for the vital business of growing vegetables and soft fruit.

Summer vegetables

Carrots

Fodder beet

Mangolds

Farm buildings

Orchard

Soft fruit

Duck housing

Pigs

Timber

Wheat

Winter crops
Sow wheat, and potatoes or Jerusalem artichokes, as winter crops for an early harvest. When you have harvested your potatoes or Jerusalem artichokes, fold pigs on that plot and let them dig out the remnants of the roots, dung the land and plough it ready for next year's pea and bean break.

Jerusalem artichokes

grass-and-clover ley. If you were a vegetarian this might be quite a good solution. But you could not hope to increase the fertility, and thus the productiveness, of your land like this as much as you would do with animals.

THE FIVE ACRE HOLDING

The basic principles I have described for running a one acre holding will also broadly apply to larger acreages. The main difference would be that if you had say five acres of medium to good land in a temperate climate, and the knowledge, you could grow *all* the food necessary for a large family except such things as tea and coffee, which can only be grown in the tropics. And you *could*, of course, do without such things. You could grow wheat for bread, barley for beer, every kind of vegetable, every kind of meat, eggs, and honey.

Just as every person in the world is different, so is every five acre plot, but here is a possible pattern:–

Assuming one acre was set aside for house and buildings, orchard and kitchen garden, the remainder could be divided up into eight half-acre plots. It would be necessary to fence them permanently: electric fencing would do. Or, if you are a tetherer, you might tether your cows, and your pigs, and your goats if you have any, and not have any fencing at all. I tried tethering a sheep once but the poor thing died of a broken heart so I wouldn't recommend it.

The rotation could be something like this: *grass (for three years) – wheat – roots – potatoes – peas and beans – barley, under-sown with grass-and-clover – grass (for three years).*

This would only leave you, of course, one and a half acres of grassland, but it would be very *productive* grassland, and in a good year it could be supplemented with something like: a ton of wheat; twenty tons of roots; four tons of potatoes; half a ton of peas or beans; three quarters of a ton of barley.

You might well manage to get two tons of hay off your grassland, and then have enough "aftermath" (grass which grows after you have cut the hay) to give grazing to your cows until well into the autumn.

There are a thousand possible variations of this plan, of course. Flexibility is the essence of good husbandry. You could, for example, take potatoes after your ploughed-up grassland, and follow that with wheat. You could grow oats as well as barley, or oats as well as wheat. You could grow some rye: very useful if you have dry light land, or want good thatching straw, or like rye bread. You could grow less peas and beans. You could try to grow all your arable crops in four half-acre plots instead of five and thus leave two acres for grassland instead of one and a half. You might find you had some grassland to spare in your "home acre" – in your orchard, for example, if your trees were standards and therefore too high to be damaged by the stock. Of course if you were in maize growing country you would grow maize, certainly instead of barley, maybe instead of roots or potatoes. A good tip is to seek out farming neighbours,

and ask them which crops grow best in your area.

As for stock – you might well consider keeping a horse to help you do all that cultivating, or you might have a small garden tractor instead. Your ploughing could be done with pigs. With five acres you might well consider keeping enough sows to justify a boar. Four is probably the minimum: we kept six sows and a boar for many years and they were astonishingly profitable. Indeed, in good years and bad, they paid all our bills for us: the Irish call the pig "the gentleman who pays the rent" and one can see why. But pigs won't pay you very well unless you can grow a great deal of their food for them. You could look upon your pig herd, whether large or small, as your pioneers: they would plough up your half acre of grass every year for you, plough your stubbles after corn, clean up your potato and root land after harvest, and generally act as rooters-up and scavengers.

Poultry, too, would be rotated about the holding as much as possible. Put on wheat or barley stubble they will feed themselves for some time on spilled grain, besides doing great good scrapping out leatherjackets and wireworm. Following the pigs after the latter have rooted up a piece of land they will also do good by eating pests and will do themselves good too. Ducks, geese, turkeys, tame rabbits, pigeons: your five acres will provide enough food and space for them all, and they will vary your diet.

I would recommend keeping two cows, so you would have ample milk all the year, you would have enough milk to make decent hard cheese during the summer to last you through the winter, and enough whey and skimmed milk to supplement pig and poultry feed. If you reared one calf a year, and kept him eighteen months or two years, and then slaughtered him, you would have enough beef for family use. That is, if you had a deep freeze. If you did not, then you could sell your bullock and use that money for buying beef from the butcher, or, much better, you could make an arrangement with several small-holder neighbours that you each took turns to slaughter a beast, then divided the meat up amongst you so it could all be eaten before it went bad. In a cold winter you can keep beef at least a month.

Sheep, on such a small acreage, are a more doubtful proposition because they need very good fencing and also it is uneconomic to keep a ram for less than say six sheep. But you could keep some pet ewes, get them mated with a neighbouring ram, rear the lambs and keep yourself in mutton and wool.

The above is only an introductory outline of how a prospective self-supporter might organize a five acre holding. Each person will wish to adapt according to his circumstances, the size of his family or his community, and the nature of his land. But the main body of this book is aimed at providing him with as much practical help as possible in selecting and managing his acreage, his crops and his livestock, and in making them the productive agents in his search for the good life.

Food from the Fields

"He gave it for his opinion, that whoever
could make two ears of corn or two blades of grass to
grow upon a spot where only one grew before,
would deserve better of mankind."
SWIFT

Clearing Land

Unless your holding is big and you plan to farm a proportion of it on the "dog and walking stick" principle, one of your first priorities will be to see if you can gain any extra usable land by clearing overgrown wood and bush land. Such land is worth clearing as long as it is not on a ridiculously steep slope, or is irretrievably boggy or is covered in boulders. Clearing land is hard but rewarding work, although it can be extremely expensive and time consuming.

Pigs and goats

Your pig is your best pioneer. If you concentrate pigs in bush land they will clear it for you with no effort on your part at all. They won't, of course, remove trees, but all brambles, gorse and undergrowth generally will yield to their snouts and they will manure the land at the same time. If there are any stubborn areas of thicket try throwing some corn into them and the pigs will soon root them out.

Goats will kill small trees, and big ones too if they are concentrated, by barking them, and they will prevent trees from coming back. They will not of course get the trees out, any more than pigs will. You will have to do that.

Clearing woodland

Stumping woodland may well cost you more than buying new land unless you happen to live in a country that has a large government subsidy for this work. But if you can spend the time and the vast effort needed, you can stump old woodland, and to produce fertile land where no cultivatable land was before is a worthy endeavour. Consider first, though, whether it would not be better to replant old woodland as new woodland and farm it as forest (see p. 33).

The most expensive method of stumping is to hire a mechanical excavator. One of these, plus a driver, costs a lot to hire but undoubtedly does a lot of work in an hour. It leaves the trees pulled out, higgledy-piggledy, one on top of the other. You are then left with the formidable job of slashing out the usable timber and burning the "slash", as the small branches are called. And to do the latter operation when the wood is green is a much harder job than you might think, but you have got to do it before you can cultivate the land.

It is cheaper to haul stumps out with a tree-jack or monkey-winch. You might hire or borrow one of these, or buy one if you had a lot of land to clear but they cost several hundred pounds. There are many varieties of them. Alternatively you can dig stumps out with spade and mattock, but this is very laborious. Or you can blow them out with gunpowder, gelignite, or other explosive. This involves driving a hole as deep down under the stump as you can get it and pushing your charge down there. A *lifting* explosive is the best thing to use: black gunpowder is fine if you use enough of it. Ammonol

Hand tools
If you haven't got pigs or machines to clear your land, you can do it by hand, but you need the right tools.

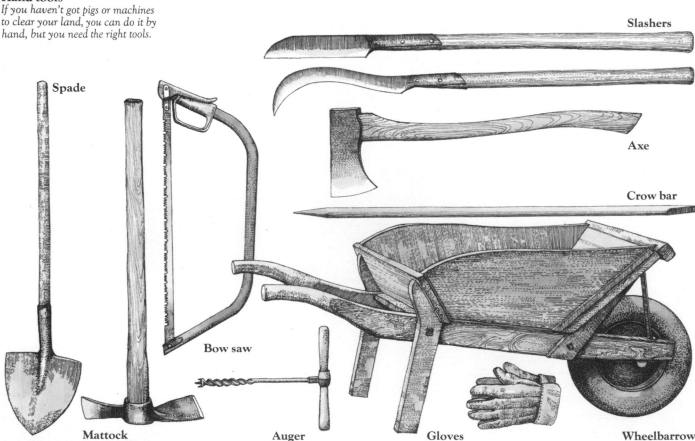

Slashers

Spade

Axe

Crow bar

Mattock

Bow saw

Auger

Gloves

Wheelbarrow

is excellent or any "high-expansion-ratio" explosive. Thus it is better to use "open-cast" gelignite than ordinary rock-breaking gelignite. As for quantities – this is entirely a matter of judgment and trial and error. Two pounds (0.9kg) of ammonol might lift a big oak right out of the ground; it would take ten pounds (4.5kg) of black gunpowder to do the same thing. But get somebody who has used explosives before to help you.

A more accessible method for most of us is sodium chlorate, which is a common weed killer, much used by terrorists for the manufacture of their infernal machines. If you drill holes in the stump and fill them with sodium chlorate, put some cover over the holes to stop the rain from getting in, and wait a month, you will find that the stump has become highly inflammable. Build a small fire on the stump and it will burn right away.

Removing rocks

Rocks can be very obstructive, particularly on boulder-clay or glacial till in which boulders have been left by the retreating ice in a completely random fashion. Again, the mechanical excavator can deal with these if they are not too big, hauling them out and dozing them to the side of the field.

You can lift quite large rocks, of several tons or more, with levers. Dig down around the rock, establish a secure fulcrum at one side of it – a railway sleeper will do, or another rock – insert a long beam of wood or steel girder – a length of railway line is ideal – and raise that side of the rock a few inches. Now pack small rocks under the big rock, let the latter subside, and apply your lever to the other side. Do the same there. Continue to work your way round the rock, raising it again and again the few inches made possible by your lever and packing small stones under it each time you have gained a bit. You will eventually work your rock to a point above the surface of the surrounding ground.

Once you have got a boulder out you may be able to roll it to the side of the field, again using levers. If it is too big for this you can try lighting a big fire under it, heating it right through, and then throwing cold water on it. This should crack it.

Breaking rocks

If you can get them explosives are the easiest way of breaking rock. Plastic high explosive is the best of the lot, but any fairly fast gelignite is fine. Drill a hole in the rock and put in your explosive. An ounce (28g) of gelignite splits a huge rock. You can drill rock with a compressor and rock drill, or you can do it by hand with a jumper – a steel bit like a long cold chisel – and a heavy hammer. You drive the jumper into the rock with the hammer, turning the jumper after every blow, and pouring water into the hole you are making from time to time. Wrap a rag round the jumper to stop the rock paste thus formed from splashing up in your face. But, as I said before, if you have never used explosives I strongly advise you to get somebody who has used them to come and help you the first time.

Using a monkey-winch
Use the base of one tree as a hold-fast and attach the wire rope as high as you can to the tree you want to pull out. Cut through as many roots as you can and then pull the tree over.

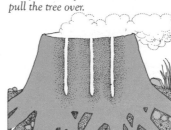

Blowing up a stump
Put your charge in a hole deep under the stump and retreat.

Burning a stump
Drill holes, fill with sodium chlorate and cover over. Wait a month, then build a fire on top.

Levering up a boulder

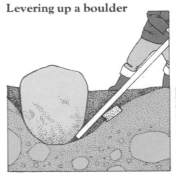

Use a rock or a chunk of wood as a fulcrum. Work a lever down beside the boulder.

Raise the boulder as far as possible. Prop up with stones. Take lever and fulcrum to the other side.

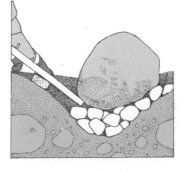

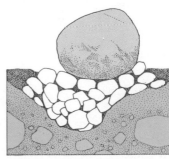

Repeat the process over and over, gaining a few inches each time.

Once the boulder is out, roll or lever it off your field.

Draining Land

If you are lucky your land will not need draining at all. Much land has porous subsoil and possibly rock through which water can percolate, perhaps has a gentle slope, and is obviously dry. But land with an impervious subsoil, very heavy land, land that is so level that water cannot run away from it, or land with springs issuing out in it, may well need draining. Badly-drained land is late land, meaning it will not produce plants early in the year. It is cold land and it is hard to work. You cannot cultivate it when it is wet – particularly if it has clay in it. In short, it will not grow good crops.

You can tell wet land even in a dry summer by the plants growing in it. Such things as flag irises, sedges, rushes and reeds, all give away the fact that, although dry in the summer, it will be wet and waterlogged in the winter time and should be drained.

Cut-off drains

Often, on sloping land, you can drain a field by digging a ditch along the contour above it (see illustration). The effect of this ditch is to cut off and take away the water that is percolating down from above. The rain that actually falls on the field is not enough to cause it to become waterlogged: it is the water that drains down from above that does the damage.

Springs

You can drain springs by connecting them by ditch or land drain (see illustration) to a stream that will carry the water away. You can see where springs are by wet patches or by water-loving plants. If there is a large waterlogged area around the spring common sense might tell you to make a larger hole around the mouth of your pipe and fill it with stones.

Land drains

Level land can be drained simply by lowering the water table. The water table is the level at which the surface of the underground water lies. It will be higher in the winter than it is in the summer, and in severe cases may be above the surface. You lower it by digging ditches, or putting in land drains, to take the water away. You can even do this with land below sea-level, by pumping water from the deepest ditches up into the sea, or to raised-up rivers that carry it to the sea.

Obviously heavy soils (soils with a big clay content) need more draining than light soils, but even sand, the lightest of all soils, can be waterlogged and will then grow nothing until it is drained. The heavier the soil is the closer together your drains will need to be, for the less is the distance water can percolate. A very few drains will suffice to drain light or sandy soil. If you have had no experience it will pay you to get the advice of somebody who has: in countries with government drainage officers these are the obvious choice. There can often be heavy grants for draining, too.

There are three main types of land drain: open ditches, underground drains and mole drains. An open ditch is just what it says. You dig, or get dug by machine, a ditch with

Three situations where you need drains
A. Water runs downhill through porous soil or rock before hitting an impervious layer. This forces it, generally sideways, to the surface where it emerges as a spring. B. An impervious subsoil prevents rain sinking. C. Absolutely flat land has no slope to allow drainage.
The plants on the right are sure signs of wet land: (left to right) marsh orchid, marsh violet, flag iris, marsh marigold, jointed rush, wood sedge, common rush and bulrush.

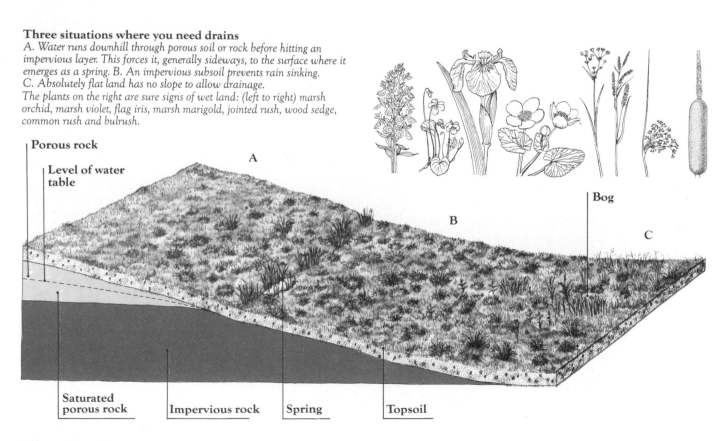

Porous rock

Level of water table

Bog

A

B

C

Saturated porous rock

Imperivous rock

Spring

Topsoil

The mole drainer
A torpedo-shaped steel object at the bottom of a narrow blade is dragged through the soil. The narrow slot made by the blade fills in but the drain remains. The drain lasts much longer in clay than in soft sandy soil.

The chisel plough
The chisel plough, or subsoiler, cuts a series of deep, evenly spaced furrows in the soil. This works very well with heavy clay, where the furrows last and ensure free drainage.

The uses of drains and ditches
A cut-off ditch will intercept water draining downhill, and lead it round your field to a receiving ditch at the bottom. An underground drain can be used to drain a spring, and a series of underground drains – herring bone pattern is ideal – can take sufficient water away to lower your water table. You want to get the water table at least 18 inches (46 cm) below the surface. Four feet (1.2 m) is ideal.

Cut-off ditch

Underground drains lowering the water table

Receiving ditch

Underground drain capturing spring water

Draining a spring
Dig down to the spring. Lay a pipe or dig a ditch to carry the water away. If the spring covers a large area fill in around your pipe with some stones.

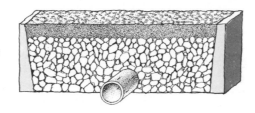

battered (sloping) sides. On light land (sandy soil) the batter wants to be much less steep than on heavy land because heavy land supports itself better. Common sense will tell you how much to batter. If the sides fall in it is too steep.

Depth too is a matter of reasoned judgment. If the ditch is deep enough to lower the water table sufficiently for the crops to grow happily it is deep enough. You certainly don't want standing water in the soil at less than 18 inches (46 cm) from the surface: better if you can lower the water table to four feet (1.2m). If you are having to dig the ditch by hand you won't want it too deep. And remember open ditches need flashing-out (clearing of scrub and weeds) every year or two and cleaning with a spade every five to ten years. They also need fencing.

Underground drains are of many types (see illustrations). As long as they are deep enough not to be affected by deep ploughing or cultivating, and their slope is continuous to the outfall so that they don't silt up in the dips, they will require no maintenance and should last for centuries. Mole drains (see illustration) do not last for more than five to ten years – less in sandy land.

But draining is simple common sense. Imagine what is going on down there. Dig try-holes to find how deep the water table is and where the springs are. Arrange to drain that water away to the nearest stream or river or whatever, or even let it debouch into waste-land below your land, and you will have well-drained productive land.

Plastic pipe drain

Semi-circular tile drain

Stone culvert drain

Bush drain

Underground drains
Stone culvert drains and tile drains are naturally porous. Plastic pipe drains have slits in them to let the water in. The Roman bush drain, simply bushes covered with earth, can be reinforced with a piece of perforated corrugated iron.

Irrigating Land

Almost wherever you live your crops will benefit by irrigation, and in some countries they just won't grow without it. The luckiest cultivators in the world are those who live in a hot dry climate but have plenty of water for irrigation. They have far better control over their husbandry than people who live in high rainfall areas. They need have no serious weed problem: they simply kill their weeds by withholding water from them when the land is fallow. They can drill their seed in dry dust before they water it, and then immediately flood the land to make the seed grow. They can give the crop exactly enough water for its needs throughout its growing time, and then withhold water when it comes to harvest and thereby harvest in perfect conditions. They have it made.

But the rest of us can also use irrigation to advantage. It takes 22,650 gallons of water to apply an inch depth of water to an acre (an "acre-inch"). If there is no rain during the rainy season it is nice to apply an inch (2.5 cm) a week during the period of hardest growth of the crop. In temperate climates with a fair rainfall like most of Northern Europe, and the Eastern United States, the addition of from two inches up to six (5-15 cm) during the growing season will probably be enough. In any case the irrigator cuts his coat according to his cloth. Anything is better than nothing.

If you are lucky you may be able to tap a stream above the land you wish to irrigate and lead the water down in a pipe, but unless your source is much higher than your land you won't get much pressure. On the other hand, contrary to popular Western belief, you don't really need a lot of pressure: you only need the water. By the simple means of laying a hose on the ground and moving it about from time to time, as patch after patch gets flooded, you can do a great deal of good. You can do more good by letting water run down furrows between your rows of crops, moving the hose each time the water reaches the bottom of another furrow.

Sprinkle irrigation

Broadly there are two kinds of irrigation: sprinkle irrigation and flood irrigation. Western farmers tend to go in for the

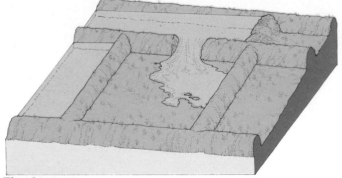

Flood irrigation
Sloping beds, previously levelled, with a water channel at their head, are separated by little earth bunds. You make a dam across the channel at the first bed, break the bund separating channel from bed, close the gap once the bed is flooded, destroy the dam and repeat the process.

former. They use pumps and either "rainers," rotary sprinklers, or oscillating spray lines, all of which need considerable pressure to make them operate. This is fine if you can afford the equipment, afford the fuel and have the water, which does not have to be above the field. But all this is expensive, and not for the ordinary self-supporter. Personally I could never see the point of squirting water up in the air at some expense just to have it fall down again, and have always practised some form or other of flood irrigation.

Flood irrigation

In countries where irrigation is really understood, and these are the countries where it is really needed, flood irrigation is what is used. If you have a stream running next to a field, it is not difficult to get a little petrol pump and a hose, and to move the pump along the bank of the stream as one stretch of the field after another is irrigated. Alternatively, you may have a stream at a higher level than the field.

Ideally the land should be either terraced in perfectly level beds, or, if the field has a natural gentle slope, levelled into gently sloping beds with bunds separating each bed from the next. (A bund is a small earth bank not more than a foot high.) You can grass these bunds, in which case they are permanent, or level them down each year and build them up again. If you are working with tractors you will probably level them, because it gives you more room to manoeuvre. At the head of all the sloping beds is a water channel. To irrigate you build with a spade a little dam of earth about a foot high across this channel at the first bed, and break the bund which separates the channel from the bed with the spade. You sit there, in the sunshine watching the butterflies, until the water has meandered down the bed, covered all of it and has got to the botttom. If your bed is not properly levelled, and has no crop in it, you can use your spade to level it so as to spread the water evenly. On a hot day this is a delightful job.

Now you will have already built small dams level with each of the other beds. When the first bed is watered you close the gap in its bund, break its dam down, break a hole in the bund of the second bed, and let the water run into there. And so you go on.

Of course this pre-supposes that the water in your head-channel is higher than your beds. What if it is lower? Then you must do what many a Chinese or Egyptian does: just raise it that few inches. You can do this with a bucket, very laboriously, or a hundred other devices that ingenuity will lead you to. A small petrol pump might be one of them, a tiny windmill another.

If your field is very steep it is obvious that beds sloping down it will not do for flood irrigation. You will have to terrace it. This will involve stone or at least turf retaining walls and is a tremendous job. And if you have a very big field you may need two or more head channels on different contours, because the water won't be able to meander down from the top of each bed to the bottom.

Making Use of Woodland

The most useful trees for the self-supporter are, in order of importance, sweet chestnut (the best tree in the world for timber), oak, ash, and larch. In North America you would add hickory, sugar maple and black cherry. If you have a saw bench capable of ripping down trees, then softwoods or any of the timber hardwoods are useful too.

Hardwoods and softwoods

When considering timber for purposes other than fuel, points you should look out for are: a fairly quick rate of growth, hardness and resistance to rot, and what I will call "cleavability" or "splittability."

For very many farm and estate uses it is better to cleave wood rather than rip-saw it (saw it along the grain). Cleaving is quicker, cheaper, the resulting wood is stronger, and lasts longer. Why? Because when you rip-saw you inevitably cut across certain of the grain, or wood-fibres. When you cleave, your cleavage always runs between the grain, which avoids "cross-graining" and leaves undamaged grain to resist the weather.

Sweet chestnut cleaves beautifully. It is fast growing, straight, hard and strong. It also resists rot better than any other tree. Oak cleaves well too, but not as well as chestnut. The heart of oak is as hard and lasts as long, but the white sap-wood on the outside – most of a small tree – is useless. Oak is extremely slow growing and needs good soil to grow at all. Ash on the other hand is tough, and resilient, but will rot if put in the ground. It is straight, grows fast, and splits well. Above the ground, but exposed to the weather, it will last a long time if you oil or creosote it every now and then. It makes good gates or hurdles. Larch is unusual in that it is a conifer but not an evergreen. It is very fast growing and the best of the conifers for lasting in the ground providing it is creosoted. All the other conifers, or softwoods, that I know are hopeless in the ground if not pressure-creosoted, and then they don't last many years.

Cherry and all other fruit woods are hard, and make fine firewood. They are good for making hard things like cog teeth in water mills, for example. It is a pity to use them for posts. Hickory is the best wood for tool handles. It doesn't grow in Europe (why I don't know), and so is either imported or else ash is used, a pretty good substitute. Elm – alas now being killed off by Dutch elm disease – is good for any purpose where you want a non-splittable wood, such as for wheel hubs, chopping blocks, and butcher's blocks. It is great under water. Maple and sycamore are good for turning on a lathe, and making treen (carved objects). Walnut is a king among fine woods, and fit to harvest in a mere 150 years, though 350 is better if you have the patience to wait for it!

Firewood

Trees are your most likely source of fuel. If you have even an acre or two of woodland, you will find that, with proper management, the trees in it will grow faster than you can cut them down for your fire. A piece of woodland is the most efficient solar heat collector in the world.

The forester's essential tools
Fell your tree with axe and saw. Use hammer and wedge, or club and froe for splitting. Adze and draw-knife are for stripping and shaping.

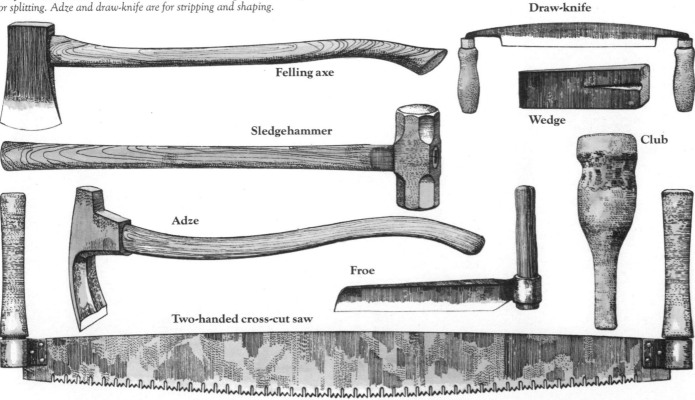

Felling axe

Draw-knife

Wedge

Sledgehammer

Club

Adze

Froe

Two-handed cross-cut saw

Making Use of Woodland

Ash is the best of all firewoods. "Seer or green it's fit for a queen!" The loppings of felled ash are excellent. It burns as well when newly cut as when mature. Oak, when seasoned, is a fine and long-burning firewood, but it grows far too slowly to be planted for this purpose. Silver birch is good for firewood, though not for much else. It burns very hotly when seasoned, and it grows fast. Conifers aren't much good for firewood. They spit a lot and burn very quickly, but in the frozen north, where there's nothing else, that's what people have to use. Birch is better as firewood, and it will grow further north than any other tree. All the weed woods, like alder and goat-willow, are very sluggish when green, but can be burned when dry, though even then they don't burn well or give out prolonged heat. But what else is there to do with them? Any wood in the world will burn. But if you are planting trees especially for firewood plant ash, and then coppice it.

Coppicing means cutting down all your trees when they are about nine inches (23 cm) in diameter, and then letting them grow again. They will "coppice" by putting up several shoots from each bole. Cut these down again in about twelve years and they will grow once more. This twelve-yearly harvesting can go on for hundreds of years, and in this way you will harvest the greatest possible quantity of firewood from your wood-lot.

Planting trees

Plant trees very close together and they will grow up straight and tall, reaching for the light. Five foot (1.6m) by five is fine. When they become crowded you thin them and get a small preliminary harvest. In winter plant trees at least three years old. You can buy them from a nursery, or the Forestry Commission, or you can grow them yourself from seed. Keep the grass and rubbish down every summer for three or four years, so the trees don't get smothered. Saw off low branches from the growing trees to achieve clean timber without knots. Feed with phosphate, potash, and lime if needed. Muck or compost will make them grow faster.

In existing woodlands uproot the weed trees (alder, goat-willow, thorn) to give the other trees a better chance. Wet land favours weed trees, so drain if you can. Keep out sheep, cattle and goats to give seedlings a chance. Cut out undergrowth if you have time, or try running pigs in the wood for a limited period. They will clear and manure it and they won't hurt established trees. They will also live for months in the autumn on acorns or beech mast.

Seasoning wood

Stack the planks as they come out of the log, with billets of wood in between to let the air through. Kiln-drying is a quick way of seasoning, but time is better. Some wood (e.g. ash) can be laid in a stream for a few weeks to drive the sap out. This speeds seasoning, but some trees do take years to season. If you want woods for cabinet-making, for example, there must not be any subsequent movement. But for rough work, gates, or even timbers for rough buildings, seasoning is not so important.

Always remember to treat trees as a crop. Don't hesitate to cut mature trees when they are ripe, but always plant more trees than you cut down.

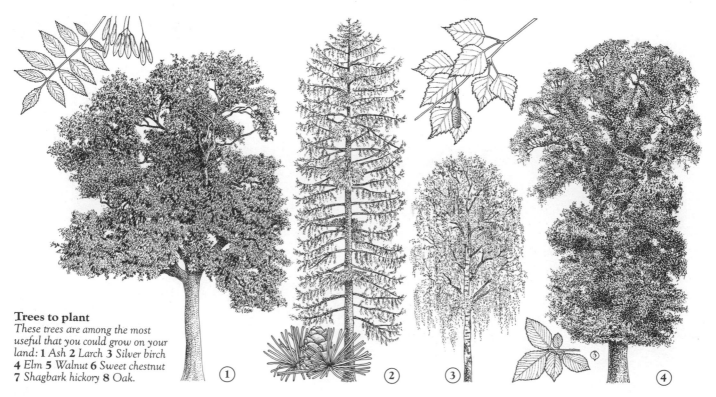

Trees to plant
These trees are among the most useful that you could grow on your land: **1** *Ash* **2** *Larch* **3** *Silver birch* **4** *Elm* **5** *Walnut* **6** *Sweet chestnut* **7** *Shagbark hickory* **8** *Oak.*

(1)   (2)   (3)   (4)

Felling a tree

Trim off all roots and buttresses with your axe. Then use the axe to cut a "face" (forester's term for a deep V-shaped notch) in the side towards which you want the tree to fall. Then begin sawing from the other side, making your cut a few inches above the deepest part of the face. When the tree "sits on" your blade so you can't move it use your sledgehammer to drive a wedge in behind your saw. Carry on sawing until you are close to the "face" and the tree is about to fall. Then, pull

out your saw, bang the wedge further in and over she goes. A jagged piece of wood, called the "sloven" will be left sticking up from the stump. Trim it off with your axe.

Riving with wedge and sledge-hammer

Wedges and a sledgehammer are the best tools for "riving", or splitting, large logs. Use the sledge-

hammer to drive a wedge into the end grain of the log. Then drive more wedges into the cleft thus

made until the log splits right down its length. Never use an axe as a wedge. The handle will break.

Riving with froe and club

For riving smaller wood the ideal tool is a froe. Whack the blade into the end grain with a club or mallet. Work the blade further into the

wood by levering sideways with the handle. You won't have got far before the wood splits down its

length. This is much quicker than using wedges.

Sawing planks

A pit-saw is a time-honoured tool for sawing logs into planks. One man stands on the log; the other is down a pit dodging the sawdust. Band saws and circular saws are easier but more expensive.

Seasoning planks

Stack planks as they leave the log with spacers to let the air through. Leave for at least 18 months.

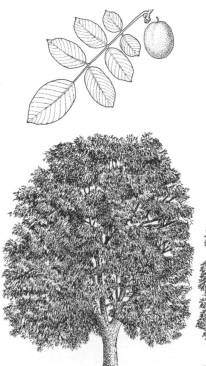

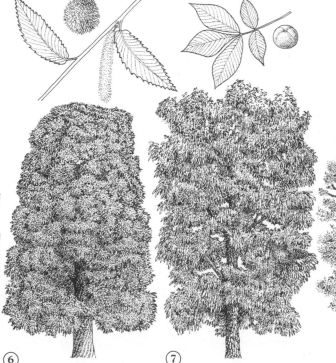

⑤　　　⑥　　　⑦　　　⑧

Hedging & Fencing

Domestic animals can be herded: that means kept where they are supposed to be by human beings. But the self-supporter will of necessity be a busy man. Fences will not only relieve him and his wife and children from the time-consuming task of herding, but will give him a useful tool for the better husbanding of his land. Without the fence you cannot fold sheep or cattle on fodder crops; you cannot concentrate pigs on rooting; you cannot even keep goats and chickens out of your garden.

Quickthorn hedge

The cheapest and most natural barrier you can build is a quickthorn hedge. Quick means alive, and such a hedge is established by planting thorn bushes, generally whitethorn (may), close enough together in a long line. Seedling thorns, about six inches (15 cm) high, can be planted in two lines, staggered, nine inches (23 cm) between the two rows but eighteen inches (46 cm) between the plants in the rows.

You can buy the plants from nurseries or grow them yourself from haws, the seeds of the hawthorn. But the hedge must be protected from stock for at least four years, and this is what makes a quickthorn hedge so difficult to establish. Animals, particularly sheep and even more particularly goats, will eat a young quickthorn hedge. Therefore some other sort of fence – probably barbed wire – must be established on both sides of a new quickthorn hedge: an expensive business.

Laying a hedge

But once the quickthorn hedge is established it is there, if you look after it, for centuries. You look after it by laying it. That is, every five years or so, cutting most of the bushes' trunks half way through and breaking them over. The trunks are all laid the same way – always uphill. They are pushed down on top of each other, or intertwined where possible, and often held by "dead" stakes driven in at right angles to them. Sometimes the tops of these are pleached with hazel or willow wands twisted through like basketry. In due course the pleaching and the dead stakes rot and disappear, but the hedge puts out new growth and can be very stock-proof.

The quickthorn hedge is a labour intensive way of fencing, but labour is all it uses, and it lasts indefinitely. Also it looks nice, gives haven to birds and small animals, and serves as a windbreak: very important in windy countries. In days of old it supplied, with no extra work, faggot-wood, used for heating bread ovens and other purposes, to say nothing of black-berries. You can often restore old hedges to efficiency on a new holding by laying them, judiciously planting here and there an odd thorn bush to fill in a gap.

Dry-stone wall

If there is freestone (stone that cleaves out of the quarry easily in fairly even slabs) in your district you have probably already got dry-stone walls. Dry means without mortar in this con-text. If you have them you will need to maintain them. If you

haven't but you have the stone on your land you can build some. It is backbreaking but costs nothing. You need tons of stone – much more than you think you are going to need – and a good hand and eye. Dig a level foundation trench first, then lay the stones carefully, breaking all joints, keeping sides vertical, and fitting the stones in as snugly as you can. Dry-stone walls can be quite stock-proof. They are enormously expensive in labour and need repairing from time to time.

Stone-hedge

It is possible to build a cross between a wall and a hedge. You find these in districts where the natural stone is rounded or boulder-shaped, not the rectangular slabs which are found particularly in limestone country. Two stone walls are built with a pronounced batter – that is they lean inwards towards each other. The gaps between the stones are filled in with turf, and the space between the two walls is filled with earth. A quickthorn hedge is then planted on top. After a year or two grass, weeds and scrub grow from the earth and the turf. The wall is quite green and not, to be quite frank, very stock-proof. If you look at a hundred such hedges I'll warrant you'll find a discreet length of barbed wire or two, or even sheep-netting, along ninety of them. These wall-hedges aren't really much good. So if you have them, fortify them with barbed wire to keep your animals in.

Wattle-hurdle

If you can get stakes from your own trees a wattle-hurdle fence is free except for labour, and fairly quick to erect, but it doesn't last long. You drive sharpened stakes into the ground at intervals of about nine inches (23 cm) and pleach, or weave, pliable withies (willow branches), hazel branches, holly, ivy, blackberry or other creepers between the stakes so as to make a continuous fence. The weaving material soon dries out and cracks and gets rotten and you have to ram more in and the stakes themselves, unless of chestnut or heart-of-oak or other resistant wood, rot after a few years and break off. Where stakes or posts are expensive or hard to come by it is an extravagant form of fencing.

Post-and-rail

A post-and-rail fence is stronger and, unless you are able to grow your own wood, more economical. It consists of strong stakes, either of resistant wood or else soft-wood impreg-nated with creosote, driven well into the ground, with rails of split timber nailed on to them. Abraham Lincoln, we are told, started his life as a "rail-splitter". The rails he split would have been for post-and-rail fences, for in his day that wonderful invention wire had not begun to encompass the world, and yet the new settlers spreading over North America had to have fences on a large scale. Post-and-rail was their answer. A variant of it was the zig-zag fence, the posts of which formed a zig-zag pattern. This added lateral strength. It took up more wood of course.

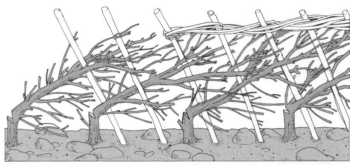

Building or repairing a hedge

Cut stakes out of your hedge so as to leave strong bushes at intervals of about a foot. Wear a leather hedging glove on your left hand. Bend each trunk over and half-cut through it near the base with a bill-hook.
Force the half-cut trunk down to nearly horizontal and try to push the end

under its neighbour so as to hold it in position. Be sure not to break it off. Take the stakes you have just cut and drive them in roughly at right angles to the trunks, interweaving them with the trunks. Pleach tops of stakes with some pliable growth such as hazel or willow. By the time the stakes have rotted the living hedge will be secure.

Overgrown hedges
Runaway hedges can be tamed with a slasher (left). Clear surrounding undergrowth with a bagging hook (above), but use a stick in your left hand. Otherwise you might lose a finger or thumb.

Using stone
A well maintained dry-stone wall is even more stock-proof than an established hedge. You need stone that comes in even, flattish slabs. Dig down about nine inches (23 cm) and make a level foundation trench. Lay the stones, neatly fitting them together. Make sure the sides are vertical and all joints are broken. If you have large round stones on your land, you can make a sort of stone hedge. Build two stone walls leaning towards each other about a foot (30 cm) apart. Plug the gaps between the stones with turf and the space between the walls with earth, and plant a hedge on top. You will probably find sheep will walk straight over it, at least until the hedge is mature. So to be really stock-proof the whole thing needs to be reinforced with barbed wire.

Steel wire

The invention of galvanized steel wire was the answer to the fencer's dream. It can be plain wire (often high-tensile), barbed wire, or netting. Plain wire is effective only if strained. Barbed wire is more effective if it is strained, but often a strand or two attached somewhat haphazardly to an old unlaid hedge is all there is between animals and somebody's valuable crop. Netting is very effective but nowadays terribly expensive. Square-meshed netting is strongest for a permanent situation, but is awkward to move very often: diamond-meshed netting is much weaker but stands being repeatedly rolled up and moved and is therefore ideal for folding sheep.

Straining wire

If you buy a wire strainer you can see easily enough how to use it, but there are several very effective ways of improvising one.

A tool much used in Africa consists of a forked stick two feet (61 cm) long, with a six-inch (15 cm) nail fastened with staples along its length just below the fork. The wire to be strained is inserted under the nail and then wrapped twice round it for firmness. You then take up the slack by twisting the stick, using the fork like the handle on a tap. Then you put the final stress on by turning the stick round the corner post, using the stick as a lever. You can get short lengths of wire quite tight enough like this, although if you are straining extremely long lengths at a time you will need a proper wire strainer, unless you pull the wire taut with a tractor.

If you strain wires on a post on a cold winter's day you may well have to strain them on a hot day next summer. Heat makes metal expand. Often, in practice, you can apply strain to wire by hauling it sideways – out of the line of the fence – to a suitable tree with another snatch of wire. This is looked upon as very infra-dig by estate managers but is often useful just the same, especially when you are trying to make a fence stock-proof down in the depths of the woods on a pouring wet day. If you can't get a wire strainer you can exert quite a little strain by using a post as a lever, or by using a block-tackle, or even by using a horse or a tractor. Many farmers use the tractor method. But do not strain wire too much. It breaks the galvanizing and takes the strength out of the wire: always use common sense.

Anchoring fences

A strained fence is as good as its anchor posts. A wire strainer, such as you can buy or borrow from a neighbour, can exert a pull of two tons, and this multiplied by the number of wires you have in your fence will pull any corner post out of the ground unless it is securely anchored. You can anchor a fence with a kicking post, a post placed diagonally against the corner post in such a way as to take the strain. The kicking post itself is secured in the ground against a rock or short post. Alternatively the strain can be taken by a wire stretched taut round a rock buried in the ground. A refinement of this, the box anchor, is the most efficient of all (see illustration).

Remember if you anchor wire to any tree that is not fully mature, the tree will gradually lean over and the fence will slacken. It is bad practice to fasten wire to trees anyway: the staples and lengths of wire get swallowed up by the growing tree and ultimately break some poor devil's saw blade. Not that many of us are quite innocent in that respect.

Electric fencing

You can get battery fencers, which work off six-volt dry batteries or twelve-volt accumulators, or mains fencers that work off the mains and will activate up to twenty miles of fencing! One strand of hot wire will keep cattle in – it should be at hip height – and one wire a foot (30 cm) from the ground will keep pigs in if they are used to it. Until they are, use two wires. The wires needn't be strong, or strained, just whipped round insulators carried on light stakes, and the whole thing can be put up or moved in minutes.

The electric fence gives the husbandman marvellous control over his stock and his land, making possible a new level of efficiency in farming.

Hurdles

Except for electrified wire-netting, which is expensive and hard to come by, sheep won't respect an electric fence. So when we wish to fold sheep on fodder fields we make hurdles (see illustration). It's cheaper than buying wire netting. Some wood that rives (splits) is necessary: ash or chestnut is fine. If you use ash you should creosote it. To erect hurdles drive a stake in at the point where the ends of two hurdles meet and tie the hurdles to the stake with a loop of binder twine. To carry hurdles put as many as you can manage together, shove a stake through them, and get your shoulder under the stake. A fold-pritch is the traditional implement for erecting hurdles, and you can hardly do the job without it.

You can make wattle-hurdles out of woven withies or other flexible timber. These are light, not very strong, don't last long, but good for wind-breaks at lambing time. To make them you place a piece of timber on the ground with holes drilled in it. Put the upright stakes of your hurdle in the holes and then weave the withies in. It is simply basket-work.

The box anchor
A fence is only really secure if its wires are strained, which means they can take a pull of two tons. Half a dozen strained wires will pull your corner posts straight out of the ground unless they have good anchors. The box anchor is the best of all. Heavy soft wire (generally No. 8 gauge) goes from the buried rocks to the second post. A cross-piece morticed in this supports the two corner-posts on which the wires are held.

Ten anchors in a field
Every stretch of strained wire fence needs an anchor, and one anchor can only take a strain in one direction. Thus each corner of your field will need two anchors, and you will need one each side of the gate.

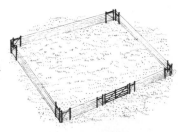

A farm gate

A cattle-proof gate for a field or farmyard is best built of split ash or chestnut. Use bolts to join the four main timbers which make up the frame, and also bolt the hinges on. Use clenched six-inch (15 cm) nails for the other joints. Drill holes for the nails as well as the bolts and pour creosote through all holes. If you have a forked timber you can use the fork as the bottom hinge, but you must put a bolt through the throat to stop it splitting. The diagonal timbers are compression members which hold the thing in shape and should be fitted as shown.

Hurdles

Hurdles are movable fences, which you can easily make yourself from any wood that splits. Use mortices to join the horizontals to the pointed uprights. Be sure that the ends of the horizontals are tapered in such a way that they apply pressure up and down and not sideways. Otherwise the uprights will split. You can drive thick nails through the joints to hold them or else use wooden dowels. Nail the cross-braces. Drill all your nail holes or you will split the timber. To erect your hurdles, drive stakes into the ground and fasten the hurdles to them with string.

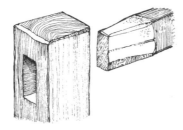

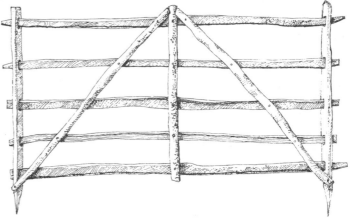

Wattle-hurdles

Wattle-hurdles can be made of split hazel or willow withies woven onto uprights. Put a baulk of timber with appropriate holes drilled in it on the ground to hold the uprights while you are weaving.

Post-and-rail fencing

Strong uprights must be well tamped into the ground. Drive all nails right through and clench them.

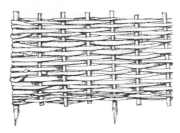

Wire netting

Wire netting is often convenient but always expensive. Square-meshed, or pig, netting (right) makes an excellent permanent fence, and coupled with a strand of barbed wire is completely stock-proof. Diamond-meshed, or sheep, netting (below) is weaker, but it can be rolled up and re-erected, which is what you need for folding sheep.

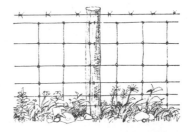

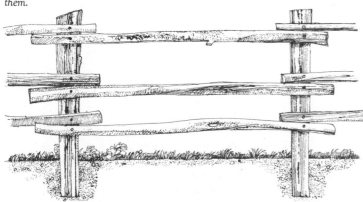

Horse or Tractor Power

There are three practical methods of powering instruments that have to be dragged over the land: farm tractors, garden tractors and animals.

Farm tractors are very large, enormously expensive unless they are very old, cost a lot to up-keep, and are not suitable for small plots of land or small gardens, because in twisting and turning in a small space the tractor wheels compact the soil to a damaging extent. I have sometimes been forced by circumstances to use a farm tractor in a garden and have always regretted it.

A small, or garden, tractor is another matter altogether. It is light – lighter than a horse – you can even pick it up if it is not too big, it does not compact the soil, it is fairly cheap to buy and to maintain. It will work comfortably in small corners and between row crops. It can often be adapted to many uses: one common type will mow grass, either by a reciprocating knife or a rotary knife, it will saw wood, drive all sorts of small barn machinery, rotovate, plough (rather inefficiently and very slowly), row crop cultivate, pull a small barrow and scrape the snow off your garden path. Many of these jobs you could

do as quickly or quicker by hand, and compared with a large tractor or a horse, a garden tractor is extremely slow.

You can plough three acres a day with a small farm tractor: five with a large one, and it doesn't matter how rough the land is. With a horse you can plough perhaps half an acre: with two horses an acre. But one horse will only pull a small plough and plough arable land. To plough grassland you need two good horses. With a garden tractor it would take you days to plough an acre and drive you mad with noise and boredom. It will rotovate old grassland but it will make pretty heavy weather of it.

Tractors have two major advantages. They are not eating or drinking when they are not being worked and they do not use up your land in their search for food. But you do have to pay for their food, even though a garden tractor uses a tiny amount. On the other hand a horse – the best example of animal power – has the advantage that it does not use fuel from off the farm, that you have to buy: it can be fuelled entirely from your land. And a horse has another advantage: it can have another horse. It is unlikely that the tractor will

Farm tractors and garden tractors
If you don't have horses a farm tractor is essential for any holding of more than ten acres. And a garden tractor makes running a garden of any size a lot easier. There are two types, those that run on wheels and those that drag themselves forward by the action of their tines. Both do a good job, but the former, if big enough, is quicker and more versatile.

The sources of traction

The most powerful source of traction, the farm tractor, is predictably the most expensive, both to buy and to run. And the cheapest, the hapless donkey, provides less traction and is slower than everything else. For the self-supporter the horse is the obvious compromise. It need cost only a tenth of the price of a tractor, and will very likely last longer. In any case if you are lucky and manage things properly it will reproduce itself before it wears out. It works quickly and provides good traction, and you can run it on fuel which you grow yourself. Your children will fall over themselves in their efforts to look after it, while you can be fairly certain you'll be the one who keeps the tractor going. The sources of traction compared here are (from left to right): a farm tractor, a garden tractor, a horse, a mule, a donkey and an ox.

Traction	Terrific	Bad	Good	Fair	Bad	Good
Speed of work	Very fast	Very slow	Fast	Fast	Slow	Slow
Ease of working	Some skill needed	Little skill needed	Much skill needed	Much skill needed	Much skill needed	Much skill needed
Fuel	A lot of diesel oil	A little petrol	Nil	Nil	Nil	Nil
Can it be fed with farm produce?	No	No	Yes, but must be good quality	Yes, even poor quality stuff	Yes, even poor quality stuff	Yes, on grass
Does it make manure?	No	No	Yes	Yes	Yes	Yes
Can it reproduce?	No	No	Yes	No	Yes	Yes
Life span	20 years if you're lucky	10 years if you're lucky	15 years	10-15 years	10-15 years	3 years
Initial cost	Enormous unless old	Expensive	Expensive	Fairly expensive	Cheap	Fairly cheap

ever be invented that can have another tractor. But a farm tractor will drive a really effective saw bench, or any barn machinery (such as mills, chaff-cutters, and the like), it can be fitted with a powerful winch for hauling trees out, or down, it will pull a large trailer or cart, it will dig post-holes, it will operate a digging arm that will dig ditches for you (but only just). So it is versatile.

Maybe we can sum the whole complicated subject up by saying: if you have only a garden probably a garden cultivator will be valuable – at least if you don't want to do everything by hand which you perfectly easily could do if you had the time. Don't think a garden cultivator is necessarily light work – some of them can be very arduous things to manage.

If you have anything over four acres – and *like* horses – a light horse might suit you very well. Once you have got your land broken up, either with pigs or with a borrowed farm tractor, a small horse will keep it that way, keep your land clean, and give you a lot of pleasure besides. But on the other hand one of the larger garden tractors would do the work equally well if not as pleasantly. A horse will eat the produce of an acre of very good land in a year, or two or three acres of poorer land. Do not be put off by people who tell you that a horse only converts such and such a percentage of the food it eats into energy. A horse wastes not an ounce of its food: what it doesn't convert into energy it puts back into the land as magnificent manure. On a very small holding you might well consider keeping a horse and buying in hay and oats, or maize, for him or her. You are thus buying-in fertility for your holding.

If you have ten or fifteen acres or over – *and* can pick up a cheap farm tractor in good condition – *and* know how to keep it going – it might well save you a lot of work. On the other hand two good horses will do the job as well, but take three times as long.

Other animals of draught include oxen, mules, donkeys, elephants, water buffalo, llamas, yaks, camels, and reindeer. I have had experience with all of these except yaks and reindeer, but the only ones that are likely to concern the self-supporter in Europe or North America are oxen, mules and perhaps donkeys.

Oxen are very good draught animals. They are much slower than horses but exert a strong steady pull. Some horses are inclined to "snatch" with a heavy load and break things – I have seen oxen sink to their knees in hauling a heavy wagon out of the sand or mud and exert tremendous traction. Oxen are growing into meat during their working lives: horses are depreciating in value, but oxen require two people to work them – horses only one. To bring things down to a smaller scale: two oxen will just about do the work of one horse, pull a very small single-furrow plough, or a row crop cultivator, or a small cart. Four oxen will pull these things much better.

Mules are very hardy, particularly for hot and dry climates (they hate mud and constant wet). They walk fast, will pull hard, can live on worse food than a horse, and I find them completely unlovable. They will not exert so much traction as a heavy horse and are inclined to snatch, kick, bite, and generally misbehave. And I don't want to have hundreds of letters from mule-lovers.

Asses, or donkeys, can exert some traction, but walk very slowly, and it is very hard to make most of them trot. They can be used (as indeed mules and ponies can) for carrying packs over ground too rough for a sled or a cart. One donkey won't pull very much at all – maybe a small row crop cultivator at best. My own feeling about donkeys – and I have travelled many hundreds of miles with them – is that you can have them, but I concede they have their uses.

The Working Horse

There is great nobility about a working horse, and great beauty too. If you want to plough your acre a day for month after month with a pair of horses you will need big horses such as the Shire, Suffolk Punch, Clydesdale, Percheron: great creatures weighing a ton and consuming an awful lot of oats and needing very good looking after. But as a self-supporter you will probably only have to plough half an acre in a day, and that occasionally. You may also wish to drive to market in a cart, perhaps go for a ride now and again, and teach your kids to ride. If this is so, something more in the nature of a Welsh Cob will suit you better, or one of those fine cob-type animals from Denmark, or Belgium. If you have very little heavy farm work to do – just pulling a light pony-plough in already arable land for example, or pulling a horse-hoe, then a light cob, or a Dale or Fell pony, will do. They are fun to ride and drive, and make a pet of too.

Feeding

Horses, like other herbivorous animals, need to be fed often: they need a feed at least three times a day while they are working and must be given at least an hour to eat each meal. Also, they should have some hay to mumble at night if they are in the stable, or else be put out on grass.

For working horses "good hay hath no fellow," as Bottom said in *A Midsummer Night's Dream*, but it must be good hay; dusty hay makes horses broken winded, mouldy hay upsets them, and too much clover hay, if too fresh, will cause them to scour (have diarrhoea).

During the summer, when grass is good, working horses may be run on grass. They graze very close to the ground and should be put on pasture after cows have eaten off the long, lush grass, or else rationed severely as to how long they have on the pasture. Do not expect a horse to work hard, or get hard, on grass alone. For grass makes horses fat and soft. Take it that a horse on grass should have six pounds (2.7kg) of oats a day for every half day that he works.

In the winter, or when grass is short, a horse is best kept in a stable and could eat: sixteen pounds (7.2kg) of hay, twelve pounds (5.4kg) of oats, and maybe some swedes or carrots or even fodder beet as well, while on medium work. A large horse on very heavy work might well have more

oats: perhaps up to twenty pounds (9.0kg) and twenty pounds (9.0kg) of hay. But whatever you do, do not overfeed a horse. If you do you will kill him. A heavy horse doing only half a day's work should never get a whole day's ration. Hay will never hurt him but grain will. A horse on a high ration, working hard and continuously, may be killed by a disease called haemoglobin urea (he pisses blood) if you suddenly knock his work off but go on feeding him the same. The old practice was, on Friday night before the weekend, to give a horse a bran mash (bran is the coarse husk that is taken off wheat to leave white flour, and bran mash is bran soaked in water) instead of the corn feed, and then to feed nothing but plenty of good hay over the weekend: to keep up the corn ration while the horse was idle could be fatal. Similarly it is not fair to expect a soft horse – that is a horse that has lived for weeks out on grass – to do immediate heavy work. You will find that if you try to do this he will sweat a lot, and puff and blow, and show signs of distress. Give him a little work each day, and feed a little more grain, and gradually harden him up.

Beans make a good feed for horses, but don't let them make up more than a sixth of the grain ration. It is very nice if you can get chaff (straw or hay cut up small by a chaff-cutter). Mix it with grain to make it last longer.

Foaling

Fillies can be put to the "horse" (horseman's word for stallion) at two years old (three might be better), and a colt can serve a mare when he is two years old. Pregnancy is slightly over eleven months. A filly or mare may work at regular work for six or seven months of her pregnancy and thereafter can do progressively lighter work "in chains" (pulling an implement with chains) until she foals. She should not work "in shafts" when far gone in pregnancy – the pressure of the shafts might harm her. A mare will probably have less trouble in foaling if she is kept working than if she is not, because she will be in harder condition. If the

The stable
In temperate climates you can leave your horse out all the year round. But you will almost certainly want to bring him indoors in cold weather, and sometimes to feed him or groom him. The ideal stable has a loose box for each horse. This keeps him away from other horses and from all the harness, grooming equipment and feed which you will keep for him.

Removing a horseshoe
First, calm your horse by giving him some food. Face away from him, and pick up his hoof in your left hand, gently sliding your hand down his leg as you do so. Use a buffer driven in with a hammer to lift the clenched nails round the hoof. Scrape the hoof clean with a hoof pick. Then lever the shoe up all round with pincers, before finally pulling it off.

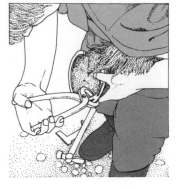

The Working Horse

mare is out on grass in the winter, and not working, she should be given a small ration of hay and maybe a little oats (not more than four pounds or 1.8kg a day), as well as winter grass. In summer grass should be enough.

After foaling, a mare should not be asked to work for at least six weeks: suckling the foal is enough for her. The mare might do very light work after six weeks. But wait until four months – preferably six – before weaning the foal. Once the foal is weaned – taken right away from his mother and kept out of hearing – the mother should be put into work immediately in order to dry off her milk. If you don't want to work the mare you can leave the foal on as long as you like. If you do wean the foal he should be given say four pounds (1.8 kg) of oats a day and four pounds (1.8 kg) of hay.

Breaking a foal

Colt foals should be castrated by a vet at about a year old, but this should never be done in the summer when the flies are about, nor in frosty weather. A foal can be broken (trained) at about two and a half years old. But it is never too soon to get a halter on a foal (the first day is OK) to teach him to be led about. Foals have a great sense of humour and can be great fun. If you make a fuss of a foal and get him really tame he is far less trouble to break. And the foal's feet should be lifted often, to accustom him to this necessary procedure.

To break him, get a bit into his mouth and drive him in front of you with a whip and long reins. After a few lessons get a collar on him. When he gets used to this, hitch him to some not too heavy object like a log or a set of harrows and get him to pull. Then put him next to an older horse and get them both to pull, say, a plough. Wait until he is pretty calm before trying him in shafts: the experience of being confined in shafts and having a rattling cart behind him may be too much for him.

Kindness and firmness and common sense are the qualities needed for breaking horses, and it is absolutely essential that you should not be frightened of the horse, for if you are the horse will sense it immediately and you will never break him. If you have great trouble breaking a horse try keeping him away from other horses in a loose box (a room in which he is kept loose) for a week or so, and spend some time each day with him, talking to him, feeding him, handling him and getting to know him. He will then get used to you.

Shoeing

If a horse is to be worked at all hard he must be shod, perhaps every six weeks. The hooves grow under the shoes. If the latter have not worn too much they can be taken off, the feet trimmed and the shoes nailed on again. Shoeing is a highly skilled job, but any horseman should be able to pull shoes off a horse's feet. Nailing on, though, should only be done by a skilled man: it is easy to lame a horse – perhaps for life – by driving a nail in the wrong place.

Harnessing a horse
1 Use a halter to lead your horse for harnessing. Then take it off.

2 Have the collar in easy reach and the bridle hung on the crook of your left arm. Hold the horse over his nose and fit the collar over his head upside down. Then strap the hames (the curved metal or wooden strips which take the strain) to the collar. Tighten them at the top.

4 Fit the saddle, or ridge pad, and tighten the girth, but not so much that the horse's wind is constricted. Sometimes the britchin will be kept fastened to the girth.

3 Slide on the bridle. To get the bit in the horse's mouth you may have to force his teeth apart by pushing your fingers in at the side. It takes practice.

5 Here the britchin is being put on separately. The crupper, a loop of leather that goes round the tail, must go on when the britchin is right back. It is then eased forward and strapped on to the saddle, if it is not already so strapped.

Ridge pad
Ridge chain
Hip strap
Hip strap
Britchin
Hames
Tug
Shaft
Belly chain
Girth strap

The fully harnessed horse
The horse is now taken to the cart or implement and shut in. In other words he is backed between the shafts and the tugs are hooked to the harness. Then the ridge chain which holds the shafts up is fastened and lastly the britchin chains. The tugs pull the implement or cart forward. The britchin chains hold it back if it tries to go too fast. A belly chain is passed from shaft to shaft under the horse's belly to prevent the shafts from skying if the cart or implement is back-loaded.
See that all is well adjusted before you move off. The shafts must not pinch the horse, the britchin must indeed take the weight of the cart going downhill, and the tugs, not the ridge chain, must exert the forward pull on the shafts.

Preparing Land & Sowing

If you threw some seeds on grassland, or in a wood, all that would happen is that the birds would eat them. In order to sow seeds with any hope of success you have got to do two things: eliminate the competition of existing plants, and disturb the soil so that the seed can get into it. If possible, in fact, bury the seed, although of course not too deep.

The most usual method of preparing grassland or other land with an indigenous vegetation on it is by ploughing or digging. But if you have pigs, use them. They will do the job even better than a plough. If I plough old pasture to sow a grain crop I plough it so as to turn it over as completely as possible, although it still stands up in ridges. Then I drag disc harrows up and down the furrows for two passes, so as not to knock the ridges back again. At this stage I would add any fertilizer, such as lime or phosphate, that the land might require. Then I would disc again across the furrows. The reason for using a disc harrow at this juncture is that it cuts the hard turf furrows of the old grassland to pieces – instead of dragging it out as a spike harrow would do.

A pass or two with the spike harrow works the land down to a fine seed bed. It must not be too fine for winter-sown corn, nor even for spring-sown if it is wheat or oats. Barley needs a much finer tilth than either. I then broadcast the seed, that is sow it by hand, but if I had a seed drill I would drill it. Remember if you drill seed too deep it will become exhausted before its shoots can get to the surface and it will die. So the smaller the seed the shallower it should be. Three times the diameter of the seed is quite far enough. I would then harrow once again. A pass with a roller, completes the sowing process. With row crops hoe between the rows when the seedlings are about six inches (15 cm) high and then the gate can be shut until harvest time.

No-ploughing and no-digging

The no-ploughing or no-digging theory is now very popular. The adherents of this theory claim that the land should never be ploughed or dug because it is bad to invert the soil. Inverting the soil upsets the soil life, putting surface bacteria down so deep that they die, bringing deeper organisms to the surface where they die.

No-diggers and no-ploughers have great success, provided they have very large quantities of compost, or farmyard manure, with which to mulch their land. The seeds are virtually sown under a covering of compost.

My own experience shows that for bringing grassland into cultivation either the plough, or the pig's snout, is essential. The next year, if you still wish to keep that land arable, you can often get away with cultivating only, or even harrowing or other shallow cultivations. The idea of very heavy mulches of compost is fine – providing you can get the compost. But the land itself will never produce enough vegetable material to make enough compost to cover itself sufficiently deeply and therefore you will have to bring vegetable matter in from outside.

1 Use pigs or a plough
For bringing grassland into cultivation the pig's snout is unbeatable. And a pig does something a plough can't. He manures the land as he digs it. Otherwise plough.

2 Then use a harrow
Disc harrow.first up and down the furrows, then across. Next use a spike harrow to produce the right tilth for your seed.

3 Sow the seed
Broadcasting is simply scattering the seed on the ground in the biblical manner. A seed drill drops the seed down pipes so that it is buried and safe from birds.

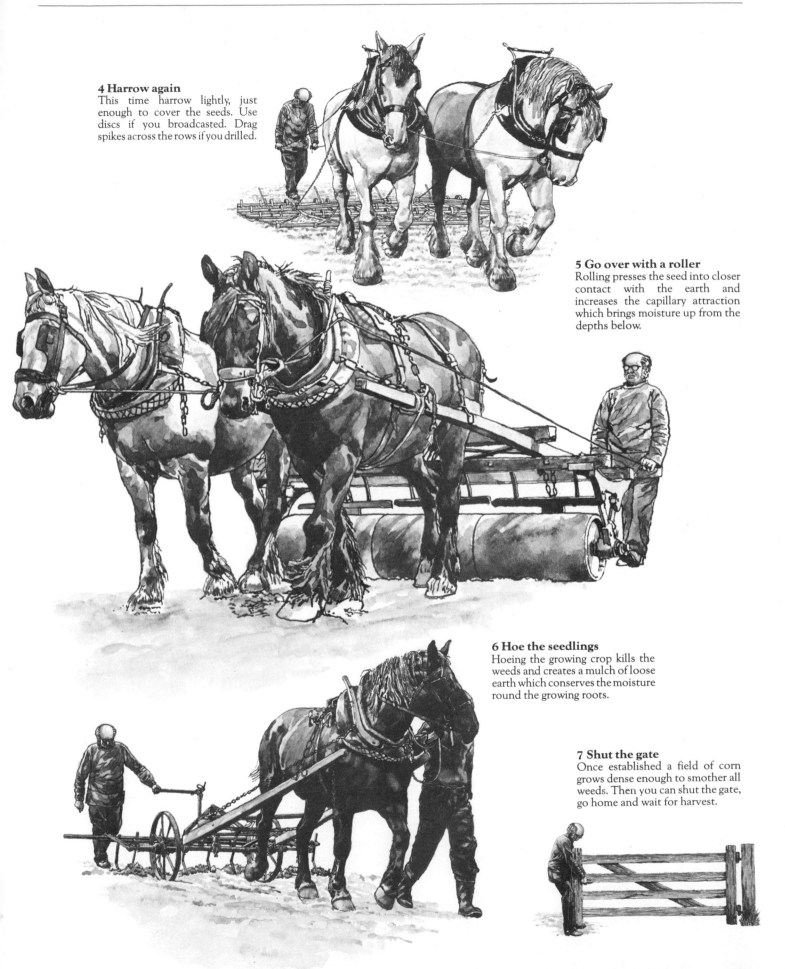

4 Harrow again
This time harrow lightly, just enough to cover the seeds. Use discs if you broadcasted. Drag spikes across the rows if you drilled.

5 Go over with a roller
Rolling presses the seed into closer contact with the earth and increases the capillary attraction which brings moisture up from the depths below.

6 Hoe the seedlings
Hoeing the growing crop kills the weeds and creates a mulch of loose earth which conserves the moisture round the growing roots.

7 Shut the gate
Once established a field of corn grows dense enough to smother all weeds. Then you can shut the gate, go home and wait for harvest.

Preparing Land & Sowing

Ploughing

The plough that Western Man has used since Iron Age times has three main working elements: the coulter, the share, and the mould-board or breast (see illustration). In Africa, Australia, and parts of America, a similar plough, the disc plough, is much used. This is not to be confused with the disc harrow. It is a large, very dished, steel disc, dragged through the soil at a certain angle. The angle is such that the leading-edge of the disc acts as a coulter, the bottom edge acts as a share and the belly of the disc acts as a mould-board. It is very good on trashy land.

Using the fixed-furrow plough

Now if you consider what happens when you actually take a fixed-furrow plough out into a field and begin to plough, you will realize that the operation is not so simple as you might think. Suppose you go into the middle of one side of the field and plough one furrow. Then what do you do? If you turn your horse or tractor round, face the other way and go back, you will either simply plough the slice you have ploughed out back into its furrows so you are back where you started from, or you will plough the other side of it and build up a ridge of two slices bundled up against

A horse or oxen-drawn fixed-furrow plough
This is the classic plough of which all others are mere variations. The essential parts are: the coulter, which is a vertical or slightly sloping knife which goes through the soil in front and cuts a vertical slot; the share, a blade which cuts a horizontal slice underneath the furrow to be ploughed; and the mould-board, or breast, which is that beautifully curving blade of wood or metal which takes the slice of earth cut out by the other two members and turns it over and lays it against the slice already turned. The plough's big wheel goes along the furrow, the small one stays on "land". The two hakes adjust depth and position. The coulter is sometimes a sharp steel disc and on some ploughs used on light crumbling land does not exist at all. Some ploughs also have a skim coulter, or skimmer, a sort of miniature plough which goes ahead of the main one turning over the vegetation on top of the soil.

How the plough cuts
A properly adjusted plough will cut a roughly rectangular slice out of the soil, and turn it almost upsidedown so that it rests on its predecessor, as shown right.

each other, and under the ridge will be unploughed ground.

The way to avoid the piece of unploughed ground is to plough your first furrow, then turn round and plough it back again with the piece of ground underneath it too. Then turn round again and plough the next furrow up against the first two. You have then made a ridge. You then simply go round and round this ridge, every time ploughing your furrow towards the ridge. It will be seen that, when you do this, you get further and further away from the ridge, and each time you have to go right round it. You soon find yourself having to travel a huge distance along the headland to get to where you are to start the furrows going back again. So what do you do then?

You go even further along the headland, and plough out another "setting-out" furrow as the first furrow of a stetch of land is called, and make another ridge. (A stetch is the area of ploughed land around a single ridge.) You then plough round that one. As soon as you come to the last furrow of the first stetch you go back and travel on further beyond your second stetch and "set-out" a third stetch. And so on. The ridges are traditionally 22 yards (20 m) apart.

It will be seen now that you will end up with a field with parallel furrows running down it, and in between each pair

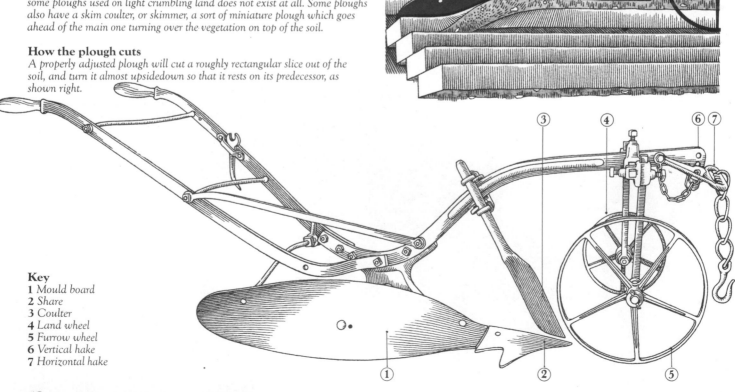

Key
1 *Mould board*
2 *Share*
3 *Coulter*
4 *Land wheel*
5 *Furrow wheel*
6 *Vertical hake*
7 *Horizontal hake*

of furrows parallel ridges. In other words you have gathered the soil at the ridges and robbed it out of the furrows. If you go on doing this year after year you will end up with the typical "ridge-and-furrow" land of parts of the English Midlands. On wettish heavy land this pattern of field has an advantage: the furrows, running up and down the slope, serve to carry the surface water away, and crops growing on the ridge part are well above the water table. In most parts of Southern Europe and America, though, it would be criminal thus to plough up and down the slopes. It would lead to gully-erosion.

Turnwrest plough

Now if you want a simple life, and don't want your soil gathered into ridges, there is another kind of plough that will suit your needs and that is the turnwrest, or two-way plough. This has two ploughing bodies, one in the ground and the other up in the air. One turns the furrow to the right, the other to the left. With this you simply plough one furrow, turn round, swing the two bodies over so they change places and plough back again. And when you do this both furrows are laid the same way. You avoid all the complications of "setting-out," "gathering-up" and all the rest of it and when

you have finished your field is quite level, with no "lands" or stetches at all. Many tractor ploughs are of this type nowadays, and the famous Brabant plough, widely used in Europe and drawn by horses or oxen, is also a turnwrest. The Brabant is a marvellous instrument. I have a tiny, one-horse one and it is worth its weight in gold.

Incidentally the ancient belief in the necessity of turning the soil deeply enough to bury all rubbish completely is becoming more and more discredited. Organic farmers, even in England and the Eastern States of the USA, prefer to leave their compost or manure on top of the soil rather than to plough it in. It is a fact that the enormous earthworm population in soil that has been organically farmed for some time drags all vegetable matter down into the soil without our help. Except for my potato field, I am tending more and more to leave manure on the surface and to disturb the soil deeply as little as possible. But, whatever his theories in this respect, the practical grower finds himself forced, occasionally, to plough or to dig.

Sowing

There is no rule of thumb in farming, particularly when it comes to sowing seed. Examine the soil after every operation

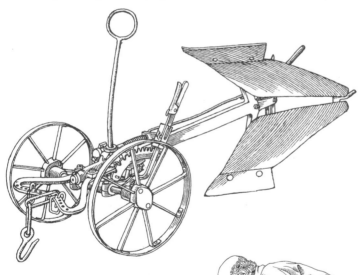

The Brabant turnwrest plough
The Brabant turnwrest is the best animal-drawn plough yet invented. When it is properly adjusted the ploughman need not even hold it; the ring above it is for the plough-line or reins. The great advantage of this and all turnwrest ploughs lies in their two ploughing blades. One turns the furrow to the right, the other to the left. You plough a furrow, turn round, fling the blades over as shown right and your next furrow will fall the same way as the first one. All the problems of ridges and "setting out" are avoided.

Ploughing with fixed-furrow and turnwrest ploughs
With a fixed-furrow plough (see above left), plough your first furrow, then turn round and come back the other way ploughing the piece of ground underneath your first furrow. This will turn your first furrow over again with the second one on top of it. Turn round again and plough the piece of ground on the other side of the hole left by your first furrow, piling it up against the first two forming a ridge. Plough round and round the ridge, going up one side and down the other so that the furrows all face in towards the ridge, resting on each other. Make a new ridge, a sensible distance from the first one – about 22 yards (20 m) away – and start again. The turnwrest plough (above right) avoids these complications. By turning the blade over each time you turn round to go back the other way, you can plough from one side of your field to the other, and have all your furrows leaning the same way.

– remember the needs of the seed and the plant. If the seed is too shallow the birds will get it or it will dry out, that is if the soil is dry and dusty on top. If it is too deep it will use all its energy pushing its shoot up to the light and will die before the life-giving sun's rays can give it more energy. If the land is too wet the seed will drown. If it is too sticky the seed will not be able to push out its roots and shoots. The plant itself needs open soil, which permits the air to circulate and the water to rise.

Don't forget that temperature is most important for seed germination. I knew an old farmer in Suffolk who used to drop his trousers in the spring and sit on his soil to see if it was warm enough to sow spring barley. He could sense the temperature, humidity and so on with his bare backside more sensitively than he could with his hand. To drill his seed in too-cold ground was only to have it rot, or the birds get it, or the hardier weeds grow away from it and smother it. To plant it too late was to have a late and not very heavy crop of barley. To get it just right he had to use his buttocks. He grew very good barley.

Hoeing

Having sown or planted your crop, you may have to "keep it clean," which is the farmer's way of saying suppress the weeds among it. Some crops don't need this because they grow quickly and densely, and smother the weeds by denying them light and soil space. You can often get away without hoeing cereals. But row crops (see pp. 82-88) do need hoeing. There are two kinds of hoeing: hand hoeing and mechanical hoeing. The hand hoe is simply a blade on a stick with which you cut through the surface of the soil. Mechanical hoeing is the pulling of mounted hoe blades along between the rows of the crop by animal or tractor power. This only cleans the ground between the rows. It cannot do it in the rows but between the plants, because no machine has yet been invented which can tell the difference between a weed and a crop plant. It takes the eye of man, or woman, to do that. Therefore, even if you horse or tractor hoe, you will still have to hand hoe as well, at least once.

There is another consideration about hoeing. Not only does it kill the weeds but it also creates a mulch of loose

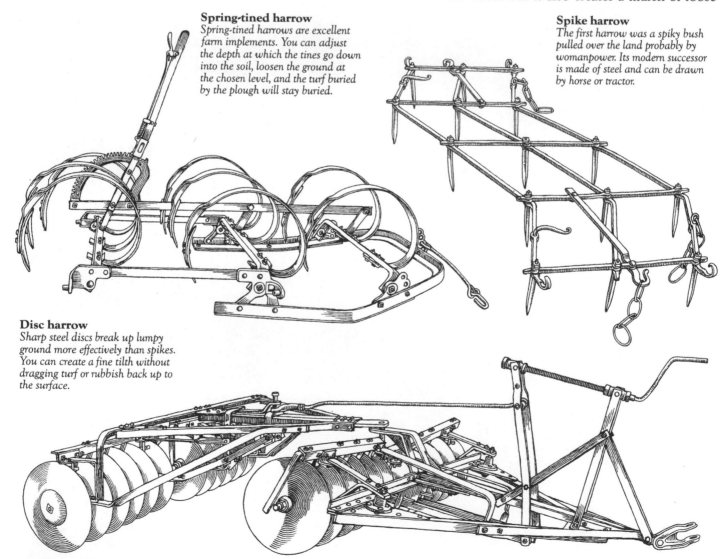

Spring-tined harrow
Spring-tined harrows are excellent farm implements. You can adjust the depth at which the tines go down into the soil, loosen the ground at the chosen level, and the turf buried by the plough will stay buried.

Spike harrow
The first harrow was a spiky bush pulled over the land probably by womanpower. Its modern successor is made of steel and can be drawn by horse or tractor.

Disc harrow
Sharp steel discs break up lumpy ground more effectively than spikes. You can create a fine tilth without dragging turf or rubbish back up to the surface.

earth. This mulch conserves the moisture in the land, for it breaks the capillary crevices up which water can creep to the surface. It is very nice to see loose, broken-up soil on the surface rather than a hard pavement. It is true that some crops – onions are one, brassica, or cabbage-tribe, plants are another – like firm soil, but once they have got their roots in, it is best to shake up the surface around them. This lets the rain and air in and stops the moisture coming to the surface and evaporating too quickly. In Suffolk old countrymen say: "a hoeing is as good as a shower of rain." Experience shows that it is, too, and you cannot hoe too much.

Weeds

Selective weed sprays, or pre-emergence weed sprays, are the agribusinessman's answer to weed suppression in row crops. We organic farmers don't use them, because we cannot believe that it is good to douse our soils year after year and decade after decade in what are, after all, nothing more nor less than poisons. Also the hoe can do it, not only just as well but much better.

Weeds have been defined as "plants in the wrong place." Wrong, that is, from the husbandman's point of view. From their point of view they might be in the right place. But do not become paranoiac about them. Weed competition, it is true, can ruin a crop. The weeds are so much more vigorous, and fitted for their environment, than our artificially induced crops can be. But also, under other circumstances, they do no harm and often do good. Bare, naked soil, with no crop on it, should be anathema to the husbandman. A good covering of weeds is as good as a crop of green manure. Green manure is any crop that we plant merely in order to plough in again. A good crop of chick-weed, fat-hen, or many another annual weed, is just as good. And, in the summer when weeds are rampant no matter how many times we hoe, when you go along the rows and either hoe weeds out, or pull them up, and let them lie down between the crop rows to rot, you realize that they do a lot of good. They form a mulch, which covers the soil and stops the drying winds from getting at it, and eventually they rot and the earth-worms drag them down and turn them into humus.

Seed drill and basket
A seed drill sows seed evenly and also buries it. If you scatter seed by hand which you can do from a basket or a sack, you will need about half as much seed again, because the birds will eat the extra.

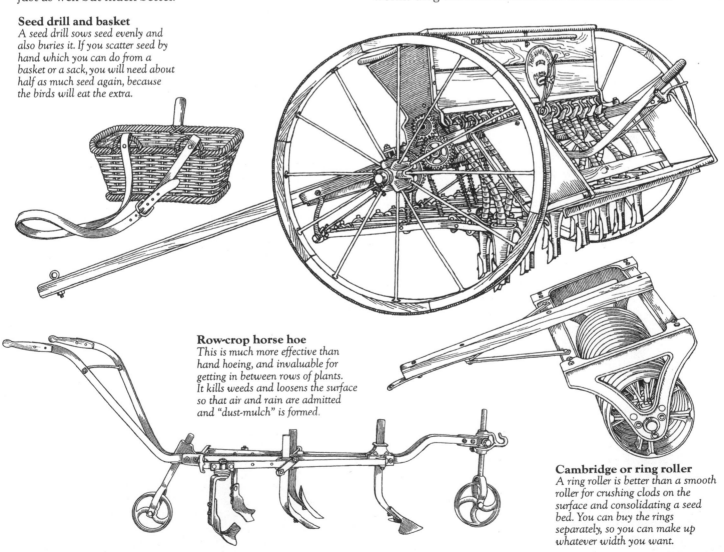

Row-crop horse hoe
This is much more effective than hand hoeing, and invaluable for getting in between rows of plants. It kills weeds and loosens the surface so that air and rain are admitted and "dust-mulch" is formed.

Cambridge or ring roller
A ring roller is better than a smooth roller for crushing clods on the surface and consolidating a seed bed. You can buy the rings separately, so you can make up whatever width you want.

Harvesting

The crown of the year is harvest time, and if a man cannot enjoy that he is unlikely to enjoy anything. He sweats and toils, along with his friends and neighbours, to gather in and make secure the fruit of his year's labours. The work is hard, hot, sometimes boisterous, always fun, and each day of it should be rewarded with several pints of home-brewed beer.

All the cereals with the exception of maize are harvested in exactly the same way. When the crop is ripe, but not so ripe that it will shed its grain prematurely, the straw is cut. This may be done by sickle, scythe, mower (reaper), reaper-and-binder, or combine harvester.

Sickling a field full of corn is unbelievably tedious. A scythe used by a skilled man will cut two acres in a day, and if you can fit a cradle to it (see illustration), it will dump the cut corn in sheaf-sized piles. Wet the blade at regular intervals with a rough stone, or hammer sharp as Alpine farmers do.

A grass mower, whether horse or tractor drawn, will cover a field fairly quickly leaving cut corn all over the place. It must then be gathered into sheaves. A reaper-and-binder ties the sheaves for you, but it is a dirty great cumbersome machine and needs three horses to pull it for any length of time. If you are growing corn for your own and your family's consumption, you should not need to grow much more than an acre. It is certainly not worth owning a reaper-and-binder to harvest such a small area, and it's hardly worth borrowing one either.

Sheaf

Sheaves are bundles of a size you can conveniently grab, tied around the belly either with string, or with a fistful of the corn itself. To tie a sheaf with corn rub both ends of the fistful to make it pliable, put it round the bundle which is gripped betweeen your legs, twist the two ends together tightly, then tuck the twisted bit under the part round the sheaf (see illustration). The reaper-and-binder, of course, ties its own sheaves, with string.

Stook

You then walk along the field and stand the sheaves up into stooks or traives. Six or eight in a stook is normal. Take two sheaves and bang the heads together so that they lean into each other at an angle and do not fall down. Lean two or three more pairs against the first two. Leave them like that for a week or two so that the corn can dry out in the sun and wind, and the grain can become dead ripe.

Mow

In wet climates the practice is then to form a mow, which is intermediate between a stook and a stack, or rick. To make a mow stand about twenty sheaves up on their butts leaning inwards in a solid circle. Then start building another solid circle on top of the first lot starting from the middle. You can build in a spiral if you like. Lay the sheaves of this second layer closer to the horizontal, with the ears inwards towards the middle. To stop these sheaves slipping snatch a handful of

1 Cut the corn
If you cut corn by hand it is quicker and easier to use a scythe rather than a sickle.

2 Tie it into sheaves
Take an armful of corn and tie it tightly round with string or a handful of corn.

3 Make stooks
Lean six or eight sheaves together to form a stook. Leave for a week or more to dry.

4 Build a rick
Get your corn into a rick before the bad weather comes: it can be circular or rectangular. Thatch the top, or cover to protect against rain.

7 Store the grain
You can keep grain in sacks, bins, jars, or on a special grain floor: anywhere as long as it is absolutely dry and proof against vermin.

6 Winnow the grain
To separate the grain from the chaff, you can use the time-honoured method of throwing the whole lot into the wind. The lighter chaff will blow further than the heavier grain.

5 Thresh your corn
Threshing by hand is best done with a flail, two sticks of different lengths joined by a piece of leather. But you can beat your corn against any hard surface to get the grain out of the ears.

corn from each sheaf and tuck it under the band (string or corn tie) of the next sheaf.

Arrange all the time that the centre of the mow shall be higher than the outside edges. Put layer after layer on like this, drawing each layer in a little so that the mow rises steeply to a point. It will then be crowned by, say, four sheaves with their ears upwards waving in the wind like flags. Very pretty. Any rain that blows into it will run downhill along the sloping straws and onto the ground.

Rick

But before the stupendous gales of winter blow up you should get the corn out of the mows and into ricks or stacks, in your stackyard. When working on a fairly small scale stacks are better circular. You lay the sheaves horizontally, ears inwards, layer after layer, always keeping your centre firm and

high. Work from the centre out this time, and do not pull in as you did with the mow until the eaves are reached. Then pull inwards sharply until the apex is reached. You must then thatch this rick (see p. 241), or provide it with some waterproof cover, just on top. Corn will keep well in such a rick for years, as long as the rats don't get into it. To keep rats away you can build a raised platform on staddle stones.

Grain in the stook, mow and rick is maturing naturally all the time, slowly ripening and drying out, and it is better grain than grain cut and threshed with a combine harvester.

Threshing

Then you must thresh your grain. This is the business of knocking the grain out of the ears. You can do this by bashing the ears on the back of a chair, putting them through a threshing drum, beating them with a flail, or driving horses or oxen about on them. Paddy is often threshed in Sri Lanka by men trampling it with their feet, all holding on to a horizontal bar to steady themselves, and singing like hell as they do it.

A threshing drum is a drum revolving round which knocks out the grain. A flail is two sticks linked together: the longer stick, which you hold, may be anything – ash or hickory is fine; the short stick, with which you wallop the grain, is often holly. The link which joins them can be leather, and eel-skin was a traditional thing for this, being very tough. (Eel-skin is excellent for "leather" hinges as well.) You try to lay the short stick flat on the ears of the corn.

Winnowing

After you have threshed, or knocked out, the grain, you must winnow it. Traditionally, this is done by throwing the grain, which is mixed up with chaff, broken bits of ear and straw,

Hand tools
Time-honoured equipment works well and is adequate for the homesteader. Cutting with sickle or scythe is arduous and time consuming, but it produces better grain than that cut and threshed with a combine harvester.

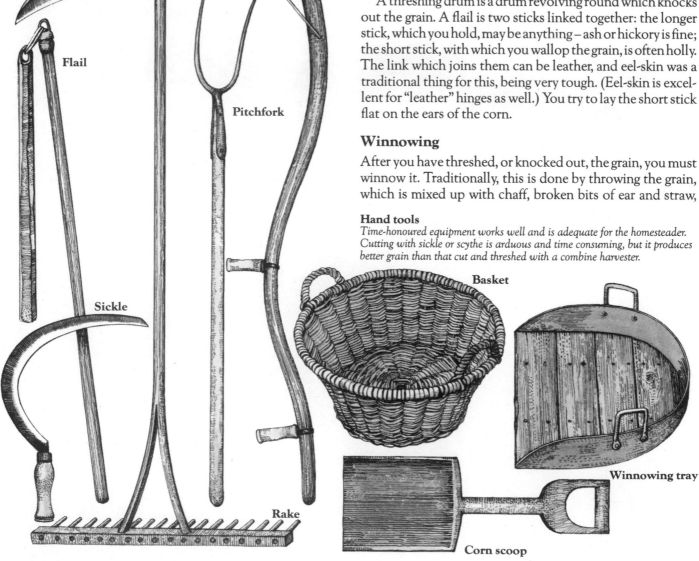

Scythe

Flail

Pitchfork

Sickle

Rake

Basket

Winnowing tray

Corn scoop

thistle seeds and all the rest of it, up into the air in a strong breeze. The light rubbish blows away, and the grain falls in a heap on the ground. Common sense suggests you do this on a clean floor, or else have a sheet of canvas or something similar on the floor to catch the grain. The chaff – the stuff that blows away – can be mixed with corn and fed to animals.

A winnowing machine, though, is a machine that has a rotating fan in it which produces an artificial wind to winnow the grain. It also has a number of reciprocating sieves. These extract weed seeds, separate small ("tail") corn from large ("head") corn, and thoroughly clean the grain. They can be turned by hand or power.

Storing

When grain has been harvested naturally by the above means it will keep indefinitely provided it is kept dry and away from vermin. You can store naturally-dried corn in bins, on a grain floor, in big Alibaba jars, in sacks: anything will do provided rats and mice and other vermin cannot get to it.

The processes described above are just the same for wheat, barley, oats, rye, field beans, rice, buckwheat, sorghum, millet, linseed, oil-seed rape, and many other seed crops.

Combining

Harvesting by combine is another kettle of fish. Here the machine cuts the corn and threshes and winnows the grain in one operation, while moving round the field. It saves an awful lot of labour. In countries with dry summers, like Canada, the grain comes straight off the combine dry enough to store, but in damper climates it either has to be dried artificially, or stored hermetically while still moist, in a grain silo or sealed in a polythene bag.

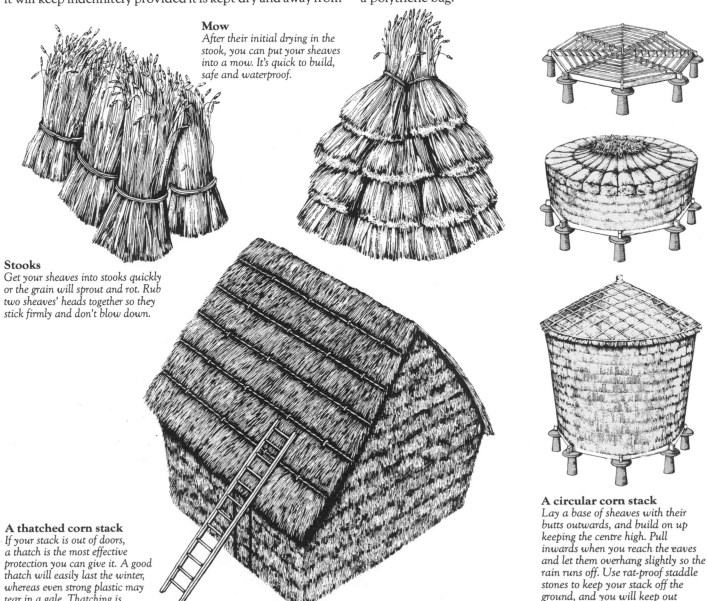

Mow
After their initial drying in the stook, you can put your sheaves into a mow. It's quick to build, safe and waterproof.

Stooks
Get your sheaves into stooks quickly or the grain will sprout and rot. Rub two sheaves' heads together so they stick firmly and don't blow down.

A thatched corn stack
If your stack is out of doors, a thatch is the most effective protection you can give it. A good thatch will easily last the winter, whereas even strong plastic may tear in a gale. Thatching is described on pp. 240-241.

A circular corn stack
Lay a base of sheaves with their butts outwards, and build on up keeping the centre high. Pull inwards when you reach the eaves and let them overhang slightly so the rain runs off. Use rat-proof staddle stones to keep your stack off the ground, and you will keep out damp as well as rats.

The Cereals

Cereals are the staff of life for most of mankind. Even our milk and our meat derive largely from them. They are grasses nurtured and bred by man so that their grain is large and nourishing. Except in parts of the tropics where such roots as tapioca and yams are the staple carbohydrate, and in wet cold places where the potato plugs the gap, wheat, barley, oats, rye, rice, maize and sorghum are what keep us all alive and kicking.

The cereals have all been bred from wild grasses, and bred so far away from their parent stocks that they are now distinct species. In fact it is sometimes difficult to guess which wild grass a particular cereal is derived from, and, in some cases, maize for example, the wild species is now probably extinct.

It was inevitable that the seeds of the grasses should become mankind's staple food. After all – grass is the most widespread of plants, its seeds copious and nourishing and easily stored. When the Bushmen of the Kalahari find a hoard of grass seed in an ants' nest, stored there by the industrious insects for their future supplies, the Bushmen steal this seed, roast it on a hot stone, and eat it themselves. Our stone age ancestors no doubt did the same. And it is but a short step to harvesting the grass oneself and threshing the seed out of it. Then it was found that if you put some of the seed into the ground, in the right conditions, it would grow where you wanted it to. Agriculture was born and with it civilization, made possible by the ability of Man to grow and store the food he has grown reliably.

Many smallholders feel that grain growing is not for them: it requires expensive machinery, is difficult, and cannot be done effectively on a small scale. This is just not so. Anyone can grow grain, on no matter how small a scale, provided he can keep the birds off it. Harvesting can be done quite simply with the sickle or even an ordinary carving knife. Threshing can be done over the back of a chair and winnowing outdoors in the wind. Grinding can be done with a coffee grinder or a small hand-mill. Baking can be done in any household oven. It is very satisfying to eat your own bread baked from grain you have grown and milled yourself, from your own seed.

When the Roman armies wanted to conquer Britain they waited until harvest time, so that their soldiers could spread out over the country, reap the native wheat, take it back to camp and make bread out of it. If the Roman legionaries could do it with such apparent nonchalance, there is no reason why we cannot do it too.

It is fortunate that the grasses are widespread: they grow in practically any climate our Earth affords, and therefore Man has been able to find, and adapt, one particular grass to suit each area. Thus, if we live in the wet tropics, we may choose rice; the dry tropics, sorghum; temperate heavy lands, wheat; temperate dry and sandy lands, rye; cold and rainy lands, oats; temperate light fiend, barley; and so on. There is an improved grass for practically every area and climate in which Man can survive.

Sorghum
Sorghum vulgare

Rice
Oryza sativa

Maize
Zea mays

Barley
Hordeum distichum

Rye
Secale cereale

Wheat
Triticum vulgare

Hard wheat
Triticum durum

Oats
Avena sativa

Wheat

Ever since Stone Age man found that he could bang the grass seeds collected by seed-collecting ants between two stones and eat them, men have used cereals for food, and in all those parts of the world where wheat will grow, wheat is the favourite.

Hard and soft wheat

Hard wheat grows only in fairly hot and dry climates, although there are some varieties that are fairly hard even if grown in a colder climate. It is much beloved by commercial bakers because it makes spongy bread full of holes. It holds more water than soft wheat and a sack of it therefore makes more bread. In temperate climates soft wheat grows more readily and makes magnificent bread: a dense bread perhaps, not full of huge holes, not half water and wind – but bread such as the battle of Agincourt was won on.

Sowing

Wheat grows best on heavy loam or even clay soil. You can grow it on light land, and you will get good quality grain but a poor yield. It will also grow on very rich land, but it must have land in very good heart.

In temperate climates wheat – and it will be one of the varieties called winter wheat – is often sown in the autumn. Winter wheat grows quite fast in the autumn, in the summer-warmed soil, then lies dormant throughout the winter, to shoot up quickly in the spring and make an early crop. In countries, such as Canada, where the winter is too severe spring wheat is grown and this is planted in the spring. It needs a good hot summer to ripen it, and will come to harvest much later than winter wheat. If you can grow winter wheat do so. You will get a heavier crop and an earlier harvest.

I prefer to get winter wheat in very early: even early in September in Britain, because it gets off to a quick start, beats the rooks more effectively (rooks love seed wheat and will eat the last seed if they get the chance), and makes plenty of growth before the frosts set in. Frost may destroy very young wheat by dislodging the soil about its roots. If the early-sown wheat is then "winter-proud" as farmers say, meaning too long, graze it off with sheep. Graze it off either in November or in February or March. This will do the sheep good and will also cause the wheat to tiller – put out several shoots – and you will get a heavier crop. You can sow winter wheat in October and sometimes even in November. The later you sow it the more seed you should use.

Spring wheat should be sown as early as you can get the land ready and you feel the soil is warm enough. I would say not before the beginning of March although some people sow it in February. The earlier you sow it the more you will lose from rooks, who have little other food at that time of the year, and the longer it will take to get established. But wheat needs a long growing season and therefore, the earlier you sow it the better. In other words, if you don't want a very late harvest, as always in farming, you have got to find a compromise between tricky alternatives.

Wheat needs a fairly coarse seed bed, that is, it is better to have the soil in small clods rather than fine powder. For autumn-sown wheat the seed bed should be even coarser than for spring-sown. This is so that the clods will deflect the winter rain and prevent the seed from being washed out and the land becoming like pudding.

So plough, if you have to plough, shallowly, and then do not work your land down too fine. In other words, do not cultivate or harrow it too much. Aim at a field of clods about as big as a small child's fist. If you are planting wheat after old grassland, plough carefully so as to invert the sods as completely as you can, and then do not bring them up again. Disc the surface, if you have discs, or harrow it with a spring-tined harrow, or ordinary harrow if you haven't got that. But do not harrow too much. Then drill or sow into that. The earlier you can plough the land before you put the wheat in the better, so as to give the land a chance to settle.

You can either drill wheat, at a rate of about three bushels of seed to the acre, or else broadcast it at about four bushels to the acre. Whichever you do it is a good thing to harrow it after seeding and also to roll it – that is if you don't think the rolling will break down the clods too much. If it is wet don't roll it. Discing is quite good after broadcasting seed – but only do it once – if you do it twice you will bring the seed up again.

Care of growing crop

You can harrow wheat quite hard when it has started to come up but is not more than six inches (15 cm) tall. After you have harrowed it may look as if you have ruined it, but you haven't. You will have killed several weeds but not the wheat, and the harrowing does good by opening up the surface of the ground. If frosts look as if they have lifted the surface of the ground in the early spring you can roll, preferably with a ring roller, but only if the ground is pretty dry.

Jethro Tull invented a seed drill and developed "horse-hoe-husbandry." His idea was to drill wheat and other cereals in rows a foot (30 cm) apart (there was much experimentation with distances) and then keep the horse-hoe going up and down between the rows. Very good results were achieved. The practice has been discontinued because developments in husbandry have enabled the farmer to clean his land, meaning free it from weeds, more thoroughly. It is therefore not so necessary to weed the wheat. In any case, a good crop of wheat that "gets away" quickly will smother most weeds on reasonably clean land. Agribusiness-men of course use selective weed poisons to kill weeds in wheat. I used them only once and have seldom had a crop of any cereal that has suffered badly from weed competition. Selective weed poisons are only necessary to cover up the effects of bad husbandry.

Wheat is harvested in the way pictured on pp. 52-53.

Milling Grain

Modern industrial grain milling is enormously complicated, and aims to remove everything from the flour that is ultimately used for bread except just the pure starch. The milling of wholemeal, on the other hand, is very simple: all you do is grind the grain: nothing is taken out and nothing is put in. Wholemeal flour also has more of every beneficial thing, except pure starch (carbohydrate) than white flour has. And wholemeal bread is better for the digestion than white bread because it has roughage. Here is a percentage comparison:

	Protein	Fat	Carbo-hydrate	Calcium	Iron	Vitamin B1	Ribo-flavin	Nicotinic acid
White flour	2.3	0.2	15.6	4	0.2	0.01	0.01	0.2
Whole-meal	3.1	0.6	11.2	7	0.7	0.09	0.05	0.6

There are four types of mill for grinding grain. Two of them are of little use to the self-supporter: the hammer mill, which will smash anything up, even feathers, but does not make very good flour; and the roller mill, as used in huge industrial mills, where steel rollers roll against each other and the grain passes between. The other two types – the stone mill and the plate mill – are both suitable for anyone who wants to make his own bread.

Stone milling

The stone mill is one of the oldest and most basic types of mill. It consists of two stones, one of which turns on the other which remains stationary. The grain is passed between the two, generally being dropped down a hole in the top, or runner stone. The art of milling with stones, and particularly that of making stone mills, has nearly died out. The sooner it is revived the better. However, in response to the new demand for such devices, several firms have put miniature stone mills on the market, both hand and electrically driven. These make very good flour, and they will grind very fine or coarsely as desired; the finer you grind the longer it will take.

Plate milling

There are also some good hand-driven plate mills available. A steel plate with grooves cut in it revolves, generally vertically, against a stationary steel plate. Flour ground slowly with one of these seems just as good as stone-ground flour. If you have a tractor or a stationary engine, the ordinary barn plate mill found on nearly every conventional farm is quite satisfactory for grinding bread flour provided you don't drive it too fast. If it goes too fast it heats the flour (you can feel it coming hot out of the spout). Heating the flour like this spoils the flavour.

There is one thing to remember that makes the milling of all grain much easier. That is – dry the grain first. In a warm, dry climate this may not be necessary, but in a damp climate it makes a great difference. When you are nearly ready to

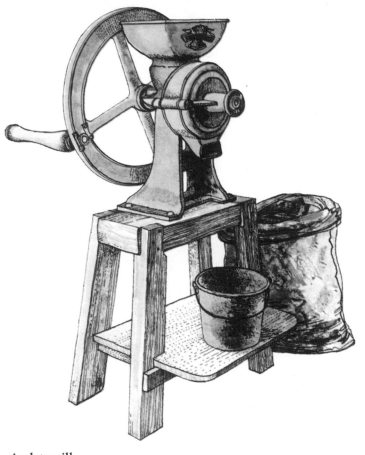

A plate mill
This little hand plate mill is perfectly adequate for a small family, and grinds fine flour. Stone mills may be marginally better, but take skill to dress and operate.

grind your wheat, keep it in a jute bag over your stove, or furnace, or dry the day's supply on a tray over the stove, or in a warm oven: anything to get the grain quite dry. Don't cook it of course. If you mill grain in larger quantities a kiln is not a bad idea, and it is also useful for kilning malt which I describe in detail on p. 69.

There is no reason why anybody, even somebody living in a tenth floor apartment, shouldn't buy a small stone or plate mill and a sack of wheat from a friendly farmer, and grind his own flour and make his own bread. Do not believe it when people tell you to do so does not pay. Whenever we have kept accounts about bread-making we have found it pays very well. You get your bread for considerably less than half of what you would pay in a shop and it is much better bread.

Bread made from freshly ground wheat and baked by home baking methods is superb bread. You are not interested in trying to sell as much holes and water as you can, as is the commercial baker. Your bread will be a lot denser than bought loaves, but well leavened nevertheless, and, if your oven was hot enough, well cooked. It will take far less of it to feed a hungry man than it takes of shop bread, and if you consistently eat your own good bread you, and your family, will stay healthy and your visits to the dentist will be mere formalities.

Making Bread

There is white bread and wholemeal bread, and many gradations between the two, and there is leavened bread and unleavened bread, and again many gradations. There is sourdough and soda bread, pitta bread and flat bread, but the great thing for the self-supporter to remember is that whatever kind of bread he chooses to make, and whatever kind of grain he makes it from, the process is simple. It is also fun, and even the most ham-fisted cook can take pleasure and pride in his efforts.

Undoubtedly the first breads were unleavened and undoubtedly the first person who discovered yeast discovered it by accident. If you make a dough with flour and water without yeast or baking powder and then bake it, you will be left with something very like a brick. People got over this by rolling the dough out very thinly and cooking it that way. (In Baghdad to this day you will see bakers putting great sheets of thin dough – as big as small blankets – into enormous cylindrical ovens.) But no doubt one day someone mixed up some dough, didn't cook it immediately and found the stuff began to ferment. What had happened was that wild yeasts had got into it and were converting the sugar (in the flour) into alcohol and carbonic acid gas. The alcohol evaporated, but the carbon dioxide blew the glutinous dough up into bubbles. This unknown ancient took up the bubbling doughy mass and placed it upon his hot stone or maybe into a little hollowed-out stone oven and made the first leavened bread.

It was then found that bread could be made not in thin sheets but in thick loaves, and was still good to eat. Furthermore, it was discovered that leavened bread stays palatable longer than unleavened bread: good home-baked wholemeal bread can taste fine for five days or more, while unleavened bread tastes very dreary unless you eat it when it is still absolutely fresh.

Yeast

How long it took mankind (or womankind) to suss out the true nature of that lovely stuff yeast, we will never know. But certainly they must have found that if they were lucky enough to get a good strain of wild yeast in their dough they could go on breeding it – simply by keeping a little raw dough back from each baking to mix in with the next batch of bread. The old pioneers in the Wild West were called "sourdoughs" because they made their bread thus. And even today, people out of touch with bakers' shops and yeast suppliers commonly make bread with sourdough (see p. 64).

If you live near a baker *always* buy your yeast fresh. It should be a creamy putty colour, cool to the touch and easy to break, with a nice yeasty smell. Don't buy any that is crumbly or has dark patches. It will keep for one week to ten days in a screwtop jar in the fridge. Or cut it into one inch cubes and freeze it. Both yeast and bread freeze well.

If you cannot obtain fresh yeast, you can still make a perfectly good bread with dried yeast. This is widely available in packets, and it will keep for up to three months. But it is a good idea to test dried yeast if you have had it around for some time. Drop a few grains into a little warm liquid dough mix; if it is still "live" it will froth in under ten minutes.

If you are using fresh yeast for any recipe specifying dried yeast, always double the quantity. Or halve it if the recipe asks for fresh yeast and you are using it dried.

Yeast flourishes in a warm atmosphere in temperatures between 48–95°F (9–35°C), but strong heat – over 140°F (60°C) – will kill it. Set your dough to rise in a warm place: on top of the stove, in the airing cupboard, even under the eiderdown on the bed.

If you are brewing beer, you can use your beer yeast for your bread-making. Conversely, you can use your bread yeast in your beer-making. Neither is ideal because they are two different sorts of yeast but we have done it often and we get surprisingly good beer and good bread.

Kneading

A word about kneading. Kneading is important because it releases the gluten and distributes the yeast right through the dough. Don't be afraid to treat your dough fiercely when you knead it. Push and pull it about until it seems to take on a life of its own, becomes silky and springy in your hands. Then leave it alone to rise. When it has risen enough it should jump back at the touch of a finger.

Keeping

If you don't have a freezer keep bread in a dry, cool, well-ventilated bin. Don't put it in an airtight container or it will go mouldy. Make sure the bread is quite cool before you stow it away or the steam in a warm loaf will make it turn soggy. Keep your flour in a dry, dark, cool cupboard.

There's much more to bread than white sliced or wholemeal. And we should all be thankful for that. Bread can be made from soya, rye, wheat, corn, sorghum or oats. If you vary your grain, you vary your bread. It's as simple as that. Have it leavened or unleavened, plain or fancy, or try a mixture of flours. Bread at its most basic, as we have just seen, is simply yeast, flour, salt and water. Add milk, butter, eggs, sugar, honey, bananas, carrots, nuts and currants and you will enrich your bread, change its taste and texture. Roll it in wholewheat grain, or poppyseed, sesame, dill, celery, caraway, sunflower or aniseed as you please. Brush it with milk, paint it with egg yolk, shine a currant loaf with sugar syrup. Knot it, twist it, plait it. Experiment, and you will find that being your own baker is one of the great joys of the self-sufficient way of life.

On the following pages a variety of breads you can make in your own home are described.

The home bakery
Baking bread is one of the most satisfying processes of the self-sufficient life. Simple ingredients, traditional equipment and common sense are all you need.

Making Bread

Bread made with different flours

For people who grow rye, barley, oats, maize, rice, sorghum and the rest, it is useful and interesting to try some breads made with these grains, or with them mixed with wheat flour. It must be remembered that of all the grains only wheat has enough gluten to sustain the gas generated by the living yeast sufficiently to make fairly light, or risen, bread.

You can try a combination of two or three different flours, but it is usually worth adding some wheat flour. And always add salt. Oil, butter, lard or margarine help to keep bread moist. Water absorption varies with the sort of flour. Here is a rundown of the different flours:

Wheat flour Wheat flour is rich in gluten, which makes the dough stretch and, as it cooks, fixes it firmly round the air bubbles caused by the leavening.

Rye flour Rye flour gives bread a nice sour taste, and can be used on its own, although a lighter bread will result if ½ or ⅓ of the flour is wheat flour. Maslin, flour made from rye and wheat grown together and ground together, was the staple English flour of the Middle Ages. Only the rich ate pure wheaten bread.

Barley flour Barley flour alone makes very sweet tasting bread. A proportion of ⅓ barley flour to ⅔ wheat produces good bread. If you toast the barley flour first your bread will be extra delicious.

Oatmeal Oatmeal is also sweet and makes very chewy damp bread, which fills you up nicely. Use ½ oat and ½ wheat flour for a good balance.

Cornmeal Bread made from cornmeal has a crumbly texture. Try ½ cornmeal and ½ wheat flour.

Ground rice Ground rice bread is a lot better if the rice is mixed half and half with wheat flour.

Cooked brown rice Like the whole cooked grains of any other cereal, cooked brown rice can be mixed with wheat flour to make an unusual bread.

Sorghum By itself sorghum (or millet) flour makes a dry bread. Add wheat flour and you will get nice crunchy bread.

Soya flour Soya flour too is better mixed with wheat. The soya flour adds a lot of nourishment.

Bread made without yeast

Unyeasted bread is really solid stuff, quite unlike yeasted bread which is, after all, half full of nothing but air. To my mind it can only be eaten cut very thin. Warm or even boiling water helps to start softening the starch in the flour. Kneading helps to release the gluten. If unyeasted dough is allowed to rest overnight the bread you make will be lighter, as the starch will soften more and a little fermentation will begin. The carbon dioxide released will provide a few air holes.

I suggest the same proportions of whole wheat to other flours as with yeasted bread. Other ingredients need be nothing but salt and water, and perhaps oil to brush the tops of loaves. Knead well, and leave to prove overnight.

Unyeasted bread may need longer and slower cooking than yeasted bread. It will also need good teeth.

Here are some recipes for different breads:

Standard wholemeal bread

I never measure my flour because what matters is getting the dough to the right consistency and flour absorbs more or less water according to its fineness, quality, etc. But for people who must have exact quantities of everything this is what Sam Mayall, an experienced English baker, who grows and mills his own wheat, uses:

2½ lbs (1.1 kg) of wholemeal flour
1 oz (28 g) salt
½ oz (14 g) dried yeast
2 teaspoons soft brown sugar
1¼ pints (0.7 litres) water

Put the flour and salt in a basin. Put the yeast in a bowl, add the sugar and some warm water. Leave in a warm place to rise.

When the yeast is fermenting well add it to the flour and the rest of the water, and knead it till it is soft and silky in texture. Return it to the basin and leave it to stand in a warm place until it has about doubled its size. Knead it again for a few minutes and mould into loaves. Place in warmed greased and floured tins, and, if it is soft wheat flour, leave it to rise for five minutes. If it is hard wheat flour, allow longer, up to 20 minutes. Put in an oven of 425°F (218°C) for 45 minutes.

Maize bread

Maize bread tastes good. It is crunchy and rather gritty and should have a nice brown crust. You will need:

1½ pints (0.8 litre) boiling water
2 lbs (0.9 kg) maize flour
2 teaspoons baking powder
3 eggs (optional)
½ pint (0.3 litre) buttermilk (optional)

Mix the maize meal with the baking powder and pour on the boiling water. Adding eggs and/or buttermilk improves the bread. Bake in a greased tin at 400°F (205°C) for about 40 minutes.

Sorghum bread

This is a rather dry bread, and only really worth making if sorghum is all you've got. Sorghum is much better mixed with wheat flour. You need:

12 oz (340 g) sorghum flour
1 teaspoon baking powder
1 teaspoon salt

Mix the ingredients and wet with warm water to make a stiffish dough. Bake for about 50 minutes in a moderately hot oven at 350°F (177°C).

Oat bread

In those damp parts of the world where nothing else will grow, oat bread is common. It is heavy and sweet-tasting. To make it you will need the following ingredients:

1 lb (0.5 kg) rolled oats or oat flour
3 oz (84 g) sugar or honey
1 tablespoon salt
4 oz (114 g) butter
1 pint (0.5 litre) boiling water (a little less if you use honey)
1 oz (28 g) yeast or ½ oz (14 g) dried yeast

Mix the dry ingredients well, rub in the butter and add the boiling water. Dissolve the yeast in a little tepid water. When it begins to froth mix it well in with the other mixture. Leave to rise for a few hours. Then dump dough on a floured board and knead for about ten minutes. Cut and shape into rounded loaf-sized lumps, and allow for some expansion. Put on a baking tray in a warm place and allow to expand for about an hour. Then bung in a very hot oven of 450°F (232°C) for 45 minutes. Test as usual by tapping the bottoms of the loaves to see if they are hollow. Stand to cool on a wire tray so that the air can circulate all round them.

Making bread

If you can boil an egg, you can bake bread. There is absolutely nothing difficult about it. To make six medium loaves, take 4½ pints (2.3 litres) of water, warmed to blood heat, 2 ounces (56 g) of salt, 2 ounces (56 g) of brown sugar, 1 tablespoon of fresh yeast (or half this amount of dried yeast). You can even use yeast from the bottom of your beer kive.

table and dump the dough into the middle of all this.

Put all the ingredients into a large mixing bowl. When the yeast has dissolved pour in enough flour to make a fine sticky mash. Stir this well with a wooden spoon until the spoon will just about stand upright.

Cover with a cloth and leave it over night in a warm place where it will be free from draughts.

Come morning the yeast will have the dough spilling over with enthusiasm. Heap some dry flour on to a

Sprinkle dry flour on top of the dough and it is ready for kneading. Start by mixing the dry flour with the wet dough.

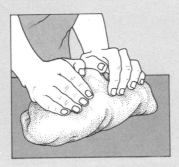

The aim is to make a fairly stiff dough, dry on the outside. You do this by pushing the dough away from you with the palms of your hands (above) and then pulling it towards you again (below). This is kneading and it is a very sticky process. When the dough sticks to your hands – and it will – fling on some flour. Whenever it feels sticky, sprinkle flour. Push and pull and fling on the flour until you have a dry, satisfying little ball. Roll it about to your heart's content. After 10 minutes the fun has to stop. It is nearly ready for baking.

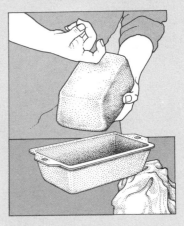

Divide the dough into six equal portions. Grease the baking tins and shape your dough. Fill the tins just three-quarters full. Score patterns on top with a knife and leave covered about 1 hour in a warm place.

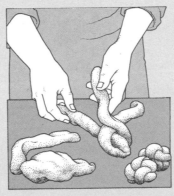

If you want to be more decorative make a plaited loaf. Divide the dough into three, make each sausage-shaped and plait. Just like that. If you want to, brush the top with milk to make it shiny and sprinkle with poppy seeds.

Shape little rolls with the left-over dough. Put them on a baking tray and leave on top of the stove to rise. After half an hour put them in a very hot oven 450°F (232°C). In ten minutes you will have a taste of things to come – and magnificent rolls for breakfast.

Now take up your bread tins *very* carefully. If you jog them they will collapse and you will have solid bread, so *gently* ease them into a hot oven 425°F (218°C). Half an hour later take a look to see if they are cooking evenly. Change them round if necessary. Wait another 15 minutes and they should be done.

To test them tap the bottoms. If they sound hollow they are done. Or push in a skewer – it should come out clean. If it doesn't it is not a disaster; put them back for a few more minutes.

When you are sure your loaves are good and ready take them out and stand on top of their tins to air. Bread rises (and yeast ferments) best at 80°F (27°C). Yeast will die at any temperature much over 95°F (35°C) and it won't multiply under 48°F (9°C). So the place where you set the bread to rise must fall within these temperatures. Usually the top of the stove is ideal. The oven should be – well, hot. Not counting the time you spend waiting for things to happen you probably don't spend more than half an hour working at it, and the result is six beautiful wholemeal loaves.

Making Bread

Rye bread

Rye bread, which is black bread, is fine when you get used to it, but it is pretty solid stuff. You need:

3½ lbs (1.6 kg) rye flour
1 oz (28 g) yeast (or ½ oz dried yeast)
1 tablespoon sugar
1 tablespoon melted butter
2 teaspoons salt
1½ pints (0.8 litre) warm water

Mix flour, sugar and salt. To the water add yeast and butter and stir the whole into the flour. Knead well, cover closely and leave in a warm place for 8 hours, perhaps in the airing cupboard overnight. Then shape into loaves and leave to rise until they have doubled in size. Bake at 350°F (177°C) for 1-1½ hours.

Sourdough

Sourdough uses a baking system which, once started, means you never need to buy yeast. You have to bake once every week however, to keep the sourdough going. It was very handy for the pioneers and goldminers of the old Wild West, who managed to have fresh leavened bread every day without having any yeast.

Rye flour is good to use in sourdough, both because it is naturally sour, and because bacteria that help to make sourdough find rye very encouraging. Use all rye flour or all wheat flour, or else mix rye, or any other flour, with wheat flour.

Begin by saving a fair sized lump of dough, about the size of a large fist, from an ordinary batch of bread dough. This is your "first starter". Keep it covered with a cloth in a warm place for 3 or 4 days. After this it should begin to smell pleasantly but definitely sour.

Now mix this starter with 1 lb (0.5 kg) flour (one of the sorts described above) and ¾ pint (0.4 litre) of warm water. This will make a sloppy batter. Leave it in the bowl, covered with a cloth in a warm place overnight. Next day, it should be bubbly. At this point, if you are going to make more sourdough bread in the future, put by your "regular starter", say enough to fill a jam jar. Keep it in a cool place, firmly covered until you need it again. It will keep at least a week.

Now to make sourdough bread, add to the spongy mixture:

3 tablespoons honey
2 teaspoons salt
½ pint (0.3 litre) milk (sour if you have it)
2 lbs (0.9 kg) flour (rye or otherwise)

Knead until the dough is really smooth and elastic. Shape two loaves and place them on baking sheets. Oil them, and leave them to prove until they have doubled in size. This takes longer than for ordinary dough, as the yeast is wild. Heat oven to 400°F (205°C). Bake the loaves for 30 minutes then reduce the heat to 375°F (190°C) until the bread is done.

Very good sourdough pancakes can also be made, using some of your starter to make the same sloppy dough as for the bread. Then instead of making bread, next morning add one egg, a little oil, enough milk to make the batter creamy, a pinch of bicarbonate of soda and some honey or brown sugar to sweeten. Make the pancakes in the usual way.

Soda bread

This is another bread which needs no yeast, and it takes no time to rise, as it does it in the oven.

1 lb (0.5 kg) flour
1 level teaspoon bicarbonate of soda
2 level teaspoons cream of tartar or ½ oz (14 g) baking powder
1 knob of butter or margarine
about ½ pint (0.3 litre) sour milk, buttermilk, or fresh milk
½ teaspoon salt

Mix the dry ingredients, rub in the butter, and mix in the milk lightly with a knife until you have a stiff broken-looking dough. Form it into a round, slightly domed shape, and put on a floured tin. Brush with milk, and make a cross on top with a knife. Bake in a hot oven 400°F (205°C) for 20 to 30 minutes.

Optional extras: 1-2 teaspoons sugar and 1 or 2 eggs beaten into the milk, to make a special, deluxe version.

Malt loaf

This is a sweet, dark brown, delicious sticky bread. You can add dried fruit or not as you like. If you do, use about 2 oz (56 g). Sultanas are best.

1 lb (0.5 kg) flour (wholemeal)
Pinch salt
1 oz (28 g) yeast or ½ oz (14 g) dried yeast
about ½ pint (0.3 litre) milk and water, milk alone or water
2 tablespoons malt extract
2 tablespoons black treacle or golden syrup
2 oz (56 g) butter

Put flour and salt in a basin. Cream the yeast in a little of the milk or water, which should be warm, and add it to the flour. Add treacle, malt, butter and then enough milk or milk and water to make a firm breadlike dough. Knead until it all looks well mixed together (it will be rather sticky).

Leave in a bowl covered with a damp cloth, to rise until it's doubled in size. Put the dough into loaf tins, so that they are half filled. Leave to prove until the dough reaches the tops of the tins. Bake at 375°F (190°C) for 45-50 minutes. To give a proper finish paint the tops with a hot milk and sugar syrup as soon as they come out of the oven.

This keeps well. Some say it's even better after a day or two.

Norwegian flat bread (Flat brød)

Flat breads are a sort of cross between a potato crisp and an Indian papadum. They taste pretty good. This recipe will make 12 large flat breads:

3 lbs (1.4 kg) potatoes
1 lb (0.5 kg) rye flour

Before you go to bed boil the spuds and mash them. Then knead the rye flour and warm mashed potatoes together until you have a smooth dough. Go to bed. In the morning knead again with more flour if the dough seems sticky, then roll it out, as thinly as possible, into big circles which will fit a large frying pan. Bake them over a gentle heat and turn several times until they are quite dry. Cool on paper. They should then be quite crisp.

Soft cakes (Letser)

These are a variation on flat breads. Cook as above but before they become quite hard, (after only 2 or 3 turns) wrap them up in a cloth to keep warm. Eat them with sour cream, something you are always likely to have plenty of. Sprinkle them with sugar if you want them to look pretty, fold them over and cut them in triangles. Keep warm until they are eaten.

Greek pitta bread

This is the bread you get in Greek restaurants that looks like flat slippers.

Use ordinary bread dough made from wheat flour, water, salt and yeast, and work in some oil if you like soft pittas. When the dough has doubled in size after the first kneading, divide it up into lumps about the size of tennis balls. Work them into nice smooth balls, then sprinkle flour on the table and with a rolling pin, or an old bottle, roll each one in one direction only so that it flattens into an oval shape, about ¼ inch thick.

Leave them to prove (rise again) in a warm place lying between two floured cloths. Heat your oven and some greased baking sheets to 450°F (232°C) – really hot. Then splash each pitta with cold water just before you bake it. Bake for 5 to 10 minutes. They should, just be starting to colour and puff up, but they mustn't go brown or they will get too hard.

Cool them and wrap them in cloths to keep them soft. Reheat them in the oven. They were designed to go with kebabs, humus, and taramasalata, but they are equally good with rollmops (see p. 207), pickled onions (see p. 188), or just plain butter (see p. 101) and jam (see p. 190).

Doughnuts

You won't eat a shop doughnut again after you have made your own. The problem is you need a lot of very clean fresh oil.

They are made from a normal bread dough but as well as this, include the following ingredients during the mixing:

2 oz (56 g) melted butter
1 egg
2 oz (56 g) sugar
milk instead of water
pinch of salt
1 lb (0.5 kg) flour
1 oz (28 g) yeast or ½ oz (14 g) dried yeast

The dough should be smooth and soft, but not sticky. It doesn't have to be kneaded at this stage. Leave it to rise, covered with a cloth, in a warm place for about one hour.

Knead it vigorously, till it feels right (about 4-5 minutes). Make it into pieces about the size of a large walnut, or roll it out on a floured board and cut rings using a large glass for the outside and a bottle top for the inside. Don't worry if they look small, they more than double in size during cooking. Once again, leave them in a warm place to prove for 20 minutes. Cover them with a cloth to keep the warmth in and the dust out.

Fry them both sides a few at a time in deep boiling fat. The spherical ones turn themselves over at half time, leaving a pale ring round the equator. Drain them then roll in caster sugar. Eat them at once. You can push jam into them if you want some extra flavour.

Making pasta

A book I have seen lists sixty-eight distinctive kinds of what I would call, simply, spaghetti, with splendid names like: amorini (little cupids), agnolotti (fat little lambs), mostaccioli (little grooved moustaches) and vermicelli, which means, horribly, little worms. But it is all the same thing: white wheat flour, preferably from durum wheat, a hard wheat that grows in Italy and North America. This is kneaded into a stiff dough, forced through an appropriate mould by a machine, or rolled thin and cut by hand, and then dried ready for cooking. The stuff you buy has been dried first by a fan, and then in an oven.

You can make perfectly good pasta by kneading some white flour with a little water very thoroughly into a stiff dough. Roll it out very thin with a rolling pin, adding more dry flour whenever the dough sticks to either table or roller. Then gently roll the thin sheet into a Swiss-roll shape and cut thin slices off across the grain. Dry these carefully over a fire, or very gently in a slow oven. Cook exactly like spaghetti you buy in a shop.

Making chapatis

Chapatis are thin sheets of unleavened bread which form the staple diet of most of the people of West Pakistan and North India. They make one wonder if yeast is such a good idea after all. They are delicious, and don't forget that the healthiest and most long-lived people on Earth live on a diet of un-leavened wholemeal bread, yoghourt, beer, vegetables and spices, and a little meat. Chapatis go well with spicy or sharp-tasting food but are also good spread with butter and eaten hot by themselves. The only argument against chapatis as a staff of life is that you have to make them fresh for each meal, and they are a little trouble. But if you are used to doing them, and have what is needed at hand, they don't take long.

You need: wholemeal wheat flour, salt, water, an open fire, a rolling pin or an old bottle and a cast iron plate. The hub-cap off a motor car does at a pinch which is why so few cars in North India have hub-caps. In some regions of India, chapatis are made with different flours. Millet, barley and chick-pea flours are all commonly used and have very interesting flavours.

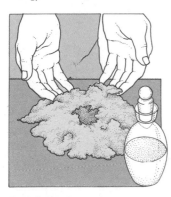

Egg noodles
Egg noodles are a richer form of pasta, but they are also easier to make. Make a well in the top of a mound of flour and break an egg, or eggs, into it. One egg to 8 oz 228 g) of flour is the norm.

Put a little olive oil in and roll the dry flour over the top of the egg.

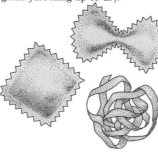

Then knead together with your hands, adding a tiny bit of water if it is too dry or else another egg. Dust well with dry flour. Roll out very thin, adding more flour if the dough sticks. As with ordinary pasta roll the dough up like a Swiss-roll and cut thin slices across the grain. Just hang up to dry.

Permutations with pasta
Of course you can make pasta any shape you like, and you don't have to boil it. You can make small shapes and cook them in soup; you can make large flat slices and bake them with a huge variety of different flavoured sauces; or you can make containers and stuff them with meat, cheese, fish, vegetables or what you will.

Chapatis
Mix an ounce (28 g) of salt with 4 lbs (1.8 kg) of flour. Mix the flour into a stiff dough, divide it into egg-sized lumps, take a lump and roll it out quite flat, very thin, and round. Indians, and you when you get experienced, can do it without the rolling pin. They just pat it flat between their hands.

As you finish rolling each one throw it on the hot grid-iron, which must be so hot that spit sizzles on it, but not red-hot.

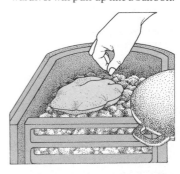

Turn the chapati over as soon as the first side is brown. When the second side is done, throw the chapati on the embers of the fire with the first side you cooked down-wards. It will puff up like a balloon.

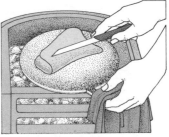

Immediately flip it upside down, leave it like that for a few seconds, pull if off, blow the air out of it by pressing it, smear it all over with a little butter or ghee, and eat quickly.

Oats & Rye

OATS

Oats will grow in a damper climate than wheat or barley, and on wetter and more acid land. Thus it is a staple human food in Scotland, which led Dr Johnson to rib his friend Boswell about how in Scotland men lived on what in England was only thought fit to feed to horses. Boswell replied: "Yes – better men, better horses." In North America and Europe oats tend to be grown in damper, colder places, and often on glacial drift, where the land may be heavy, acid and not very well drained. Oats and potatoes have enabled people to live in areas where no other crop would have grown.

Sowing

In wetter areas it is most usual to sow spring oats: in drier and warmer areas winter oats are preferred and give a heavier yield and also are less attacked by frit fly, a common pest of oats. The only trouble with winter-sown oats is that it is likely to be eaten by birds. If it is possible to sow while other people are harvesting their spring-sown crops, it stands a better chance of survival because the birds are tempted by seeds dropped elsewhere. The cultivation of oats is exactly the same as that of wheat (see p. 58).

Harvesting

But whereas barley should be allowed to get completely ripe and dry before harvesting, oats should not. There should still be a bit of green in the straw. Oats are far better cut and tied into sheaves with sickle, scythe, reaper, or reaper-and-binder, than they are combined, for combining knocks out and wastes a lot of the grain. When cut and bound it should be stooked and then "churched" three times. Churching is the old farmers' way of saying that it should be left standing in the stook for at least three Sundays. The purpose of this is to dry the straw thoroughly, and any grass growing among it, and to dry the grain itself, so that the grain will not go mouldy in the stack.

Many old-fashioned farmers, including me, feed oats to horses and cattle "in the sheaf". In other words we do not thresh the grain out but simply throw animals complete sheaves. One per beast per day during the winter, plus grass, will keep bullocks and dry cows looking fine. The animals eat straw and all. Oat straw, whether threshed or not, is the best of all the straws for feeding: good oat straw is better feed than poor hay. But of course working horses should be fed on the grain alone as well. You will find more details about feeding horses on p. 42.

Milling

The Scots, and other sensible people, mill oats thus. They kiln it, that is put it in a kiln (see p. 69) until it is quite dry. It must be completely dried, so they kiln it at quite a high temperature: this is the most important part of the operation. They then pass it between two millstones set at quite a distance apart. This gently cracks the skin of the oats off. They then winnow it (see p. 54). This blows the skins away and leaves the grain. Finally they pass it through the stones again, but this time set them closer to grind it roughly, not too fine. This is oatmeal, and it has fed some of the best races of men in the world.

There are two ways of making porridge with it, very different but both equally efficacious. One is: sprinkle the meal into boiling water, stirring the while, and the moment the porridge is thick enough for your taste take it off the fire and eat it. The other is: do this but then put the closed pot in a hay-box and leave it overnight. (A hay-box is a box with hay in it. You bury the pot in the hay when the porridge is boiling and, because of the insulation, it cooks all night.) Eat it in the morning. Eat porridge with milk or cream, and salt: never with sugar, which is a beastly habit, and not what porridge is about at all.

RYE

Rye is the grain crop for dry, cold countries with light sandy soil. It will grow on much poorer, lighter land than the other cereals, and if you live on rough, heathy land rye might be your best bet. It will thrive in colder winters than other cereals and stands acid conditions.

You might well grow rye to mix with wheat for bread: a mixture of rye and wheat makes very good bread. Rye alone makes a dense, dark, rather bitter bread, very nutritious and eaten in large quantities by the peoples of Eastern Europe. It seems to do them good.

Sowing

You can treat rye in exactly the same way as the other cereals (see p. 58). If you plant it in the autumn and it grows very quickly, which it often does, it is very advantageous to graze it off with sheep or cows in the winter when other green feed is scarce. It will grow very quickly again and still give you a good crop. It doesn't yield anything like as well as wheat, though, whatever you do. Rye is often used for grazing off with sheep and cattle only. A "catch crop" is sown, say after potatoes have been lifted in the autumn. This is grazed off green in the spring during the "hungry gap" when a green bite is very welcome. Then the land is ploughed up and a spring crop put in. Its ability to grow well in the winter is thus utilized. One advantage of rye as a winter-sown crop is that it does not seem to be so palatable to birds as other grains. Wheat and oats both suffer badly from members of the crow family: rye seems to escape these thieving birds.

Harvesting

Rye ripens earlier than other grains. Cut it when it is dead ripe, and it will not shed much. The straw is good for bedding and is a very good thatching straw. This year I am growing rye specifically for thatching.

Oatcakes

Oatcakes are thin savoury biscuits, good by themselves and especially good with cheese or home-cured ham. You need:

4 oz (114g) fine or medium oatmeal
1 teaspoon melted dripping
½ teaspoon salt
½ teaspoon bicarbonate soda
hot water

Mix the oatmeal, the soda and the salt. Make a well in the centre, add the melted dripping and enough hot water to make a soft mixture. Turn out on to a pastry board well dusted with meal and form into a smooth ball. Knead and roll out as thinly as possible. Rub with meal to whiten cakes. Put on a hot griddle or greased baking sheet and cut into four or eight pieces. Bake at 350°F (177°C) until the edges curl. Toast until slightly brown under the grill.

Porridge

The very best breakfast food for cold winter mornings, warming, nourishing and quick to make. For two or three people use:

4 oz (114g) porridge oats
    (if you use ordinary oats you must soak them overnight)
¾ pint (0.4 litres) cold water or milk and water
salt to taste

Put water, or better still, milk and water into a saucepan and add oats and salt. Bring to the boil and simmer for 3-4 minutes stirring all the time. This quantity gives two helpings.

Muesli

This of all things can be made to everyone's individual taste. Mix oats, or any flaked cereal, dried nuts, sugar and any fresh fruit you fancy. Some people like to soak it in milk overnight. Personally I like it fresh and crunchy and covered in fresh cream.

Water biscuits

I've always found water biscuits a bit bleak, but the women in the family seem to like them and they are wholesome: the biscuits as well as the women. You need:

oatmeal (or any flour, but oatmeal is best)
salt to taste
water

Mix the ingredients to a firm, rollable dough. Roll out thinly (about ¼ inch or 6 mm). Cut into squares or circles, any size you like. Prick the surface in a pattern, and bake on greased sheets at 350°F (177°C) until crisp.

Roasted or toasted flakes

You can make them with any flaked grains. Oats, barley and millet flakes are the most common. They are very simple to cook. All you need is a fire, and a clean, dry frying pan. Simply put the flakes in a pan and heat them until they just turn colour. They go nice and crisp and taste nutty, and are mouthwateringly good served with stewed fruit and cream.

Pancakes

Oatmeal pancakes are very good, but you can make pancakes from any flour or from flaked grains. The principle is the same. To make about a dozen oatmeal pancakes you will need the following ingredients:

8 oz (228g) oatmeal
2 eggs
¾ pint (0.4 litres) milk and water
salt or sugar
a little butter or oil

Make a creamy batter from oatmeal, egg, milk and water. Season with salt or sugar, depending on whether the pancakes are to be savoury or sweet. Leave the batter to stand for two hours before cooking. Grease a frying pan and heat it well. Pour enough batter into the frying pan to just cover the base and fry until the surface is no longer shiny. Then flip it over. If you are brave toss it, otherwise turn with a palette knife. Fry the other side until the pancake can be slid out dry and rustling. It only takes a couple of minutes to make.

Serve up filled with chopped meat, fish, vegetables, jam or just plain with lemon juice and/or sugar.

You can make a more interesting lighter pancake if you add yeast to your mixture and leave it to go foamy. Another variation is to use beer as your liquid.

Oat flake loaf

This is a vegetarian form of meat loaf and makes a complete meal in itself. Eat it hot with a dark soya sauce thickened with corn or soya flour. Otherwise it is good with a spicy tomato sauce, or it goes down nicely with a meat stew. You will need:

3 measures oat flakes
    (9 oz or 255 g will make a loaf for 4 or 5 people. Instead of oats you can use barley or millet flakes.)
3 measures water
1 or 2 sliced leeks, onions or both
1 clove garlic
chopped parsley
oil
salt

Fry the onions, leeks and garlic slowly in a little vegetable oil until they are just beginning to go brown. Put them aside and fry the flakes in a little oil. Let them start to burn, but do not let them burn too much. Stir in the water when the flakes are nicely coated with oil. Add salt and stir over a medium heat, until it thickens and becomes fairly solid. Stir in the onions and leeks and dump the lot in a greased earthenware casserole. Leave the top slightly rough and splash it with a little water. Bake it at 400°F (205°C) for 1 hour. The top should be slightly brown and the inside soft and moist.

Rye grain and vegetables

If you can, soak the rye grain overnight, or at least for two hours before cooking. If you can't, don't worry, but the cooking will take longer. Boil the grain with at least 4 times its volume of water. Cook it until each grain has swollen to

splitting point. Drain off the surplus water, which is very good for soup, and mix the cooked grain with some lightly fried vegetables, such as carrots, onions, turnips, cabbage or whatever you have. Add salt after cooking, not before. Eat the mixture on its own as a vegetarian meal or as an accompaniment to meat.

Rye toast

This is excellent for parties, and goes down well with cheeses, rollmops, pickled cucumbers and so on. You need:

1 loaf rye bread
butter
lemon juice
assorted fresh herbs

Cut the loaf of bread into very thin slices, and bake it in a low oven, 250°F (121°C), until it is really dry and crisp. This should take about one hour. Meanwhile, chop up a handful of fresh green herbs very finely and mix them with melted butter and lemon juice. Paint this mixture on the toast with a pastry brush. (You can make a pastry brush with a short piece of dowel, some pig's bristles and a length of cotton.) Put the bread back in the oven for ten minutes to allow the herb and butter mixture to penetrate the toast.

You can store rye toast for several days in a cool, dry place and then reheat it in the oven when you want to use it.

Rye dropscones

These really are mouthwatering, and if you, or your lady, can make them when your kids have their friends round, so much the better. You need for about ten scones:

4 oz (114g) rye flour
2 eggs
pinch of salt
some milk

Mix the flour, the yolks of the eggs and the salt with enough milk to make a creamy batter. Beat the two egg whites stiffly and mix them in. Heat and grease a griddle and make drop scones in the usual way by dropping a spoonful of the mixture on the griddle and letting it sizzle for a few seconds on each side. Serve up hot spread with butter.

Rye and honey biscuits

You can have these thick and doughy, or thin and crisp. Either way the taste is unusually good. You need:

8 oz (228g) rye flour
2 tablespoons honey
water
1 oz (28g) yeast or
½ oz (14g) dried yeast

Dissolve the yeast in water. Then add this liquid to the flour and honey to make a thick dough. Leave this overnight to rise. Next day roll out the dough and press out biscuit shapes. Bake for 15 minutes in an oven at 425°F (218°C) to make well-risen scone-like biscuits. To make thin, crisp biscuits roll thinner and then bake them on a griddle.

Barley

Barley has two principal purposes: one is feeding animals and the other is making beer. It doesn't make good bread because the protein in the grain is not in the form of gluten, as it is in wheat, but is soluble in water. It will not therefore hold the gases of yeast fermentation and so will not rise like wheat flour will. You can mix barley flour with wheat flour though, say three to one wheat to barley, and make an interesting bread.

Barley will grow on much lighter and worse soil than wheat, and it will also stand a colder and wetter climate, although the best malting barley is generally grown in a fairly dry climate.

Sowing

The old saying goes: "sow wheat in mud and barley in dust!" My neighbour says that the farmhands used to come to his old father and say: "Boss, we must get in the barley seed. The farmer over the valley is doing it." "Can you see what horses he's using?" said the old man, who couldn't see very well. "The roan and the grey gelding." "Then don't sow the barley" said the farmer. A few days later the same exchange took place, but when the farmer asked what horses his neighbour was using the men answered: "I can't see them for dust." "Then sow the barley," said the farmer.

Don't take this too literally, but barley does need a much finer seed bed than wheat. There is such a thing as winter-sown barley, but most barley is spring-sown, for it has a much shorter growing season than wheat. It grows so quickly that it will come to the sickle even if you plant it as late as May, but any time from the beginning of March onwards is fine, so long as the soil is warm and sufficiently dry. As I explained before, a certain Suffolk farmer used to drop his trousers and sit on the land before he drilled his barley, to see if the land felt warm and dry enough. Where I live we have a festival, in the town of Cardigan, called Barley Saturday. This is the last Saturday in April. We are all supposed to have got our barley in by then, and to celebrate there is a splendid parade of stallions through the streets of Cardigan and the pubs are open all day.

Barley, particularly for malting for beer, should not have too much nitrogen, but needs plenty of phosphorus, potash and lime. I broadcast barley seed at the rate of four bushels, about 2 cwt (101 kg) to the acre. If I drilled it I would use less: about three bushels, or 1½ cwt (76.2 kg). Drilling it would probably be better but we haven't got a drill, and in fact we get very good results by broadcasting. Of course after drilling or broadcasting you harrow and roll just as you do for wheat. Excepting that the seed bed should be finer the treatment is exactly the same as for wheat, but one tends to sow barley on poorer ground.

Harvesting

Harvesting is the same as for wheat (see pp. 52-53). If you harvest it with a combine harvester it must be dead ripe.

They say around here: wait until you think it is dead ripe and then forget all about it for a fortnight. An old method of harvesting barley is to treat it like hay, which isn't tied into sheaves but left loose. You turn it about until it is quite dry, then cart it and stack it loose just like hay. You can then just fork it into the threshing machine.

If you do bind it into sheaves, you should leave it in the stook for at least a week. But however you cut it do not do so until the ears have all bent over, the grains are hard and pale yellow and shed easily in your hand, and the straw is dry. You can then put it into mows (see p. 52) and the straw can be fed to livestock. It is better for feeding than wheat straw which is useless, but not so good as oats. It is no good for thatching, and not as good as wheat straw for litter or animal bedding.

The grain is the beer-grain *par excellence*, but most of the grain gets fed to pigs and cattle. It can be ground (best for pigs) or rolled (best for cattle). If you haven't got a mill, just soak it for 24 hours. If you want to eat it, try:

Barley soup
This is one of the self-supporter's staple meals, not just a soup. It's warm and nourishing. You can vary the vegetables according to what you've got. Add more carrots if you haven't got a turnip and so on. You need:

2 oz (56g) washed husked barley
1 lb (0.5kg) stewing mutton
2 quarts (2.3 litres) water
1 teaspoon salt
3 or 4 carrots
2 or 3 leeks
3 or 4 onions
1 big turnip or
1 big swede

Put the whole lot in a stewing pot. Season slightly, cover and simmer for three hours. Stir occasionally to make sure nothing is sticking to the bottom. Take out the meat at the end of the cooking time, remove the bones and chop into mouthsized lumps. Put them back in the soup. Add chopped parsley if you've got it.

Northumberland barley cakes
If you haven't got a deep freeze, these will keep a lot longer than bread. They are like huge thick biscuits and make a very good between-meal snack. You need:

1 lb (0.5kg) barley flour
1 teaspoon salt
½ teaspoon bicarbonate of soda
¼ teaspoon cream of tartar
½ pint (0.3 litres) buttermilk or skim milk

Bung all the ingredients in a mixing bowl and stir into a soft dough. Make this into balls and press them out until they are about 10 inches (25cm) across and ¾ of an inch (2cm) thick. Bake on a griddle until the cakes are brown on one side. Turn over and brown the other side. Serve up cold, cut in pieces and spread with butter.

Barley pastry
This is very light and crumbly and good for fruit pies and flans, and for the dentist's nightmare and child's delight, treacle tart. Take any shortcrust pastry recipe, substitute barley flour for wholewheat flour and slightly reduce the amount of fat. For example, with 8 oz (228g) of barley flour use 3 oz (84g) of fat instead of 4 oz (114g). Roll out and cook in the same way as you would pastry made with wheat flour.

Malting Barley

Something that has contributed over the millennia to keeping humans human, even if it sometimes gives them headaches, is the invention of malt. One imagines that very soon after men discovered grain, they also discovered that if you left it lying about in water the water would ferment, and if you drank enough of it, it would make you drunk. In fact you can make beer out of any farinaceous grain whatever. During the war we had a Company Brewer in every company of the King's African Rifles. He brewed once a week, and would brew beer out of absolutely any kind of grain or grain meal that he could lay his hands on. Most of it was pretty horrible stuff but it kept us sane.

Later on in history some genius discovered that if you sprouted the grain first, it made better beer and made you even more drunk. He didn't know the reason for this of course, but we do. It is because alcohol is made from sugar. Yeast, which is a microscopic mould or fungus, eats sugar and turns it into alcohol. It can also do the same, in a much more limited way, with starch. Now grain is mostly starch, or carbohydrate, and you can make an inferior sort of beer out of it before it sprouts by fermenting it with yeast. But, if you cause the grain to sprout, that is start to grow, the starch gets turned, by certain enzymes, into sugar. It then makes much better, stronger beer much more quickly. Thus, to make beer, we civilized people sprout our barley before we ferment it. This process is known as malting, and the sprouted grain is known as malt. You can malt any grain, but barley, being highest in starch, makes the best malt.

Malting barley

Put your barley, inside a porous sack if you like, into some slightly warm water and leave it for four days. Pull it out and heap it on a floor and take its temperature every day. If the latter goes below 63°F (17°C) pile it up in a much thicker heap. In the trade this is called "couching" it. If the temperature goes above 68°F (20°C) spread it out more thinly and turn it often. Turning cools it. Keep it moist but not sodden: sprinkle warmish water on it occasionally. Remember you want to make it grow. After about ten days of this the acrospire, or shoot of the grain (not the root, which will also be growing), should have grown about two-thirds the length of the grain. The acrospire is to be seen growing below the skin of the grain. Couch it for twelve hours when you think it has grown enough.

Kilning the malt

After this you must kiln the grain. This means bringing it to a temperature of 120°F (50°C) either over a fire or stove, or in an oven with the door open to keep the hot air moving through the grain. Keep it moving in the kiln, which is simply a perforated steel plate over a fire, until it is dry.

Kilning for different beers

Now the colour and nature of beer can be altered one way or the other by the extent of the kilning of the malt after it has been sprouted. This kilning is necessary to kill the grain. If you didn't kill it it would go on growing into long gangly shoots. Kilning also makes it keep, and you almost always have to keep it before you use it. If you just put it, wet and growing, in a bag it would rot. Not only would it be useless, it would also smell nasty.

A light kilning makes a light-coloured malt and consequently a light-coloured beer, while heavier kilning makes darker malt and darker beer. If you want to make lager, keep the temperature down to slightly under 120°F (50°C). If you want dark ale take it up as high as 140°F (60°C), but not over. Why not over? Because over would kill the enzymes which are to go on turning even more starch into sugar when you mash the malt.

The maltster watches his malt in the kiln, constantly turning it and looking at it, and he stops the kilning at the right stage for the kind of beer he intends to make. You can stop kilning when you can bite a grain and it cracks between the teeth, but if you want a darker beer you simply go on kilning until the grains turn browner. If you want stout you actually go on kilning until the grain turns nearly black – but do not allow the grain in the kiln to go over 140°F (60°C). Just give it longer, that's all.

When you have kilned enough just crush the grain in a mill: don't grind it fine. Now you have malt and you are ready to start brewing your beer.

Malting barley
Soak the grain for four days. Pile it in a heap on the floor and by alternately spreading it out and piling it up again, or "couching" it, keep it at a temperature between 63°F (17°C) and 68°F (20°C). You will need to do this for about ten days, until a shoot about two thirds the length of the grain can be seen growing beneath the skin of the grain. Dry the grain completely in a kiln (below right), crush it in a mill and you have malt.

Making Beer

Before Tudor times there were no hops in Britain and the stuff people drank, fermented malt, was called ale. At about that time hops were introduced from the Continent and used for flavouring and preserving ale, and the resultant drink was called beer. Beer is bitterer than ale was and, when you get used to it, much nicer. Nowadays the nomenclature has got confused and the words beer and ale are used indiscriminately. However, it is well worth growing your own hops.

Soil for hops

Hops like a deep, heavy, well-drained loam and liberal manuring, preferably with farmyard manure. But they will produce some sort of a crop on most land, provided they are well dunged and the land is not waterlogged, and if you grow your own hops for your own beer some sort of a crop is all you need: you need pounds, not tons.

Planting hops

Clean your piece of land thoroughly first. Make sure you get out all perennial weed roots and grass. Beg, borrow, or steal a dozen bits of hop root. Bits of root about a foot in length are fine. Hops produce an enormous mass of roots every year and an established hop plant just won't miss a foot or two of root.

Plant these bits of root at intervals of two or three feet (61 cm), with plenty of farmyard manure or compost. Arrange horizontal wires, some high and others down near the ground. Put vertical strings between the wires for the hops to climb up: three or four strings for each bit of root. When the hops begin to grow they will race each other up the strings and you can place bets with your family on the winner – they grow so fast you can almost see them move. Watch for aphids. If you get them spray with derris, nicotine, pyrethrum or other non-persistent insecticide.

Harvesting hops

Pick the flowers when they are in full bloom, and full of that bitterly-fragrant yellow powder which is the virtue of the hop. Dry the flowers gently. If you put them on a wire, hessian, or other perforated surface over a stove, that will do. When they are quite dry store them, preferably in woven sacks.

The above directions are for a homesteader to grow enough hops for his beer. They are not instructions for a commercial hop-grower. The growing of hops on a commercial scale is quite different, and is, therefore, a highly specialized profession.

Malt and malt extract

You *can* brew beer from malt extract, which you can buy from the chemist, or in "brewing kits" from various enterprises. The beer you brew will be strong (or can be), will taste quite good (or can do), but it will not be the same as real beer brewed from real malt. The best beer will be the stuff you brew from the malt you have made yourself (see p. 69). But you can also buy malt in sacks, and this is preferable to malt extract. The difference between beer brewed from malt and beer brewed from malt extract is great and unmistakable, and if you once get used to beer brewed from malt you will not be content to go back to extract beer – nor to the liquid you buy from the pub.

Brewing beer

In the evening, before you go to bed, boil ten gallons (45.5 litres) of water. While it is boiling make a strainer for your mash-tub, kive, brewing vat or whatever you call it. This is a tub holding twenty gallons, but with the top cut off. You can make the strainer by tying a bundle of straw, or hay, or gorse leaves with a piece of string, poking the string through

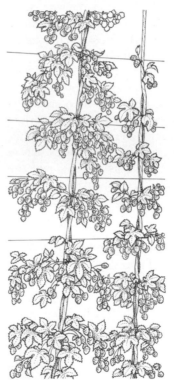

Grow your own hops
Hops must be given strings to grow up, otherwise they get into a hopeless mess and the harvest is drastically reduced. Fix horizontal wires to stout posts and then arrange vertical strings between the wires, three or four to each root planted. The hops will do the rest. You just watch and keep them clear of aphids if necessary. Harvest when the flowers are in full bloom (above). Inside they will be full of bitter yellow powder – sweet nectar to a serious home brewer.

the tap-hole of the kive, pulling it tight so as to haul the bundle hard up against the hole inside, and banging the tap in. The tap then holds the piece of string. Or, if you like, you can have a hole in the bottom of your kive with an ash stick pushed down into it to close it. When you pull the ash stick out, of course, it opens the hole. If you lay a layer of gorse then in the bottom of your kive, some straw on top of this, then a flat stone with a hole in the middle of it, and then poke your ash stick through this hole, you have a magnificent strainer.

Beermaking implements
Brewing your own beer gives you an excuse to collect a lot of beautiful implements. There's nothing better than barrels and stone jars for storing beer, and a barrel with the top sawn off makes the best kive or brewing vat. Hops are vital unless you want to make old-fashioned ale. And you'll need a thermometer, weighing scales and a kettle for sparging.

When the water has boiled let it cool to 150°F (66°C). Then dump one bushel (about half a hundredweight or 25.4kg) of cracked malt into it and stir until the malt is wet through. This is called "mashing" and the malt is now the "mash." It is most important that the water should not be hotter than 150°F (66°C) because if it is it will kill the enzymes. Cover the kive up with a blanket and go to bed.

Early in the morning get up and open the cock, or draw the ash stick, to allow the wort, as the liquid is now called, to run out into buckets. Pour it from the buckets into the boiler, together with a pound (0.5 kg) of dried hops tied in a pillowcase, and boil it. While the wort is dribbling out, "sparge" (brewer's word for sprinkle) the mash with boiling water. (You don't care about the enzymes now – they have done their work and converted the rest of the starch into sugar.) Go on sparging until ten gallons (45.5 litres) of wort have drained out. Much of the original ten gallons has been absorbed by the mash.

Boil the ten gallons of wort, and the hops in the pillow case, for an hour. If you want the beer to be very strong add say six pounds (2.7 kg) of sugar now, or honey if you can spare it. Or, another way of cheating, is to add six pounds (2.7 kg) of malt extract. But you needn't add anything at all. You will still get very strong beer. Clean the mash out of the kive and set it aside for the pigs or cows.

Transfer the boiling wort back into the clean kive. Take a jugful of wort out and cool it by standing it in cold water. When it is hand hot, say about 60°F (16°C), dump some yeast into it. This can be yeast from a previous fermentation, or yeast you have bought especially for beer. Bread yeast will do but beer yeast is better. Bread yeast is a "bottom-fermenting" yeast; it sinks to the bottom in beer. Beer yeast is "top-fermenting" and is marginally better.

The faster your bulk of wort cools now the better. An "in-churn" milk cooler put into the wort with cold water running through it is very helpful. If you haven't got this you can lower in buckets of cold water, but be sure no water spills out and that the outside of the bucket is clean. Quick cooling allows less time for disease organisms to get into the wort before it is cool enough to take the yeast.

When the main body of the wort has cooled to 60°F (16°C) dump your jugful of yeasty wort into it and stir. This is the time when you should pray. Cover up very carefully to keep out all vinegar flies and dust.

Try to keep away from the stuff for at least three days. Then skim the floating yeast off. Otherwise it will sink which is bad. When it has stopped fermenting, after five to eight days, "rack" it. That means pour it gently, without stirring up the sediment in the bottom, into the vessels in which you intend to keep it and cover these securely. From now on no air must get in. You have made beer.

You can use plastic dustbins instead of wooden or earthenware vessels, but I don't like them. If you use wooden vessels though, you must keep them scrupulously clean.

If you do want your beer windy, like the stuff you buy in pubs, bottle it in screw-top bottles just before it has finished fermenting in the kive.

Small beer

When we read of our ancestors always drinking beer for breakfast, and drinking it pretty consistently throughout the rest of the day too, we must remember that they were not drinking the kind of stingo that I have described the making of in the last few pages, but small beer. Small beer is a pleasant, slightly alcoholic malt drink. Nobody is going to get drunk on it, but it is very good for you. And it comes as a natural by-product of ordinary beer.

Brewing small beer

Make beer in the way described above, but do not sparge the mash with boiling water and draw the resultant brew out of the bottom of the kive. Instead, after you have drained the ten gallons (45.5 litres) of wort to boil up for your real beer, you pour ten gallons of boiling water on your mash. You let this ten gallons stand in the mash while you finish your work with the first lot of beer.

But you will realize that you will need two kives to make small beer, for your first kive is now occupied by your mash and ten gallons of water. You have got to have another kive ready for the wort of your first beer, now busily bubbling in the boiler with a pillow-case of hops in it. So you transfer the first beer to the new kive, then drain the small-beer wort out of the first kive, and boil it for an hour in the boiler with the hops in it. Meanwhile, you clean the spent mash out of the first kive to give to the animals and return the boiled small-beer wort to it. Then wait until it gets cool enough to take yeast, and dump a pint or two of the first batch of wort into it to start it. Cover it up and leave it to ferment like the other lot.

But remember, it won't keep like real beer. What keeps beer is its alcohol content, and small beer is weak stuff. You must drink it up within a fortnight or it will go off. But you can drink it in fairly large quantities, and you will get plenty of help from your neighbours.

Distilling

If you get a big copper with a fire under it, half fill it with beer, float a basin on the beer, and place a shallow dish wider than the copper on the top of the copper, you will get whisky. Alcohol will evaporate from the beer, condense on the under-surface of the big dish, run down to the lowest point of it and drip down into the basin. It is an advantage if you can run cold water into, and out of, the top dish to cool it. This speeds up condensation.

If distilling is illegal in your part of the world and some inquisitive fellow comes down the drive, it doesn't take a second to be boiling clothes in the copper, making porridge in the floating basin, and bathing the baby in the big flat dish. And what could be more innocent than that?

Beer making

To make consistently good home-brew you must start off with scrupulously clean kives and barrels. They should be scrubbed, scalded and then disinfected by exposure to wind and sunlight. Choose a quiet evening and boil up 10 gallons (45.5 litres) of water in your copper.

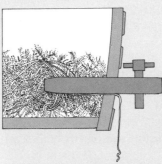

While you are waiting for the water to boil make a strainer for the kive. Tie a small bundle of gorse, hay or straw with a piece of string and drop it in the kive, poke the loose end through the bung-hole and pull hard. Then bang in the tap (wooden cock).

When the water boils let it cool to 150°F (66°C) and pour half into the kive.

Dump in 1 bushel (½ cwt or 25.4 kg) malt, the rest of the hot water and stir thoroughly.

Then tuck the kive up for the night. Cover with a clean sheet and a blanket. The enzymes in the malt plus the water will then go to work extracting the malt sugar.

Next morning, open the cock and drain the "wort" (liquid) into a bucket, or even better into an "underbuck," the traditional wooden vessel.

Now "sparge" (sprinkle) the spent malt with kettle after kettle of boiling water to remove all sugar, until 10 gallons of wort have drained out into the bucket. And thence into the boiler.

Pack 1 lb (0.5 kg) of hops into a pillowcase and plunge it into the wort. If you want to cheat by stirring in sugar, honey or malt extract (7 lbs or 3.2 kg to 10 gallons or 45.5 litres of wort) now is the time to do it. Boil for at least one hour. Meanwhile get on with cleaning out the kive. The mash makes splendid food for pigs or cows.

Draw a jugful of boiling wort and cool quickly by immersing in icy water. When it has cooled to 60°F (16°C), plop in your yeast. Either packet beer yeast (about 1 oz or 28 g will do) or a couple of tablespoons of "barm" which you have strained off the top of your last brew and kept covered in a cool place. Then transfer the rest of the boiling wort back into the kive.

Cool the bulk of the wort as fast as you can by lowering bucket after bucket of cold water into it, but don't spill a drop if you want your beer to be worth drinking.

As soon as the bulk of the wort has cooled to being hand-hot, 60°F (16°C), pour in the "starter", the jugful of foaming yeasty wort and stir. Cover with blankets to keep out vinegar flies and leave for 3 days.

Then skin off the "barm." When it has stopped fermenting (5-8 days) "rack" it. In other words pour off, without stirring up the sediment, into your storage vessels. Cork.

Maize

Besides the potato, and that horrible stuff tobacco, the most important contribution the New World has made to the Old is maize. The first white settlers in America called it Indian corn, and this was shortened to corn, and corn it now is. In England it is maize, although gardeners also refer to it as sweet corn.

Maize is grown for several purposes. First, for harvesting when the grain is quite ripe, and ready to be ground to make human or cattle food. Secondly, for harvesting before the ears are ripe to be eaten, boiled and with lashings of butter, as "corn-on-the-cob." The grain in the unripe cobs is still soft and high in sugar, because the sugar has not yet turned into starch for storage, but is still in soluble form so that it can move about the plant. Thirdly, maize is grown for feeding off green to cattle in the summer time, long before the grain is ripe, just as if it were grass. Fourthly, it is grown for making silage. This is done when the grain is at what is called the "cheesey," or "soft dough" stage. To make silage the stems must be well cut up or crushed, in order that they can be sufficiently consolidated.

Maize will grow to the "corn-on-the-cob" stage in quite northerly latitudes, but it will not ripen into hard ripe grain (the grain is nearly as hard as flintstones) except in warmish climates. It is always planted in the spring and likes a warm, sunny summer but not one that is too dry. It will stand considerable drought, and the hotter the sun the better, but in dry climates it needs some rain or irrigation.

Sowing

Maize likes good but light soil: heavy clays are not suitable. It must be sown after the last danger of frost as it is not at all frost-hardy. So plant one or two weeks after the last probable killing frost. You will need 35 lbs (15.8 kg) of seed for an acre, sown about three inches (8 cm) deep. Space between rows can be from 14 inches (36 cm) to 30 inches (76 cm): do what your neighbours do in this respect and you will not go far wrong. There should be about nine plants to a square yard.

Care of crop

Birds are a terrible nuisance, particularly rooks, and will, if allowed, dig up all your seed. Threads stretched about four feet (1.2 m) above the ground on posts hinder the rooks (so they do you when you want to hoe), and shooting the odd rook and strewing its feathers and itself about the land puts them off for a short time. Rooks are a menace and there are far too many of them: the idea put about by rook-lovers that they are not after your seed but after leatherjackets is arrant nonsense, as the most cursory examination of a dead rook's crop will show.

Harvesting

Harvesting ripe cobs by hand, as the homesteader is most likely to do, is delightful work. You walk along the rows, in a line if there are several of you, rip out the ears and drop them in a sack slung over your shoulder. Then tread the straw down with your foot so you can see where you have been (the straw is as high as you are). When you get hungry light a fire of dried maize straw, or sticks, throw some cobs on it, without removing their sheaths, and when the sheaths have burnt off and the grain is slightly blackened, eat them. They are quite unlike the admittedly delicious "sweet corn" or "corn-on-the-cob" and are food for a king – or a hungry harvester (who has presumably got good teeth).

Maize in the garden

In cold latitudes you can grow maize for "sweet corn" in your garden. Plant it under cloches or else plant it in peat pots indoors and then carefully plant out pots and all after the last frost. Or you can plant direct into the ground after the last frost, say with two seeds in a station, stations a foot (30 cm) apart and two feet (61 cm) between rows. Plant in blocks rather than long thin lines because this helps pollination.

Maize likes well-dunged ground. Water it if the weather is really dry. Pick it when the silk tassels on the ears go from gold to brown.

Cooking maize

Boil in the sheaths (at least I do) for perhaps a quarter of an hour. Eat it off the cob with salt and oodles of butter. This is food that I challenge anybody to get tired of. For years we Seymours ate tons of it. It was our staple diet for the whole of the autumn. It is a crop that must be eaten as soon as possible after harvesting: if it is kept, the sugars begin to harden into starch and the fragrant elements of the succulent grains disappear.

Polenta or cornmeal mush
This can be made with ground maize or ground sorghum. It comes from north Italy and is rather stodgy unless well buttered and cheesed after cooking, but it is quite delicious. You need for six people:

8 oz (228 g) cornmeal
2 teaspoons salt
2½ pints (1.4 litres) water
3 teaspoons grated cheese and butter

Boil the water in a large pan with salt. Then sprinkle in the cornmeal, stirring all the time to prevent lumps. Keep on stirring. After 30 minutes it is so thick it is leaving the sides of the pan. Mind it doesn't brown on the bottom. Stop cooking and spread it out on a dish. Cover it with blobs of butter and grated cheese, and push it under the grill for a few minutes. It's very good by itself, and even better served up with fried spicy Italian sausages and plenty of tomato sauce.

Polenta gnocchi
Cook polenta as in the recipe above, but at the end of cooking stir in two beaten eggs and some grated cheese, and, if you want to make it more exotic add 4 oz (114g) of chopped ham as well. Turn it all on to a flat wetted dish and spread it out so that it is about ¼ inch (1 cm) thick.

Next day cut it into squares, lozenges or circles about 1½ inches (4cm) across. Lay these overlapping in a thickly buttered, ovenproof dish. Dot with more butter, heat in the oven or under the grill and serve sprinkled with more cheese.

Rice

Rice, before it is milled, is called "paddy" by English-speaking people in Asia. There are for practical purposes two sorts: rice that grows in water or "wet" rice, and "upland" rice. The latter grows on open hillsides, but only in places with a very high rainfall such as the Chin Hills of Burma. Ordinary, or wet rice is grown on a large scale in the United States and in southern Europe, and there is no doubt that its cultivation could be extended to more northern latitudes. It will grow and ripen in summer temperatures of over 68°F (20°C), but these must cover much of the four to five months that the crop takes to grow and ripen.

It might well be that some of the upland rice varieties would grow in northern latitudes. The reason why we of the northern latitudes do not attempt to cultivate them may be because we are congenital wheat-eaters and do very well without rice. The wheat-eating peoples of India have a strong sense of superiority over the rice-eaters and look upon rice as food fit only for invalids!

Sowing

The best way to grow rice on a small scale is to sow the seed broadcast on a dry seed bed when the ground has warmed up in the spring, rake it well in, and then flood the seed bed but only just. As the shoots grow, always try to keep the water level below the tops of the plants. Rice survives in water by virtue of its hollow stem, which takes oxygen down to the rest of the plant.

When the plants are about eight inches (20 cm) tall pull them out in bunches and transplant them in to shallow standing water in an irrigated field. Simply dab each plant into the soft mud four inches (10 cm) away from its neighbours. Billions of paddy plants are planted like this every year in India and China. Keep the paddy field flooded (never let it get dry) until about a fortnight before you judge the grain ripe enough to harvest. Then drain the field and let the grain ripen in the dry field.

Harvesting

Harvest with the sickle, thresh as you would other corn (see pp. 52-53), "hull" (separate grain from husk) by passing through a plate mill or stone mill with the plates or stones open enough to hull the grain without cracking it, and you are left with "brown rice," that magical perfect food of the yin-yan adherents. It is in fact a good grain, very rich in starch but lower in protein and also in several other qualities than wheat.

If you mill the brown rice more closely you get pearled rice, which is generally and wrongly called polished rice. This is almost pure starch and a very incomplete foodstuff, even less nutritious than white wheat flour which is saying a lot. A further process, called polishing, produces true polished rice which is what most of us buy in the shops. If you live on practically nothing else but pearled or polished rice you get beri-beri. So the sensible thing to do, if you live on rice, is to eat brown rice and not go to the trouble of removing the bran, which is the most nutritious part of it, and feeding it to the pigs.

Cooking rice

Unlike most other grains rice does not need grinding before it is cooked. The Western way to cook your own home-milled rice is to wash the grain well in cold water and strain, then bring 1 pint (0.6 litres) of water to the boil, add a teaspoonful of salt, and throw in 6 oz (170 g) of rice. Bring this to the boil again and then allow it to simmer by reducing the heat. Cover the pan and simmer for fifteen minutes. When the rice is tender, eat it. It will have absorbed all the water.

I personally use the Indian method which is to bring much more water than you really need to the boil, throw the rice in, bring to the boil again, allow to simmer until the grain is tender (but not reduced to that horrible stuff: rice pudding!) which will be in about a quarter of an hour, strain the water out, toss the rice up a few times in the strainer, and eat it. Each grain will be separate if you do this properly and the rice will be perfect.

You can colour and flavour rice very nicely by tossing a pinch of saffron into the rice while it is cooking. For brown rice, you need to allow forty to fifty minutes cooking time.

INDIAN RICE

North American wild rice (*Zizania aquatica*), or Indian rice, can be harvested when it is ripe, and dried in hot sun or else "parched" by heating over a fire or kilning. This can be boiled or steamed and eaten, preferably with meat. It is very nutritious, but very laborious to harvest.

Risotto

This is usually made with rice, as the name implies, but it is very good made with whole millet or with pearl barley. You need:

1 measure grain (1 lb or 0.5 kg should feed 8-10 people)
2 measures hot water or good clear stock
a little oil, salt and pepper
a variety of firm vegetables, such as onions, green peppers, peas, carrots etc.

Use a solid pan with a lid (earthenware is good). Slice the vegetables and lightly fry them in a little oil. Put them aside in a separate dish when they are soft and slightly brown. Put some more oil in the pan and tip in the dry grains. Stir them until they are well-oiled and start to turn colour.

Put the cooked vegetables back in the pan with half the hot water or stock. Season well. Turn the heat low, or put the pan in a moderate oven, closely covered, for 15-30 minutes. Then, add the rest of the broth, stir and cook another 15-30 minutes until all the liquid is absorbed, and the grains are soft and tender, but separate. Times vary with the hardness of the grain.

Rice griddle cakes

A good way of using up left over boiled rice or rice pudding.

½ pint (0.3 litres) milk
4 oz (114 g) warm cooked rice
1 tablespoon melted butter or oil
2 eggs, separated
4 oz (114 g) wheat flour and a pinch of salt

Mix the milk, rice and salt. Add the egg yolks, the butter and the flour, and then, stiffly beaten egg whites. Heat a griddle and drop the mixture in spoonfuls onto it. Cook both sides.

Sorghum

SORGHUM

Sorghum is a very complicated matter: there are many different varieties, and hybrids, and at least four distinct species. Of the four main types of sorghum, sweet sorghum, which can grow as high as 14 feet (4.2 m), is grown for sugar, much as sugar cane is; grass sorghum is grown for grazing, silage, hay, and so on; grain sorghum is grown for grain; and broom sorghum is grown for making brooms.

Grain and grass sorghum are grown extensively in the United States in the Great Plain areas, both as livestock feeds and for industrial purposes. They are not crops commonly grown by the self-supporter, but they could be, and grain sorghum, unthreshed, is magnificent for feeding to poultry. It is sometimes used by African villagers for this purpose, the heads being thrown down in the straw for the hens to scratch out. Sorghum porridge, as anyone who has lived in Central Africa can testify, is far superior in flavour to "mealie pap", or whatever the local name might be of the maize meal porridge which is the staple diet of many Africans.

Grain sorghum is a healthy grain and many people believe that the Africans who live on sorghum are healthier than those that live on maize; but wherever maize will grow, it is grown in preference to sorghum. This is because where the rainfall is high enough for it, maize produces more grain. Furthermore where alfalfa, clover, and so on will grow, sorghum is not grown for fodder crops.

Sowing grain sorghum

The seed bed for sorghum must be fine, weed-free and not too trashy. In higher rainfall areas land is generally prepared for sorghum by ploughing in the fall, and discing and harrowing the next spring. In drier areas spring cultivation is kept to a minimum to avoid loss of water. Seed is drilled, for grain production, in rows from 20–40 inches (51–102 cm) apart: the greater distances being in the drier climates. You sow it about a fortnight after you would maize.

Sorghum likes hot weather. It is no good trying to grow it in cool climates, for it won't germinate at all under 45°F (7°C) and won't really get going under 60°F (16°C). The ideal temperatures for sorghum are 75°F to 80°F (24°C to 27°C). It is a hardy crop under these conditions, and is more resistant to insect pests like grasshoppers than other cereals.

In drier areas drill about three pounds (1.4 kg) of seed to the acre: in wetter areas perhaps about five (2.3 kg).

Sowing grass sorghum

If you want to grow grass sorghum, and it does make good hay, you can broadcast the seed at a rate of 40 lbs (18.1 kg) to every acre.

Care of crop

When any sorghum is sown in rows you should hoe it to stop weed competition. Once the plants have grown plenty of foliage the weeds will be kept down naturally.

Harvesting

Harvest sorghum when it is dead ripe (you can leave it until the first frost). Thresh and winnow grain sorghum just like other grains.

Stock grazing sorghum grass can get prussic acid poisoning, so don't let them graze it until the plants are eighteen inches (46 cm) high when the acid content is lower. And don't graze for three days after a frost.

PEANUTS

Peanuts are a tropical American legume but they can be grown as far north as Massachusetts. They are an extremely valuable food plant, being very rich in many of the B vitamins that are hard to obtain from vegetable sources. They are also rich in oil and are, in fact, grown for its production on a large scale in the Americas, China, and Africa.

What they like is a growing season of at least four months with hot weather and about twenty inches (51 cm) of rain distributed throughout the period. They need an acid soil, and a sandy one, and it is fortunate that these things often go together. So never lime for peanuts.

Sowing

Seed from plants grown in a cold climate gives better results than seed from plants grown in the tropics, and many growers save their own seed. You can plant shells and all, or you can shell and plant the separate nuts.

If you plant unhulled nuts plant them eight inches (20 cm) apart in rows thirty inches (76 cm) apart. In the colder North plant only an inch and a half (4 cm) deep: in the warm South four inches (10 cm) deep. In northern climates you must plant the seed at about the time of the last frost so as to give them as long a growing season as possible but between April 10 and May 10 is considered about right. It is a hard crop to keep clean, so hoe and weed frequently.

Harvesting

Harvest before the first frost kills the vines, but after the leaves have started to yellow and the inside of the shells have begun to colour. Dry by hanging the vines in an airy shed or by spreading out on wire netting.

Save seed from the best plants. Thresh the nuts out of the vines, but don't husk them. Store in old oil drums that have some holes punched in them to allow for ventilation.

Peanut butter

You can make peanut butter by roasting the nuts at 300°F (149°C) to 325°F (163°C) for twenty minutes, turning occasionally. Then put them through a mincing machine or a meat grinder. You may have to do this several times. It depends how crunchy you like your peanut butter. Add a little salt and a dessert spoonful of honey per pound (0.5 kg). Then mix in peanut oil (or any other vegetable oil) until it reaches a spreadable consistency.

Growing Crops for Oil

If you have a small piece of land not taken up with growing food it is well worth planting some crop which will produce vegetable oil.

OIL SEED RAPE

Oil seed rape will grow in temperate climates. You plant it like kale (see pp. 84–85) and harvest it when it is still fairly green. Pull the plant out of the ground, dry it in a stack, thresh it and then crush the seeds to get the oil out. The residual "cake" can be fed to stock, but only in small quantities, as it can upset their stomachs.

FLAX

The seed of the flax plant is linseed which is very rich in oil, and a good feed for livestock in itself. It is high in protein as well as in fat. If you crush the seed in a mill or else scald it in hot water, you will have an excellent food for young calves, a good replacement for milk. This is good for most sick animals, and is fairly laxative. Linseed, mixed with wheat or mixed corn, makes a perfect ration for hens. As you can grow half a ton to the acre it is a crop well worth growing. It can be crushed for oil, but the oil is not very edible and is chiefly used in the manufacture of sundry products such as soap, paint and printer's ink.

I shall deal with the production of flax for cloth and fibre on p. 230.

SUNFLOWERS

Thirty-five percent of sunflower seed is edible oil, which is good for margarine, if you must have the stuff, and for cooking oil. Sow the seed one week before the last likely frost. Plant a foot (30 cm) apart in rows three feet (91 cm) apart. Harvest the crop when about half the yellow petals have fallen off the flowers. Cut so that you leave a foot (30 cm) of the stem on, and hang the flowers downwards in bunches under a roof.

To get the oil out you will have to crush the seed. Or you can feed the seed direct to poultry at a rate of one (28 g) to two ounces (56 g) a day, and it is very good for them. You needn't even take the seed from the flowers. Just chuck them the complete flowers. You can sprout sunflower seed, then remove the husks and eat them.

POPPIES

Poppies can be grown for oil seed, as well as for more nefarious purposes, and up to 40 gallons (182 litres) of oil can be got off an acre. It is good cooking oil, burns in lamps with a clear smokeless flame, and the residual "cake," after the oil has been removed, makes excellent stock feed.

In a temperate climate sow the seed in a fine seed bed in April. Sow it fairly thinly, say three inches (8 cm) apart in rows one foot (30 cm) apart. Harvest by going along with a sheet, laying it on the ground, and pouring the seed into the sheet from the heads. Go along about a week later and do it

Pressing oil
Crack the seeds and wrap them in cloth to make "cheeses", which are cheese-shaped bundles. Pile them into the press, clamp down and turn the handle.

again. Or you can thresh the seed out in the barn with a flail. I grew two long rows of poppies once and harvested about a bushel of seed from it, but the kids ate the lot. Whether they got high on it I never found out. My kids seemed to be high most of the time anyway.

Olives and **walnuts** both make fine oil. You will find details about growing olives on pp. 178-179.

Extracting the oil

One method used by primitive men in hot climates to get the oil out of olives, oil-palm and other oleaginous fruits is to pile the fruit in hot sunlight on absorbent cloth. The oil exudes and is caught by the cloths which are thereafter wrung out. The process sounds most insanitary but is effective.

The other non-technological method is pressing. Before pressing, the seed must be cracked in a mill (plate or stone), or with a pestle and mortar. The cracked seeds are then put in what cider-makers call "cheeses" – packs of crushed seeds lapped round with cloth. The cheeses are piled one on top of the other in a press. The whole lot is then pressed and the oil is exuded. If you haven't got a press you can rig one up with a car jack. If the cracked seeds are pressed cold, the oil is of better quality than if they are heated first, but there is slightly less of it. The pressed residue is good for stock feed.

Grass & Hay

By far the most important, and the most widespread, crop grown in the world, is grass. Its ubiquitousness is amazing: it grows from the coldest tundra to the hottest tropic, from the wettest swampland to all but the driest desert. In areas where it only rains once every five or ten years, grass will spring up within days of a rainstorm and an apparently barren and lifeless land will be green. This is why grass has been called "the forgiveness of nature."

All the cereals are of course grasses: just grasses that have been bred for heavy seed yields. Sugar cane is grass and so is bamboo, but when a farmer speaks of grass he means the grass that grows on land and provides grazing for animals, and can be stored in the form of hay and silage.

Now the confusion here is that what the farmer calls "grass" is actually a mixture of all sorts of plants as well as grass. Clover is the most obvious and important one, and most "grassland" supports a mixture of grass and clover, and very often clover predominates over grass. Therefore whenever I write of "grass" I would ask the reader to know that I mean "grass and clover." Grass itself, too, is not just grass. There are many species of grass, and many varieties among the species, and it is of the utmost importance which species you grow.

Managing grassland

You can influence the make-up of the grass and clover species on your grassland by many means. For example, you can plough land up and re-seed with a chosen mixture of grass and clover seeds. But these will not permanently govern the pasture. According to how you manage that grassland so some species will die out, others will flourish and what the farmer calls "volunteer" grasses – wild grasses from outside – will come in and colonize. But essentially the management of the grassland will decide what species will reign.

If you apply heavy dressings of nitrogen to grassland you will encourage the grass at the expense of the clover. If you go on doing this long enough you will eventually destroy the clover altogether. The reason for this is that, normally, the clover only survives because it has an unfair advantage over the grasses. This advantage is conferred by the fact that the clover has nodules containing nitrogen-fixing bacteria on its roots and can thus fix its own nitrogen. The grasses cannot. So, in a nitrogen-poor pasture the clovers tend to predominate. Apply a lot of nitrogen and the grasses leap ahead and smother the clover. Alternatively, if you put a lot of phosphate on land you will encourage the clovers at the expense of the grass. Clover needs phosphate: grass nothing like so much. Clover-rich pasture is very good pasture and it also gives you free nitrogen.

If you constantly cut grassland for hay, year after year, and only graze the "aftermath" (what is left after you have cut the field for hay) you will encourage the coarse, large, vigorous grasses like perennial ryegrass and cocksfoot, and

you will ultimately suppress the finer grasses and clover, because these tall coarse grasses will shade them out. On the other hand if you graze grassland fairly hard, you will encourage clover and the short tender grasses at the expense of the tall coarse ones. If your land is acid you will get grasses like bent, Yorkshire fog, mat grass and wavy hair grass that are poor feeding value. Lime that land heavily and put phosphate on it and you will, with the help of mechanical methods too and perhaps a bit of re-seeding, get rid of these poor grasses and establish better ones. If land is wet and badly drained you will get tussock grasses, rushes and sedges. Drain it and lime it, and you will get rid of these. Vigorous and drastic harrowing improves grass. It is good to do it every year.

Improving old pasture

You may inherit grass in the form of permanent pasture which has been pasture since time immemorial. Often this is extremely productive, and it would be a crime to plough it up. But you can often improve it by such means as liming, phosphating, adding other elements that happen to be short, by drastic harrowing (really ripping it to pieces with heavy spiked harrows), subsoiling, draining if necessary, heavy stocking and then complete resting, alternately grazing it and haying it for a season, and so on.

Now if you inherit a rough old piece of pasture, or pasture which because of bad management in the past is less than productive, the best thing to do may be to plough it up and re-seed it. You can do this in several ways. You can "direct re-seed it," that is plough it and work it down to a fine seed bed, sprinkle grass and clover seed on it, harrow it, roll it, and let it get on with it. You can do this, according to the climate in your locality, in spring, summer or autumn. What you need is cool, moist weather for the seed to germinate and the plants to get established. Or you can plough up, sow a "nurse crop," and sprinkle your grass seed in with it. The nurse crop can be any kind of corn or, in some cases, rape. When you harvest the corn you will be left with a good strong plant of grass and clover.

Seed mixture

As for what "seed mixture" to use when establishing either a temporary ley, which is grassland laid down for only a year or so, or permanent pasture, go to your neighbours and find what they use. Be sure to get as varied a mixture as you can, and also include, no matter what your neighbours and advisers say about this, some deep-rooting herbs such as ribgrass, plantain, chicory, yarrow, alfalfa and

The balanced pasture
Some of these plants are almost certain to be found in a good pasture.
Left to right, top row: Meadow fescue (Festuca pratensis);
Perennial rye-grass (Lolium perenne); Cocksfoot (Dactylis glomerata);
Timothy (Phleum pratense); Italian rye-grass (Lolium multiflorum).
Bottom row: Burnet (Sanguisorba officinalis); Lucerne (Medicago sativa);
Red clover (Trifolium pratense); Ribwort plantain (Plantago lanceolata).

burnet. You can rely on them to bring fertility up from down below, to feed your stock in droughts when the shallower-rooting grasses and clovers don't grow at all, and to provide stock with the minerals and vitality they need. On deep, lightish land, alfalfa by itself, or else mixed with grasses and clovers, is splendid for it sends its roots deep down below. What if it does die out after a few years? It has done its good by bringing nutriments up from the subsoil and by opening and aerating the soil with its deep-searching roots.

HAY

Grass grows enormously vigorously in the first months of the summer, goes to seed if you don't eat it or cut it, then dies down and becomes pretty useless. In the winter, in northern climates, it hardly grows at all. In more temperate climates though, it may grow pretty well for ten months of the year provided it is not allowed to go to seed.

Now there are two ways of dealing with this vigorous summer spurt: you can crowd stock on the grass to eat it right down, or you can cut the grass and conserve it. The way to conserve it is to turn it into hay or into silage. You can then feed it to stock in the winter.

Hay is a more practical proposition for the average self-supporter. You should get two tons of good hay off an acre of good grass. The younger you cut grass for hay the less you will have of it but the better it will be. Personally I generally cut hay before my neighbours, have less, feed less, but the cattle do better on it. In France and in places where a very labour-intensive but highly productive peasant agriculture prevails, grass is cut very young, made into hay very quickly, and then the grass is cut again, maybe three or four times, during the season. The resulting hay is superb: better than any silage, but the labour requirement is high.

Haymaking

To make hay: cut the grass before, or just after, it reaches the flowering stage. If it has begun to go to seed you will get inferior hay. Then pull it about. Fluff it up and keep turning it. Let the wind get through it and the sun get at it. If you are very lucky it may be dry enough to bale, or, if you are making it loose, to cock, in three days. Then bale it or cock it and thank God. The chances are, in any uncertain climate, that you will get rain on it, which is always bad for it, and then you have the job of turning it about again to get it dry again. In bad years you may have to go on doing this for weeks, and your hay will be practically useless for feed when you finally get it in.

Cocking

A cock is a pointed-topped dome of hay that you build with a fork. It sheds most of the rain and allows a certain amount of in-cock drying, but if the grass is too green, or wet from rain, you may have to pull the cocks open again and spread the hay about to dry. Then, if rain threatens, throw it up in the cock again. If you are worried about too much moisture in hay that you have cocked, thrust your hand deep inside. If the hay in there is hot, or feels wet and clammy, you must spread that hay about and dry it again. You can only stack it when it is dry enough – that is when it is no longer bright green and feels completely dry.

Baling

A bale is a compact block of hay which has been rammed tight and tied with string by a machine called a baler. You mustn't bale hay until you are sure it is dry enough. If you bale when it isn't dry it will heat in the bale and the hay will be spoiled. Once the hay is baled there is nothing you can do with it. Just get those bales inside as soon as you can: they will shed a certain amount of light rain. But once rain gets right into them you have had it. You will have spoiled hay.

There is a great armoury of machines, both tractor and animal-drawn, for dealing with hay. There are machines

Haycocks and tripods

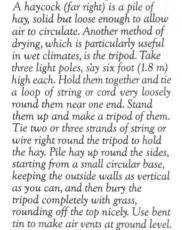

A haycock (far right) is a pile of hay, solid but loose enough to allow air to circulate. Another method of drying, which is particularly useful in wet climates, is the tripod. Take three light poles, say six foot (1.8 m) high each. Hold them together and tie a loop of string or cord very loosely round them near one end. Stand them up and make a tripod of them. Tie two or three strands of string or wire right round the tripod to hold the hay. Pile hay up round the sides, starting from a small circular base, keeping the outside walls as vertical as you can, and then bury the tripod completely with grass, rounding off the top nicely. Use bent tin to make air vents at ground level. There must be at least one on the windward side.

for tedding (fluffing-up), windrowing (gathering together into long loose rows), turning (turning the windrows over) and raking. But all you need if you don't have too much hay, or have enough labour, are some wooden handled rakes and some pitch forks. You can make the best hay in the world with just these. You can ted the hay with the pitch forks, rake it into windrows, then rake three or four windrows together, cock these with the forks, load the cocks on to a cart with the forks, and ultimately stack it. Haymaking in summer-wet climates is always a gamble; a triumph if you win, and something to put up with if you lose.

Tripoding

In wet climates the tripod (see illustration) is a useful means of drying wet hay. Grass that has only had maybe a couple of days of air drying can be tripoded, even if it looks quite green, for the air continues to get through it in the tripod. I have seen hay left on the tripods in bad weather for a month, but it does not necessarily make very good hay after that sort of treatment.

SILAGE

If you take grass, clover, lucerne, crushed green maize, kale, or many other green things, and press them down tight in a heap from which you exclude the air, it will not go bad, as you might think, but will ferment into a food very nourishing to animals. In fact good silage is as good as the very best of hay. And of course, because you can cut your green crop at any stage of growth you can cut it young when its protein-content is highest, so it makes good feed. Grass you can cut again and again during the season, instead of waiting until it is fully grown as most people do when they make hay.

Making silage

To make your silage you need some machinery. At its most basic, a mower and a buck-rake. You mow the grass when it is quite young and green, haul it together with the buck-rake, load it in a cart or on a trailer, take it and dump it on your silage heap. Ideally, though, you need a forage harvester, which, towed behind a tractor, cuts the grass and blows it into an accompanying trailer, pulled by another tractor (so you need two tractors). You then take it to the heap. Most small-scale self-supporters will not consider silage, because it is rather a large-scale enterprise. Further, the bigger the silage heap the less surface area there is compared to volume and therefore the less spoilage there is to the silage. If you do decide to make it on a small scale, you must enclose the heap pretty completely: walls all round it and a roof on top, for air spoils silage.

Consolidate your heap after every day's cut by driving a tractor up on top of it or leading a horse across, and ultimately cover the complete heap over with a plastic sheet weighted down with tons of straw bales, hay bales, or old motor-car tyres. If you can, build your heap in a shed to keep the rain off. But you can make silage out of doors, by enclosing the stuff in a bag, like a huge balloon, of plastic, and again weight that down, probably with old motor tyres. You can make marvellous silage by stuffing lawn clippings tight into plastic fertilizer bags, sealing them and leaving them for a while to ferment.

Feeding silage

You then feed it, come winter, by exposing the open end and letting the animals feed from a "face." You control the animals, to stop them from trampling on the stuff, either with "tomb-stones" which are a row of posts or concrete blocks through which they can poke their heads and get at the silage in a controlled manner, or with an electric fence. You give them another slice every day. Nobody can say that any *aesthetic* pleasure can be derived from silage, but cows like it.

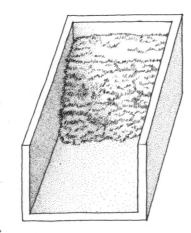
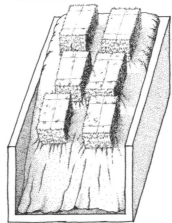
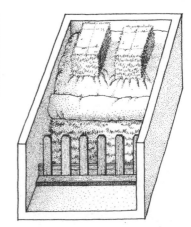

Silage
If you compress green vegetation into a tight heap, provided that the sugar content is high it will not rot but will ferment and become silage, a nutritious animal food. It is best made on a large scale, as the less surface area there is in relation to volume the less waste there will be. Young grass is ideal but any green crop will do. Build up a pile enclosed within three walls and preferably with a roof. Each time you add to your heap consolidate it by running it over with a tractor or horse. When the heap is complete cover it with a plastic sheet, weigh it down and leave it until winter when you can feed it to animals by exposing one end.

Pile in greenstuff
Make sure that the greenery is tightly compressed so that all air is excluded from the silo.

Cover and weigh down
Weigh down the completed pile with heavy objects on top of a plastic sheet to keep out air and rain.

Open up for feeding
Expose the open end to the animals, but limit them to a daily ration by erecting a row of "tomb-stones."

Row Crops

In Europe in the Middle Ages there was an annual holocaust of animals every autumn. It was impossible to feed all these extra animals during the winter, so most of them were killed off in the autumn and either eaten then or salted down. Salt meat was about all that medieval man had in the winter or, indeed, until the first lambs could be killed in the early summer. And milk, too, was in very short supply.

The introduction of the turnip changed all this. If a proportion of your land was put down to turnips you could continue to feed and fatten animals all through the winter, and also keep up the milk yield of your cows. And the turnip was followed by all the other root crops.

With "roots" I am including all those crops known as fodder crops, such as kale, cow cabbages and kohl-rabi, as well as those crops of which the actual roots are the part of the plant that we grow to eat or to feed to our stock. This simplification is justified because all these crops can take the same place in our rotation, and serve the same purpose which is, broadly, to feed our animals in the winter time when there is very little grass. And we can eat some of the roots as well.

These plants all have this in common: they store up energy in the summer so that they can lie dormant during the winter, and then release this energy early in the spring to flower and produce seed before other, annual, plants are able to do so. They are in fact biennials. We use them by making use of this stored nourishment for our winter feeding.

TURNIPS AND SWEDES

Swedes have a neck, are more frost-hardy than turnips, and store better, being less prone to disease. Turnips yield slightly more. Both these closely related plants are members of the brassica family, and thus are liable to club-root, a fungus disease, sometimes called "finger-and-toe" in turnips and swedes. This is a killer and can reduce your yield very drastically and even to nothing. If your land is infected with it don't grow turnips and swedes.

Sowing

Turnips and swedes are sown quite late: swedes in May perhaps, and turnips about a fortnight later. In very dry and warm areas it is better to sow later still, for with early sowing in such areas there is a tendency for "bolting" to occur. Bolting is when the plant skips a year and goes to seed at once, when it becomes useless. But turnips and swedes are of most use in the wetter, colder areas.

The seeds are small and therefore want a fine seed bed. Get it by ploughing in the autumn and cross ploughing as early as you can in the spring. Or, if you can't plough in the autumn, then plough for the first time as early as you can in the spring and plough again, or rotovate, cultivate and "pull your land about" with whatever tines or discs you may have or can borrow. Then drill in rows, preferably with a precision drill. This will drop seed in one by one at a set interval. If you drill with such a drill at the rate of a pound (0.5 kg) an acre this will

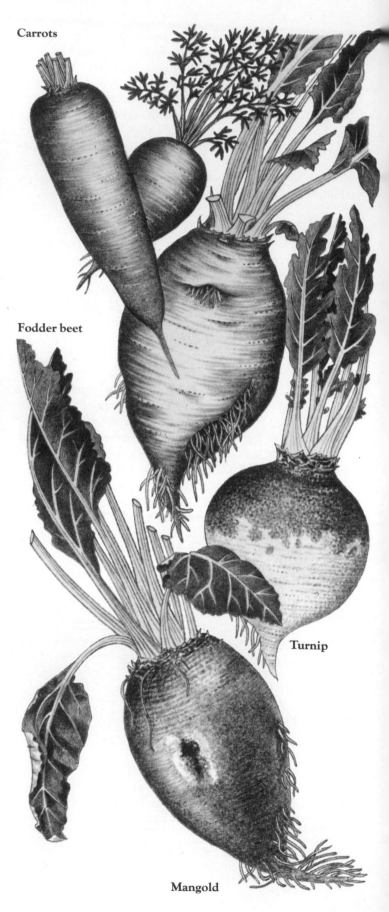

Carrots

Fodder beet

Turnip

Mangold

Cow cabbage

Kale

Kohl-rabi

Field beans

White mustard

Jerusalem artichoke

Potatoes

be about right, but to do this you must use graded seed. You can buy such seed at a seed merchant: it is much more expensive than ordinary seed, which you can grow yourself, but as it goes much further it is cheaper in the end. In wet climates it is an advantage to sow on raised ridges which can be made with a "double Tom" or ridging plough.

Singling

If you haven't got a precision drill, then drill the seed in rows as thinly as you can and rely on "singling" when the crop has declared itself. Singling means cutting out with a hoe all the little seedlings except one every nine inches (23 cm). You can't go along with a ruler so, as the plants are at all sorts of intervals, you will end up with some closer than nine inches and some further apart, but broadly speaking it doesn't matter that much. This singling of course cuts out the weeds as well as the surplus plants. You will then have to hand-hoe at least once more, possibly twice, during the growth of the crop, to cut the weeds out in the rows, and you will save labour if you can horse-hoe, or tractor-hoe, several times as well. Horse-hoeing is a very quick operation and does an enormous amount of good in a short time, but of course, in the end, you will always have to hand-hoe as well because the horse-hoe can't get the weeds between the plants in the rows.

Harvesting

You can leave turnips and swedes out in the field until after Christmas if you like, except in countries which have deep snow or very heavy frost. You can feed the roots off to sheep by "folding", moving the sheep over the crop, every day giving them just enough to eat off in a day by confining them behind hurdles or wire netting. You will have to go along, however, either before the sheep have had a go at them, or afterwards, and lift the turnips out of the ground with a light mattock. Otherwise the sheep leave half the roots in the ground and they are wasted.

You lift the crop pulling by hand and twisting the tops off. Then you can clamp (see p.182) or you can put them in a root cellar. Swedes are more nutritious than turnips and I think are the better crop to grow. They are also sweeter and pleasanter for you to eat.

MANGOLDS

Mangolds are like huge beet and crops of fifty tons of them to the acre are perfectly possible. Scientists say "they are nearly all water", but experienced farmers answer to this: "yes – but what water!" For they know that the moment you start feeding mangolds to cows the yields of milk go up. They are not suitable for humans to eat but make good wine. They are grown more in warmer, drier places than turnips are, but they are pretty hardy.

Sowing

It is best, especially on heavy land, to plough for mangolds the previous autumn. You must then work the land down to a good seed bed in the spring, and then drill at the rate of 10 lbs (4.5 kg) of seed to the acre as near the first of April as you are able. If it is a cold wet season you may not be able to get a seed bed till May, but it is not much good sowing the crop after the end of May: better sow turnips instead. Drill in rows about 22 inches (56 cm) apart and single out to about 10 inches (25 cm) apart in the rows. Then hoe and horse-hoe as for turnips.

Harvesting

Lift in the autumn before heavy frosts set in, top, put in little heaps covered with their own leaves until you can cart and clamp. In the old days farmers used to slice the mangolds in machines. Now we know that cattle can do it just as well with their teeth. Don't feed mangolds too soon: not until after New Year's Day. They are slightly poisonous until mature.

FODDER BEET

Fodder beets are very like mangolds, but smaller and far more nutritious. They are very high in protein, and are excellent for pigs, cows, or even horses. Personally I think they are a better grow. Sow and thin exactly like mangolds, but thin to eight inches (20 cm). To harvest – break the tap-roots with a beet-lifter or break out with a fork before you pull. Top with a knife, put in small piles, cover with leaves against frost, and cart to clamp when ready.

CARROTS
Sowing

Carrots need a fine seed bed just like turnips, and not too much fresh muck: it makes them fork. Carrots will not thrive on an acid soil, so you may have to lime. Sow them in rows a foot (30 cm) apart, or up to 18 inches (46 cm) if you intend to horse-hoe a lot, and sow the seed as thinly as you can. You may then avoid singling, but the crop takes a great deal of labour in hand-weeding, as it grows very slowly, far slower than the weeds in fact.

Harvesting

In places with mild winters you can leave the crop in the ground until you want it, but if you fear hard frosts lift it by easing out with a fork and then pulling. Twist the tops off; don't cut them. Then clamp or store in sand. It is really too laborious a crop to grow for stock feeding, but it does make very good stock feed, particularly for pigs. You can fatten pigs on raw carrots and a very little high protein supplement as well, and they will live on just raw carrots. And, of course, they are an excellent human food: very rich in vitamin A.

KALE

The most common of the myriad kales are: Marrowstem, Thousand-headed, Rape kale, Hungry-gap kale and Kohlrabi, and there are lots of other curious kales in different parts of the world.

Sowing

Drill in rows about 20 inches (51 cm) apart, or broadcast, but drilling gives a better yield and if you have a precision drill you can save seed. Sow from two to four pounds (0.9 – 1.8 kg) of seed per acre. Drill most kales early in April, although drill Marrowstem in May so that it does not get too woody. Thin and hoe in rows and you will get a heavier crop, particularly of Marrowstem kale. Kale likes plenty of manure.

Harvesting

You can fold kale off in the winter. It is more used for folding to cows than to sheep – it is a marvellous winter feed for milking cows. Let the cows on to it a strip at a time behind an electric fence. Or you can cut it with a sickle and cart it to feed to cows indoors. Use Marrowstem first and leave hardier kales like Hungry-gap until after the New Year. After you have cut, or grazed off, a field of kale the pigs will enjoy digging up the roots. Alternatively you can just plough in.

RAPE

Rape is like a swede but has no bulb forms. It is good for folding to sheep or dairy cows. It can be sown (generally broadcast – not drilled) in April for grazing off in August, or can be sown as a "catch crop" after an early cereal harvest to be grazed off in the winter but then it won't be a very heavy crop. Rape is too hot a taste for humans, so you can't eat it as a vegetable, although a little might flavour a stew.

COW CABBAGES

These are very similar to ordinary cabbages. Establish them like kale, or if you have plenty of labour you can grow them in a seed bed and transplant them out by hand in the summer. This has the advantage that you can put them in after, say, peas or beans or early potatoes, and thus get two crops in a year: a big consideration for the smallholder. You can get a very heavy crop but remember cow cabbages like good land and plenty of manure.

You can clamp cabbages. All the above brassica crops are subject to club-root, and must not be grown too often on the same land. Cow cabbages make splendid human food too, and are fine for sauerkraut (see p. 187).

MUSTARD

There are two species: *Brassica alba* and *Brassica juncea*, white and black mustard. They can be grown mixed with rape for grazing off with sheep; or grown alone for the same purpose; or grown as a green manure to be ploughed into the land to do it good; or harvested for seed, which you can grind, mix with a little white wheat flour and moisten as required to produce the mustard that goes so well with sausages.

Remember that mustard is cabbage-tribe though, and is therefore no good for resting the land from club-root. I would never grow it as green manure for that reason. It is not frost-hardy.

Cleaning crops

It must be understood that all the above crops, excepting rape and mustard when these are broadcast and not drilled in rows, are cleaning crops, and thus of great value for your husbandry. Being grown in rows it is possible to horse-hoe and hand-hoe, and this gives the husbandman a real chance to get rid of weeds. So, although you may think that the growing of these row crops is very hard work, remember that it is hard work that benefits every other crop that you grow, and I would suggest that you should grow a crop in every four years of your arable rotation.

POTATOES

Where potatoes grow well they can be, with wheat, one of the mainstays of your diet, and if you have enough of them you will never starve. They are our best source of storable vitamin C, but most of this is in the skins so don't peel them. You can even mash them without peeling them.

Seed potatoes

For practical purposes, and unless we are trying to produce a new variety of spud and therefore wish to propagate from true seed, potatoes are always grown from potatoes. In other words we simply plant the potatoes themselves. This is known as vegetative reproduction, and all the potatoes in the world from one variety are actually the same plant. They aren't just related to each other: they are each other.

We can keep our own "seed", therefore, from one year to the next, but there is a catch here. The potato is a plant from the High Andes, and grown at sea level in normal climates it is heir to various insect-borne virus diseases. After we have planted our potato "seed" (tubers) year after year for several "generations" there will be a build-up of virus infections and our potatoes will lose in vitality. Hence we must buy seed potatoes from people who grow it at high altitudes, or on wind-swept sea-islands, or in other places where the aphids do not live that spread these diseases. An altitude of over 800 ft (244 m) is enough in Britain for growing seed potatoes: in India most seed comes from Himachayal Pradesh, from altitudes of over 6000 ft (1829 m). The cost of seed potatoes now is enormous, and anybody who has land over 800 ft (244 m) would be well advised to use some of it for growing seed. In any case, many more of us ought to save the smallest of our tubers for "once-grown seed" or even "twice-grown seed". After we have carried on our own stock for three years, however, it will probably pay to import fresh seed from seed-growing areas rather than risk the spread of disease.

EARLY POTATOES

Potatoes that grow quickly and are eaten straight from the ground and not stored are called "early potatoes." To grow them you should chit, or sprout, them. They should be laid in shallow boxes, in weak light (at any rate not in total darkness for that makes them put out weak gangly sprouts) at a temperature between 40°F (4°C) and 50°F (10°C). A cold greenhouse is generally all right. It is an advantage to give them artificial light to prolong their "day" to 16 hours out of the 24. This keeps the "chits" green and strong and less likely to break off when you plant the spuds.

Planting

Beware of planting too early, for potatoes are not frost-hardy, and if they appear above the ground before the last frost it will nip them off. On a small garden scale you can guard against this to some extent by covering them with straw, or muck, or compost, or cloches. If they do get frosted one night go out early in the morning and water or hose the frost off with cold water. This will often save them.

Plant earlies by digging trenches nine inches (23 cm) deep and two foot (61 cm) apart, and putting any muck, compost or green manure that you might have in the trenches. Plant the spuds on top a foot (30 cm) apart, and bury them.

Actually you will get the earliest early new potatoes if you just lay the seed on the ground and then ridge earth over them (about five inches or 13 cm deep is ideal). You couldn't do this with main crop because the spuds grow so large and numerous that they would burst out of the sides of the ridges and go green. Spuds go green if the light falls on them for more than a day or two and then become poisonous: green potatoes should never be eaten nor fed to stock. The fruit of the potato plant, and the leaves, are highly poisonous, being rich in prussic acid.

Potatoes are usually planted by dropping them straight on muck, then earthing them up. But more people are now ploughing the muck in the previous autumn. Twenty tons of muck per acre is not too much. And always remember potatoes are potash-hungry. Non-organic farmers use "artificial" potash: organic ones use compost, seaweed, or a thick layer of freshly-cut comfrey leaves. Plant the spuds on top of the comfrey; as the leaves rot, the potato plants help themselves to the potash that they contain.

Harvesting

You might get a modest five tons to the acre of early potatoes, increasing the longer you leave them in the ground: but if they make part of your income the earlier you lift them the better. You can fork potatoes out, plough them out, or lift them with a potato-lifter.

MAIN CROP POTATOES

The potato plant has a limited growing season, and when this stops it will stop growing. So it is best to let your main crop potatoes grow in the most favourable time of the year. This means the summer, and it is inadvisable to plant them too early. Plant them in April and you won't go far wrong. Easter is the traditional time in England.

Planting

If you use bought seed you can be a bit sparing with the amount: perhaps a ton an acre. Where you are using your own seed perhaps a ton and a half. Main crop potatoes should be planted 14 inches (36 cm) apart, in rows 28 inches (71 cm) apart if the seed averages $2\frac{1}{2}$ ounces (70 g). If the seed is smaller, plant it closer: if it is bigger, plant it further apart. You will get the same yield either way. If you plant by hand you can control this very accurately. Ideally seed potatoes should go through a $1\frac{3}{4}$-inch (5 cm) riddle and be stopped by a $1\frac{1}{2}$-inch (4 cm) one. Anything that goes through the latter is a "chat," and goes to the pigs.

If you have a ridging plough, horse-drawn or tractor-drawn, put the land up into ridges. Put muck or compost between the ridges if you have it to put, although it would be better if you had spread it on the land the previous autumn. Plant your seed in the furrows by hand and, if you lack the skill or equipment to split the ridges, and by God it takes some skill, do not despair. Simply harrow or roll the ridges down flat. This will bury the potatoes. After about a fortnight take your ridging plough along again, and this time take it along what were, before you harrowed them flat, your ridges. So you make what were your ridges furrows, and what were your furrows ridges.

If you haven't got a ridging plough use an ordinary plough. Plough a furrow, plough another one next to it and drop your spuds in that. Plough another furrow, thus burying your spuds, and plough another furrow and drop spuds in that. In other words plant every other furrow. Don't worry if your planted rows aren't exactly 28 inches (71 cm) apart. Potatoes know nothing of mathematics.

Care of crop

Drag the ridger through once or twice more whenever the weeds are getting established. This not only kills the weeds, it earths up the spuds, gives them more earth to grow in and stops them getting exposed and going green. If you haven't got a ridging plough, and are skilful, you can ridge up with a single-furrow plough.

Go through the spuds with the hand-hoe at least once to kill the weeds in the rows, but after you have done this, and thus pulled down the ridges, ridge them up again. Up to ten days after planting you can harrow your potato field to great advantage to kill weed seedlings, but after that be careful because you might damage the delicate shoots of the spuds It is all a matter of common sense. You want to suppress the weeds and spare the spuds. When the potatoes meet over the rows they will suppress the weeds for you and you can relax, but not completely. You are afraid of blight.

Blight

Blight is the disease that, helped by absentee landlords, killed two million Irishmen in 1846, and you can be as organic as all get-out and if it is a blight year you will still get blight. Now if you do get blight, don't despair; you will still get a crop. The virulent strain that killed the Irishmen, by killing their only source of food, has passed by now. But your crop won't be such a big one.

You will know you have blight if you see dark green, water-soaked patches on the tips and margins of the leaves. If you see that, spray immediately, for although you cannot cure a blighted plant by spraying, you can at least prevent healthy plants being infected. These patches soon turn dark brown and get bigger, and then you can see white mould on them. Within a fortnight, if you do nothing about it, your whole field will be blighted and the tops will simply die and turn slimey. Now the better you have earthed up your ridges the fewer tubers will be affected, for the blight does not travel down inside the plant to the potatoes but is washed down into them by rain.

Commercial farmers spray the blighted tops with 14 gallons (63.6 litres) of BOV sulphuric acid to 85 gallons (386.4 litres) of water, or else some of the newer chemicals. This burns them off and the blight spores do not get down to your spuds. I cut my tops off with a sharp sickle (it has to be sharp, else you simply drag the spuds out of the ground when you cut) and burn them. Don't lift your spuds for at least a fortnight, preferably longer, after the tops have been removed. This is so that they don't come in contact with blighted soil.

But, of course, you will never get blight, for you will have sprayed your "haulms" (tops) with Bordeaux or Burgundy Mixture, or one of the modern equivalents, before the first blight spore settled on your field, won't you? To make a Bordeaux Mixture, dissolve four pounds (1.8 kg) copper sulphate in 35 gallons (159.1 litres) of water in a wooden barrel, or in plastic dustbins. Then slowly slake two pounds (0.9 kg) freshly burned quicklime with water and make it into five gallons (22.7 litres) of "cream." Slowly pour the "cream" through a sieve into the copper sulphate solution. Make sure that all your copper has been precipitated by putting a polished knife blade in the liquid. If it comes out coated with a thin film of copper you must add more lime.

Burgundy Mixture is stronger and more drastic. It has 12½ pounds (5.7kg) washing soda instead of lime. These mixtures must be used fresh, because they won't keep long. Spray with a fine spray very thoroughly. Soak the leaves above and below too. All the spray does is prevent spores getting in. Do it just before the haulms meet over the rows and again, perhaps a week later. An alternative is to dust with a copper lime dust when the dew is on.

Blight attacks vary in date: it needs warm, moist, muggy weather, and in some countries agricultural departments give blight warnings over the radio. If you do get muggy weather when your spuds are pretty well grown, spray for blight. You will get half as big a crop again as if you didn't. You can help prevent blight by not allowing "rogue" potatoes

to grow: in other words lift every single potato from your fields after harvest, for it is these rogues that are the repositories of blight. Pigs will do this job for you better than anything else in the world, they will enjoy doing it and they will fertilize the land too.

Harvesting

Harvest as late as you can before the first frosts, but try to do it in fine weather. Fork them out, plough them out, spin them out or get them out with an elevator digger, but get them out. Leave them a day or half a day in the sun after lifting for the skins to set. Don't give them more than a day and a half or they will begin to green.

Storing

Clamping (see p. 182) is fine. Stacking in a dark shed, or a dark root cellar, is OK. The advantage of clamping is that if there is blight in your spuds, or any other spud disease, you don't get a build-up of the organisms as you would in a permanent building. Do what your neighbours do. In intensely cold winters clamping may not be possible: no clamp will stop the frost, and potatoes cannot stand much frost or they will rot. On the other hand, if they are too warm they will sprout. If possible they want it just above freezing.

JERUSALEM ARTICHOKES

As a very few plants of these would give us more tubers than we would care to eat, they are seldom grown on a field scale except by a few wise people who grow them to be dug up and eaten by pigs. They are wonderful for this purpose, and provided the pigs have enough of them they will do very well on artichokes alone and a little skimmed milk or other concentrated food. Half a pound (0.2 kg) a day of "pig nuts," plus unrestricted rooting on artichokes should be enough for a dry sow.

Sowing

Drop them in plough furrows 12 inches (30 cm) from each other, and the furrows should be three feet (91 cm) apart. Put them in any time after Christmas, if the land is not frozen and not too wet, and any time up to April. It doesn't much matter when, in fact. They won't grow until the warmer weather comes anyway and then they will grow like mad. They will smother every imaginable weed and after the pigs have rooted them up the land will be quite clean and well dunged too. But beware: the pigs will never get the very last one, and next year you will have plenty of "rogues" or "volunteers." In fact, if you leave them, you will have as heavy a crop as you had the year before. I sometimes do, but never for more than two years running. They will grow in practically any soil and don't need special feeding, although they like potash. If you just put them into the ground and leave them they will grow whatever you do.

Beans are distinguished from peas and the other legumes because they have a square hollow stem instead of a round solid one. There are hundreds of kinds and varieties of beans throughout the world. The various kinds of "runner" beans: scarlet runners, french beans, snap beans and so on, are seldom grown on a field scale, so I will deal with them as garden vegetables (see pp. 149–152).

FIELD BEANS

The crop which supplied most of the vegetable protein for the livestock of northern Europe and North America for centuries, and which should still do so today, is the field bean, tic bean, horse bean, or cattle bean: *Vicia vulgaris.* This is a most valuable crop, and it is only neglected nowadays because vast quantities of cheap protein have flooded into the temperate zones from the Third World. As the people of the latter decide to use their own protein, which they sadly need, temperate-zone farmers will have to discover the good old field bean again.

It produces very high yields of very valuable grain, and it enriches the soil in two ways: it is a legume, and therefore takes nitrogen from the air, and it forms deep tap roots which go well down and bring up nutrients, and themselves rot down afterwards to make magnificent humus. It is a most beneficial crop to grow, good for the land, and gives excellent yields of high-protein grain.

As with other grains, there are two sorts of field bean – winter and spring. However, farmers classify beans as "grain" or "corn".

Soil

Beans don't want nitrogen added, but they do benefit greatly by a good dressing of farmyard manure (muck) ploughed in as soon as possible after the previous crop has been harvested. In land already in good heart they will grow without this. They need lime though, as do all the legumes, and if your land needs it you must apply it. They need potash very badly and phosphates to a lesser degree. Non-organic farmers frequently apply 80 units of phosphorus and 60 units of potash, but we are more likely to rely on good farming and plenty of muck.

The seed bed need not be too fine, particularly for winter-sown beans. In fact a coarse seed bed is better for the latter because the clods help to shelter the young plants from the wind throughout the winter. In very cold climates you cannot grow winter beans because very hard frost will kill them. You will get heavier crops from winter beans than from spring ones, less trouble from aphids, a common pest of the crop, but possibly more trouble from chocolate-spot, a nasty fungus disease.

Sowing

You can sow with a drill, if you have one, provided it is adapted to handle a seed as big as the bean, or you can drop the seed in by hand behind the plough. Plough shallowly (four inches or 10 cm) and drop the seed in every other furrow, allowing the next one you plough to cover them over. I find this method very satisfactory as the seed is deep enough to defy the birds. Jays will play havoc with newly sown beans, simply pulling the young plants out of the ground.

Care of crop

By all means hoe beans. Horse-hoe or tractor-hoe between the rows and try, if you can, to hand-hoe at least once in the rows. They are a crop that can easily suffer from weeds.

Harvesting

Wait until the leaves have fallen from the plants and the *hilum,* or point of attachment of the pods to the plant, has turned black. Cut and tie the crop with a binder if you have one. If not, cut with the sickle and tie into sheaves. You have to use string for this because bean straw is difficult to tie with. Stook and leave in the stook until the crop feels perfectly dry (maybe a week or two). Then stack and cover the stack immediately, either by thatching it or with a rick-cover, or else stack it indoors. A bean stack without a cover will not keep the rain out, and if it gets wet inside the beans will be no good to you.

Threshing

Do not thresh until the beans have been in the stack at least four months. Many farmers like to leave the stack right through to the next winter before they thresh it, because beans are better for stock after they are a year old. Thresh just as you would wheat, with a flail or in a threshing drum.

Feeding to animals

Grind or crack the beans before feeding. Mix them as the protein part of your ration. Horses, cattle, pigs, sheep and poultry all benefit from beans. Cattle will pick over the straw and eat some of it. What they leave makes marvellous litter (bedding) and subsequently splendid manure.

SOYA BEANS

Soya beans, or soybeans, are grown in vast acreages in China and the United States in the warmer latitudes. They don't, as we all discovered a year or two ago, do much good in the climate of southern England and we must wait until a hardier variety is bred, if it can be, before we can grow them. In climates where they can be grown, sow or drill them well after the last possible frost about an inch (2.5 cm) deep, 10 inches (25 cm) apart in the rows and with the rows three feet (91 cm) apart. Keep them well hoed because they grow very slowly at first. Their maturing time can be anything from three to five months depending on the climate. If you need to, you can extend the season by covering them with glass or plastic. If you pick them young you can eat the pods whole. Otherwise shell them for the three or four beans inside. The same instructions apply to Lima beans.

Food from Animals

"A couple of flitches of bacon . . .
are great softeners of the temper, and promoters
of domestic harmony."
COBBETT

The Living Farmyard

Just as I advise against monoculture when it comes to planting crops, so I would urge you not to specialize in one animal, but to keep a wide variety. This is the only way to make the best use of your land's resources and to take advantage of the natural ways in which your animals help each other. Your cows will eat your long grass, and then your horses, sheep and geese can crop your short grass. After that your pigs will eat the roots and at the same time plough the field ready for sowing with grain crop, which all the animals, especially the hens, can eat. Pigs of course thrive on whey, and skimmed milk from butter making, and cows' milk can nourish orphan foals or lambs. Your different animals will protect each other from disease as well, for organisms which cause disease in one species die when eaten by another.

Cows, horses, sheep and goats
Ruminants – cows, sheep and goats – are the animals best equipped to turn that basic substance, grass, into food in the form of meat and milk. Horses, I hope, will not be exploited for meat or milk, but for their unique ability to turn greenstuff into power. Amongst themselves these animals divide up the available food very efficiently, and in so doing they work to each other's benefit. A lot of horses kept on a pasture with no other animals will not thrive; with other animals they will. It has been said that if you can keep twenty cows on a given piece of pasture, you can keep twenty cows and twenty sheep just as well. Cows will eat the long, coarser grass and the sheep and horses will clean up after them by nibbling what they leave close to the ground. Goats, which are browsers rather than grazers, fill a useful niche because they will eat bark, leaves, brambles and bushes, and if you want your land deforested they will do that as well.

Geese
Geese will compete directly with the ruminants for grass, but, like the ruminants, though less efficiently, they will turn grass into food in the form of meat. At the same time they will improve your pasture. It is well worth keeping a few, for the more you diversify your grazing species the better.

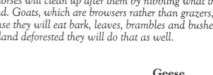

Ducks

Your ducks will eat a lot of food which will otherwise yield you no benefit: water plants, frogs and other aquatic creatures. And they will patrol your garden and eat that unmitigated nuisance, the slug.

Pigs

The pig is a magnificent animal and really the pioneer on your holding. He will eat anything, and in his efforts to find food he will plough land, clear undergrowth and devour all surpluses, even your washing-up water.
As William Cobbett wrote in his Cottage Economy: "In short, without hogs farming could not go on; and it never has gone on in any country in the world. The hogs are the great stay of the whole concern. They are much in small space; they make no show, as flocks and herds do; but without them cultivation of the land would be a poor, a miserably barren concern."

Chickens

Chickens are essentially graminivorous, or at least they prefer to live on seed. They will pick up all spilled grain in your harvest fields, eat the "tail corn", the grains which are too small to grind, and eat weed seeds. They will follow the pig, when that splendid animal is rooting away in the ground, and snap up any worms, wireworms, leatherjackets or whatever else he turns up. And they will keep the rats away by pecking up spilled seed from corn ricks.

The Cow

There are four classes of cows: dairy cows, beef cows, dual purpose cows and just cows. Fifty years ago there were some magnificent dual purpose breeds in Europe and America but economic circumstances caused them to die out as the pure dairy and pure beef animals took over. This is sad, from the point of view of the self-supporter, and from every other point of view in fact, because beef should be a by-product of the dairy herd and not an end in itself.

One cow produces one calf every year, and she's got to do that if she is to give milk. If she is a beef cow all she can do is suckle this one calf, unless she has twins of course, until it is old enough to be weaned. But if she is a dual purpose cow she can have a good beef calf, provide him with enough milk, and provide you with enough milk as well. And if she is a pure dairy cow she will have a calf a year and provide enough milk for it and more than enough for you, but the calf won't be a very good one for beef.

Now, half the calves you have are likely to be male, and, of the other half that are female, only half will be needed as replacements for the dairy herd. Therefore ultimately you will be forced, whatever you do, either to sell the three-quarters that are not wanted for beef, or to kill them for beef yourself. Otherwise your ox population will build up on your piece of land until there is no room for you or anybody else.

What breed?

But we can and do eat dairy cattle. Most of Britain's beef now comes from the Dutch Friesian, called the Holstein in the US. These cattle are large, bony and give an awful lot of poor milk, meaning milk low in butter-fat. They are hardy and their calves, although from dairy animals, give good beef.

Then at the opposite end of the scale there are the Channel Island breeds. Of these the Jersey makes the best house-cow. They are small, don't give as much milk as the Friesian, but it is the richest milk there is. Their calves make poor beef

and are practically unsaleable, but they are good to eat all the same. I've had them.

If you can get a good old-fashioned dual purpose breed I would say get it every time. The Danish Red is fine, the old Red Poll is too, or the dual-purpose Shorthorn. From these you will get good milk and good beef. But there is no cow more tractable, or indeed loveable, than the little Jersey, and if you want a friend as well as a milk supply I strongly recommend her.

Buying your cow

How do you get a cow in the first place? Nothing can be more difficult. You see, if a person who owns a herd of cows wishes to sell one of them you can be sure of one thing. It is the worst cow in his herd. It may just be that a farmer wants to sell a cow or two because he has too many, and wishes to reduce his herd, but even if he does it for this reason, and his herd is a good one, you can still be sure that the ones he culls will be the worst in the herd. Generally, if a farmer sells a cow, it is because there is something wrong with her.

There are a few let-outs from this Catch 22 situation. One is the farmer who for some reason (maybe because he has been translated to another world) is selling up. His whole herd will be put up for auction and the good cows will be sold along with the bad. Another is the person (maybe a fellow self-supporting freak?) who has reared one or more heifer calves with the object of selling them "down calving". Down calving means that the cow has just calved and is therefore (another cowman's term) "in full profit", in other words giving a lot of milk. In this case you can buy a cow which has just calved for the first time, and she is just as likely to be a good cow as any other cow you might buy. The person selling her is not selling her for the usual reason, because she is bad, but because he has bred her up especially to sell.

Apart from carefully examining the heifer herself in such

The Friesian
The archetypal dairy cow. Big, heavy-yielding, hardy, and given the right bull will produce fine beef calves.

The Jersey
The classic house-cow. Affectionate, hardy, with the richest milk in the world, but not so good for beef.

cases, also examine the mum. It always pays to examine a prospective future mother-in-law before proposing to a girl. You get an idea of how your beloved is likely to turn out in her maturer years. The same applies to heifers.

There is one disadvantage about thus buying a first-calver, at least there is if you are new to cows. You will both be learners. She will be nervous and flighty, and may kick. You will be the same. She will have tiny teats, and you may not get on very well together.

So if you are a learner maybe you had better get some dear old duck with teats like champagne bottles, kind eyes, and a placid nature. What does it matter if she is not the world's champion milker? What does it matter if she only has three good "quarters"? (Each teat draws milk from one quarter of the udder). Provided her owner is honest, and he says she is healthy, and doesn't kick, she will probably do for you. Now here are a few points to consider when you buy a cow:

1 Feel the udder very carefully and if there are any hard lumps in it don't buy her, because it probably means that she has, or has had and is likely to get again, "mastitis" very badly. (Mastitis is an extremely common complaint. One or more teats gets blocked, and the milk you get is useless). But if you are getting a cow very cheaply because she has got a "blind quarter" (one quarter of her udder with no milk in it) then that is a different matter. As long as you know about it.

2 Make sure she it TT (tuberculosis tested) and has been tested, and found free from, a disease called brucellosis. In many countries both these tests are obligatory, and it is illegal to sell milk from cows found infected with either. In any case, it is damned foolish.

3 If the cow is "in milk", in other words has any milk in her udders, try milking her. Try each teat fairly carefully. Make sure she doesn't kick when you milk her and handle her, although of course common sense will tell you that, because you are a stranger, and because maybe she has been carted to some strange market or sales place, she will be more than usually nervous. Make sure she has some milk in each quarter. If you are buying her from her home ask the vendor if you can milk her right out (save the vendor the trouble!) and then you will really know how much milk she gives.

4 Look at her teeth because they will tell you how old she is.

5 See that she is quiet enough and tame enough to let you put your arms round her neck and stroke her behind the ears.

6 Make sure she has that indefinable but nevertheless very real "bloom of health" about her.

7 If you are a real beginner, ask some kindly cow-knowing neighbour to go with you and advise you. If the neighbour is really into cows do what he says.

Having got your cow get her home and make her comfortable. Spoil her a little. Tie her up in your cowshed, give her some good hay, some oats or barley meal or cow-cake: give her time to calm down. In the evening milk her.

Feeding

"Agriculturalists" work out the feeding of cows by saying that a cow needs a certain amount of food for her "maintenance ration" and a certain amount more for her "production ration". That is, we work out what it will take to maintain the cow healthily if she is giving no milk and then add some according to how much milk she is giving.

Maintenance ration

Twenty pounds (9.0 kg) a day of good hay will maintain a large cow during the winter. Twelve pounds (5.4 kg) would maintain a small cow like a Jersey. You can take it that, if you feed a cow nothing else but fair quality hay for her maintenance ration she will need 33 cwt (1676 kg) of hay for the winter if she is a big girl like a Friesian, or 21 cwt (1167 kg) of hay if she is a Jersey. Now, if we want to feed other things besides hay for maintenance, these are the hay equivalents:

The Red Poll
A good old-fashioned dual-purpose cow, producing plenty of good milk and good beef too.

The Hereford
Recognized all over the world as a fine beef animal, good for crossing with other breeds for beef.

The Cow

A ton of fairly good hay is equivalent to:
  ¾ ton of very good hay
  4 tons of kale or other greens
  5 tons mangolds
  3 tons fodder beet

Production ration

Now to give "maintenance plus one gallon" the winter's ration should increase to: 45 cwt (2286 kg) for a Friesian and 33 cwt (1676kg) for a Jersey. The daily ration therefore goes up to 27 lbs (12.9 kg) hay or its equivalent for a Friesian, and 20 lbs (9.0 kg) for a Jersey.

Now you can reckon that if you feed 3½ lbs (1.6 kg) of a mixed "concentrate" ration for each gallon (4.5 litres) that the cow produces over the first gallon, that will do. And the concentrate could be:
  2 parts barley (rolled)
  1 part oats (rolled)
  1 part beans (broken or kibbled)
To each ton of concentrates you can add if required:
  20 lbs (9.0 kg) limestone
  20 lbs (9.0 kg) steamed bone flour
  20 lbs (9.0 kg) salt
Cows kept naturally on organically-farmed pastures and hay are unlikely to suffer from mineral deficiencies, but if you ever did get "grass-staggers" or hypo-magnasemia, or any other diseases that your vet told you were due to mineral deficiency then you would have to add the missing element either to the diet of the cows or to the land. Seaweed meal is an excellent source of all minerals. You can just dump some seaweed on your pasture from time to time, and allow the cows to nibble it and lick it if they want to. They will not suffer from mineral deficiency if they do this.

All this means that if, in an average winter situation, you feed your cows, say, 30 lbs (13.6 kg) of kale or other greens a day and 12 lbs (5.4 kg) of hay for her maintenance plus one gallon, and, say, 3½ lbs (1.6 kg) of the above suggested "concentrate" for her production ration for every gallon over the

first, you will not go far wrong. But, use what food you've got. Use common sense and watch the milk bucket. If the milk goes down feed more and you should be all right.

Summer feeding

In the summer, if you have plenty of good grass, grass alone should give maintenance plus up to four gallons (18 litres). A cow yielding over this would have to have 3½ lbs (1.6 kg) concentrate per gallon over four gallons, but I hope you wouldn't try to keep such a cow. You don't want a ridiculous lot of milk, and very high yielders need a vet in almost constant attendance and have to be cared for like invalids. But grass varies enormously in value, and, if you suddenly find her milk yield dropping off, give her a little concentrate (even a pound or two) and see what happens.

Stockmanship is a matter of constant keen observation and common sense. Look at your animals: learn what the "bloom of health" means. Watch their condition. Are they getting fatter or thinner? Watch their milk yield, watch how hungry they seem to be. The "stockman's eye" may not be given to everyone but it can usually be acquired.

Milking

Milk your cow twice a day, ideally at twelve hourly intervals. Wash the cow's udder and teats in warmish water. Thoroughly wash your own hands. Then dry well with a towel. The more you massage the udder in doing so the better. Clean the rear end of the cow generally so that no dung or dirt will fall into your pail. Give the cow something nice to eat. Sit down beside her on a stool and grasp the two front teats in your hands. Or, if you are an absolute beginner, grasp one teat with one hand. Squeeze high up the teat with your thumb and forefinger so that the milk that is in the teat cannot get back into

The cowshed
The modern cowshed has a concrete manger in front of the cows, a concrete standing area for the cows to stand or lie on, and a dunging passage behind the cows. There must be a drain somewhere in the dunging passage to take liquids away. Any food-bins in the cowshed should be securely latched in case a cow slips her tie.

Milking a cow
Sit down on the right-side of the cow, grip the bucket at an angle between your knees, and grasp the two front teats in your hands. To milk, squeeze the top of the teat with the thumb and forefinger to stop the milk from going back up to the udder, then squeeze progressively downwards with the rest of the fingers to expel the milk.

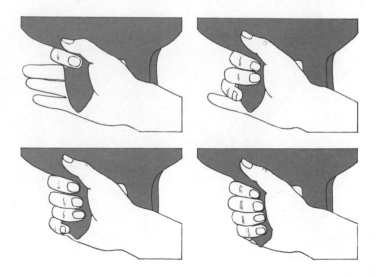

the "bag", as farmers call the udder. Common sense will tell you how hard to squeeze. Next, keep holding on with your thumb and finger, and squeeze the teat successively with your second, third, and little fingers, so as to expel the milk downwards out of the teat. Release the teat and repeat the operation. It sounds easy but it is difficult.

It is as well to practise on a dummy teat so as to get the necessary rhythmic motion. It takes a week to learn to milk. It is much the best to begin on an old cow who is used to being milked and who won't mind if you fumble.

Housing

The modern milking shed is a concrete-floored building arranged so that the cow can be tied up to a vertical post. This has a ring on it that can slide up and down so that the cow can lie down if she likes. She is supposed to dung in the "dunging passage" and you are supposed to clean it every day.

But in my view all this is bowing down too far to the great god "hygiene". If you keep your cow in a house for all or part of the time and throw in plenty of dry straw, bracken or other bedding, every day, the dung will slowly build up and you will have the most magnificent muck. Your local Dairying Officer will excommunicate you if you milk cows in such a house and you would certainly not be allowed to sell milk or any milk product in any so-called civilized country; but in fact the milk you get from a cow milked on "deep litter" will be as clean as any milk in the world, provided you observe the other rules of hygiene. We milked our cows for eight years like this, cleaning the muck out about once a year, and the cows were indoors at night in the winter. Our milk, butter and cheese were perfect.

A refinement is to have a house for milking the cow or cows and another house for them to sleep, eat and rest in. This can be cleaned out regularly, or it can be strawed every day and the dung left for months. It will be warmer and pleasanter for the cows than the milking stall, and they can be left free. If you have silage (see p. 81) the "silage face" can be one end of it so the cows feed themselves.

As to when to house: our cows only come into the cow-shed to be milked, and to finish their hay. Winter and summer, night and day, they are out on the bare hillside except for an hour morning and evening when they come in to be milked and to eat. In the summer they don't want to come in. They want to stay out and eat grass. We don't feed them in the summer – except maybe a pound or two of rolled barley to make them contented. If there is plenty of grass, grass is enough for them. We don't go in for very high yielders, nor should any self-supporter.

In the winter they come in eagerly because the grass is of little value and they are hungry. In bad weather I would prefer to leave them in all night and only turn them out in the day-time, and then, when the weather is really foul, keep them in some days too. But to do this I would need an awful lot of straw. In really cold climates cows have to be housed all winter. Do what your neighbours do. But don't keep them in half the winter and then turn them out. And when you do turn them out in the spring be careful about it. Wait for fine weather, and only push them out for short periods at first. Too much grass may upset stomachs not used to it, and sudden exposure to weather can give cattle a chill. And if you can keep cows out all winter, that is if any of your neighbours do, it is far less trouble.

Mating

A small cow might be mated at 15 months: a large cow at 20 months. A cow will only take the bull, or the artificial in-seminator, when she is "bulling" or on heat. This condition occurs at intervals of 21 days in a non-pregnant heifer or cow, and continues each time for about 18 hours. You must watch for signs of bulling and then get the cow to a bull or have her artificially inseminated immediately, certainly by the next day at the latest.

Signs of bulling are: she mounts other cattle or other cattle mount her; she stands about mooing and looking amorous; she swells slightly at the vulva; she will let you put all your weight on her back and apparently enjoy it. It may be a good thing to miss the first bulling period after calving, so as to give

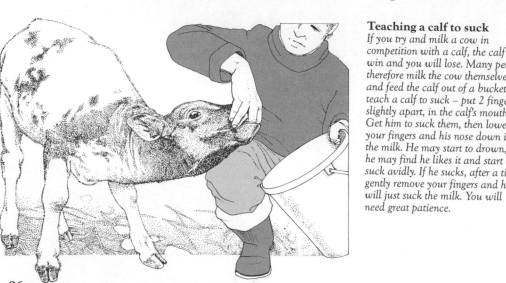

Teaching a calf to suck
If you try and milk a cow in competition with a calf, the calf will win and you will lose. Many people therefore milk the cow themselves and feed the calf out of a bucket. To teach a calf to suck – put 2 fingers, slightly apart, in the calf's mouth. Get him to suck them, then lower your fingers and his nose down into the milk. He may start to drown, or he may find he likes it and start to suck avidly. If he sucks, after a time gently remove your fingers and he will just suck the milk. You will need great patience.

the cow a rest, but make sure you don't miss the second one.

If there is a bull running with the cows there is no trouble. He knows what to do and when to do it. But if there is no bull you will just have to use your eyes, that is all. Then, you may take her to a neighbour's bull, or bring him to her, or, in countries which have "AI" (artificial insemination) simply telephone the relevant authority.

Calving

Leave her alone, out of doors, and you will probably find her one day licking a little calf that has just been born quite easily and naturally. Outdoor cows very seldom have trouble with calving. But watch the two for a few hours until you are quite sure that the calf has got up and sucked. If the calf doesn't suck within an hour, be worried. Get it up and hold it to the teat and make it suck, and if necessary tie the cow up.

Cows calve up in the bare mountains in winter and rear their calves perfectly happily in the snow. As long as the calf runs out with the cow, and the cow has enough to eat, and the weather isn't too awful, he is all right. But as soon as you bring him indoors – and if you want the cow's milk you will have to – you have upset the ordinary workings of nature and you must keep the calf warm and out of draughts. He must suck from his mother for at least three days, because this first milk has colostrum, or beestings, a mixture of chemicals, organisms and antibodies which are essential for the health, nay survival, of the calf.

Then you can either take the calf right away from the cow, and keep him out of earshot if possible, or at least in a separate building, or you can keep him close to the cow's head so that she can see him, while you milk the cow. The easiest way for you to get your milk is to take the calf right away, milk his mother yourself, and she, after perhaps a night of bellowing for her calf, accepts the situation. She is not a human, and has a very short memory, and very soon accepts you as her calf-substitute. I have ended up with a wet shirt many a time because I could not stop an old cow from licking me while I milked her!

Meanwhile what do you feed the calf on? Well, if you have enough milk, feed the calf on the following mixture: the mother's milk, at a rate of 10% of weight of calf (if the calf weighs 50 lbs give him 5 lbs of milk), plus added warm water (one part water to three parts milk). Feed him this mixture twice a day out of a bucket (see illustrations opposite) and serve it at blood heat.

After about a week or two see that the calf has got some top-quality hay to nibble if he feels like it. After a month try him with "cake," rolled barley or other concentrates, and always have clean water available for him. After four months wean him off milk altogether and feed him 4 lbs (1.8 kg) hay and 3 lbs (1.4 kg) concentrates, or let him out on a little clean grazing. By six months he should be getting 6 lbs (2.7 kg) hay and 3 lbs (1.4 kg) concentrates, unless by then he is on good clean grazing.

A cow's teeth reveal her age
A mature cow has 32 teeth of which eight are incisors. All eight are on the lower jaw, and munch against a hard layer of palate called the dental pad. Within a month of birth a calf has grown eight temporary incisors. These will slowly be replaced, until at age five the mature cow has eight permanent incisors. Age can therefore be determined by the number of temporary and permanent incisors present in a cow's jaw. The age of cows over five can be gauged by the wear on their teeth (by the age of twelve only stumps remain), and by the roughness of their horns. But beware cattle dealers who sandpaper cows' horns to make them look young.

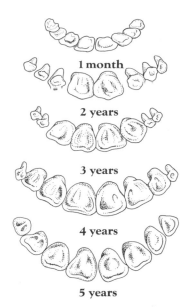

1 month

2 years

3 years

4 years

5 years

"Husk" is a killer disease and a calf who has grown up outdoors with his mum will be naturally immune. But before you put a calf reared indoors out to graze you must inject him with an anti-husk serum got from the vet, and feed him very well, on hay and concentrates as well as grass, until he has built up an immunity to husk. Don't turn motherless calves out in the winter time anyway, whatever you do.

There are other ways of rearing small calves and still getting some milk for yourself. If you are very lucky you can find another cow who has her own calf at heel and fool her into thinking she has had twins. Then you can turn her, her calf and your new calf all out together to pasture. This is the ideal solution because the new calf is absolutely no more trouble and will thrive exceedingly. But such cows are rare. So another solution is to select a foster mother, tie her up twice a day and force her to give milk to the new calf as well as her own. Many cows are pretty complacent about this, others fight like hell. If she fights you may have to tie her legs up to stop her hurting the calf. To get a young calf to suck a cow, put two fingers in his mouth and gently lead him up to the teat. Don't try to heave him forward from behind: that's useless.

Another way of getting milk for yourself and keeping the calf happy is to milk some milk out of the mother and let the calf suck the rest. Or, you can let the calf run with his mum in the day, keep him away at night, and milk the cow in the morning. There are many ways of playing this game.

The whole subject of cows may seem to the beginner to be very complicated. Well, it is complicated, and there is absolutely no substitute for making friends with a knowledgeable neighbour and asking him for help and advice. As for diseases of cows, these are many and various, and if your cows suffer from disease you must send for the vet. But cows that are not unnaturally heavy yielders, and that are kept as naturally as possible (not over-fed but not under-fed and allowed out as much as climate permits) will very seldom become ill.

Making Butter & Cream

The dairy is not where you milk cows, but where you process milk. Most homesteaders have to make do with the kitchen. We made butter, cheese, yoghourt and so on in ours for twenty years, pretty successfully. But it is a messy and difficult business doing dairy work in the kitchen, and a special room is a great convenience and luxury.

The dairy should be as cool as possible and very airy. Working surfaces should be marble, slate or dowels (round wooden rods). Ideally the dairy should have a concrete or tiled floor, with a drain for taking the water away. You must be able to swill it down with plenty of cold water and sweep the water out. Concrete rendering requires a very fine finish. Use four parts of sand to one of cement on the floor, and five to one on the walls. Smooth it off very carefully with a steel trowel. It is better not to whitewash or paint it. The ceiling should not have any cracks in it, or it will let down the dust.

There should be hot and cold water, with the hot preferably boiling, as sterilization is the most important thing. There should be a big sink and I prefer a draining board made with dowels. The water then drains straight down on to the floor through the gaps between the dowels, and the air comes up into the utensils.

Dairy hygiene

Don't go to a lot of trouble to get milk, and then let it go bad because of lack of hygiene. Always avoid keeping anything in the dairy that is not absolutely necessary, because everything catches or retains dust. Wear clean white overalls when you are working. The other rules are simple. They apply to all milk containers and are as follows:

1 Physically remove any cream, milk, dirt etc., which may be adhering to the vessel either inside or out, with water and some sort of brush. It doesn't matter whether the water's hot or cold.

2 Scald the vessel inside with boiling water.

3 Rinse the vessel well with cold water to cool it down.

4 Turn the vessel upside down somewhere where it can drain and where the air can get into it.

5 Leave it upside down until you want it. Never wipe any dairy utensil with a cloth or rag, no matter how clean you think the cloth is.

Always clean dairy utensils the moment they are empty, but if you do have to leave them for some time before washing them, fill them with clean cold water. Never leave utensils wet with milk. Remember that milk is the perfect food for calves, babies, and bacteria! The moment milk leaves the teat of the animal, bacteria attack it and it begins to go sour. If they are the wrong sort of bacteria it will not go sour but bad. Sour tastes nice, but sour. Bad tastes horrible. Enough bacteria of the sort that you need (chiefly *Bacillus lacticus*) will occur naturally in any dairy.

Dairy equipment

A cream separator or settling pans are a great advantage.

Mount the separator on a strong bench. You will need a butter churn (any device for swishing cream about), and a butter-worker (see opposite) or a flat clean table, ideally marble or slate for working butter.

A cheese vat is a great labour-saving device. It is an oblong box, ideally lined with a stainless steel jacket. The cheese inside the vat can be heated or cooled by running hot or cold water through the jacket. There should be a tap at one end and it should be easy to lift the vat so that the liquid whey which accumulates during cheese-making can be drained off.

You will also need a cheese press, a chessit and a follower, unless you are going to make nothing but Stilton, which doesn't need pressing. The chessit is a cylinder open at the top and full of holes to let out the whey. The follower is a piston which goes down into it and presses the cheese. And the press itself is a complex combination of weights, levers and gears which can put pressure on the follower, and therefore the cheese, inside the chessit.

Cheese presses are now hard to come by, but you can improvise. Drill holes in the bottom of an empty food can or an old saucepan. This is your chessit. Cut out a metal disc to fit inside it. This is your follower. Your pressing will have to be done with weights, which can be bricks, rocks, encyclopedias – anything that is heavy.

Other requirements will be a dust-proof cupboard for keeping thermometers, an acidimeter, and a fly-proof safe for your butter and cream cheese. Hard cheese should not be stored in the dairy, because it is generally stored over long periods and it would get in the way.

CREAM

If you leave milk alone the cream will rise to the surface and you can skim it off. You do this with a skimmer, which is a slightly dished metal disc with holes in it to let the milk run out but retain the cream. Or if you leave the milk in a shallow dish with a plug hole in the bottom, you can release the milk and leave the cream sticking to the dish. Then you simply scrape the cream off.

Alternatively, you can use a separator: a centrifuge which spins out the heavier milk, leaves the lighter cream and releases them through separate spouts. Cream put through a separator is 35 percent butter fat (15 percent more than skimmed cream). Milk should be warm to separate.

The colder the milk is the quicker the cream will rise to the surface. It is a very good thing to cool milk anyway, as soon as it comes from the cow. Cooling it slows up the action of the souring organisms. And of course the wider and shallower the pan that you settle the milk in, the faster the cream will rise to the surface.

Devonshire or clotted cream

Leave fresh milk for twelve hours, then heat it to 187°F (92°C), and immediately allow it to cool. Leave for 24 hours, then skim. What you skim is Devonshire cream.

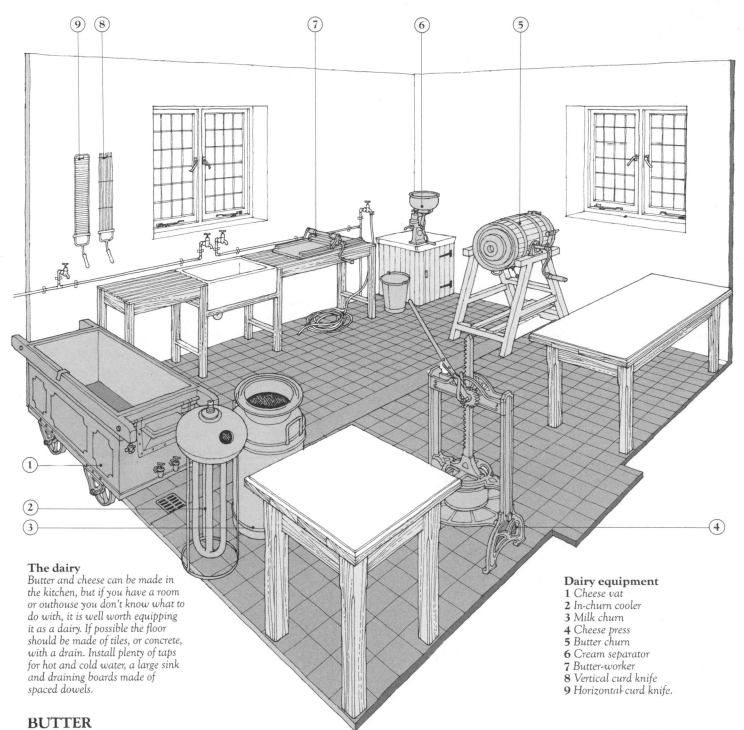

The dairy
Butter and cheese can be made in the kitchen, but if you have a room or outhouse you don't know what to do with, it is well worth equipping it as a dairy. If possible the floor should be made of tiles, or concrete, with a drain. Install plenty of taps for hot and cold water, a large sink and draining boards made of spaced dowels.

Dairy equipment
1 *Cheese vat*
2 *In-churn cooler*
3 *Milk churn*
4 *Cheese press*
5 *Butter churn*
6 *Cream separator*
7 *Butter-worker*
8 *Vertical curd knife*
9 *Horizontal curd knife.*

BUTTER

Butter is made by bashing cream about. But it will not work until the cream has "ripened": in other words, until lactic acid bacteria have converted some of the lactose, or milk sugar, into lactic acid.

Commercially, cream is pasteurized to kill all bacteria, lactic acid included, and then inoculated with a pure culture of bacteria. We can't, and don't want to be, so scientific, but we make equally good butter by keeping our cream until the oldest of it is at least 24 hours old. It can be kept twice as long as this if everything is clean enough. We add more cream to it at every milking, at a temperature of more or less 68°F (20°C). Then we make sure the last lot of cream has gone in at least twelve hours before we start churning it.

The best-known churn is simply a barrel in which the cream is turned over and over so it flops from one end to the other and bashes itself. But there are churns, like the blow churn, which have paddles that whirl round to beat the cream. You can make butter on a tiny scale by beating it with a wooden spoon or paddle, plunging a plunger up and down in a cylinder or using an egg-beater. Anything, in fact, which gives the cream a good bashing. If the cream is more or less at the right stage of acidity, and at the right temperature, it will "come", meaning suddenly turn into little butter globules, in as little as two or three minutes. If it hasn't come in ten minutes, take its temperature and if it is wrong bring it to 68°F (20°C). Then try again.

Making Butter & Cream

It doesn't matter how sour the cream is when you churn it, provided it's not bad. Taste it. If it's bad, it's useless. When the butter has "come", drain the butter milk out. (If your cream has been kept right it's the most delicious drink in the world.) Then you must wash the butter. Washing should be continued until every trace of cream or butter milk or water has been removed.

There is a fine thing called a butter-worker, which is a serrated wooden roller in a wooden trough. This squodges the water out. Keep putting more cool, clean water on and squodging until the water that you squodge out is absolutely clean and clear without a trace of milk in it. Your butter is made when the last drop of water has been pressed or squeezed out of it. From now on, don't expose it to the light or the air too much, and if you keep it wrapped it will last much longer.

If you want salty butter, you can use brine for the last washing, or you can sprinkle dry salt on the butter and work it in thoroughly. If, on tasting, you find the butter is too salty, you can wash some of the salt out. If you wash too much out you can put some more back. It's as simple as that.

If you haven't got a butter-worker don't despair. Do your washing and squodging on a clean board with a "Scotch hand" or a wooden paddle. Very few beginners at butter making ever wash the butter enough, and so their butter generally has a rancid taste, particularly after a week or so. Squodge, squodge and squodge again.

To keep butter, incorporate $2\frac{1}{2}$ percent of its own weight of salt in it, and do it in this way: scald out an earthenware crock, tub or barrel. Dry it outside in the wind and sun. Then throw a handful of butter into the bottom of the vessel as hard as you can, in order to drive all the air out of the butter. Keep on doing this, sprinkling more salt in after each layer and pummelling the butter down with your fist to drive out the air. When your crock is full, or you have no more butter, cover the butter with a sprinkling of salt and some grease-proof paper or other covering. It will keep for months. If it is too salty, simply wash some salt out before you eat it. It will be just as good as fresh butter. But remember that it must always be well washed in the first place.

Ghee

Ghee is a great Indian standby. Put butter in a pot and let it simmer gently over a slow stove for an hour. Skim off the scum. Pour the molten butter into a sterilized container, cover from the air, and it will keep for months. It won't taste like butter. It will taste like ghee. It's very good for cooking, and helps to give real curries that particular taste.

YOGHOURT

Yoghourt is milk that has been soured by *Bacillus bulgaricum* instead of the more usual *Bacillus lacticus*. To make two pints (1.1 litres) of yoghourt, put two pints of milk in a bowl. The bacteria need a warm climate. So if it's too cold for them, you should warm your milk to about blood heat. Stir in two tablespoons of a good live yoghourt that you have bought in a shop, and at this point mix in any fruit and nuts that you want for flavouring, though to my mind nothing beats a bowl of natural yoghourt served up with a spoonful of honey.

Cover the mixture, and keep it at blood heat for two or three days. A good method of keeping it warm is to bury it in straw. When it has gone thick it is yoghourt.

Take some out every day to use, and put the same amount of fresh milk back and so keep it going. But the milk should be very clean and fresh, the vessel should be sterile, and you must keep it covered. It may go bad after a while. If it does, start again.

Thick milk or curds and whey

If you leave clean milk alone in the summer it will curdle, and become "curds and whey" such as Miss Muffett was eating when she had that unfortunate experience with the spider. Curds and whey are slightly sour and delicious to eat. Sprinkle cinnamon on, or a little salt.

ICE CREAM

Ice cream made with cream is very different from the stuff you buy from itinerant vendors and is really worth eating.

Pure frozen cream is pointless. Ice cream should be sweet and fruity; white of egg, gelatine, and even egg yolks can be used to enrich the texture. A typical recipe is: 1 lb (0.5 kg) strawberries, 4 oz (114 g) sugar, $\frac{1}{4}$ pint (0.2 litres) water, $\frac{3}{4}$ pint (0.4 litres) single cream or $\frac{1}{2}$ pint (0.3 litres) double cream. Use the following method.

Make a syrup of the sugar and water. Mash up the strawberries and strain the pips out, and when the syrup has cooled pour it into the strawberry mash. Add the single cream as it is, or if you use double cream beat it first and fold it in. Then you have to freeze it.

This can be done with a deep freeze, a refrigerator, or even with just ice. If you do it with ice you must mix the ice with salt, because salt makes the ice colder. Two pounds (0.9 kg) of ice to one (0.5 kg) of salt is about right. William Cobbett, in his marvellous *Cottage Economy*, described how to preserve ice from the winter right through the summer in a semi-subterranean ice house, insulated with a great thickness of straw, and with a provision for draining off the water from melting ice.

To freeze ice cream with ice you need a metal container, with a good cover on it for the ice cream and some means of stirring it when it is inside the container. This container must be buried in a larger container filled with the ice/salt mixture. The latter must be well insulated from the outside air.

To freeze ice cream in your fridge set the fridge at its coldest and put the ice cream mixture in the ice compartment. Open it up and stir it from time to time to prevent large ice crystals forming. A deep freeze can be treated just like the ice compartment of a fridge.

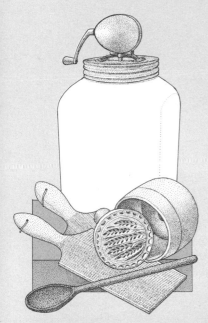

Making butter

Butter is made by bashing ripened cream. So a churn of some kind is essential. To shape the finished butter use two wooden paddles, called "Scotch hands," or, better still, an old-fashioned wooden butter mould.

I use a blow churn. Fill the churn with cream and turn the handle.

When the butter "comes" or coagulates, drain off the butter milk.

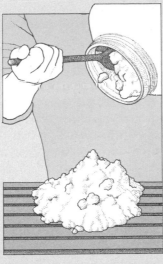

Dump butter out on a clean draining-board or on a butter-worker.

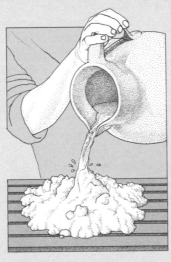

Wash the butter thoroughly by repeatedly mixing with cold water and squeezing.

Squodge, or press, to remove all water and traces of butter milk.

Add salt to taste, or if you want to keep the butter long, add a lot.

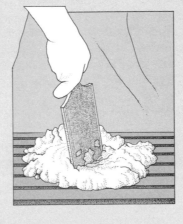

Work the salt well in. You can always wash salt out again.

Shape the butter with wetted "Scotch hands," making sure you squeeze any remaining water out. The secret of making good butter is to wash and squeeze all milk and water out of it.

There are various charming moulds and wooden blocks for the final shaping and imprinting of butter. With this mould you pack the butter in tightly, so as to fill in all the airholes.

Then it may even take two of you to force the butter out on to grease-proof paper.

The mould impresses a picture on the butter. You can get thistles, cows, wheat sheaves and many other designs.

Making Cheese

A pound (0.5 kg) of cheese has 2000 calories of energy in it. Meat from the forequarters of an ox has a mere 1100. And cheese, hard cheese at any rate, is easy to store and, within certain limitations, improves with age. Cheese is made from milk whose acidity has been increased either by an additive, or by simply being left in the warm so that it does it itself. The extra acid causes the formation of curds and whey. Cheese is made from the curds. The whey is drained off and can be given to the pigs.

SOFT CHEESE

Soft cheese is made by allowing milk to curdle, either just naturally which it does anyway in the summertime, or by adding rennet. Rennet is a chemical which occurs in the stomachs of calves and has the property of curdling milk. Milk curdled with rennet is called junket. Milk which curdles naturally forms curds and whey.

If you simply hang up some curds and whey in a muslin bag, the whey will drip out and the curds will turn to soft cheese. This is tasteless without flavouring, but seasoned with salt and herbs, or garlic, or chives, it is delicious. Eat it quickly because it won't keep long and is therefore no good for preserving the summer glut of milk for the winter.

Cream cheese

Cream cheese is simply soft cheese made with curdled cream instead of curdled milk. The result is smoother, richer and more buttery.

Poor man's cheese

Poor man's cheese got its name because it could be made from the milk of one cow. A lot of it was eaten in England in the Middle Ages.

Warm some milk slowly in a pot and let it curdle. Leave the curds in the whey overnight and drain the whey off in the morning. Then cut up the curd, salt it, tie it up tightly in a linen cloth and leave it all day to drip. Re-tie it more tightly in the evening and leave it to hang for a month. You can eat it at the end of the month and it will taste even better if you work some butter into the curd and leave it for three or four months to mature.

HARD CHEESE

Hard cheese is important as a method of preserving the summer flush of milk for the winter and also as a very valuable source of protein and a marvellous food. Everyone needs cheese and lacto-vegetarians can scarcely do without it. Hard cheese is difficult to make and better cheese is made from the milk of many cows than from the milk of but one cow. The reason for this is that, for bacteriological reasons, the best cheese is made from the milk from two milkings only: the evening's milking and the following morning's. If you have to save up more than those two milkings to get enough milk to make a cheese you will almost certainly run into trouble with such things as over-acidity and "off" flavours – the cheese will have a nasty taste.

Cheddar

If you make cheese on a fairly large scale, say from the milk of six or seven cows, you should have certain equipment and do the job scientifically. Over the page I describe how to make hard cheese if you have approximately five gallons (22.7 litres) of milk from two milkings and don't feel the need to be too scientific. A marvellous cheddar cheese can be made in this way, but luck, as well as skill, and common sense come into it. If you don't make good cheese using the method overleaf you will have to try using *starter* (see p. 104).

Caerphilly

Once you have made cheddar successfully, you might enjoy trying to make other cheeses. Caerphilly originated as a semi-hard cheese made by the wives of South Wales coal miners, for their husbands to take down the pit. It is an easy cheese to make, but will not keep as long as cheddar.

To make Caerphilly, strain the evening's milk into a vat and cool it if the weather is hot. Next morning skim off the cream and add a starter to the milk at a rate of about ½ percent of the milk. Warm the cream of last night's milk and pour it in together with that morning's milk. The purpose of skimming last night's cream off and warming it up and putting it back again is that only in this way will you get it to mix back with the milk and enrich the cheese.

Heat the vat to 68°F (20°C). Measure the acidity with an acidimeter. When it reaches 0.18 percent add a teaspoon of rennet extract to every five gallons (22.7 litres) of milk. About forty-five minutes after rennetting the curd will be ready for cutting. Cut both ways with the vertical knife but only one way with the horizontal knife. After cutting leave for ten minutes, gradually raising the temperature of the vat to 88°F (31°C): the "scalding". When this is complete, and there is 0.16 percent acidity, draw the whey off, scoop the curd into coarse cloths and leave it in a dry vat to drain. After half an hour cut the curd into three inch (8 cm) cubes, tie again in the cloths, and allow to drain another half hour.

Mill the curd (break it up into small pieces) and add 1 oz salt (28 g) to every 3 lbs (1.4 kg) curd, mix well, and put it in cloth-lined chessits or moulds. About 10 lb (4.5 kg) of curd go into each chessit and the chessits are traditionally fairly small and of flattish section: not the huge half-hundredweight cheddar ones. Two hours later apply pressure of four hundredweight (203 kg). Next morning take the cheeses out, turn and put on fresh cloths, put back in the press and give them five hundredweight (254 kg). That afternoon turn again, put on more clean cloths, and apply 15 hundredweight (762 kg) for the night. Next day take out and store it for a month at as near 65°F (19°C) as you can get, turning it two or three times a week and wiping it with a cloth dipped in salt water. After that it is ready to eat.

Cheese implements
These are the simple hand implements you need to make that pure and superb substance – cheese. The larger items, such as the cheese vat and cheese press, will be found in the dairy.

Key

1 Rennet
2 Skimmer
3 Curd knife
4 Thermometer
5 Chessit
6 Follower
7 Muslin
8 Mould
9 Cooking pan
10 Straw mat
11 Settling pan

Stilton

Stilton is a blue-moulded cheese, and it is not pressed. Properly made it is one of the finest cheeses in existence, but made in a commercial factory as most of it is nowadays, it is pretty boring stuff. It can be eaten fresh, in which case it is not blue, or it can be matured to make that rich blue cheese beloved of the gourmet at about Christmas time.

A Stilton cheese should be made from about fifteen gallons (68 litres) of milk. You can make it either with the one curd system (with just one batch of curds), or with the two curd system. If you don't get fifteen gallons of milk with one milking use the two curd system. Let the evening's milk curdle, and let the morning's do the same. Mix the two together and the rest of the process is the same.

With the one curd system take fifteen gallons (68 litres) of milk straight from the cow and put it in a tub or vat. Get the temperature to 85°F (30°C) or thereabouts. Add one teaspoon of rennet extract to every five gallons

(22.7 litres) of milk. Dilute the rennet with ½ pint (0.3 litre) of cold water before adding it to milk. After an hour and a half try dragging the dairy thermometer upwards through the curd. If it leaves a clean cut and no curd sticks to it then the curd is ready for cutting. But don't cut it. Ladle it out into vessels lined with coarse cheese cloth so that the whey can drain through the cloths but not away completely, because you have left the plug in the vessel or sink. About three and a half gallons (15.9 litres) of curd should go into each cloth, and the curd should be ladled out in fairly thin slabs. After ladling the curd should be left there, soaking in its own whey for an hour and a half.

Then pull out the plugs and let the whey run away, and draw the corners of the cloths tighter around the curds. Replace the plugs and let the curds have a second draining for half an hour. If the curd feels soft leave it longer in the whey: if it is firm draw the plugs and drain the whey off.

Now keep tightening the cloth round the curd – hauling

one corner of the cloth around the other three corners and pulling tight. Each time you do this you gently expel some whey. Do it five or six times. When the curd contains 0·18 percent acidity turn it out of the cloths. Pile the bundles of curd up on top of each other, then cut into cubes about three inches (7.6 cm) square.

Keep turning the pile every half hour until the acidity reaches 0.14 or 0.15 percent. This may take from two to four hours. If you haven't got an acidimeter just go on until the curd is fairly solid but still moist and has a nice flaky look about it when it's cut.

Now break the curd up into small pieces as for other cheeses, add an ounce (28 g) of salt to every three pounds (1.4 kg) of curd and mix well. Place the curd in hoops, or moulds. Your fifteen gallons (68 litres) of milk should have produced about twenty-six pounds (11.8 kg) of curd. The mould should hold this amount. Place it on a wooden board. By now the curd should be cool, not more than 65°F (19°C). Don't press, just let it sink down.

Take the cheese out and turn it twice during the first two hours, then once a day for seven days.

When the cheese has shrunk away from the sides of the mould take it out and scrape the surface of the cheese with a knife to smooth it. Then bandage it tightly with calico. Put it back in the hoop and mould. Take it out of the mould and re-bandage it every day for three days. Then take it to the drying room which should have a good draught and be about 60°F (16°C). Take the bandage off once or twice to help drying, and leave it off for a day. Then put it on again.

After fourteen days remove the cheese to a cellar, again about 60°F (16°C), but with not too much draught, and plenty of humidity. Leave it there for four months before eating it. Many Stilton makers pierce the cheese all over with copper needles at some stage during this ripening process to get the famous blue mould to grow inside it. It is all a long and involved process, but the resulting cheese is one of the great gastronomic experiences, not to be confused in any way with eating "stilton" bought from the supermarket.

SEMI-SOFT CHEESE

Semi-soft cheese is another sort of thing altogether, and as far as I know native to the Continent of Europe. Pont-l'Evêque is one of the best. To make it take six pints (3.4 litres) of 12 hour-old milk. Heat to 90°F (32°C) and add a teaspoonful of cheese-maker's rennet diluted with three times its own volume of water. Leave for half an hour to curdle. When the curd seems firm enough, which is when it comes cleanly away from the side of the vat, cut it both ways with a curd knife as for hard cheese. Spread a cheese cloth over a wooden draining rack and ladle the curd on to the cloth. Fold the corners of the cloth over the curd and gently squeeze. Progressively increase the pressure until you get a lot of the whey out.

Place a mould, which is just a collar 1½ inches (4 cm) deep and about 6 inches (15 cm) square (Pont-l'Evêque is traditionally square but the shape doesn't matter), on a straw mat on a draining board. After your curd has been draining about an hour in the cloth break the curd up and put it in the mould in three layers, with a layer of salt between each. Use two ounces (56 g) of salt for the six pints (3.4 litres). Pack the curd well down and into the corners.

When the mould is full turn it upside down on to another straw mat on another board. Both mats and boards should have been washed in boiling water. Repeat this turning process every ten minutes for an hour.

Turn the mould upside down again once a day for three days. Then take the cheese out of the mould and scrape the surface gently with a knife.

You can eat it there and then, but it is far better if you can keep it at a temperature of more or less 58°F (15°C) for two weeks, turning it on to a clean mat daily. The outside of the cheese will be covered with mould.

Wrap the cheese in waxed paper and keep for another month, turning it over each day. Before eating or selling scrape the mould from the surface. The outside should then be quite firm but the centre should be soft and buttery and utterly delicious.

Starters

Starters, which are batches of milk rich in lactic acid bacteria, can be bought, but you can also make them at home.

Take a quart (1.1 litres) of milk from a healthy cow and allow it to get sour in a clean well-ventilated dairy. Don't include the very first milk to come from the cow. See that the udder, and you, are washed thoroughly before milking. Strain the milk straight from the milking bucket into a sterilized container. Leave this fresh milk in the dairy for 24 hours. It is best if the temperature of the dairy is about 70°F (21°C). This quart of milk becomes almost a pure culture of *Bacillus lacticus*.

Then put some fresh milk through your separator, if you have one (don't worry if you haven't got one). Heat this milk to exactly 185°F (85°C) and cool it quickly to 70°F (21°C). This pasteurizes it. Skim the top off your first quart of milk and give it to the cat. Pour the rest of the first quart into the new, now pasteurized, milk. This inoculated milk must be covered with a cloth and kept for 24 hours at about 70°F (21°C). This is then your starter. By adding a pint (0.6 litres) of this every day to a new lot of pasteurized milk you can keep the culture going for months.

You will get better results with your cheese-making if you do use starter, for it starts the lactic acid bacteria working much more quickly and enables them to defy competition from unworthier organisms. After a few weeks, however, it may be best to give your current starter to the pigs and make a new batch as described above, for too many other bugs will have got into it.

Making a hard cheese

Put the evening's milk in a settling pan and leave it overnight. In the morning skim the cream off with a skimmer, put it in a separate pan and heat it to 85°F (30°C). Pour it back into the milk and stir it in.

Now add the morning's milk. This is the time to put in *starter* if you have any. Gently heat the milk to a temperature of 90°F (32°C).

Put one teaspoonful of rennet in a cupful of cold water and pour it in.

Stir with your hand for about five minutes. As soon as the milk begins to cling to your fingers stop stirring.

Immediately start stroking the top of the milk with the fleeter. This stops the cream rising to the surface. Stroke gently for about five minutes. After this the curd should be set enough to trap the cream.

When the curd feels firm to your hand (about fifty minutes after you have stopped stirring), cut it with curd knives or a long-bladed kitchen knife, into cubes about ¾ inch square.

Warm the milk – now "curds and whey" – *very slowly*, not quicker than one degree F in three minutes, to 100°F (38°C). If you haven't got a cheese vat the best way is to scoop a saucepanful of whey out, heat it and pour it back again. As you do this stir *very gently* with your hand.

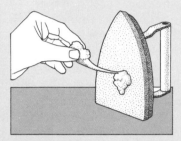

Pitching raises the acidity of the curd. You simply leave the curds to soak in the whey, and test every now and then for *acidity*. If you haven't got an acidimeter use the hot iron test. Take a bit of curd, touch it on a hot iron so that it sticks and draw it away. If the thread is less than half an inch long when it breaks leave the stuff to go on pitching. When the thread breaks at just about half an inch the acidity is right (0.17 to 0.18), and you can drain off the whey.

A cheese-mill is two spiked rollers working against each other, to break the curd into small pieces. If you haven't got a mill you must laboriously break the curd up into small pieces (about the size of walnuts) with your fingers. Mix an ounce (28 g) of fine salt into every four pounds (1.8 kg) of curd.

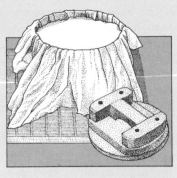

Line your chessit with cheese cloth, put your bits of curd into it, cover with the cloth, put on your follower, and apply pressure.

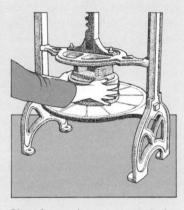

If you have a cheese press apply the pressure with this, otherwise improvise. For the first six hours twenty to thirty pounds (9.0-13.6 kg) of pressure is enough, then pull the cheese out, wash the cheese cloth in warm water and wring it out, wrap again and replace the cheese upside down. Put on half a hundredweight (25.4 kg) pressure. After a day turn the cheese and replace it. After another day turn it and give it half a ton pressure for two days, turning it once.

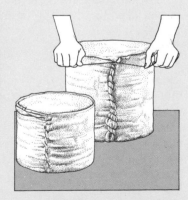

Paste with flour and water, and wrap with calico or clean cloth. Store at about 55-60°F (13-16°C). Turn every day for a week and thereafter about twice a week.

Beef

If you have a big enough deep freeze you can kill an ox and stow it away for future use. But don't make the mistake of putting all the meat in the deep freeze. Keep plenty of it out to eat unfrozen. You will only kill beef in the autumn or winter of course, because there are too many flies about in the summer. Good beef needs a week of hanging in a cold, airy larder to mature before you eat it anyway, and a fortnight in cold weather. So keep quite a lot out of the deep freeze. If you haven't got a deep freeze, you have several options.

If you kill a calf, say six months old (it is a terrible waste of resources to kill a very small calf), you will get an immature but nevertheless very tender and delicious "baby-beef". If you do it in a cold winter and you are a fair-sized family, you may well be able to eat the whole animal. If you have another self-supporter nearby, your problem is immediately halved. Let him have half your calf and he will let you have half his three months later.

But the longer you keep a bullock, up to three years old, the more meat you will get for the food that you put into him. So how can you kill adult cattle for beef, when you aren't a large community, and you don't have a deep freeze?

Well, there is such a thing as the salting tub. You can salt down the lot, just leaving out what you want to eat fresh. Plenty of people have sailed round the world on a diet of almost nothing but salt beef, and lived to tell the tale. You will find salt beef is delicious. An occasional silverside, for example, boiled and eaten with carrots, parsnips and other gew-gaws, is beyond compare. But to eat your way through an entire salt ox would be a heavy task, to say the least. So there are several options open to you.

One is to rear and fatten your bullock, and sell him. Another is to rear him to what is known as "store" condition (adult but not fat), then sell him to someone who will fatten him. With the money you get you can buy small joints of beef from the butcher as you want it. But you will find you are paying at least twice as much for your meat as you got for it, and you soon discover who makes the money in farming.

The other alternative is to be the butcher yourself. Kill the ox, or take him to a slaughterhouse, and sell him off in joints to your neighbours.

Slaughtering an ox

Before killing an ox you should really starve him for twelve hours, but it's not the end of the world if you don't. Bring the ox quietly into where you are going to kill him. Then either shoot him with a small bore rifle (which almost always means a .22) or with a humane killer. If you shoot him, he never knows anything is going to happen to him. Shoot just above the point at which imaginary lines from alternate eyes and horns cross.

The ox will fall immediately and lie on its side. Beware, all animals have violent death throes and those hooves can be dangerous. Once he's fallen stand under his chin with one leg pushing the chin up so as to stretch the head upwards, and the other leg in front of and against the forelegs. If the animal starts to lash out with his forelegs now he cannot hurt you.

With the throat thus stretched, stick a pointed knife through the skin at the breastbone and make a cut a foot (30 cm) long to expose the windpipe. Then stick your knife right back to the breastbone, pointing it at an angle of about 45 degrees towards the back of the animal. Make a deep cut forwards as long as your other incision. Your knife will now be along one side of the windpipe. This cut will sever several main veins and arteries and the animal will bleed. If you have a block-tackle you should haul the animal up by the hind legs at this juncture to assist bleeding. Catch the blood and, if you don't like black pudding, add it to the pigs' mash or dump it on your compost heap.

Skinning an ox

Skinning is the most difficult part of the whole process, and you will wish you had seen an expert on the job. Lower the animal to the ground to skin it.

Skin the head first. You can do this with it lying flat on the ground, but it makes it easier if you cut through the nostrils, push a hook through the hole, and haul the head just off the floor with the block-tackle. Slit the head down the back, from the poll to one nostril by way of the eye and simply skin away until you have skinned it. I am not going to pretend this is an easy job, nor a very pleasant one, but there is a lot of very good meat on an ox's head and you can't just throw it away.

When you've skinned it, grab the lower jaw and stick your knife in the neck close to the head. Cut just behind the jaws first, then disjoint the atlas bone, the top bone of the vertebral column, and take the head off.

Lay the carcass straight on its back with some wedges. Sever the tendons of the forelegs, cutting from the back, just below the dew claws. Slit the hide of the leg from this point to just above the knee. Skin the shank. Cut through the lower joint or, if you can't find it, saw through the bone. Skin all the legs out to the mid-line of the body. Slit the skin right down the belly, and haul as much of the skin off as you can. Use a sharp, round-pointed knife for this and incline the blade slightly so the edge is against the skin and not the meat. Hold the skin as taut as you can while you use the knife. Skin both sides as far as you can like this.

Open the belly now, putting the knife in just behind the breastbone and protecting the knife with the hand so you don't pierce the paunch. Slit the abdominal wall right down the centre line to the cod or udder. Don't puncture the paunch! Then cut along the breastbone and saw along its centre. Saw through the pelvic bone at the other end.

Now cut the tendons of the hindlegs and the hock-bone, make loops of the tendons, and push the ends of your gambrel, which is a wooden or steel spreader, through them. Haul the hind quarters clear of the ground with the tackle.

Slit the hide along the underside of the tail, sever the tail near the arse and haul the tail out of its skin. Ox-tail soup.

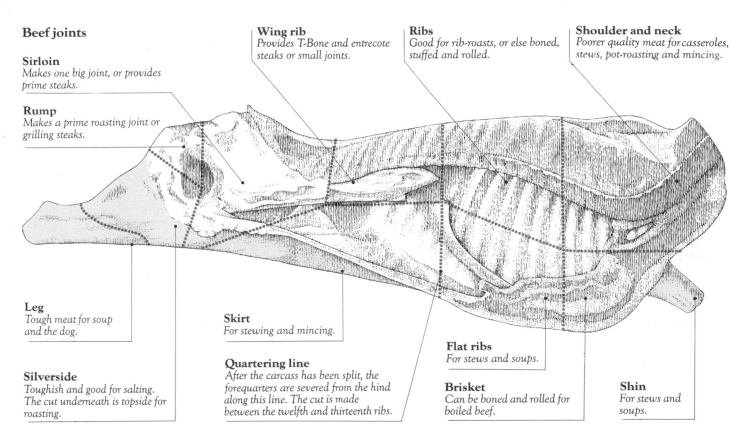

Beef joints

Sirloin
Makes one big joint, or provides prime steaks.

Rump
Makes a prime roasting joint or grilling steaks.

Wing rib
Provides T-Bone and entrecote steaks or small joints.

Ribs
Good for rib-roasts, or else boned, stuffed and rolled.

Shoulder and neck
Poorer quality meat for casseroles, stews, pot-roasting and mincing.

Leg
Tough meat for soup and the dog.

Skirt
For stewing and mincing.

Silverside
Toughish and good for salting. The cut underneath is topside for roasting.

Quartering line
After the carcass has been split, the forequarters are severed from the hind along this line. The cut is made between the twelfth and thirteenth ribs.

Flat ribs
For stews and soups.

Brisket
Can be boned and rolled for boiled beef.

Shin
For stews and soups.

Now skin out the rump. This is easier to write than to do. Remember not to stick your knife into the meat, or nick the skin. Both meat and skin are very valuable. Leave the fell, the membrane under the skin, on the meat to protect it. Difficult. Hoist the rear quarters higher as you find it convenient. Rip the skin off where it will rip – spare the knife.

Gutting an ox

With a pointed knife cut right round the rectum (bung) so as to separate it from the rest of the animal. After it is free, tie a piece of binder twine round it, tight, so that nothing can fall out of it. Then cut it free from the backbone. Now haul the beast up fairly high and pull the rectum and other guts forwards and downwards so they flop out. Cut the liver out carefully, and remove the gall bladder from it. Hang the liver on a hook, wash it, and hang it up in the meat safe.

Pull out the paunch, or guts and stomach, and all the machinery, and let it flop into a huge dish. You can clean the stomach thoroughly by putting it in brine, and then use it for tripe. The intestines make good sausage skins. But don't eat the reticulum or "bible" stomach (it looks like the leaves of a book inside).

Haul the carcass right clear of the ground now. Cut out the diaphragm, the wall between chest cavity and abdomen. Heave out the heart and lungs, and hang them up. The lungs (lights) are for the dogs, but the heart is for you.

Rip the hide right off the shoulders and fling a few buckets of cold water into the carcass. Go to bed, after a hefty meal of fried liver; only the offal is fit to eat at this stage. In the morning, split the carcass right down the backbone with a cleaver if you have faith in yourself, with a saw if you haven't. Wash the two halves of the carcass well with tepid water and trim to make it look tidy.

At this point I would strongly advise most people to enlist the aid of a butcher. Jointing is a complicated process, and there is no substitute for watching an expert do it. If the meat is for yourself and not for sale to the public, you could say that it doesn't matter how you cut it up. On the other hand, you want to make the best use of the animal you have spent three or four years fattening for this moment. And you can't really improve upon the recognized butcher's cuts.

Salting beef

The traditional salting tub has a loose round board with holes in it beneath the meat, and another such board on top of the meat. You can put a stone on the top board to keep the meat down, but never use a metal weight.

To make your brine, boil salted water and allow to cool. Test the brine for strength; if a potato will not float in it, add salt until it does.

For silverside, prick all over with a needle, rub with brown sugar, and stand for 24 hours. Then immerse in the salting tub for eight to ten days.

You can pickle tongue by spicing the brine with, say, parsley, thyme, celery, cloves, a lemon and an onion or two, and then soaking the tongue in it for six days.

Goats

In some dry countries the goat is called the "desert-maker" because it destroys what scrub there is and prevents more from growing. But where the goat is controlled it can fill a place in a mixed ecology, and if you want to discourage re-afforestation it has a very useful part to play. In cut-over woodland, for example, the goat can go ahead of the other animals as a pioneer, suppress the brambles and briars, prevent the trees from coming back, and prepare the way, perhaps, for the pig to come and complete the process of clearing the old forest for agriculture.

Goats will thrive in deciduous woodland (perhaps one to an acre), and give plenty of milk, but they will, have no doubt of it, prevent any regeneration of trees. In coniferous woodland goats will find very little sustenance, but on heather or gorse-covered mountainsides they will thrive, and there is no doubt that a mixture of goats and sheep in such situations would make better use of the grazing than sheep alone. Goats, concentrated enough, will clear land of many weeds, and they will eat vegetation unsuitable for sheep and leave the grass for the sheep.

For the self-supporting smallholder the goat can quite easily be the perfect dairy animal. For the person with only a garden the goat may be the only possible dairy animal. This is because goats are very efficient at converting roughage into milk and meat. Goat's milk is not only as good as cow's milk, in many respects it is better. For people who are allergic to cow's milk it is much better. For babies it is very good. It makes magnificent cheese because its fat globules are much smaller than those of cow's milk and therefore do not rise so quickly and get lost in the whey. It is harder to make into butter, because the cream does not rise within a reasonable time, but with a separator butter can be made and is excellent. On the other hand, milking goats takes more labour per gallon of milk than milking cows, however you do it, and so does herding, or fencing, goats.

Fencing and tethering

Restraining goats is the goat keeper's chief problem, and we all know goat keepers who also try to be gardeners and who, year after year, moan that the goats have – yet again – bust into the garden and in a few hours completely ruined it. Young fruit trees that have taken years to grow are killed and the vegetables absolutely ravaged. But this annual experience has no effect whatever on the beliefs of the true goat keeper. Next year he will win the battle to keep goats out of his garden. What he forgets is that the goats have twenty-four hours a day to plan to get into his garden, and he doesn't.

Three strands of electric fence, with three wires at 15 inches (38cm), 27 inches (69cm) and 40 inches (102cm) above ground level, will restrain goats, and so will a 4-foot (1.2m) high fence of chain link with a support wire at 4-foot 6 inches (1.4m) and another support wire lower down. Wire netting will hardly deter goats at all.

Tethering is the other answer. Where you can picket tether goats along road verges, on commons, and so on, and thus use grazing where you could use no grazing before, you must be winning. But it is unfair to tether any animal unless you move it frequently; above all, don't keep putting it back on the place where it has been tethered before except after a long interval. Goats, like sheep, soon become infested with internal parasites if they are confined too long on the same ground. By tethering you are denying the animal the right to range and search for clean, parasite-free pasture. Picket tethering is very labour-intensive, but for the cottager with a couple of goats and plenty of time it is an obvious way to get free pasture.

Another form of tethering is the running tether. A wire is stretched between two posts and the tether can run along the wire. This is an obvious way for strip-grazing a field, and also a good way of getting rid of weeds that other animals will not touch.

Toggenburg
A fairly small Swiss goat. Yields well and can live on grass.

Anglo-Nubian
Gives very rich milk, but in relatively low quantities.

Saanen
A large goat of Swiss origin capable of high yields, if given good grazing.

Feeding

A kid should have a quart (1.1 litres) of milk a day for at least two months, but as he gets older some of this may be skimmed milk. A reasonable doe should give from three to six pints (1.7 to 3.4 litres) of milk a day. In the winter a doe in milk should have about two pounds (0.9kg) a day of very good hay (you should be able to raise this – about 750 lbs or 340 kg a year – on a quarter of an acre) one or two pounds (0.5-0.9kg) of roots or other succulents, from one to two pounds (0.5-0.9kg) of grain depending on milk yield. Goats should have salt licks available. It is a mistake to think that goats will give a lot of milk on grazing alone: milking goats need good feeding. They will, for example, thrive on the silage you can make by sealing grass clippings in fertilizer bags (see pp. 80-81). As for the grain you feed to your goats: a good mixture, such as you might feed to dairy cows, is fine, or you can buy "cake," or "dairy nuts" from a merchant (and *pay* for it too). All debris from the market garden or vegetable garden can go to goats, but it is better to crush, or split, tough brassica stems first. Feed them their concentrates individually, or they rob each other.

Housing

Goats are not as winter-hardy as cows and cannot be left out all the time in north-European or North American winters and expected to give any milk. They don't like cold and hate rain. High-yielding goats (which personally I should avoid) need very high feeding and warm housing, but medium yielding ones must have shelter from the rain, and an airy but fairly draught-proof shed to sleep in o'nights. Giving them a table to lie on, with low sides to exclude draughts, is a good idea and if they are lying in a fierce down-draught of cold air adjust the ventilation until they are not. Maybe a board roof over the table to stop down-draughts would be a good idea.

Otherwise you can treat milking goats much the same as you treat cows. Dry them off eight weeks before kidding. But a goat may milk for two or three years after kidding without kidding again.

Rearing orphans

One possible good use for goats is rearing orphans of many kinds. Goats are excellent for suckling other animals: calves thrive better on goat's milk than they do on their mother's, and it would be reasonable, if you kept cows, but had some wilderness or waste land on which cows could not thrive, to keep a flock of goats on the bad lands and use them for suckling the calves so that you can milk their mothers. Goat milk is very digestible, and pretty good milk anyway, and orphan piglets, for example, which don't take very kindly to cow's milk, will thrive on goat's. Calves will suck straight from the nanny. Lambs will too but don't let them – they may damage her teats and give her mastitis. Milk her yourself and bucket feed the lambs. Milk the nanny and feed the

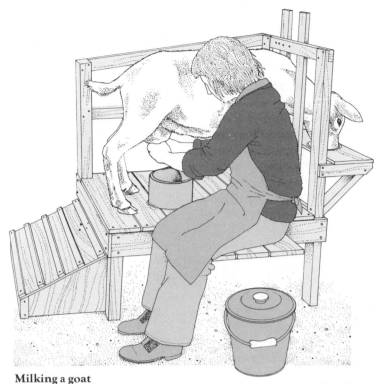

Milking a goat
You can milk a goat that is standing on the ground, just as you would milk a cow (see p. 94). But because goats are so much smaller a stand helps. Coax her into position with some hay or grain.

milk to piglets through a bottle. You can rear foals on goats. The suggestion has been made that a suitable person could make a living – or half a living – by running a goat-orphanage – not for orphan goats but for other animals. Neighbours soon get to know such things, and orphan lambs are ten a penny in the lambing season in sheep districts and very often a sow has too many piglets.

Billy kids

Billy kids come whether you want them or not, and in the end you have to find something to do with them. What you can do is castrate them and then eat them. The most humane way to castrate a goat or anything else is to use rubber rings, put on with an "Elastrator," which you can buy from any agricultural suppliers. A billy becomes very male at three months, whereas a lamb does not develop specific male characteristics until about six months. Therefore many of us who produce fat lamb don't bother to castrate, but male goat kids should be castrated unless you intend to eat them before three months or they will become strong tasting. In my opinion, a goat wether (castrated billy goat) tastes as good as any mutton, particularly if you lard it well, or marinate it in oil and vinegar, or oil and wine, for it is short of fat compared to sheep. Up to six months old, it lends itself very well to roasting with various herbs or spicy sauces. If the billy goat has not been castrated, the meat has a strong gamey taste, and it is best to marinate it for three days in wine and vinegar and then curry it. Cooked in this way it is delicious. As a general rule though, it is better to castrate if you are going to eat it.

Pigs

The pig fits so well into the self-supporter's economy that the animal almost seems designed with that in mind. It is probably the most omnivorous animal in the world and will thrive on practically anything. It is even more omnivorous than man, because a pig can eat and digest grass while we cannot. A pig will not thrive on grass alone, but it can make it a substantial part of its diet. And it will convert virtually anything that you grow or produce on the farm into good meat. Throw any vegetable matter, of whatever kind, to a pig, and he will either eat it – converting it within hours to good meat and the best compost in the world – or he will tread it into the ground, dung on it, and turn it into compost that way. Put a pig on rough grassland, or scrubland, that you wish to bring into cultivation, and he will plough it for you, and root it up for you, and manure it for you, and at the same time extract sustenance from it to live and grow on.

Feeding

The self-supporter should aim to produce all the food he needs to feed his pigs from off his farm. Barley meal, maize meal, potatoes, jerusalem artichokes, carrots, fodder beet, parsnips, turnips or swedes: these are all crops that may be grown to feed pigs, and if supplemented with skimmed milk or whey you have a pretty good diet. I have fattened pigs very successfully on boiled potatoes and skimmed milk, and they will fatten on raw potatoes too. I have fattened them on raw carrots and separated milk. Wheat "offals", such as bran and middlings, are good too, but there is no doubt that either barley meal or maize meal have no peers when it comes to fattening pigs. Even then they must have a "protein supplement" which may well be whey or separated milk, though any other high protein food will do: meat meal or fish meal, cooked meat or fish, bean meal or any other high-protein grain. Soya is excellent for fattening pigs. If pigs are out of doors they don't want mineral supplements. If they get some fresh greens, some milk by-products, scraps, they don't want vitamin supplements. Let sows run out over plenty of land, and in summer they will get nearly half their sustenance from grass, if they are not in milk. Keep sows or growing pigs on artichokes, or a field of potatoes, or a field from which potatoes have been harvested, or any other crop, and they will get half their food from that.

But for milking sows, or sows in late pregnancy, animal protein is absolutely essential, as it is the only source of vitamin B 12. A good rule for rations is that breeding sows, out of doors on grass and with access to scraps, surplus vegetables, and so on, will need two pounds (0.9kg) a day of concentrate such as barley meal and some protein, but six pounds (2.7kg) a day when they farrow. If they are indoors or having concentrates only, you can double these amounts. When the baby pigs are three weeks old or so you can start "creep feeding" them: that is, allowing them through holes in a fence too small for the sow to where they can eat concentrates unrestricted. Fattening pigs can be given as much as they can eat until they are about 100lbs (45.0kg) in weight (half grown) after which their ration should be restricted or they will get too fat. Restrict them to what they will finish in a quarter of an hour. If they take longer than that, give them less next day; if they wolf it all in five minutes and squeal for more, increase their ration. Feed them like this twice a day. Do not restrict their intake of roots, vegetables, and suchlike, but only of concentrates. At all times watch your pigs, and if they look too thin, or too hungry, feed them more.

I have kept pigs successfully for over thirty years with nothing more elaborate than some rolled barley, skimmed milk, maybe at a push some fish meal, some bran, plenty of roots and vegetables and whatever else there is to give away.

The pig bucket

And now I must touch on the high art of the pig bucket. For the man with a thousand sows the pig bucket is irrelevant, but for the self-supporting family fattening a pig or two in the garden to kill, or with one or two dear old breeding

Gloucester Old Spot
A fine and beautiful English breed evolved originally for living in apple orchards and woodlands. It is hardy, prolific, and a fine baconer.

Wessex Saddleback
Also known as the British Saddle-back, this is a hardy out-door breed popular for crossbreeding.

Welsh
A popular commercial breed because it's white, long, and lean. It is a reasonable outdoor breed.

Pig housing
A pig house should be very strong, either movable or else easily dismantled and re-erected, and, if possible, free. Mine are made of scrap corrugated iron nailed to bush timber. Walls and roof can be double iron sheets with insulation (old paper bags or bracken, for example) stuffed between. When piglets are three weeks old, make a gap in the fencing that is too small for the sow but large enough for the piglets to get through and "creep feed" on concentrates.

Hurdles
Two hurdles lashed together with straw between, and covered with netting, make good pig house walls.

Farrowing rail
Piglets sometimes get squashed by their mothers. But if you fix a farrowing rail, 10 inches (25 cm) from the floor and 10 inches (25 cm) from the walls, your piglets can sleep under it, protected from the sow's bulk by the rail.

sows who become almost part of the family themselves, the pig bucket is very relevant indeed.

Nothing should be wasted on the self-sufficient holding. The dustman should never have to call. Under the kitchen sink there should be a bucket, and into it should go all the household scraps except such as are earmarked for the dog or the cats. When you wash up develop the "pig bucket technique." This means scraping all scraps first into the sacred bucket; then dribble – rather than run – hot water from the tap over each plate and dish so that the water carries all grease and other nutriments into a bowl (helped by a brush). Throw this rich and concentrated washing-up water into the pig bucket. Then finish washing the dishes any way you like and let that water run down the sink. The concentrated washing-up water from the first wash is most excellent food, and should not be wasted on any account.

Housing and farrowing
Except when sows are actually farrowing or have recently farrowed, they can live very rough. If they have plenty of straw or bracken and are kept dry, with no through draughts, and if possible with well insulated walls and roof in cold climates, they will do very well. Several sows together are,

generally speaking, much happier than one sow alone.

However when a sow farrows she must have a hut to herself. It needs to be big enough for her to turn round in comfort. If you like, you can have a farrowing rail, which prevents the sow from lying on the piglets, but we kept six sows for eight years and only lost two piglets during all that time from crushing. The books say the sow should have no litter when she farrows. All I can say is we give our sows access to litter, and they carry as much as they want of it indoors and make an elaborate nest. What they don't want they chuck out. It is delightful to watch a sow making her nest, and there is no doubt that she is most unlikely to have any trouble if she is able to go through all her rituals before farrowing, and is then left alone in peace to farrow, with no other pigs jostling her, and no over-anxious owner fussing her like an old hen. Sows eating their piglets, or lying on them, are generally products of an artificially organized system. If you break the chain of instinct here you do so at your own risk.

Heat, the period when the sow wants the boar, occurs at twenty-one day intervals, as in the cow. I do not like to put a gilt, or young female pig, to the boar until she is nearly a year old. Gestation is 116 days. Where do you get the boar?

Pigs

If you keep six sows or more you can afford the keep of a boar so you can buy one, and let him run with the sows. If you have fewer sows you can take a sow to a neighbour's boar when she needs it.

Litters can vary from six piglets to twenty; ten is about average but we used to have twelves (and rear twelves) with monotonous regularity when we kept sows out of doors. We are keeping them again now after an interval of ten years when we preferred to buy weaners from neighbours to fatten. If you buy weaners (piglets from eight to twelve weeks old), you won't have to have a sow at all. We have often bought and fattened three weaners, sold one and eaten two, and the one we sold paid for the two we ate.

Slaughtering

The traditional way to kill a pig is to stick it in the throat, but I don't recommend this. Although I see nothing wrong with killing animals for meat, I see everything wrong with making them suffer in any way. If we kill an animal we should do so instantaneously, and the animal should have no inkling that anything nasty is about to happen to it.

Lure your pig into the killing room, put a little food on the floor, and shoot the pig in the brain with a .22 rifle. You can use an humane killer (captive bolt pistol), but then you must be very quick and skilful, because the killer must be in contact with the pig's head when you fire it, and the pig may, and probably will, move away. With a rifle you can stand well back, aim at the pig's brain, and the animal has no idea that anything is going to happen before it is stone dead.

Immediately the pig has dropped stick it. Squat squarely in front of the recumbent pig while someone else holds it on its back, stick the knife just in front of the breastbone, and when you feel the bone let the knife slip forward to go under it. Then push the knife in a couple of inches and slice forwards with the point of the knife towards the head. This severs the artery. Now look out: a nervous reaction takes place. The pig appears to come to life and thrashes about, so take care not to be cut by its hooves. If you want to catch the blood to make black pudding you have got to be quick. Some people get a strop on one of the pig's hind-legs after they have shot it and haul it up with a block-tackle before sticking it. This enables you to catch the blood more easily and makes the pig drain better. Personally I am not a lover of black pudding so the blood falls into a bed of straw or spoiled hay which ultimately goes on the compost heap. Waste not want not, and your blood is a fine activator of your compost.

Scraping

Now you have got to scrape your pig. To do this you must scald him, and this is a ticklish operation. You can either dip your animal right into hot water, or you can lie him on the floor or a scraping bench, and baste him with hot water. If you dip him, leave him in water of 145°F (63°C) for five minutes and then haul him out and scrape him. You can only do this if

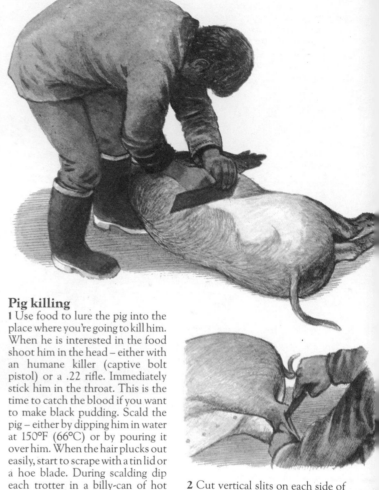

Pig killing

1 Use food to lure the pig into the place where you're going to kill him. When he is interested in the food shoot him in the head – either with an humane killer (captive bolt pistol) or a .22 rifle. Immediately stick him in the throat. This is the time to catch the blood if you want to make black pudding. Scald the pig – either by dipping him in water at 150°F (66°C) or by pouring it over him. When the hair plucks out easily, start to scrape with a tin lid or a hoe blade. During scalding dip each trotter in a billy-can of hot water and then pull off the toenails with a sharp hook.

2 Cut vertical slits on each side of the tendons of the hind legs in order to insert the gambrel.

3 Split the breast-bone. First, cut down to the bone with a knife, then saw through it.

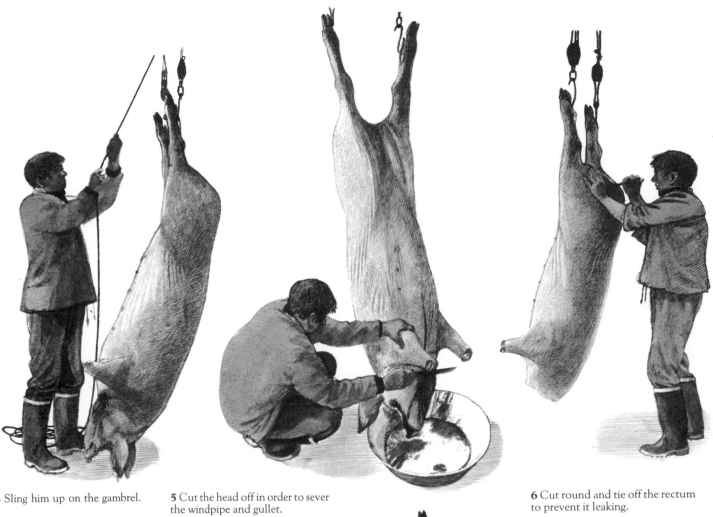

4 Sling him up on the gambrel.

5 Cut the head off in order to sever the windpipe and gullet.

6 Cut round and tie off the rectum to prevent it leaking.

9 Saw down the back-bone so as to cut the pig completely in half. Leave him to hang in an airy place overnight.

7 Slit along the line of the abdomen without cutting the guts. Have a large receptacle on the floor.

8 Haul out the innards. Keep the pluck (heart, pancreas and lungs) separate. Throw a bucket of cold water inside the carcass.

you know your water is going to stay at this temperature (pretty well exactly). If it is a few degrees too cold it won't loosen the bristles. If the water is going to start cooling as soon as you put the pig in then you should have it at 150°F (65°C) to start off with, but if you have it this hot then you must keep moving your pig around, and from time to time pull him out. Why? Because for some reason if the water is too hot it sets the bristles, and once they are set they are hell to get out at all. The way to tell if they are ready is to keep trying them: pull at a few and when they come out easily then is the time to scrape.

The other method – which we use, not having a bath big enough to immerse a whole hog in – is to lay the pig on its side and carefully and slowly to pour hot water over a small part of him. This water should be 150°F (65°C) when it comes from the jug, so it should be slightly above this when it goes into it.

The joints of a pig

Trotters
Trotters can be cooked up for brawn, or boiled separately and eaten with vegetables.

Ham
The ham makes a huge joint of prime roast pork, or it can be salted and smoked to make a cured ham.

Back
A large pig's back can be cured as bacon. On a smaller pig it may go for chops. On a large baconer it can be cut into good roasting joints.

Belly
A baconer's belly can be salted whole for bacon. The thin end is sometimes pickled in brine. The thick end makes prime bacon. On a porker the belly makes chops.

Spare ribs
The spare ribs can be roast, or cut into chops. The shoulder can make a joint, or it can be cured to make second-rate bacon.

Hands
The hands can be roasted, or cut up for sausage meat.

Jowl
The jowl is used for sausage meat.

Keep pouring gently, and from time to time try some bristle with the thumb and forefinger. When the bristle begins to lift, scrape. Scrape furiously. It is better not to use a knife. A sharpened hoe-head, or a metal saucepan lid is sharp enough. Off comes the bristle, off also comes the outermost skin of the pig, and no matter what colour your pig started off as, he will become white as snow.

Keep working until the pig is absolutely clean. Put the legs right into the jug of hot water; then take them out and pull the horny toes off with a hook. You really need two or three good men and true to scrape a big hog, with one boy to bring on the hot water and another to fetch the home-brewed beer (vital on this occasion). The head is difficult: if necessary set fire to some straw with methylated spirits, hold the head over the flame to singe it, and scrub with a wire brush. When finished douse the pig with cold water to get rid of all the loose skin and bristles and any blood.

Hanging

Then hang the pig. An inch or two above the foot on the back of the hind leg is a tendon. Cut down each side of this with a vertical slit through the skin and then raise the tendon out with your fingers. Don't cut the leg above the hock as beginners do; this is barbarous and spoils good meat. Insert each end of your gambrel (see illustration) through the two tendons in the legs.

Now, don't haul that pig off the ground until you have sawn through the breastbone or sternum! Cut down to the breastbone with a clean knife, then split it, right down the middle, with a saw. If you try to do this after you have hung up the pig all the guts will come flopping out and make the operation very difficult. Then lay on to the fall of that tackle and heave away! Up goes your pig. Cut off the head. Cut it just behind the ears, at the first spinal bone (the atlas) and you shouldn't have to use the saw. Put the head straight into brine (salt and water).

Before you have hauled the pig up too high, cut round the bung, which is the anus. Cut right round it so as to sever it from the pig, but so as not to pierce the rectum. Tie a string round it to prevent the shit coming out. Now, haul the pig up further to a convenient height, and score a light cut right down from between the hams (haunches or hind legs) to the stick-cut in the throat. Don't cut through the abdominal wall! Cut right down it, keeping the guts back from the knife with your hand. You don't want to pierce the guts or stomach. Cut through the H-bone that joins the two hams, if necessary with the saw, but don't cut the bladder. Then gently haul out the rectum, the penis if it's male, the bladder, and all the guts, and flop the lot out into a huge basin. The penis and rectum can be thrown away, or to the dogs, but the rest is all edible or useful stuff.

Do not waste the guts. They need a good wash, after which you should turn the intestines inside out. You can do this by inverting them on a smooth piece of bamboo or other wood.

Jointing a pig

This pig is a baconer, because it's too large for eating entirely as fresh pork. Therefore most of it will be cured and preserved as bacon, ham, sausages, and so on. You will of course take a joint or two to eat as fresh pork, and if you have a deep freeze, this may be a larger proportion. But remember that a baconer is a fat animal and his meat is not so suitable for eating fresh as is that of a little porker.

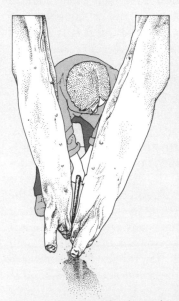

Split the carcass right down the backbone. A butcher might use a cleaver all the way, but amateurs will probably do better with a saw.

The leaf fat comes away very easily. It makes the best and purest lard. Next take out the kidneys.

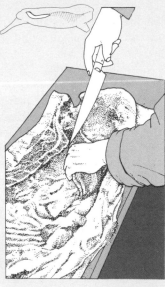

The tenderloin lies inside the backbone. It is delicious wrapped in the "caul", stuffed and roasted. The caul is that white, fatty membrane which supports the intestines.

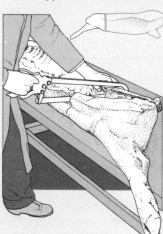

Cut the flesh of the ham.

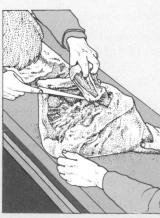

Then remove the H-bone, which is one half of a ball and socket joint, to leave a clean, uncut joint.

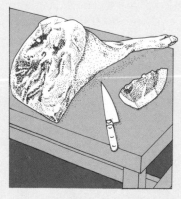

The ham must be trimmed so that a clean surface is left for salt to penetrate. It is important to work salt into every crevice.

This trotter is being cut off at the hock joint. You can saw the shank off *below* this joint to leave a cleaner surface for salting.

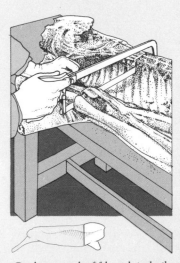

Cut between the fifth and sixth ribs to part the shoulder from the side, or flitch. The shoulders can be salted whole, or else boned and used for sausages.

Next saw off the chine, or backbone, and joint it.

You can leave the ribs in the salted flitch. I like to cut them out and use them for soup. The rest of the side is salted for bacon.

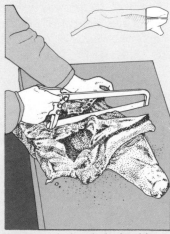

You can salt the whole shoulder, or you can halve it. Roast the top and salt the bottom.

Pigs

Then scrape their mucus lining off with the back of a knife against a board. Get them quite clean and transparent. Lay them down in dry salt now and they will come in, in due course, for sausage skins or "casings". The bladder can be filled through a funnel with melted lard, which will harden again and keep for months.

The stomach is edible as well as the intestines; together they are called "chitlings" or "chitterlings" and are quite nice. Turn the stomach inside out, wash it and put it down in dry salt until you want it. Don't waste the head or the feet, for they make excellent brawn (see p. 117).

Rescue the liver, which you can eat the same night, and peel out the gall bladder, which you can throw away. The heart should come away with the lights (lungs), and this is called the "pluck". Hang it on a hook. Carefully remove the caul – a beautiful filmy membrane that adheres to the stomach – and throw this over the pluck. The lungs are an extra treat for the dogs, while you can eat the heart. Throw several buckets of cold water inside and outside the carcass, prop the belly open with some sticks pointed at both ends, eat some fried liver, finish the home-brew, and go to bed.

In the morning the carcass will be "set" (stiff) if the weather is cold enough (and if it isn't you shouldn't be killing a baconer) and you can split it right down the backbone. A butcher does this with a cleaver – if you are a beginner, you may like to do it with a saw. Take each half off, lay it on the table, and cut it up, as per illustrations.

In the United States people cut up the pig the night they kill it much more than we are accustomed to in Britain: they split the carcass, haul out the leaf fat, and even trim much of the fat off the hams, while the hog is still hot. This is said to give the carcass a better chance to cool. I find that carcasses cool easily enough in the British climate and that they are easier to handle when set.

BACON AND HAM

Most of a big pig should be turned into bacon and ham, for there is no better way known to mankind of preserving large quantities of meat. The ham is the thick part of the pig's hind leg – the rump in fact. Bacon is the side of the pig. The shoulder can be cured too, or used for joints or sausage meat. But by far the most valuable parts of the pig are the two hams.

There are two main methods of salting pig meat – brine curing and dry curing.

Dry curing

We have a slap-happy method of doing this, which consists of simply rubbing salt and sugar into the meat, then burying it in salt, then leaving bacon sides for two weeks in the salt, and hams for three. It is better to do it more scientifically, because you save salt and the meat is not so salty when you eat it. We get over the problem of excess salt by slicing our bacon first, then soaking the thin slices for ten minutes or so in warm water before frying them.

The proper way to do it, if you are going to be more scientific and efficient about it, is to use the following mixture for every 100 lbs (45.0 kg) of meat:

   8 lbs (3.6 kg) salt
   2 lbs (0.9 kg) sugar

Prepare this mixture with extreme care. Take half of it and put the rest aside. Use the half you have taken to rub the meat very thoroughly all over, rind-sides as well. Stuff salt hard into the holes where the bones come out in the hams and shoulders, and into any cavities. Success lies in getting salt into the meat quickly: it's a race between salt and bacteria. If the latter win you may lose an awful lot of very valuable meat. Unless the weather is too warm (36°F or 2°C is an ideal temperature, but don't let the meat freeze), if you follow these instructions the bacteria won't win. Cover all surfaces with the salt and leave on a salting tray, or a shelf, or in a box (but if in a box there must be holes in it to allow the "pickle" – juice drawn out of the meat by the salt – to drain away), with all the joints carefully packed on top of each other. Be careful when you do this first salting to put roughly the right amounts of salt on each piece: not too much on the thinner bacon sides but plenty on the thick hams.

After three days give another good rubbing with half the remainder of the salt (i.e. a quarter of the whole). Put the meat back in a different order to ensure even distribution of the salt all round. After another week haul out again and rub well with the last of the salt mixture. Put it back. Now leave it in the salt for two days per lb for big joints such as hams and 1½ days per lb for small joints and bacon. If you say that roughly a big side of bacon should cure for a fortnight and a large ham for three weeks you won't be far wrong.

Take the joints out at the allotted time, scrub them lightly with warm water to get the loose salt off, string them, and hang them up for a week or a fortnight in a cool dry place. Then either smoke them or don't smoke them as the fancy takes you. Unsmoked or "green" ham and bacon taste very good, although personally I like them smoked. It's really all a matter of taste.

Brine curing

For every 100 lbs (45.0 kg) meat you should mix:

   8 lbs (3.6 kg) salt
   2 lbs (0.9 kg) sugar
   5 gallons (22.7 litres) boiled but cooled water

In theory thicker joints, like hams, should have a stronger brine – the above mixture with 4½ gallons (20.4 litres) of water – and the thinner joints, like bacon and bath-chaps which are the jowls of the pig, should have the mixture in 6 gallons (27.3 litres) of water. Put the meat in the brine, make sure there are no air pockets, put a scrubbed board on top and a big stone on top of this to keep the meat down (don't use an iron weight), and leave in the brine for four days per pound of each big joint. Thus you ought to weigh each joint before putting it in, and pull each one out at its appointed date. Bacon and small joints should only be left for two days per pound. After four or five days turn the joints round in the brine, and again every so often. If, in hot weather, the brine becomes "ropey" (viscous when you drip it off your hand) haul the meat out, scrub it in clean water, and put into fresh brine.

When you have hauled the meat out of the brine wash it in fresh water, hang it up for a week in a cool dry place to dry, then, if you want to, smoke it. You can eat it "green", i.e. not smoked at all. It should keep indefinitely, but use small joints and bacon sides before hams. Hams improve with maturing: I have kept them for two years and they have been delicious. Bacon is best eaten within a few months.

Cured hams and shoulders should be carefully wrapped in grease-proof paper and then sewn up in muslin bags and hung in a fairly cool dry place, preferably at a constant temperature. If you paint the outside of the muslin bags with a thick paste of lime and water so much the better. Like this they will keep for a year or two and improve all the time in flavour until they are delectable. Bacon can be hung up "naked" but should then be used within a few months. Light turns bacon rancid, so keep it in the dark. Keep flies and other creepies off all cured meat. Some country people wrap hams and bacon well, then bury them in bran, oats, or wood ashes which are said to keep them moist and improve the flavour.

Smoking

Smoking helps to preserve the meat, helps it dry out, and probably helps it mature quicker. It is also much easier than people seem to think. If you have a big open chimney, simply hang the meat high up in it well out of reach of the fire, and leave it there for about a week, keeping a wood fire going the while. There is a lot of mysticism about which wood to use for smoking: the Americans swear by hickory, the British will hear of nothing but oak. In my experience it matters very little provided you use hard woods and not pine.

Whatever you use don't let the temperature go above 120°F (50°C); 100°F to 110°F (39°C to 43°C) is fine. Building a smoke-house is a matter of common sense and a little ingenuity. For years we used a brick out-door lavatory, ty-bach, jakes, or loo. (We didn't use it for its original purpose of course.) We had a slow-combustion wood-burning stove outside, with the chimney pipe poking through the wall of the jakes, and we hung up the meat from lengths of angle-iron under the roof. It does seem a pity though not to make use of the heat generated by the smoking fuel, so surely it is better to have your burning unit inside a building, even if the smoke chamber itself is outside. Often a slow-combustion wood-burning stove can heat a house and, with no increase in fuel consumption, it will automatically smoke whatever you like.

There are two kinds of smoking: cold-smoking and cooked-smoking. The latter is common in America and Germany but almost unknown in Britain. It consists of smoking at a higher temperature, from 150°F to 200°F (65°C to 93°C), so that the meat is cooked as well as smoked. Meat thus smoked must be eaten within a few days because it will not keep as cold-smoked meat will.

Brawn

What to do with that head, those feet, and all the other odd bits and bobs such as the tongue and jowls if they are not to be smoked? Brawn is the answer, or pork-cheese as it is called in some countries. Just put all meat – bones, skin and all – into a pan (although it is a good idea to put the bits of skin in a muslin bag so you can draw them out after all the goodness has been extracted from them) and boil and boil. Let it cool, break it into small pieces, boil again and add salt, pepper, and as many spices as your taste-buds suggest (marjoram, coriander, allspice, cloves, caraway are all acceptable). Boil up again, and pour into moulds such as pudding basins. The fat will rise to the top and form a protective covering and the brawn will keep a long time. Eat sliced cold. In a deep freeze of course it will keep indefinitely. You can pour it straight into plastic bags before freezing.

Sausages

Sausages that won't keep are subjects for a cookery book. Sausages that keep, however, are very much the self-supporter's interest. To some people, these are more commonly referred to by the name of "salami".

Take two parts of lean meat (say pork, or half pork and half beef) and one part of pork fat. You can even use salt bacon fat. Mince the lean meat finely and the fat less so. Marinate this meat in wine or vinegar overnight if you like. For 3 lbs (1.4 kg) of this mixture add:

1 oz (28 g) salt
2 teaspoons pepper
3 cloves garlic crushed up
any spice you particularly like (I suggest paprika, or ground chilli powder)
a glassful of red wine or vinegar (if you haven't marinated the the meat)

Mix all this up well and stuff it into your casing (cleaned pigs' or oxes' guts, or other sausage casing bought from a butcher). To my mind the bigger the casing the better. Hang it in a cool, dry place; if you want to smoke it do so for say twelve hours, but this isn't vital. Then hang it up again in a cool, dry place – 60°F (16°C) is ideal, but never more than 70°F (21°C) – and it will keep for months. Eat it raw, sliced. It is better after it has cured for a month or two at least; you can eat it fresh but it is not so good. Do not be worried at eating "raw meat": all salami and other "continental sausages" you buy are raw meat.

There are a hundred recipes such as the above for making sausages that keep. But the principle is always the same. Observe it and you will get successful sausage. There is one serious disadvantage: although it is alleged to keep you can never keep it. People find it far too delicious and they will eat the lot in no time.

Sheep

Sheep have a great advantage for the lone self-supporter without a deep-freeze. In the winter time, a family can get through a fat lamb or a small sheep without it going bad. It is not that it keeps better than other meat but just that the animal is smaller and you can eat it more quickly. However, I have kept mutton for a month, and in a climate where the day temperatures rose to over 100°F (39°C) in the shade. But the days were dry and the nights were cold. At night I hung the mutton outside, in a tree – though out of reach of four-legged prowlers – and then, very early in the morning, brought it in and wrapped it in several thicknesses of newspaper to keep out the heat. The mutton was perfectly edible. You could do this in any climate where the nights are cold enough and the days are not muggy – and you could do it with any meat.

Sheep have two other advantages: they provide wool, and in various parts of the world they provide milk too. I have milked sheep, very often, and it is a very fiddly job. The milk tastes no better, and no worse, than cows' or goats' milk.

The chief disadvantage about keeping sheep on a very small scale is the problem of getting them tupped (mated). It doesn't pay to provide grazing for a ram if you have fewer than say half a dozen sheep. If you buy a ram to serve your sheep you pay quite a high price for him, and when you sell him after he has served them, or next year say, you only get "scrap price": very little. And if you eat him you will find him very tough. I have just eaten a three-year old ram and I know. So tupping is a problem with very small flocks of sheep.

Broadly, there are two quite sensible things you can do. You can keep some pet ewes and take them to a kindly farmer's ram to get them tupped in the autumn, or you might be able to borrow a ram. If you put a chest-pad on the ram with some marking fluid on it, or – in the old-fashioned way – rub some *reddle* (any coloured earth or dry colouring matter) on the ram's chest you can see when all your ewes are served and then return the ram. Alternatively, you can buy "store"

lambs. Most hill farmers cannot fatten their lambs off in their first summer sufficiently to get them ready to sell, and so they sell them as "stores". There are huge store marts in most hill-sheep countries. If you buy say 20 store lambs in the autumn, and keep them either on good winter grass or on rape, turnips or other winter fodder crops, maybe allowing five lambs to the acre, you will probably find that you not only get your sheep meat for nothing but you make a profit too. You can achieve this by killing one whenever you want some lamb to eat, and selling the fat lambs you haven't killed in the very early spring. If you also feed the store lambs a little concentrate (say 1 lb or 0.5 kg a day of crushed barley and oats, or alternatively 2 lbs or 0.9 kg a day of maize and hay) they will fatten very readily.

Feeding

Sheep do well on pasture that has not had sheep on it for six months or so, because such pasture is free from sheep parasites. Five sheep will eat as much grass as a bullock, so an acre of good grass in the summer will easily support five sheep, but the stocking rate should be very considerably less in the winter for the grass doesn't grow. Sheep are very good for grass in the winter time – they "clean it up" after cows have been grazing on it all summer, because they graze much closer than cows. Sometimes you can fold sheep to great advantage on a "catch crop" of winter greens, turnip, rape or hardy-greens. This would be put in after a crop harvested fairly early in the summer. But you may decide you want this fodder for your cows.

During the winter the pregnant ewes need surprisingly little food, and if you have even a little grass they should do on that. In very cold climates of course they need hay, and possibly corn, as well. People in very cold countries often winter ewes indoors and feed them entirely on hay, corn, and possibly roots. If you feed sheep, and they have no grass, a ewe will need about 4lbs (1.8kg) hay daily if there is nothing

Dorset Horn
A uniquely useful breed because it can lamb twice a year.

Border Leicester
A classic English sheep, a prolific breeder and good for mutton and wool.

Southdown
A very small sheep, and therefore useful for the small self-supporting family.

Lambing

The shepherd should not have to interfere at all, but if there is too long a delay in a birth the lamb or the ewe may die. The vigilant shepherd should try to prevent this.

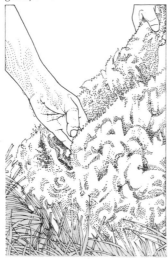

If you see the forefeet, but the ewe cannot give birth after an hour, tie a soft cord round the feet and pull gently when she strains.

Pull more and more strongly while the ewe is straining, but don't pull when she isn't.

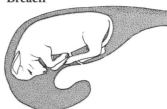

As the lamb's body appears support it with your free arm. When he is half out twist slightly to relieve the pressure.

Abnormal presentations

There can be many abnormal presentations. The shepherd must feel with his hand to find which one he is dealing with. In the case of twins both trying to get out together he must gently push one back. Sometimes with a single lamb he must push the lamb back and adjust the limbs or the head. The whole thing is a matter of common sense and sympathy for lamb and mother. The lamb or lambs must be disposed so the head is not backward and the limbs are not doubled up.

Twins

Breach

Twisted head and limbs

Wash your hands and the ewe's hind quarters. Lubricate your hand and her vulva with boiled linseed oil or carbolized oil.

If the presentation is normal, grab the forelegs and pull the lamb out but with care.

If you can't see anything introduce the hand carefully while the ewe is not straining.

Make sure the new lamb's nostrils are free of mucus, and leave him for the mother to lick.

---

else, or say ½lb to 1lb (0.2-0.5kg) a day plus 15 to 20lbs (6.8-9.0kg) roots. They will do on this without any corn or concentrates at all. They must not be too fat when they lamb, else they will have lambing difficulties, but also they must not be half-starved.

In the spring, as soon as the ewes have lambed, put them on the best grass you have got, and preferably on *clean* grass: that is grass that has not had sheep on it for some time. The grass is very nourishing at this time of the year and the lambs should thrive and come on apace. Within four months most of them will be fat enough either to eat or to sell to the butcher as "fat lamb".

Tupping

In cold climates sheep are generally tupped, or mated, in the autumn. If you have a flock of ewes it is best to cull them before mating: that is pull any out that are so old that their

teeth have gone. A full-mouth ewe, which has eight incisor teeth up, is four years old and should already have had three lambs. She may go for another year or two, or she may not, depending on the state of wear of her teeth.

Before putting the ram in with the ewes you should flush the flock. This means keeping them on very poor pasture for a few weeks, then putting them on very good pasture. Then put the ram in. All the ewes will take the ram then in fairly quick succession and you will not have a very drawn-out lambing season. A ram can serve up to sixty ewes in the tupping season. The gestation period is 147 days. Some people try to get ewes to lamb very early so as to catch the early lamb market, but unless you intend to lamb indoors, and with very high feeding, I would not recommend this. I like to see lambs coming in late February or March, and I find the later ones soon catch the poor little half-frozen winter lambs up and pass them.

Sheep

Lambing

Watch them carefully when they start to lamb. Leave them alone to get on with it: they generally can. But if a ewe is in labour for more than an hour and obviously cannot void her lamb give her help. Get the ewe into a small pen where you can catch her. Lay her down (if she is not already down). Wash your hand very well in carbolic oil or boiled linseed oil. See if the lamb's forefeet are just showing. If so work them gently out, only pulling when the ewe strains. The feet are very slippery, so put a soft cord around them – a scarf or a necktie will do – and haul gently when the ewe strains: haul slightly downwards. If you are not winning, insert your hand very gently into the vagina, feeling along the forelegs, and make sure that the head is not bent backwards. If it is, push the lamb back gently and try to pull the head forwards. The lamb should then come out.

The ideal presentation is forefeet first, then nose. There are many bad presentations possible, made more complicated if there are twins, but with experience you learn to tell what's going on in there. You can get your hand right inside and feel about, but it is difficult because the uterus exerts great pressure on your hand.

But, if you only have a few ewes, and they are healthy, the chances are that you will have to do nothing with them at all.

Switching lambs

Now if a single lamb dies and you have another ewe with twins it is a good thing to fob one of the twins off on the bereaved ewe. Put the bereaved ewe in a small pen, rub the twin lamb with the dead body of her lamb, and try to see if she will accept the new lamb. If she won't, skin the dead lamb, keeping the skin rather like a jersey, and pull the skin over the live lamb. Almost invariably the foster mother ewe will accept him then. The advantage of this is that the mother of the twins "does" (feeds) one lamb much better than she would do two, and also the bereaved ewe does not get mastitis and have trouble drying up her milk. She is happy, the twins are happy, the twin-mother is happy, and you are happy.

Orphan lambs

"Poddy lambs" are one answer for the smallholder. Farmers will often let you have orphan lambs for nothing, or nearly nothing, and you can bring them up on the bottle, with a teat on it. You can give them warm cow's milk, diluted with water at first, later neat. Goat's milk is better than cow's milk, but don't let them suck the goat direct – milk her and feed from the bottle. Keep the lambs warm. They will grow up thinking they are humans.

Shearing

I start shearing at the beginning of July, but people further south start earlier. So see what your neighbours do. Most people don't shear the new lambs, but only the ram, the ewes, and any wethers (castrated males) left over from the previous year.

If you shear by hand you will find it much easier to sit the sheep up on a bench, or a large box. Hold her with her back towards you and practise holding her firmly with your knees, thus leaving your hands free. Clip the wool off her tummy. Then clip up the throat and take blow after blow (a blow is the shearer's term for one row of wool clipped) down the left side of the neck, shoulder, flank, and right down as far as you can get it, rolling the sheep around as you clip. When you can get no further on that side, roll the sheep over and start down the right side, hoping to meet the shorn part from the other side as you roll the sheep that way. The last bit involves laying the sheep almost right over to clip the wool near the tail. The sheep should then leap away leaving her fleece in one entire blanket.

Lay the fleece, body-side down, on a clean sheet or floor and cut away any bits of dunged wool. Fold the edges over towards the middle, roll up from the head end, twist the tail end into a rope and wrap round the tight bundle and tuck the rope under itself. If the wool is for sale, pack the fleeces tight into a "pocket" (big sack). Put the dunged bits in a separate sack and mark it "daggings". We will discuss the preparation of wool for spinning on pp. 226-227.

If people tell you hand shearing is easy, you can tell them they lie. It is back-breaking, hand shears make your wrist ache like hell, and it is extremely difficult. Keep your shears sharp and cut as close to the sheep as you can without nicking her. If you do nick her, dab some stockholm tar on the wound. Beware of her teats. Of course mechanical clippers make the job much quicker, but it is still very hard work. But shearing is *fun*: if several of you are doing it there is a great sense of camaraderie, and you have a sense of achievement when you get good at it. At first it seems quite impossibly difficult but don't give up – just persevere. You'll win in the end, if you don't bust a gut. Home-brew helps.

Sheep disease

Except on mountains, sheep suffer from a bright green blow-fly which "strikes" them, i.e. lays eggs on them, particularly on any dunged parts. It is good practice to cut this wool off them before shearing. This is called "clatting" or "dagging". But if about a fortnight after shearing you either spray or dip your sheep in some proprietary sheep dip you will protect them from fly strike for at least two or three months: in fact, probably until the cold weather comes and does away with the flies. If you don't protect them they will get struck and the maggots will eat right into the sheep and eventually kill it in the most unpleasant manner possible.

There are two other very common sheep diseases. *Fluke* is one of them. When sheep graze in wet places they pick up large worms from a certain minute fresh-water snail. These worms live in the gall ducts of the liver. So drain your land, or keep sheep from wet places. There are injections that

Food from Animals

Sheep shearing

Sheep are shorn in the summer when the weather is warm enough for the sheep not to suffer from the winter cold.

Grab the sheep by the wool on her flanks, not by the wool on her back. Pick her up and sit her down on her rump for ease of handling.

Clip all the wool of her stomach down as far as the udder. Avoid cutting the udder in a ewe or the penis in a ram or wether.

Open the wool up her throat and start shearing around the left side of her neck. Shear her head.

Keep on down the left side of the shoulder and flank as far as you can reach in that position. If you can hold the sheep with your knees your hands will be free. Hold her skin tight with your left hand. Shear as close to it as you can get with the other.

Roll the sheep over and clip down her right side. The fleece should come right off her body except at the hind quarter.

Lay the sheep flat on the ground and put your left foot over her to hold her between your legs. Finish taking fleece off the hind quarters.

Trim her tail and hind legs separately for appearance. Keep the wool from these parts separate from the main fleece.

Rolling a fleece

To roll the fleece lay it body-side down on a clean surface. Pick out any thorns, straw, etc. Turn the sides inwards and begin to roll tightly from the tail end. Twist the neck end into a rope. Tie it round the fleece and tuck under itself.

Dipping sheep

About a fortnight after shearing, sheep should either be dipped or sprayed with a proprietary mixture. Dipping is better because it really soaks in. This is for various purposes. In countries where scab is present it is often compulsory, but in most countries it is necessary to guard against "strike", or blow-fly maggot infestation. It also kills keds and other parasites.

protect against fluke too. You will know if you have it when you kill a sheep and see these worms wriggling about in the liver. The other disease is *foot-rot*, likewise a scourge of sheep in damp lowlands: sheep on mountains seldom get it. To protect against foot-rot trim the feet occasionally (better with sharp pincers than with a knife) to remove excess horn. But if your sheep have it, the best cure of all is to walk them through a foot-bath of formalin.

Mutton and lamb

You stick a sheep by shoving the knife into the side of the neck as close to the backbone and the head as you can get it. Keep the sharp edge away from the backbone and pull the knife out towards the throat. This cuts all the veins and arteries in the neck and the windpipe too. But I would never never do this until I had stunned or killed the sheep with either a .22 bullet, an humane killer, or, in want of these, a blow on the head from the back of an axe.

Skinning

With the sheep on the ground or on a bench, slice a narrow strip of skin off the front of the forelegs and the back of the

Jointing a sheep

There are a vast number of ways of cutting up any carcass, but whichever way you follow, you still end up with – meat. So it doesn't really matter much which way you do it, provided you do it neatly and cleanly.

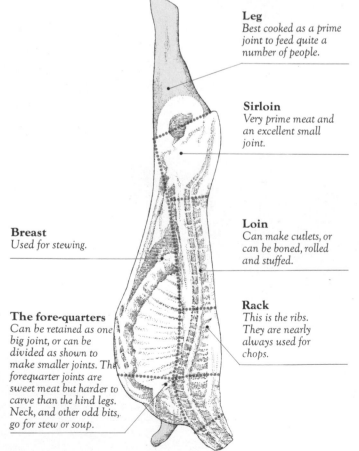

Leg
Best cooked as a prime joint to feed quite a number of people.

Sirloin
Very prime meat and an excellent small joint.

Loin
Can make cutlets, or can be boned, rolled and stuffed.

Breast
Used for stewing.

Rack
This is the ribs. They are nearly always used for chops.

The fore-quarters
Can be retained as one big joint, or can be divided as shown to make smaller joints. The forequarter joints are sweet meat but harder to carve than the hind legs. Neck, and other odd bits, go for stew or soup.

hind legs. Grasp the foreleg between your knees and raise this strip of skin off, right down into the brisket (chest). Keep the knife edge against the skin rather than the meat so as not to cut the latter. Hold the strip of skin tight away from the leg with the left hand. Do the same with the hind legs (along the back of them) as far as the anus. Then skin out the legs, still holding each leg in turn between your knees. Don't tear or cut the meat. Cut the feet off at the lowest joint, and raise the tendons of the hind legs for sticking the gambrel (hook) through. Pull the flap of skin you have raised between the hind legs off the carcass as far as it will go.

Fisting

Then "fist" the skin away from the belly. (Fisting is the forcing of your fist in between skin and sheep). Use the knife as little as possible. Keep your hand washed when you fist, and don't soil the meat. Cleanliness is essential in all butchery operations. When you are fisting a sheep skin off, make sure that you leave the "fell", or thin tough membrane, on the meat and don't take it off on the skin. On the skin it is a nuisance; on the meat it is a useful protection. Fist the skin off both rear end and brisket as far as you can. Then insert the gambrel and hoist the sheep up.

Slit the skin right down the belly, and then fist the skin off the sheep as high and low as you can. It will stick on the rump – fist here from below as well as above. Try to avoid using the knife as much as possible. If it's a nice fat lamb the skin will come off easily, but if it's a skinny old ewe, or a tough old ram, you've got problems. Free the skin with the knife from anus and tail. Then you can often pull the skin right off the sheep, down towards the shoulders, like taking a jersey off. Use the knife to take the skin off face and head. Then cut the head off at the atlas bone – right next to the skull.

Disembowelling

Cut around the anus. Pull several inches of the rectum out and tie a string round it and drop it back. Now rip the belly right down as you would do with an ox or pig (see p. 113). Protect the knife point with your finger to stop it piercing the guts or paunch. Pull the rectum down with the rest of the guts. Take the bladder out without spilling its contents, and carefully hoist out the paunch and guts and other machinery. Carefully haul the liver free from the back, and then haul the whole mass up and out of the sheep. You will have to cut the gullet to do this, and you should tie the gullet above the cut so the food doesn't drop out. Remove the liver carefully, and drop the guts into a big bowl. You can clean the guts and use all but the third stomach for tripe.

Cut down the breastbone. With a lamb you can do this with a knife, with an older sheep you may have to saw. Pull the pluck (heart and lungs) out and hang them up. Finally, wash the carcass down with cold water and go to bed.

Next morning, early, split the carcass and cut it up. You can use the small intestine for sausage casings.

Rabbits

Rabbits are a very good stock for the self-supporting family to keep. They can be fed largely on weeds that would otherwise be wasted and they make excellent eating.

Breeds

New Zealand Whites are a good breed because their skins when cured are very beautiful and the rabbits themselves are good meat. Californians are also excellent rabbits. These medium breeds are probably more economical than very large rabbits such as, for example, Flemish Giants, which eat an awful lot and don't produce much more meat. If you get two does and a buck, these should provide you with up to two hundred pounds of meat a year.

Shelter

During the summer rabbits will feed themselves perfectly well on grass alone, if you either move them about on grassland in arks, or else let them run loose in adequate fenced paddocks. The wire netting of the paddocks should be dug six inches (15 cm) into the ground to prevent them burrowing; if you have foxes you have problems. You can keep them in hutches all the year round: they can stand cold but not wet, don't like too much heat but need a cosy nest box.

Breeding

You can leave young rabbits on the mother for eight weeks, at which age they are ready to be killed. If you do this you should remove the mother six weeks after she has kindled and put her to the buck. After she has been served return her to her young. Remove the latter when they are eight weeks old and the doe will kindle again seventeen days after the litter has been removed, gestation being about thirty days.

If you keep some young for breeding replacements you must separate does and bucks at three months. Sexing rabbits is easy enough: lay the rabbit on its back, head towards you: press the fingers gently each side of where its equipment seems to be and this will force out and expose the relevant part. It will appear as an orifice in the female and a slight rounded protrusion in the male. When a rabbit the size of a New Zealand White is ready for mating she weighs 8 lbs (3.6 kg): don't keep her until she gets much heavier than this or she will fail to conceive. Always take the doe to the buck, never the buck to the doe, or there will be fighting, and always put a doe by herself when she is going to kindle. A doe should rear from seven to nine rabbits a litter, so if the litters are over twelve it is best to remove and kill a few, or else foster them on another doe that has just kindled with a smaller litter. If you do this rub the young with the new doe's dung and urine before you give them to her, to confuse her smell.

Feeding

Rabbits will eat any greens or edible roots. They like a supplement of meal: any kind of ground grain will do, but a pregnant doe should not have more than 4 oz (114 g) of meal a day or she will get fat. Assuming that rabbits are not on grass and that you are not giving them a great quantity of greenstuff, feeding should then be in the order of 3 oz (84 g) of concentrates a day for young rabbits over eight weeks old, plus hay ad lib. Eighteen days after mating the doe should be given no more hay but fed on concentrates. She should have these until her eight-week-old litter is removed from her, and at this time will eat up to 8 oz (228 g) a day. Young rabbits can have meal as soon as they are two weeks old.

Killing

To kill a rabbit hold it by its hind legs, in your left hand, grab its head in your right hand and twist it backwards; at the same time force your hand downwards to stretch its neck. The neckbone breaks and death is instantaneous. Before the carcass has cooled nick the hind legs just above the foot joint and hang up on two hooks. Make a light cut just above the hock joint on the inside of each rear leg and cut up to the vent (anus). Peel the skin off the rear legs and then just rip it off the body. Gut the rabbit by cutting down the belly and removing everything except liver and kidneys. This is known as hulking. Remove the gall bladder from the liver.

Flemish Giant
These are rather too large and unwieldy for meat production, but they are useful for cross-breeding.

Californian
A good meat rabbit weighing up to 10 lbs (4.5 kg). They are healthy and easy to rear.

New Zealand White
Another good meat rabbit, and popular with breeders for its fur which dyes well.

Poultry

CHICKENS

All hens should be allowed access to the great outdoors except in the winter in very cold climates. Not only is it inhumane to keep chickens indoors all the time, it leads to all the diseases that commercial flocks of poultry now suffer from. Some poultry keepers go to such extremes of cruelty as keeping hens shut up in wire cages all their lives. Sunshine is the best source of vitamin D for poultry, as it is for us. Hens were evolved to scratch the earth for their living, and to deny them the right to do this is cruel. They can get up to a quarter of their food and all their protein from freshly growing grass and derive great benefit from running in woods and wild places. They crave, and badly need, dust-baths to wallow in and fluff up their feathers to get rid of the mites. In twenty years of keeping hens running out of doors I have yet to find what poultry disease is, with the exception of blackhead in turkeys. Our old hens go on laying year after year until I get fed up with seeing them, and put them in the pot.

Feeding

Hens running free out of doors on good grass will do very well in the summer time if you just throw some grain. In the winter, when the grass is not growing, they will want a protein supplement. You can buy this from a corn merchant, or you can feed them fish meal, meat meal, soya meal, other bean meal or fish offal. I would recommend soya meal most of all, because soya is the best balanced of any vegetable protein. So if you live in a region where soya beans can be grown successfully, the problem of your protein supplement is easily solved.

But soya must be cooked, for it contains a substance which, when raw, is slightly poisonous. Sunflowers are good too, particularly if you can husk the seed and grind it, but they're quite good just fed as they are. You can also feed the hens lupin seed (either ground or whole), rape seed (although not too much of it), linseed, groundnut or cotton seed (but this must be cooked first), crushed or ground peas or beans, lucerne or alfalfa, or alfalfa meal. These all contain protein.

From ten days old onwards, all chickens should have access to fresh vegetables, and after all, this is one thing we can grow. So give them plenty of vegetables whether they run out on grass or not. My method of feeding hens is to let them run outdoors, give them a handful each of whatever high protein meal or grain I have in the morning, and scatter a handful each of whole grain in the evening. Wheat is best, or kibbled maize. Barley is very good, but it should be hummelled – banged about until the awns (spikes) are broken off. An equally good method is to let them feed both protein and grain from self-feed containers (illustrated). These should be placed out of the reach of rats.

If you allow hens to run out of doors, or to have access to a good variety of foods, they will balance their own rations and not eat more than they need anyway. But if hens are confined indoors, you can balance their rations like this:

Laying mash

1 cwt (50.1 kg) wheat meal
1 cwt (50.1 kg) maize meal (preferably yellow maize)
1 cwt (50.1 kg) other grain meal (oats or barley or rye)
1 cwt (50.1 kg) fish meal
30 lbs (13.6 kg) dried milk
20 lbs (9.0 kg) ground sea shells
5 lbs (2.3 kg) salt

Give them free access to this, and a handful each of whole grains to scratch out of their straw or litter.

Fattening mash for cockerels or capons

Barley meal is the best fattener for any poultry, but can be replaced by boiled potatoes. Skimmed milk is also ideal. Feed the mash ad-lib:

3 cwt (150.3 kg) barley meal
1 cwt (50.1 kg) wheat meal
½ cwt (25.0 kg) fish or meat meal
30 lbs (13.6 kg) dried milk
plus some lime (ground sea shells) and salt

Chicken breeds

As a self-supporter you will want old-fashioned broody hens, and they are hard to find nowadays because commercial breeders breed hybrids for egg production and nothing else. So you will have to search for those marvellous traditional breeds which can live outdoors, lay plenty of eggs, go broody and hatch their eggs, rear their chicks and make good table birds as well. You want breeds like: the Rhode Island Red, a good dual purpose hen, meaning it is a good layer and a good table bird; the Light Sussex, an old English breed, again dual purpose; or the Cuckoo Maran which is very hardy and lays large, deep-brown, very high quality eggs, but not in prolific quantities.

Cuckoo Maran　　**Rhode Island Red**　　**Light Sussex**

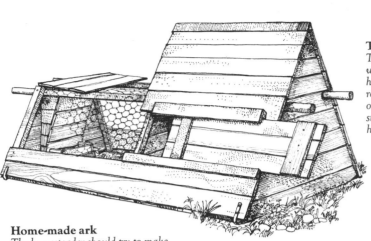

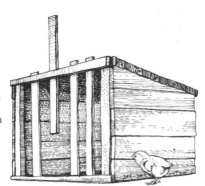

Traditional ark
This is made of sawn timber and weather-boarding, is well creosoted, has a night-house with perches, a row of nesting-boxes accessible from outside by a door, and a run. It is strong but easily movable by handles at each end.

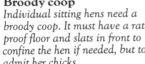

Broody coop
Individual sitting hens need a broody coop. It must have a rat-proof floor and slats in front to confine the hen if needed, but to admit her chicks.

Home-made ark
The homesteader should try to make his gear for nothing, and used fertilizer bags are free. We made this ark for nearly nothing. Thatch would work as well, and would look better.

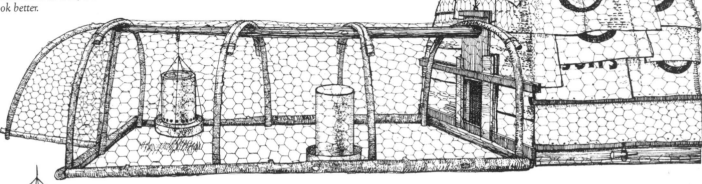

Self-feed hopper
You can buy galvanized hoppers, but you can make them yourself, for free, by hanging up an old oil-drum, bashing holes round its base to let the hens peck food out, and hang the cut-off base of a larger oil-drum underneath to catch spilled food. Hang above rat-reach.

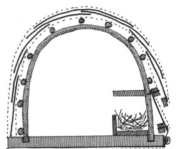

"Fertilizer-bag" ark
A layer of wire-netting over the overlapping bags keeps them from flapping. The bags can be supported underneath by closely-spaced horizontal rods of hazel, willow, etc. An inspection door for nesting boxes can be made by hanging up fertilizer bags weighted with a heavy batten across their bottoms.

Little chick mash

> 30 lbs (13.6 kg) meal (preferably a mixture of wheat, maize and oats)
> 12 lbs (5.4 kg) fish meal or meat meal
> 12 lbs (5.4 kg) alfalfa (lucerne) meal
> 2 lbs (0.9 kg) ground sea shells
> 1 lb (0.5 kg) cod liver oil
> 1 lb (0.5 kg) salt
> plus a "scratch" of finely-cracked cereals

If you give them plenty of milk (skimmed is nearly as good) you can forget all but a little of the cod liver oil, the alfalfa meal, and half, if not all, the fish meal or meat meal. If you have food that is free to you, or a by-product of something else, it is better to use that (even if the books say it is not perfect) than something you have to pay for. I am a great believer in making the best of what is available.

Free range

If hens run completely free range, it is often better to keep them in their houses until midday. They generally lay their eggs before that time, so you get the eggs before you let them out instead of losing them in the hedges where the rats get them. Hens will do pasture good if they are not too concentrated on it, and if their houses or arks are moved from time to time over the pasture. The chicken is a woodland bird, and hens always thrive in woodland if the foxes don't get them. Keep them out of the garden or you will rue the day. Obviously hens can be run very advantageously on stubble (land from which cereals have just been harvested).

Limited grass

Don't put more than a hundred hens on an acre of grassland, unless you intend to keep moving them every six months or so on to fresh grassland. If you stock more heavily you will damage the grassland, and your hens may have a build-up of parasites. It is a great advantage if you can divide your grassland, into two (a strip each side of a line of hen houses for example), and let the hens run on each strip in turn. As soon as they have really eaten the grass down on one strip let them run on the other. In the summer, when the grass grows so quickly they can't cope with it, let them run on one strip long enough to let you cut the other strip for hay. Or alternate hens with sheep, goats, cows or geese. Poultry will eat any grass provided it is kept short, but ideally it should be of the tender varieties like Timothy or the Meadow grasses. There can be clover with it, although the hens will provide enough nitrogen in their droppings.

The Balfour method

This is suitable for the "backyard poultry keeper" or the person who only has a small or limited garden. You have a pen around your hen house in which you dump plenty of straw, bracken or whatever vegetation you can get. In addition you have two (or three if you have the space) pens which are grassed down, and which can be approached by the hens from the straw yard. The hens will scratch in the straw yard and so satisfy their scratching instincts and spare the grass. Now let the hens run into one of the grass pens. Change them into another pen after, say, a fortnight or three weeks. They will get a bite of grass from this, and the grass in the first pen will be rested and have a chance to grow. The straw yard will provide half a ton of good manure a year from each hen. The old "backyard poultry yard" which is a wilderness of scratched bare earth, coarse clumps of nettles, rat holes, and old tin cans, is not a good place to keep hens or anything else.

Housing

The ordinary commercially-produced hen house, provided it is mobile, works perfectly well. If used in the Balfour or limited grassland methods described above, it doesn't even have to be mobile, unless you intend to move it from time to time into another field. Utter simplicity is fine for a hen house. Hens need shelter from rain and wind, some insulation in very cold climates and perches to sit on. Make sure the perches are not right up against the roof, and are placed so their droppings have a clear fall to the floor. The nesting boxes should be dark, designed to discourage hens from roosting in them and roofed so hens don't leave droppings in them. You should be able to reach in and get the eggs easily. There are patent nesting boxes which allow the eggs to fall down to another compartment. I think these are a very good idea; they prevent the eggs getting dirty. We now have movable hen arks (as illustrated), with an enclosed sleeping area and a wire-netted open run. They hold twenty-five hens each and cost nothing but a handful of nails, some old torn wire netting and some free plastic fertilizer bags.

In countries which have heavy snow in the winter the birds will have to be kept in during the snow period. It is not a bad idea to confine some birds in a house in which there is electric light if you want eggs in the depth of winter. Give the birds say twelve hours of light and they will think it is summer time and lay a lot of eggs; otherwise they will go off laying as soon as the days get really short.

Rearing chickens

It is always a good idea to keep a rooster among your hens, and not just to wake you up in the morning. The hens will lay just as many eggs without a rooster but the eggs won't be fertile. Also if each batch of hens has a cockerel to marshal them and keep them together out of doors, they fare better and are less likely to come to harm.

If you leave a hen alone, and the fox doesn't get her, she will wander off into the hedgerows and wander back again in a few weeks with a dozen little chicks clucking at her heels. These chicks, being utterly naturally reared, will be the healthiest little chicks you will ever see. Alternatively you can watch your hens for broodiness. You can tell when a hen is broody by the way she squats tight on her eggs and makes a broody clucking noise when you try to lift her off. Help her by enclosing her in a broody coop (a little house with slats in front of it that baby chicks can get through and the mother can't). Give her nice soft hay or something as a nest, and put a dozen fertile eggs under her. (They can be any kind of poultry egg you like). See that she always has water and food (she will eat very little). Let her out once a day for a short walk, but get her in within half an hour or the eggs will get cold. Eggs should hatch out in 21 days from start of brooding. As soon as the chicks are a few days old you can let the hen out and she will lead them around and teach them how to look for food. This is by far the best way to raise poultry, and beats any incubator. If you are just starting with hens, you can either order "day-old chicks" or "point-of-lay pullets" which are young females just about to lay. When chickens are only a day old they don't need to eat and can be packed into parcels and sent about the country with impunity. A day or two older and they would die.

Keep such pullets as you need for your flock replacements and fatten the cocks for the table. Feed all little chicks on a fairly rich diet of high protein and finely ground meal. For the first few days add ground-up hard boiled eggs and milk by-products to their ration. Wheat meal mixed with milk is also a perfect food.

Always make sure that chickens have access to enough lime, in the form, perhaps, of ground sea shells, and to insoluble grit like crushed flint. Hens running out of doors are not so dependent on artificial supplies.

Cockerels should weigh two or three pounds (0.9-1.4 kg) at eight to 12 weeks and are called "broilers". Birds or table breeds should weigh more. At 12 or 14 weeks they should weigh three or four pounds (1.4-1.8 kg), and in America are called "fryers". After this you may call them "roasters". At six or nine

Killing and preparing a chicken

Grab the legs with your left hand, and the neck with your right hand so that it protrudes through the two middle fingers and the head is cupped in the palm. Push your right hand downwards and turn it so the chicken's head bends backwards. Stop as soon as you feel the backbone break, or you will pull the head off.

Plucking
Start plucking the chicken as soon as it is dead, while it is still warm; once it gets cold the feathers are much harder to get out. Be very careful not to tear the skin.

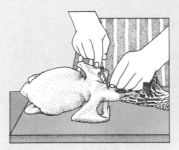

Drawing
Slip the knife under the skin at the bottom of the neck and cut up to the head.

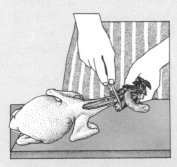

Sever the neckbone at the bottom end with secateurs or a knife.

Remove the neckbone. Insert the index finger of your right hand, move it round inside and sever all the innards.

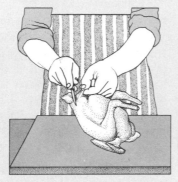

Cut between the vent and the tail, being careful not to sever the rectum.

Cut right round the vent so as to separate it from the body.

Carefully draw the vent, with attached guts, out of the tail end.

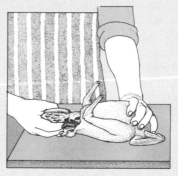

The gizzard, lungs, and heart will follow the guts.

Remove the crop from the neck end of the bird.

Trussing
If you put the bird in the oven and cooked it, it would taste just the same as if you trussed it. But to make a neat and professional job it is worth trussing properly.

Thread a large darning needle, force the chicken's legs forward, and shove the needle and thread through the body low down.

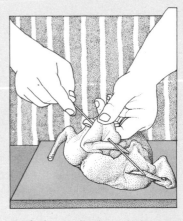

Push the needle through the wing and across the skin at the neck.

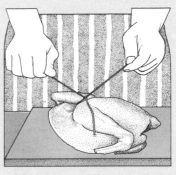

Push through the other wing and tie the ends of the thread together.

Re-thread the needle and pass over the leg, below the end of the breastbone and round the other leg.

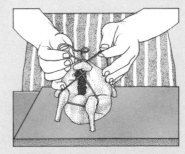

Cross the thread behind the hocks and tie around the parson's nose.

months old they are called "boilers", so are old hens culled from your laying flock. An old hen can make good eating.

Hens in lay, if good layers, will have these characteristics: bright eyes, large red healthy-looking combs and wattles, wide apart pelvic bones (fairly loose so eggs can get out) and a white, large, moist, vent. If they have the opposite, wring their necks. They won't lay you many eggs and you should certainly not breed from them. Don't stop hens from going broody.

Eggs

Eggs are much better eaten fresh, and it is quite possible to have new-laid eggs throughout the year. If you want to store eggs, clean them first and drop them into water-glass, which you can buy from the chemist.

TURKEYS

These are very delicate birds compared to other poultry. If they associate in any way with chickens, they will get a fatal disease called blackhead unless you medicate their water or their food. If you want to keep them without medicating them, you must keep them well away from all chicken-kind, and even be careful about walking from the hen run to the turkey run without changing your boots and disinfecting yourself. It's hardly worth it. Turkeys do not seem to me to be a very suitable bird for the self-supporter, unless he wants to trade them. In this case he can rear them intensively in incubators and brooders, or buy them reared from another breeder.

GEESE

These are the most excellent birds for the self-supporter. They are hardy, tough, self-reliant grazing birds and they make good mothers. The best way to start breeding geese is to buy eggs from somebody and put them under a broody hen. A hen will sit on five or six goose eggs and bring them off, but you want to make sure that she hasn't been sitting too long when you put the goose eggs under her, for goose eggs take longer to hatch than hens' do (up to thirty days or even more). During the last week of the sitting take the eggs out from under the hen every day and wet them with lukewarm water (goose-mothers get wet but hen foster mothers don't). On the day when the eggs start to pip, wet them well. Some people remove the first goslings that hatch so that the foster mother doesn't think she's done her job, and then they replace them when the last egg has hatched. I have never bothered and have always had good results.

Feed the goslings well for the first two or three weeks on bread soaked in milk (or skimmed milk). If they are fairly safe where they are, let the hen run around with them. If you fear they will get lost, confine the hen in a broody coop. I prefer the hen to run loose. When the young birds no longer need the foster mother she will leave them and start laying again.

But geese, although such fierce and strong birds, are vulnerable to two enemies: rats and foxes. Rats will pull goose eggs out from under a sitting hen or goose, and they will kill baby geese whenever they get a chance. So poison them, deny them cover, gas their holes: do anything to get rid of them. They are the enemy of everything wholesome on your farm.

Foxes just love geese. They will snatch a sitting goose off her eggs whenever they can. So they cannot really co-exist with the self-sufficient husbandman. Shoot them with a shotgun or a .22 at night. Use one of those powerful electric torches which illuminates the sights of the gun as well as the fox. If there are foxes in the area you must confine sitting geese in a fox-proof place. Adult geese, running out loose, can often protect themselves from foxes, but even so you will always lose a few.

If you start reducing the goslings' food after three weeks, they will live on grass. As adults, they don't need any food except grass, but it is a good idea to chuck them some corn in January and February when you want to feed the goose up a bit to get her to lay well. Three weeks before you intend to kill them (generally Christmas), you should confine them, and feed them liberally with barley meal, maize meal and milk if you have it to spare. They will fatten on this, and one of them will provide the best Christmas dinner in the world.

Geese pair for life, so I prefer to keep one goose and one gander together as a breeding pair, although many people keep a gander to two or three geese. They lay early: in February or March. If you leave them alone they will sit on a dozen or more of their own eggs and bring them off with no trouble at all, but if you are greedy you can keep stealing their eggs and putting them under broody hens. But hens aren't always broody as early in the year as that.

Killing a goose or turkey

Grab the bird by its legs with both hands. Keep the back of the bird away from you. Lower the head to the floor, and get someone else to lay a broomstick across the neck, just behind the head. Tread on both ends of the broomstick, and pull the legs upwards until you feel the neck break. If you hold the tips of the wings as well as the two legs the bird will not flap after it is dead. Then treat like a chicken.

DUCKS

To say that ducks don't need water is nonsense. Ducks do need water and cannot possibly be happy without it. It is inhumane to keep animals in conditions grossly different from the ones their species has been evolved to live in. So give them access to water, but keep your ducklings away from it for their first week or two until they have the natural protection of oil on their feathers. You must give them drinking water, however.

Swimming water for ducks is better if it is flowing, and renews itself. A stagnant pond is less healthy. Many eggs get laid in the water, or on the edge, and if the water is dirty the eggs, which have porous shells, can be dangerous to eat. So don't eat eggs that have been lying in filthy water, no matter how much you superficially clean them. If there is no natural water on your holding, my advice is not to keep ducks. You can, of course, create an artificial pond, either out of concrete, puddled clay, or plastic sheeting buried in earth, but if you do, make sure the water is renewable and does not become stale and stagnant.

One drake will look after half a dozen ducks and enjoy it, but ducks make rotten mothers. If you let them bring off their own eggs you must confine them in a broody coop, or they will kill the little ducklings by dragging them all over the place. Hens are much better duck-mothers than ducks are. Duck eggs hatch in 28 days.

Baby ducks need careful feeding. From hatching to ten weeks feed them as much barley or other meal as they will eat, and add milk if you have it. Feed ducks about the same as you would hens when you are not fattening them. The duck is not a grazing bird to the extent that the goose is, but ducks will get quite a lot of food if they have access to water, or mud, or are allowed to roam around. They are partly carnivorous, and eat slugs, snails, frogs, worms and insects. Don't let breeding ducks get too fat, or they will produce infertile eggs. They like a mash in the morning of such things as boiled vegetables, flaked maize, pea or bean meal, wheat meal and a little barley meal. Give them about half a handful each for breakfast, and half a handful of grain in the evening. If you find they get fat, give them less. If you find they get thin, give them more.

There are ducks (such as the Indian Runner) with very little meat on them that lay plenty of eggs, and table ducks (such as the Aylesbury) with plenty of meat but not many eggs. Then there's the Muscovy, a heavy, far too intelligent, very hardy bird, that's good to eat but has dark flesh.

You should kill your young ducks at exactly ten weeks. They are full of bristles before and after that time. They won't put on weight afterwards anyway. At ten weeks they are easy to pluck and are at their prime. You can of course eat old

ducks if you want to, but they are tougher and much fattier.

Housing for ducks can be extremely simple, but this does not mean that it should be reach-me-down. Ducks like a dry, draught-free but well-ventilated house. If it's mobile, so much the better, because otherwise the immediate surroundings get in a mess. It must also be fox and rat proof.

PIGEONS

In America squabs are a great dish. They are young pigeons killed at about four and a half weeks. The parent birds are sometimes reared intensively, in a special house with a wire run or "fly" for the birds to flap about in. Kept like this the birds should be fed on grain, with some peas included as they must have some protein. A pair of pigeons might eat up to a hundredweight of grain a year and raise up to fourteen squabs a year, so if you had a dozen pairs you would be eating squabs until you were sick of them. If they are confined in this manner you must give them grit, as well as water for drinking and bathing in, and you must attend to hygiene by having some sort of litter on the floor which you can change.

Personally I would object strongly to keeping pigeons like that and would always let them fly free. Have a pigeon loft, get a few pairs of adult pigeons (already mated) from somebody else, and before letting them loose keep them for three weeks in some sort of cage in the loft, where they can see out (this is important). Then let them out, chuck them a little grain every day, and let them get on with it. Kept like this they are no work and little expense, and in fact do very little damage to crops, although you hope they eat your neighbour's and not yours. If he shoots a few, well, that won't break you. Harvest the squabs when the underside of the wing is fully feathered. Kill, pluck, draw, and truss, as if they were chickens (see p. 127).

Aylesbury drake
The best British table breed. It is large, heavy and very hardy, and its ducklings grow exceptionally fast.

Embden gander
The Embden is a good table breed. Its feathers and down are pure white and ideal for stuffing cushions and eiderdowns.

White turkey
These can grow up to 38 lbs (17.2 kg). There is a small quick-maturing form of this breed called the Beltsville White.

Bees & Honey

Bees will provide you with all the sugar you need and as a self-supporter you shouldn't need much. A little sugar (or, preferably, honey) improves beer, and sugar is necessary if you want to make "country wines" (which I shall discuss on pp. 193-194), but otherwise the part that sugar plays in the diet is wholly deleterious. It is such an accessible source of energy that we satisfy our energy requirements too easily, and are not induced to turn to coarser foods, whose valuable constituents are less concentrated and less refined. The ideal quantity of refined sugar in the diet is: nil.

Now honey will do anything that sugar can do and do it much better. Not only is it a healthier food, for beekeepers it is also free. It is sweeter than sugar, so if you use it for cooking or wine-making purposes use about two thirds as much as you would sugar. Before the sugar-cane countries were opened up to the western world honey was the only source of sugar, and for years I lived in central Africa consuming no sugar excepting that produced by bees. These bees were wild ones of course; all Africans know how to chop open a hollow tree with bees inside it and get out the honey. Many also hang hollowed-out logs in trees in the hope – generally realized – that bees will hive in them.

Beekeeping is really a way of getting something for nothing. It is a way of farming with no land, or at least with other people's land. You can keep bees in the suburbs of the city, even in the centre of the city, and they will make plenty of excellent honey.

The medieval skep

The medieval method of keeping bees was in the straw skep. You plaited straw or other fibres into ropes, twisted the ropes into a spiral, lashing each turn to the next, until you formed a conical skep. You placed this in a cavity left in a wall, so as to protect it from being blown over or soaked from above by rain. In the autumn, if you wanted the honey, you either destroyed the bees you had in the skep by burning a piece of sulphur under them, or you could save the bees by turning their skep upside down and standing another empty skep on top of it. The bees in the inverted skep could crawl up into the upper skep. More sensibly, you could stand an empty skep on top of a full one, with a hole connecting them, and the bees would climb up. When they had done so you removed the old skep which was full of honey and comb. If you dug this comb out you could wring the honey out of it by putting it in some sort of strainer (muslin would do), squeezing it, and letting it drip.

If the skep-inversion method worked without killing the bees, then this would be quite a good way of keeping them. You need no equipment save some straw, a bee-veil, gloves, and a smoker. You get nothing like so much honey out of a skep as you do out of a modern hive, but then you could keep a dozen skeps with practically no expenditure, whereas a modern hive, at its most basic, is a fairly costly item. When hundreds of people kept bees in skeps, and probably every farm had half a dozen or more, there were a great many more bees about the countryside, and swarms were much more common than they are now. It was easy to find them and not so necessary to conserve the bees that one had.

Langstroth's method

In 1851, a Philadelphian named Langstroth discovered the key secret about bees, which was what he called the "bee space." This is the exact space between two vertical planes on which bees build their honey-comb without filling the space in between, yet still remaining able to creep through. This discovery made possible an entirely different method of keeping bees, and turned beekeeping from a hunting activity into a farming one.

The method Langstroth developed was to hang vertical sheets of wax down at the correct space apart. The bees, instead of building their comb in a random fashion, would build it on these sheets of wax. Then, with the invention of the queen excluder, which is a metal sheet with holes just big enough for the workers but not the queen to get through, the queen was kept down below in a special chamber (the brood chamber) so that she could not lay eggs in the cells above, which as a result were full of clean honey with no grubs in them. You could then remove the frames, as the vertical sheets of wax were called, with their honey, extract the honey without killing any bees or bee larvae, afterwards replacing the emptied frames for the bees to build up and fill once more.

The modern hive

Langstroth's discovery has affected the construction of the modern hive. This has a base to raise it, and an alighting board, with a narrow slit for the bees to enter. On top of the base is the brood chamber, with its vertically slung "deep" or "brood" frames. These wooden frames have foundation inside them, like canvas inside a picture frame. The foundation is sheets of wax that have been embossed by a machine with exactly the pattern made by comb-making bees. Above the brood chamber is a super, which is shallower. The queen excluder divides the two chambers. You may have two or three supers, all complete with frames fitted with foundation, one on top of the other. On the very top is a roof. The roof has a bee-escape in it, through which bees can get out but not in. There should also be a clearer-board, which is a board with a bee-valve in it. This will let bees through one way but not the other. Then you should have a bee-veil, gloves, a smoker, and an extractor, which you may be able to borrow. The extractor is a centrifuge. You put your sections full of honey into it and spin them round at great speed, which flings the honey out of the comb on the the sides of the extractor. It then dribbles down and can be drawn off.

Capturing a swarm

If you are lucky enough to come across a swarm, what you will

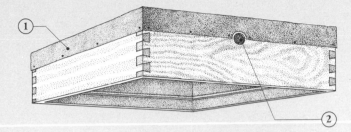

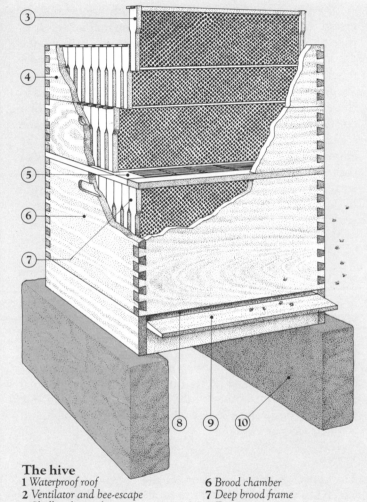

The hive
1 *Waterproof roof*
2 *Ventilator and bee-escape*
3 *Shallow honey frame*
4 *Super*
5 *Queen excluder*
6 *Brood chamber*
7 *Deep brood frame*
8 *Entrance*
9 *Alighting board*
10 *Base blocks*

Collecting honey
Take the honey-loaded super out and bang, shake and brush the bees out of it. Or else insert a clearing board the day before under the super, or supers, from which you wish to extract honey. The supers will then be free of bees when you want to take them out.

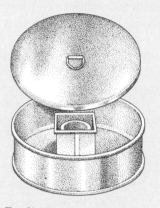

Feeding
If you take all the honey from a bee-hive in the late autumn you will have to feed the bees sugar or syrup. The feeder allows the bees to lick the syrup without getting drowned.

The skep
The original beehive, or skep, is made of twisted straw or rope sewn together into a conical shape with straw. If you use a skep your honey will be full of brood, or immature bees, because the queen can lay eggs in every cell. There is no queen excluder as there is in a modern hive. You can strain the brood out, but you kill a lot of bees. It is also impossible for the bee inspector to check a skep to see whether your bees have any diseases.

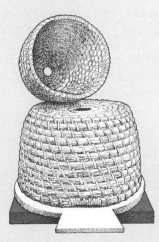

Robbing
Smoke, which is best applied with a special "smoker", quietens bees, makes them fill with honey and sting less readily. Use a screwdriver to break the top super off.

Decapping
To remove the honey cut the wax capping from the comb with a hot knife. Use two knives – heat one while you use the other.

Extracting
Put the decapped frames in the extractor. Spin very fast until the honey is all out of one side, turn the frames round and spin again.

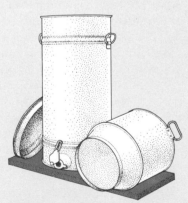

The honey tank
This is useful if you have a large number of bees. Pour the extracted honey carefully through the strainer and let it settle before drawing it off into jars or containers.

find will be a cluster of bees about the size of a football hanging on to a tree, or something similar. If it is a tree you just hold a big, empty, cardboard box under the swarm, give the branch a sharp jerk, and the swarm will fall kerplomp into the box. When this happens, turn the box upside down, put a stick under one side to keep it just off the ground, and leave them until evening. This is to let the scouts, out searching for a new home, come back to the swarm. Some ruthless people simply take the swarm away immediately. Swarming bees are unlikely to sting you, as they are loaded with honey and don't like stinging in this condition, but I'm not going to say they will never sting you.

To get a swarm into your hive, lay a white sheet in front of the hive sloping up to the entrance, and dump the swarm out on to the sheet. They should all crawl up into the hive. Make sure the queen, who is bigger and longer than the others, crawls into the hive too: without her you won't have any bees.

Bees in a colony

The fine South African scientist Marais proved conclusively that a colony of bees, for all practical purposes, is one individual. Apart from the queen, the separate bees are more like cells of an organism than like individuals. One colony mates with another and produces a swarm, the bee-equivalent of a child. The queen lays the eggs, and exerts a strong hold over the rest of the colony; kill her and if the workers can't rear another queen quickly enough from an existing grub, the colony will just die. The drones are as expendable as spermatozoa. Each one tries to mate with a young queen of another colony; whether mating is successful or not, either way the drone is killed by the workers as he is of no further use. There are about 20,000 workers in a mature colony, and they spend their lives working: gathering nectar, building cells for storing the honey, feeding the queen, nursing the young bees, ventilating and cleaning the nest, guarding it, and generally doing everything to be done. If a worker stings you she dies. Her death is unimportant, for she is not an individual, but merely a cell. Her sacrifice means nothing.

The organism survives at the expense of the individual, so if you capture a swarm you can just leave the bees to get on with it, and they will establish themselves.

A swarm of bees in May is worth a load of hay,
A swarm of bees in June is worth a silver spoon,
A swarm of bees in July is not worth a fly.

Which means that you won't reap much honey from a swarm of bees in July, but all the same do not despise one: hive it and it will establish itself and give you honey the next year.

Buying and feeding a nucleus

If you can't find swarms you can buy nuclei of bees from other beekeepers or dealers, who are fairly common in most countries; then just follow the instructions on the box. If you do this you should feed the nucleus for a while. You can do this by giving them two parts sugar to one part water in a feeder,

which you can buy and put in your hive on top of the brood chamber. In the case of a nucleus don't have a super: confine them in one brood chamber until that is full of honey and grubs before adding any supers on top.

Gathering the honey

As the frames get built up and filled with honey, and the brood chambers below with bee grubs, you may add a super, then a second super, and you may decide to take some honey. To do this take out one super, insert the clearer-board under it, and replace it. Next day go and remove the super which should be full of honey but empty of bees. Put the frames in the extractor and spin the honey out of them. You must first cut the capping off the combs with a hot knife. Each frame should be turned once to extract both sides. Then put the empty frames back in the super and return it to the bees so that they can start building on it again. Always work quietly and calmly when you work with bees. There is no substitute for joining a local beekeepers' group, or for making friends with a knowledgeable beekeeper and learning from him.

You should leave at least 35 lbs (15.8kg) of honey in the hive for the winter. I rob my bees only once: in early August. After that I leave them alone, with one empty super, and they make enough honey to last themselves the winter. My one hive gives me from 20 to 40 lbs (9.0-18.1kg). This late honey in our case is heather honey which I could not extract anyway, because it will not come out in the extractor: it has to be pressed out. People who rob all the honey from their bees have to feed them heavily all winter on syrup or candy. In fact, some commercial honey nowadays is little more than sugar turned into honey by the bees. The honey you buy from small beekeepers is generally flower honey though, and is much nicer as a result.

Wax

The cappings which you cut off the combs are beeswax, which is a very valuable substance: it makes polish, candles (the best in the world), and is good for waxing leatherwork and other purposes. Gentle heat melts the wax and it will run down a slope for you to collect, minus most of its impurities, in a container. The heat can be supplied by the sun, shining through a glass pane into an inclined box. It has been said that the reason why the monks of the Middle Ages were such a jolly drunken lot was that they had to keep lots of bees to provide the wax for their ecclesiastical candles; what could they do with the honey except – make mead of it?

Addresses

In Britain, bees can be obtained from:

BIBBA	or	The Brother Apiarist
B. A. Cooper		Buckfast Abbey
Whitegates		Devon
Thulston		
Derby		

Food from the Garden

"I have often thought that if heaven had given me choice
of my position and calling, it should have been on a rich spot of earth,
well watered, and near a good market for the productions of
the garden. No occupation is so delightful to me
as the culture of the earth."
JEFFERSON

The Food-Producing Garden

The countryman's garden of my childhood was a mixture of vegetables, flowers, soft fruit, top fruit (oh those greengages!) and very often tame rabbits, almost certainly a hen run, often pigeons and often ferrets. It was a very beautiful place indeed. Now alas it has disappeared under a useless velvety lawn and a lot of silly bedding plants and hardy perennials, but of course the owner is constrained to keep up with the people next door.

But how can we best reproduce the old cottage garden, which was one of the most productive places on Earth?

We are best to divide our garden area into six parts: seven if we insist on having a small lawn-and-flower area in which to sit among the fragrance of flowers.

One of the areas we will set aside for perennial food plants: that is plants that go on growing for year after year such as asparagus, globe artichokes, horse radish, hops perhaps (but they are very hungry and shading), comfrey, and herbs of many kinds. Another will be used for fruit canes, soft-fruit bushes, and a few top fruit trees (but remember a fruit tree really does shade and sterilize a large area of soil).

We should then divide the rest of the garden up into four parts, which can be cropped on a four year rotation.

Each yearly crop on each plot is called a "break". The four breaks are essentially: pea and bean family; cabbage family (brassica) but including swedes and turnips; roots meaning carrots, parsnips, onions, beet, celery and so on; and spuds, which means potatoes and is a very good word. More about rotation and the four plot garden will be found on p. 160.

Liming

If your land is acid it will need lime. You can test for this with a very simple device bought from any garden shop – or by asking a neighbour. You should lime before the pea and bean break. The peas and beans like the lime and the cabbage tribe that follow them like what is left of it. Lime has more time to combat the dreaded club-root disease, which is carried by brassica, if it is in the soil for a few months before the brassica are planted.

Mucking

If you have muck – farmyard manure – and I hope you have, or if you have compost, concentrate this on your potato break. The potatoes benefit enormously by it. In fact you won't grow very many without it. It is better not to put it on the root break because some roots, carrots and turnips in particular, are apt to "fork" if they have too much fresh muck. It is better not to put muck on the pea and bean break, because you lime that and lime and muck don't go very well together in the same year.

Mulching

It is quite advantageous to put a mulch, a covering of some dead greenstuff, on the surface of the soil between the cabbage-tribe plants, but only *after* you have hoed them

two or three times to suppress the weeds. If you mulch on top of weeds the weeds will simply grow through the mulch and the mulch will then impede the hoe.

Organic gardening

The aim of the organic gardener should be to get as much *humus* into his land as possible. Muck, compost, seaweed, leaf-mould, human excrement, spoiled hay, nettles, roadside cuttings, anything of vegetable or animal origin: compost it (see p. 136) and put it on the land, or just put it on the land. If you dig it in well, you dig it in. If you just leave it on top, the worms will dig it in for you.

Unless you keep animals on your garden, you will have to bring organic matter, or inorganic matter if you are not "organically minded," in from outside if you want a really productive garden. I subsidise my garden with manure made by animals that eat grass, hay and crops grown on the rest of the farm. There is much wild talk by would-be organic gardeners who think a garden will produce enough compost material to provide for itself. Well, let them try it. Let them take a rood of land, grow the bulkiest compost-making crop they can on it, compost it, and then see how far the compost it has made goes. It will not go very far.

Percentage values of organic fertilizers

	Nitrogen	Phosphorus	Potash	Calcium
Average farm yard manure	0.64	0.23	0.32	nil
Pure pig dung	0.48	0.58	0.36	nil
Pure cow dung	0.44	0.12	0.04	nil
Compost	0.50	0.27	0.81	nil*
Deep litter on peat	4.40	1.90	1.90	2.20
Deep litter on straw	0.80	0.55	0.48	nil
Fresh poultry dung	1.66	0.91	0.48	nil
Pigeon dung	5.84	2.10	1.77	nil

*Unless lime has been added

True, deep-rooting plants, such as comfrey and lucerne (alfalfa), can do great work in bringing up minerals, and phosphates and potash as well, from the subsoil to add to your soil. Trees do an even better job. But the land that is devoted to growing the comfrey or the trees is out of use for growing food crops.

Of course if your own sewage goes back, in one form or another, into the soil of your garden, one big leakage of

Organizing the self-supporting garden
However limited the space available, you only need the determination to abandon your space-wasting lawn and flowerbeds in exchange for a scheme of planned crop rotation for every inch of your garden to become a productive unit. You will save money, your end products will be fresh, and your garden will be a fine example of a dying breed: the cottage garden of yesteryear.

plant nutriments is stemmed. The old cottage gardens of the past had all their sewage returned, because the sewage system was a bucket and the contents of that were buried in the garden. Provided the ground in which they were buried was left undisturbed for a time any pathogens in the sewage would die a natural death. These country gardens owed their phenomenal fertility to the fact that the inhabitants were importing food from outside all the time, as well as eating their garden's own produce, and both lots of matter ended up in the soil.

But if you annually extract large amounts of produce from a piece of soil, and either export it or eat it and export the resulting sewage, and don't import any manure or fertilizer, the laws of nature are such that you will ultimately exhaust that soil.

It is vital that your garden be well drained, and it is an advantage if the land beneath it is not too heavy. A well drained medium loam is most desirable, but sandy soil, provided you muck it well, is very good too. Heavy clay is difficult to manage, but will grow good brassica crops. Whatever your soil is, you can scarcely give it too much muck, or other humus or humus-forming material.

Making compost

If you pile vegetable matter up in a heap it will rot and turn into compost. But to make good compost, and to make it quickly, you have to do more than this.

You can make the best compost in the world in twelve hours by putting vegetable matter through the guts of an animal. To make it any other way will take you months, whatever you do. But the principle of compost-making is this. The vegetation should be broken down by aerobic organisms. These are bacteria and fungi, which require oxygen to live. The bacteria which break down cellulose in plant matter need available nitrogen to do it. If they get plenty of available nitrogen they break down the vegetable matter very quickly, and in doing so they generate a lot of heat. The heat kills the weed seeds and disease organisms

in the compost. If there is a shortage of available nitrogen it takes the organisms a very long time to break the vegetable matter down. So in order to speed the process up as much as you can, you try to provide the things that the compost-making organisms need: air, moisture, and nitrogen.

You can provide the air by having rows of bricks with gaps between them underneath the compost and, if you like, by leaving a few posts in the heap as you build it, so you can pull them out to leave "chimneys." You can provide the moisture either by letting rain fall on the heap, or by throwing enough water on it to moisten it well. And you can provide the nitrogen by adding animal manure, urine, fish meal, inorganic nitrogen, blood, blood meal, or anything you can get that has a fairly high nitrogen content.

The natural, and traditional, way to make compost is to throw your vegetable matter (generally straw) at the feet of yarded cattle, pigs, or other animals. The available nitrogen in the form of the animal's dung and urine "activates" the compost. The urine also provides moisture and enough air gets between the straw. After a month or two, you dig the heap out and stack it carefully out of doors. More air gets into it and makes it rot down further. Then, after a few months, you cart it out and spread it on the land as fertilizer.

But if you don't have any animals your best bet is to build compost heaps by putting down a layer of bricks or concrete blocks with gaps in them, and laying coarse woody material on these to let the air through. Then put down several layers of vegetable matter, sprinkling a dusting of some substance with a high nitrogen content between them. Ten inches of vegetable matter and a couple of inches of chicken dung, or a thick sprinkling of a high-nitrogen inorganic fertilizer, would be ideal. Some people alternate lime with the nitrogen. Keep the sides vertical using walls of either wood, brick or concrete, and keep it decently moist but not sopping. When it begins to heat, keep most of the rain off it, either by shaping the top, by building a roof, or by covering it with old carpets. After a month or two, turn it, putting what was the top and the sides into the middle.

Making a compost heap

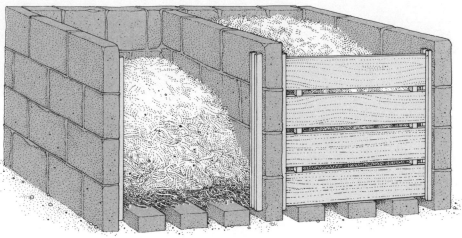

If space is no problem, make an open-layered compost heap – the larger the better, so that heat can build up inside without too much escaping. But an enclosed heap is probably more practical: you build up layers of animal and vegetable matter in a confined space, on bricks covered with twigs and small branches, and between walls. Keep the compost damp and leave gaps between the bricks for air to get through.

After another month or two, it will be fit to put on the garden. Every possible object of vegetable or animal origin should go in the compost heap.

Green manuring

Green manuring is the process of growing a crop and then digging or ploughing it in to the soil, or else just cutting or pulling the crop, and throwing it down on top of the soil. This latter form of green manuring is "mulching." Ultimately, the green matter will rot and the earthworms will drag it down into the soil in their indefatigable manner. If you dig in green manure crops you should do it at least three weeks before you sow the next crop on top of them. The only way round this is to add plenty of available nitrogen to help to rot down the green manure without it robbing the soil.

Green manuring improves the quality of the soil because the vegetable matter rots down into humus. The amount of humus added by an apparently heavy crop of green manure is smaller than you might think, but the great value of such crops is that they take up the free nitrogen in the soil. Bare soil would lose this nitrogen to the air, whereas the green crop retains nitrogen and only releases it when it has rotted, by which time the subsequent crop should be ready to use it.

It should be the aim of the organic gardener to keep as much of his land as possible covered with plants. Bare soil should be anathema unless for a very good reason it has to be bare temporarily. The old gardener's idea of "turning up land rough in the autumn to let the frosts get in it in the winter" has not proved a very good one.

Using weeds

Even weeds can be a green manure crop. If weeds grow, pull them out and let them rot, either on the surface or dug in. But don't let them seed. For one thing, "one year's seeding is seven years weeding," and for another, all green manure crops should be cut or pulled at the flowering stage, or earlier, when their growth is young, succulent, and high in protein. They then have enough nitrogen in them to provide for their own rotting down.

So look upon annual weeds as friends provided you can keep them under control. Perennial weeds (weeds that go on from year to year) should not be tolerated at any cost. They will do you nothing but harm, and will ultimately beat you if you don't beat them. I would make an exception with nettles, and also bracken. If you grow these two crops on otherwise waste land you can cut them and add them to the compost heap. They will do great good, as they are both deep rooting and thus full of material they have brought up from below.

Planting green manure

Green manure crops can be divided into winter and summer crops, and legumes and non-legumes. People with small gardens will find winter crops more useful than summer ones, for the simple reason that they will need every inch of space in summer for growing food crops. Legumes make better green manure than non-legumes, because they have bacteria at their roots which take nitrogen from the air, and this is added to the soil when they rot.

Grazing rye

Of winter green manuring crops grazing rye is probably the best. It can be broadcast at a rate of 2 oz (56g) of seed per square yard (0.8 square metre) after early potatoes have been lifted. Rake the seed in, leave it to grow all winter and then dig it in during spring. You can plant grazing rye as late as October, although you won't get such a heavy crop.

Comfrey

Comfrey is a fine perennial to grow for either green manuring or compost. Plant root cuttings from existing plants two feet (0.6m) apart in really weed-clear land in spring and just let it grow. The roots will go down into the soil as far as there is soil for them to penetrate and they will exist for a decade giving heavy yields of highly nitrogenous material, rich in potash, phosphate, and other minerals too. Over sixty tons an acre of greenstuff has been achieved, although this was probably in response to heavy manuring. Still, you might well get forty tons, and forty tons of comfrey yields about four tons of good compost, and when dug in, it makes magnificent green manure.

Other green manure and compost crops

Tares are legumes and winter crops and are therefore doubly valuable. They can be sown from August to October, and dug in next spring. As a summer crop, they can be sown any time in the spring and dug in when in flower. Mustard is a much-used green manure crop, which is sown after early potatoes are lifted. Give the dug-over ground a good raking, broadcast the seed lightly and rake it in. Dig the crop into the ground as soon as the first flowers appear. Red clover seeds are expensive but it is a fine bulky nitrogen-rich legume, which can be sown after early potatoes and dug in in the autumn. If you plant some in the spring for the purpose of keeping seed you will save having to buy any. Lupins are a large legume. Put the seeds in at six inch (15cm) intervals both ways in the spring or early summer. Here again you can save your own seed. *Tagetes minuta* is a kind of giant marigold, and is an interesting crop to plant for compost material. It grows ten feet (3m) high and has two marvellous effects. It kills eel-worm, and it wipes out ground elder and bindweed. It even suppresses to some extent the hideous couch grass or spear grass, which is the scourge of many gardens. It is too tough to be dug in as green manure and should be composted. Sunflowers make bulky compost material. The seed is planted half an inch (1cm) deep and one foot (30cm) apart both ways in the spring, and cut when it is in flower.

The Gardener's Tools

Spade A good spade, kept clean and put away after use, is essential for inverting the soil and digging in manure.

Fork The garden fork is a marvellous instrument, and many experienced gardeners use it more often than the spade. With it you can loosen up the soil, very quickly, without inverting it, incorporate compost or manure with the first few inches and fork out roots of creeping weeds like couch grass. It is also essential for digging up spuds.

Hoe There are two main types of hoe. There is the ordinary hoe, and what the English call the Dutch hoe. The former is for pulling through the soil and the latter is for pushing. The ordinary hoe is much faster, goes deeper and can tackle tougher weeds. The Dutch hoe has the advantage that you walk backwards when you use it, and so leave the ground free of footprints. For people who really have some hoeing to do, and must get on with it, I would always recommend the ordinary hoe.

Rake A rake, preferably a large steel one, is essential for raking down fine seed beds and for covering seed.

Wheelbarrow A wheelbarrow is necessary in anything bigger than a very small town garden. The old-fashioned wooden wheelbarrow, with a wooden wheel and a removable top on which light bulky loads could be carried, was a splendid and beautiful vehicle, and much better than the low steel builder's wheelbarrow sold everywhere nowadays.

Watering can Get a big galvanized iron watering can and not a streamlined plastic one that won't last five minutes.

Trowel You will need a trowel for setting out plants.

Dibber A dibber can be made by cutting down a broken spade or fork handle. You will need it for setting out smaller plants and seedlings.

Secateurs Secateurs are very useful for pruning. They are much quicker and also kinder to the plants than a knife, and they are also useful for severing chickens' neckbones when you are gutting them.

Garden line A garden line which is a light cord, rather than a string which gets tangled up, should be kept on an iron or wooden reel on which it can be wound up. This may seem a luxury, but it is very useful for getting your rows of vegetables straight.

Wheel-hoe Small wheeled tools can be a real help. A wheel-hoe is most useful; it is the equivalent of the horse-hoe in the fields. You push it up and down between the rows. This means, of course, that you still have to hand-hoe in

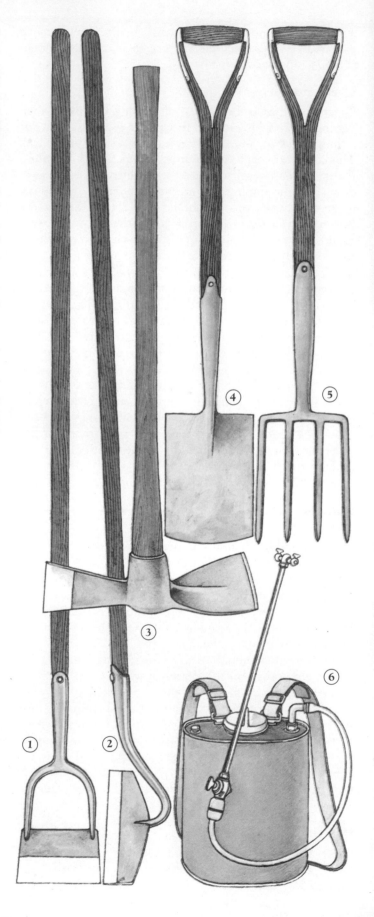

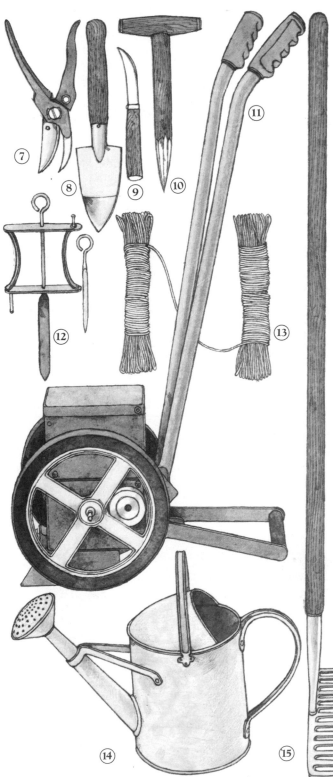

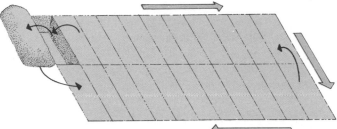

Digging

Dig a furrow at one end of your bed, and fill it with soil from the furrow you dig next. Proceed in this way to the end; then fill the last furrow with the spare soil from the first. Or split your bed and dig down one side and back the other. You then have spare soil near the empty furrow.

Before you start digging, mark off the plot to be dug with a garden line. Score a light furrow along the line and then dig your trench a foot (30 cm) wide and a spade's depth (or spit) deep.

When digging break up the earth properly, don't just turn it over on itself. Thrust your spade vertically into the ground, and with a neat twist flick the soil over into the next trench.

the rows, between the plants. There is a technique of planting such things as the larger brassica (Brussels sprouts etc), maize, and potatoes in squares, so that you can wheel-hoe both ways, at right angles. Don't be misled into thinking that you can really plough with the "plough" attachment of these instruments. It is just for scoring a small furrow to drop seeds in and it is very useful.

Drills There is a great variety of small wheeled drills on the market. Most of them just agitate the seed until it falls down through a spout which drops it below the surface of the ground. There are precision drills, however, which pick seeds up one at a time and drop them at exactly the right intervals. These are expensive, and not justified in a small garden, but on a market garden scale are well worthwhile. They save seed, and also save work thinning later. However, they won't handle all seed, and some kinds have to be "pelleted". You can buy seed already pelleted so it can be picked out by the selector mechanism of a precision drill. This seed is expensive, but you save if you use a lot.

Garden tools

1 *Dutch hoe*	8 *Trowel*
2 *Draw hoe*	9 *Pruning knife*
3 *Mattock*	10 *Dibber*
4 *Spade*	11 *Precision drill*
5 *Fork*	12 *Garden reel*
6 *Knapsack (pressure) sprayer*	13 *Garden line*
7 *Secateurs*	14 *Watering can*
	15 *Rake*

Sowing & Planting

Some people are said to have "green fingers", meaning that when they plant a seed or a plant or a tree, it grows. I suspect that this mysterious power is merely common sense and sympathy. Sympathy for the new life that you are helping to nurture. After all what does a seed want? Moisture, warmth and soil friable enough for its shoot to grow upwards and its roots downwards. This soil should be in close contact with the seed, and there shouldn't be too much soil between the seed and the light, as the plant's growth depends on the energy collected from the sun by photo-synthesis in its green leaves. This energy takes over from the energy stored in the seed when that is exhausted, and helps to protect the plant from its enemies.

Plants vary in their requirements, of course, but broadly speaking, there are two ways to establish vegetables. One is by sowing the seed direct into the ground where it is going to stay. The other is by sowing it somewhere else, and then in due course transplanting. And there are even occasions when we transplant the plants from where we sowed the seed into another bed, leave them there to grow for a while, and then transplant them again into their final bed. There are two quite sensible reasons for this seemingly laborious and time-consuming procedure.

First, by crowding the seed in a seed bed, we release the land that the plants will ultimately take up, and can use it for another, earlier crop. So nearly all our brassica (cabbage-tribe), our leeks, and those other plants that will grow through the autumn and possibly part of the winter, occupy very little ground for the first half of the summer. Then we put them in ground vacated by earlier crops, such as early spuds or peas, and so we get two crops off the land in one year. The second reason for transplanting is to give seeds a good start.

This is done by sowing seeds in a seed bed, but under glass, plastic or some other covering. This way we who live in temperate climates can start them earlier and give them an initial boost, so that they will come to harvest during our short summer. After all, many of our vegetable crops were evolved for warmer climes than the ones we grow them in.

Peat pots

There are certain crops which respond far better to being grown in peat pots before they are transplanted, rather than in flats or seed boxes. These are crops which don't like having their roots interfered with. When you plant the peat pot direct in the ground the roots will simply drive their way through the wet peat and the plant won't suffer. Maize, melons, squashes, and many other semi-hardy plants benefit from this treatment.

Soil for seed boxes

The sort of soil you put in your flats, or seed boxes, or pots, or whatever, is very important. If you just put ordinary topsoil in it will tend to crack, and dry out, and it will have insects and disease organisms in it that may flourish in the hot air of the greenhouse. This won't give you very good results.

If you can get, and afford, prepared potting composts such as the John Innes range, then get them. The expense is justified by results. These composts are carefully blended and well sterilized. If you can't, or don't want to buy them, you will have to manufacture potting composts of your own.

The fundamental ingredients of the John Innes composts are loam, peat and sand. You can make the loam by digging top quality meadow turves and stacking them, grass-side down, with a sprinkling of good compost or farmyard manure

Sowing
Fork over the ground. Mark out the rows, and stretch a garden line along each one. Drive a drill with a draw hoe at a suitable depth.

Sprinkle tiny seeds thinly. Large seeds like peas and beans should be planted at regular intervals, usually recommended by the seedsman. Water them gently.

When you have finished sowing, rake the bed all over, so that the entire surface becomes a fine tilth. This top layer of crumbly soil is the most important feature.

After you have raked the soil, tread it firmly with your feet or with the base of the rake. This ensures that the seeds are in close contact with the earth.

in between each layer of turves. Stack them in six foot layers, and leave them for from six months to a year. The loam should be sterilized. This is best done by passing steam through it. Put the loam in any container with holes in the bottom and place it over a vessel of boiling water. This will sterilize it.

Peat can be bought in bales, or it can be dug from a peat bog, and then sterilized by simply boiling it in water.

John Innes seed compost, for putting in flats or seed boxes, is, by volume: 2 parts sterilized loam; 1 part sterilized peat; 1 part coarse sand. To each bushel (25.4 kg) of the above add $1\frac{1}{2}$ oz (42 g) superphosphate of lime and $\frac{3}{4}$ oz (21 g) of ground chalk or ground limestone.

John Innes potting compost is by volume: 7 parts sterilized loam; 3 parts sterilized peat; 2 parts coarse sand. To each bushel (25.4 kg) add $\frac{1}{4}$ lb (114 g) of John Innes base fertilizer and $\frac{3}{4}$ oz (21 g) ground chalk or limestone.

And John Innes base fertilizer is by weight: 2 parts hoof and horn meal; 2 parts superphosphate of lime; 1 part sulphate of potash.

Transplanting

The same qualities are needed for transplanting a growing plant successfully as are needed for sowing seed: sympathy and common sense. Consider what a trauma transplantation must be for a plant, which is a life form evolved for growing all its life in one place. It is wrenched out of the ground, and most of the friendly earth is shaken from its tender roots which themselves are probably severely damaged. Then it is shoved roughly into some alien soil, possibly with much of its root system not in contact with the soil at all and the rest jammed together into a matted ball. It is quite amazing that trans-planted seedlings ever survive, let alone grow into mature plants.

So dig plants out gently and be sure that as much soil adheres to their roots as possible. Transplant them as gently as possible into friable soil with their roots spread naturally as they were before. Make sure the soil is well firmed, but not roughly trampled so as to break off tender roots. Then water them well. "Puddling" transplants, which means completely saturating them, is nearly always a good idea. It is drying out that kills most transplants. Of course, if we have hundreds or thousands of brassica to plant, we can't be too particular. We are forced by sheer pressure to bang them in pretty quickly, but even then it is surprising how one person will have a hundred percent success with his plantings, while another has many failures.

Putting the plant in

Plant when it is raining if you can, or when rain is promised. Put large plants in with a trowel and smaller ones with a dibber, which is basically a pointed stick. Farm labourers transplanting thousands of brassica plants go along at a slow walking pace, jabbing the dibber in beside the plant and then moving the dibber over towards it to jam the earth tight around its roots. If a moderate tug on the plant doesn't pull it out, it will be all right.

With larger or more delicate plants, such as tomatoes, broad beans (if you really have to transplant them) or sweet corn, keep a ball of soil on the roots and very carefully place them in a hole dug with a trowel. Then firm the soil around them. If you have grown them in pots, carry them in the pots to their planting station. Water them well, then take them gently out of the pots immediately before you place them in the ground.

Planting
Crowd seeds into a seed box, so that the land where they will eventually grow can bear another early crop in the meantime.

Alternatively you can plant your seeds in pots. As the seedlings grow thin them out to allow the strongest seedlings more room for their roots to develop.

When the seedlings of your first seed box look overcrowded, it is time to prick them out. This means thinning and removing to a box or bed where they have room to grow.

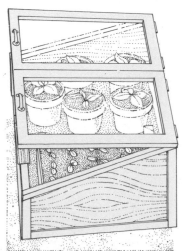

Give your seeds a good start by putting them, in pots or seed boxes, under glass. They will grow and thrive earlier than they would if left in the open air.

Growing under Cover

You can get a greenhouse which has an interior like a space module about to make a landing on the moon, with thermostats, propagators, electric fumigators and hell knows what. But if you buy this sort of equipment you are spending the money that would buy you out-of-season vegetables at the nearest greengrocers for many decades. Consider: is it really worthwhile going to great trouble and expense in order to have some vegetable or fruit ready a fortnight earlier than you would otherwise? If you are growing for market, the answer is yes.

Greenhouse production – or intensive cloche production – for sale is a very sensible and valid way of making the small amount of money that every self-supporter must have to conduct his limited trade with the rest of the world. I write books, my neighbour gives piano lessons, another makes wooden articles. If anyone wants to make under-glass cultivation his money-spinning enterprise he must get some good specialist books on the subject, which is a very complex one, and requires a great deal of knowledge to make the difference between success and complete, expensive failure.

But unless the self-supporter intends to make greenhouse production a main item of foreign exchange or money-earning, only the simplest of greenhouses is justified, with maybe some cold frames, "hot frames," or a variety of cloches. You can buy your greenhouse ready-made or build it yourself. Buying the frames with glass in them is often the best thing, for you can then build your own lean-to greenhouse. See pp. 172-173 for more details.

Cold frames

If you make four low walls and put a pane of glass on them, sloping to face the sun, you have a frame. The walls can be made of wood, bricks, concrete blocks, rammed earth, what you will. The glass must be set in wooden frames so that it can be raised or lowered. Frames are fine for forcing on early lettuces and cabbages, for growing cucumbers later in the summer, or for melons and all sorts of other things. Most of them are too low for tomatoes.

Hot frames

These are much used by the skilful French market gardeners, and are a fine and economical way to force on early plants, but they do need skill. You make a "hot bed." This is a pile of partly-rotted farmyard manure or compost. The best is stable manure: horse shit mixed with straw, mixed with an equal part of leaves or other composting material so it won't be too hot. Turn this a couple of times until the first intense heat of fermenting has gone off along with the strong smell of ammonia, then lay it down in your frame with a shallower layer of earth on top. Manure two and a half feet (76cm) deep with a foot (30cm) of soil over it is appropriate. The seed should be put in when the temperature falls to about 80°F (27°C). You can transplant plants into the bed. You would of course be doing this in the late winter or early

spring, and so as the hot bed cools the spring advances, and the heat of the sun replaces the heat of the manure, which will have gone by the time you no longer need it. You will then have lovely well-rotted horse manure.

Growing in a hot frame is not as easy as it sounds, but if you get the procedure right it is highly effective. It is sad that it is not used more often. Maybe as heating greenhouses with oil and electricity becomes more expensive it will be. Of course – you must first find your horse. A well-made compost heap with some activator will work too.

Cloches

The first cloches were bell-shaped glass bowls, and were much used in France. They were simply inverted over the plants to be forced. These were replaced by continuous cloches, which are tent or barn-shaped glass sheds placed end to end to form long tunnels. These are much cheaper, which is a good thing, because if you are half as clumsy as

Hot frame
Enough heat to last from late winter right through spring comes from a thick layer of decomposing manure or compost. Cover with a layer of soil.

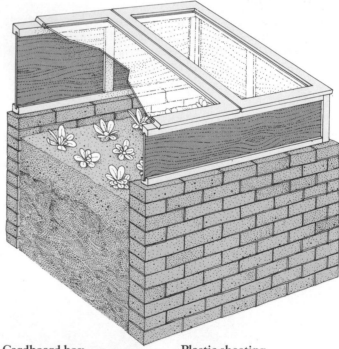

Cardboard box
A cardboard box painted black absorbs the sun's heat and aids germination.

Plastic sheeting
A transparent plastic sheet will help germination and force on early vegetables.

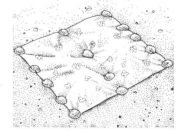

I am your cloche-managing career will be incessantly punctuated by the merry tinkling sound of breaking glass. If I just look at a glass cloche it falls to pieces, so when you reflect that you have got to hoe round crops, hand-weed, water (very necessary for crops under cloches as they do not get the rain), thin, inspect and harvest, and that the cloches have to keep coming off and going back on every time you do one of these operations, you will realize that cloche-mortality can be very high.

Polythene tunnels supported by inverted U-shaped wires were the next development. They don't shatter, but can very easily be blown away in a gale, and blown to pieces. However, they do work, and many people use them now; many market gardeners have them on a large scale. Getting them on and off enormously increases the labour involved in growing a crop, but harvesting a fortnight early may well make the difference between profit and loss. PVC by the way retains the heat more efficiently than polythene, but is more expen-

sive. And don't neglect the humble jam-jar! One of these inverted over an early-sown seed or plant of some tender species will protect it as well as any cloche. A sheet of any transparent plastic spread on the ground and weighted down on the edges with earth is fine for forcing on early potatoes and so on. When you do this sort of thing you must be careful to "harden off" the plants sensibly and gradually.

Propagators

You can use a propagator to get very early seeds going. This is an enclosed glass box with soil in it and under-soil electric heating. It produces the condition known as "warm feet but cold head" which many plants like. Tomato seed can be germinated in one of these in January in a temperate climate, but the air above it must be kept at 45°F (7°C) at least, as well as the soil being warm. A propagator is probably a worthwhile investment if you have electricity, and the time and skill to grow your own tomato plants from seed.

Cloches and a cold frame
Four walls with glass across them make a cold frame (top right). Cloches are portable and there are innumerable types: (left to right) hard plastic cloche; glass barn cloche; soft plastic tunnel cloche; simple corrugated plastic cloche; glass tent cloche.

Protecting from Pests

The weeds that grow so merrily in our gardens, in defiance of all our efforts to wipe them out, are tough organisms, and well adapted to protect themselves from most enemies and diseases. They wouldn't be there otherwise. But our crops have evolved gradually through artificial selection so as to be succulent, good to eat, and productive of high yields. As a result, their natural toughness and immunity against pests and diseases have often been sacrificed to other qualities. We must therefore protect them instead. However, avoiding attack by pests and diseases is not so easy. In fact it presents a great problem.

If you observe the principles of good husbandry, by putting plenty of animal manure or compost on the land, and by keeping to strict crop rotations (never grow the same annual crop on a piece of land two years running, and always leave the longest possible gap between two crops of the same plant), you will avoid many troubles.

You will always get pests and diseases but they will not reach serious proportions. An organic farmer I know who farms a thousand acres with never an ounce of chemicals, and whose yields for every crop he grows are well above the national average, says that in his wheat he can show you examples of every wheat disease there is, but never enough of any one for it to make the slightest difference to his yield.

A highly diversified floral and faunal environment makes for balance between species: plenty of predators of various sorts kill the pests before they get out of hand. Destroy all forms of life with poisonous chemicals and you will destroy all the predators too, so that when you do get a plague of some pest there will be no natural control, and you will be forced to use chemicals again. All the same, no matter how organically you farm, there are times when some pest or disease gets the upper hand, and when something must be done if you are not to lose the crop.

Work with nature, not against it.

Nasturtiums *repel cucumber beetle and Mexican bean beetle.*

Toads *will eat nasties such as slugs, aphids and mosquitoes.*

Thrushes *eat snails which would otherwise damage your plants.*

Hedgehogs *eat pests including millipedes that like potatoes.*

Mint *with its smell keeps white fly from beans.*

Lacewings *and their larvae destroy aphids.*

Centipedes *eat slugs' eggs and are the gardener's friend.*

Ladybirds *aren't just pretty. They consume aphids by the thousand.*

Chemical pest control

Orthodox gardeners will say use poison. You can indeed use some poison, and maybe sometimes you will have to; but surely it is far better and more skilful gardening practice to save your crops without using poison? Any fool can keep disease at bay simply by dousing his crop with chemicals, but what of the effect on other, benign, forms of life? If a chemical is poisonous to one thing you can be certain it will be poisonous to other forms of life too, and that includes human life: it will do damage even if it doesn't kill.

The only chemicals I use are Bordeaux Mixture (see p. 87) against blight in potatoes, various poisoned baits against slugs, and derris or pyrethrum or a mixture of both against caterpillars and green or black fly. Derris and pyrethrum are both derived from plants, are non-persistent, and harmless to any non-insect. I have tried calamine (mercuric chloride) against club-root but it was ineffective.

Simple methods of protection
Young plants and bushes need protection from birds. Four sticks and some soft netting can cage in a growing bush. Cover seedlings with wire netting stretched across hoops, or with a mesh of string wound on wooden pegs.

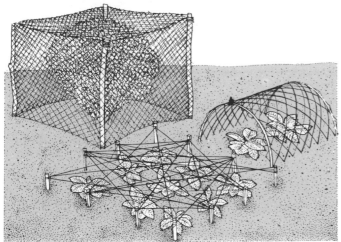

Intercropping works wonders. Carrots and onions, for example, repel each other's enemies.

Strips of sand soaked in paraffin between rows of onions will deter onion fly.

A piece of rhubarb under a brassica seedling frightens off club-root.

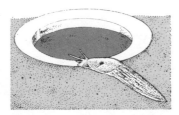

Slugs like beer. Trap them by sinking a saucerful in the earth.

Biological pest control

Very little research has so far been done into natural, or biological, means of defence, simply because there is no money to be made out of doing such research. No big company will look into ways of controlling pests and diseases which aren't going to make it any profit, and which will even operate against the profits it already makes by selling poisonous chemicals.

Lawrence D. Hills of the Henry Doubleday Association in Bocking, Braintree, Essex, England, with voluntary assistants all over the world, has in fact done some research into biological methods of pest and disease control. Many of these are merely confirmations of old and tried methods that have been used by countrymen for centuries, but some are quite new. The Association sells a little book called *Pest Control without Poisons* which is very useful. Here are some tips from it (and from other sources):

Tie sacking strips or corrugated cardboard round fruit trees in late summer and then burn complete with weevils, codling moth grubs and other nasties.

Put a very good old-fashioned grease-band around tree boles to catch nasties coming up. Most predators fly.

Cut off all dead wood from stone fruits in early summer and burn as a guard against silverleaf and die-back.

Spray winter wash on fruit trees in winter. This should only be done if needed, for it kills useful predators as well as nasties. There are many proprietary brands of winter or "tar" wash.

Use plenty of potash to prevent chocolate-spot in beans. Grow winter-sown broad beans instead of spring-sown to avoid blackfly. Pick out (and cook and eat!) the tips of broad-bean plants at the first sign of aphis attack.

Avoid carrot fly by interplanting with onions. The smell of the one is said to "jam" the smell of the other; thus you avoid both carrot and onion fly. Putting sand soaked with paraffin around carrot or onion rows is probably a better preventative. Onions from "sets" are less likely to get fly than onions from seed.

Rigorously get rid of every brassica weed such as charlock and shepherd's purse so as not to harbour club-root.

Drop bits of rhubarb down each hole before you plant out brassica seedlings, or better still, water seed beds and seedlings with rhubarb-water. The smell of the rhubarb is said to deter the club-root organism. This is an old remedy but I have never tried it.

Sink basins full of beer into the ground to trap slugs. Or save the beer and use milk and water instead.

My own experience with pests and diseases is that, except for potato blight if you don't spray, occasional plagues of caterpillars on brassicas, and occasional aphis or greenfly and blackfly attacks, there is no need to worry as long as you obey the laws of good organic husbandry which are nature's laws. A few pests on healthy crops do very little harm – certainly not enough to worry about.

Vegetables

If you grow just a few of the vegetables listed below you can eat your own fresh vegetables from early spring to late autumn. And if you grow the right things and store them (see p. 182), or if you set yourself up with a greenhouse (see p. 172) you can have your own vegetables the year round, and need never again suffer a flabby bought lettuce or a tasteless tomato in your own home.

ARTICHOKES
Globe artichokes

Use Globe artichokes are perennials and therefore a long-term proposition. I would not recommend them as the crop to feed a hungry world, but the object of the self-supporter should be to live a rich and varied life and part of this must be a rich and varied diet. Basically globe artichokes are huge thistles, and what we eat are the flower heads, and not even all of these, but just the little bit at the base of each prickly petal, and the *heart*, which lies under the tuft of prickles that are immature petals, and is delicious beyond description. Boil the whole flowers and eat with butter or oil and vinegar.

Sowing In spring plant suckers from an existing plant, each with a piece of heel of the old plant attached. Plant them four inches (10 cm) deep in good well-manured well-drained soil at three foot (91 cm) intervals.
After care Keep them well hoed.
Harvesting Spare the first year, pluck the heads the second and each ensuing year. After five or six years dig out and plant a new row somewhere else. If you plant a new row every year and scrap an old one you will never have a gap with no artichokes. Muck well every year and cover in the winter with a thick mulch of straw.

Cardoons

Use Cardoons are exactly like globe artichokes, except that they are annuals and they have slightly smaller flowers. The flowers can be eaten like globe artichoke flowers but cardoons are really grown for earthing up in the spring so that you can eat the stems like celery.
Planting Plant from seed, which is generally sown in a greenhouse in spring and then pricked out a fortnight after the last frost.

Jerusalem artichokes

Use A useful standby in winter time as a substitute for potato. They can be lightly boiled or fried in slices. They have absolutely nothing to do with globe artichokes or Jerusalem.
Planting Like potatoes, the Jerusalem artichoke grows from tubers planted in early spring. They are very easy to grow, and need only a little extra lime if your soil requires it. They are rarely attacked by pests.
After care Hoe until the foliage is dense enough to suppress weeds.
Harvesting Dig them up as you need them. They can be left in the ground throughout the winter. Save a few mature tubers to plant next year.

ASPARAGUS

Use Asparagus are perennial vegetables, so once they are planted they can't be moved each year. They take three years to get established, but it is well worth waiting. They come very early – just when you need them – and are delicious and nutritious, perhaps one of the most valuable crops you can grow. Do not be put off by any stupid puritanical ideas that this is a luxury crop and therefore somehow sinful. It is nourishing, delicious, and comes just when you don't have anything else.

Soil They like a deep light loamy fertile soil but above all it must be well drained. They will grow on sand as long as it has plenty of muck. Make absolutely sure there are no perennial weeds in your future asparagus bed: couch grass or ground-elder can ruin a bed, because they cannot be eliminated once the asparagus begins to grow. The roots get inextricably intertwined. People always used to have raised beds for asparagus, but nowadays some people plant in single or double rows. It doesn't really matter. I like a raised bed with three rows of plants, and as the years go on the bed tends to get higher because I put so much stuff on it. It is a good plan to cover it thickly with seaweed in the autumn. If it hasn't rotted down by spring take it off and compost it.
Sowing Muck really heavily in the autumn, buy or beg three-year old plants in spring and plant them eighteen inches (46 cm) apart measuring from their middles. The plants look like large spiders. Don't let them dry out before you plant them, and most important, pile a few inches of soil on top of them. Make sure the soil does not dry out, and keep weeding the bed. Don't let any weed live.
Treatment Don't cut any asparagus the first year: not a single stick. In late autumn cut the ferns down to the ground, and muck well again. The following spring you can feed well with fish meal, mature chicken dung, seaweed, or salt (yes salt – asparagus is a sea-plant), and weed again. That second year you may just have a feed or two but delay cutting until June. Muck again in the late autumn, and feed again in the spring.
Harvesting The third year when the shoots look like asparagus shoots, cut them just below the ground. You can cut away fresh asparagus ready to eat every two or three days. They soon shoot up again, and you can go on cutting until the third week in June and then stop. No more cutting, and by then you will have plenty of other green things to eat anyway. Let the tall ferns come up again, cut them down in the late autumn to confound the asparagus beetle by destroying their eggs. Then, muck them, or feed them, or both, for these are lime and phosphate-hungry plants and like plenty of humus.

AUBERGINE OR EGG PLANT

Use Aubergines have, in recent years, become more popular in Britain. They can be used for exotic dishes like moussaka and ratatouille.
Sowing Sow aubergine seeds indoors in early spring. Sow them in compost and try to keep the temperature close to 60°F (16°C). Pot out into peat pots or soil blocks about a month later.

Planting Plant them out in the open in early summer. Protect them with cloches if you live in a cool climate. When you plant them pinch out the growing points to make them branch. Or you *can* sow seeds out in your garden under cloches in late spring and still get a late crop.
Harvesting Pick them when they are a deep purple and glossy. Pick before frost sets in.

BEETROOT

Use Beetroot is a very rich source of betain, which is one of the B vitamins. Beetroot therefore keeps you healthy, particularly if you grate it and eat it raw, but it tastes a hell of a lot better cooked, although tiny immature beet are good raw.

Soil Beetroot likes light deep loam, but most soil will do.
Treatment It doesn't like freshly manured land, and wants a good fine seed bed.
Sowing Sow the main-crop in early summer, very thinly, a couple of seeds every six inches (15 cm). The seeds are multiple ones and you will have to thin anyway. Sow an inch deep (2.5 cm) in rows a foot (30 cm) apart.
After care Thin and hoe. You can eat the thinnings raw in salads.

Harvesting You can leave them in the ground until they are needed, or else until the heavy frosts set in. Or you can lift them in autumn. Twist (don't cut) the tops off, and not too near the roots, or they will bleed. Clamp, or store in sand in a cool cellar.

BROAD BEANS

Use You can pick off the tops of autumn-sown broad beans and cook them. You can eat the seeds when they are green, which is their main use. Or you can dry them for winter. It is best to rub the skins off winter-dried beans to make them more tender.

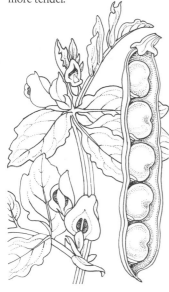

Soil They will grow in most soil.
Treatment Treat the same as you would peas (see below). Lime well and use plenty of mulch.
Sowing I like to sow broad beans in late autumn, but then the climate here is fairly moderate. If the weather got intensely cold it might nip them off but it never has yet, although once or twice in severe frost they have looked pretty sick. They perk up again though. If winter is too severe, or if you haven't been able to get seed in in the autumn, you can plant in early spring on light well-drained soil. The later you sow the more trouble you are likely to have from black-fly. Sow three inches (8 cm) deep, each seed eight inches (20 cm) from the next, in two rows eight inches (20 cm) apart. Common sense will tell you to stagger the seed in the rows. Each pair of rows should be at least two foot six (76 cm) away from the next pair.
After care In the spring, just as soon as the black-fly attack, as they inevitably will, pick the tender tops off and eat them. Hoe of course.

Harvesting Pick them as they are ready. Go on picking as hard as you can, and dry any that are left after the summer.

BROCCOLI
Hearting broccoli or winter cauliflower

Use Hearting broccoli are like cauliflower. They are a damned good winter and early spring standby, and you can have heads from late summer one year until early summer the next if you plant successionally and use a number of different varieties.

Soil They like good, heavy, firm soil, but will grow in most soil as long as it is well manured.
Treatment Like all brassica, broccoli needs lime and doesn't like acid soil. It likes deeply cultivated, but very firm soil.
Sowing Start sowing in seed beds in late spring and go on for four or five weeks.
Planting Plant out as soon as the plants are ready and you have the ground. Seedlings are ready when they are a few inches high and have made *at least* four leaves. Plant two feet (61 cm) apart in rows two feet six inches (76 cm) apart.
After care Hoe regularly until the weeds stop growing in the autumn.
Harvesting Autumn varieties can be cut in September and October; winter varieties from January to March; spring varieties up to April. To get late heads protect the curds (the white cauliflower heads) by bending leaves over them. Always cut when ripe,

and don't boil, just steam lightly. (Don't "steam launder" any brassica as hospital kitchens and private schools do. This boils the life out of them.) Steam lightly until soft but still firm.

Sprouting broccoli, purple or green.

Use These are quite different from hearting broccoli. Purple sprouting broccoli is very hardy and therefore the great standby in late winter and early spring when there is not much else about. Green broccoli or calabrese is a delicious vegetable for autumn use.
Treatment This is the same as for hearting broccoli (see above), except that green broccoli is planted in midsummer. You pick and eat the purple or green shoots when they appear. Leave the leaves until the very last and then eat them too.

BRUSSELS SPROUTS

Use Sprouts are the most useful and delicious winter green vegetable. You simply cannot have too many of them.

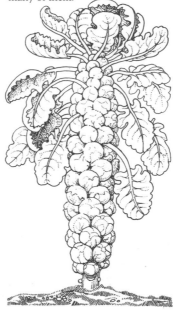

Soil They like deeply worked rich loam, but they will give a crop in most soils as long as it is deeply worked and made very firm.
Treatment Put on compost or muck the previous autumn, or plant after a well-mucked crop. If your soil is lime deficient, plant after a limed crop.
Sowing Sow in the open in seed beds during early spring, if you want late sprouts sow again in a few weeks time.
Planting Plant out in early summer three feet (91 cm) apart in rows three feet apart (91 cm). It is

useful, especially in windy places, to give each plant a stake so that it can be supported and kept straight when it grows taller.
After care Hoe when required. "Intercrop" (plant in alternate rows) if you like with lettuce or another quick-growing catch-crop, because the spaces are wide. Keep free of slugs and caterpillars. If you didn't stake the plants in spring, in autumn earth up the stems to give support and to encourage the growth of new roots.
Harvesting Early sprouts are ready in late summer, but look on them, if you live in a reasonably temperate climate, as a winter standby. Christmas dinner without sprouts is a travesty, and they should keep you going until spring. Pick off the leaves only after they have gone yellow. Use the tops of the plants after you have picked the sprouts.

CABBAGE

Use Cabbage is the most reliable of all the brassica. It is not fussy about soil and treatment, yields a heavy crop per acre and some varieties can be stored in clamp, cellar, or sauerkraut vat. What we should do without cabbages I cannot think. There are three sorts: spring, summer and autumn, and winter.

Spring cabbage
Soil Light soil is ideal.
Treatment They like fertile soil which is not acid, and it needn't be particularly firm.
Sowing Sow during the summer in a seed bed.
Planting Plant in autumn, a foot (30 cm) apart in rows 18 inches (46 cm) apart.
After care Hoe regularly, and you can top-dress with nitrogen if you want to.
Harvesting Use as spring greens

in the hungry gap – early spring – or leave a few to heart for eating in late spring and early summer.

Summer and autumn cabbage
Soil They are not very fussy.
Treatment See Spring cabbage.
Sowing Sow in late winter in a cold frame or in spring outdoors.
Planting Plant a few where there is room in early summer.
After care See Spring cabbage.
Harvesting You don't need many cabbages in summer anyway, but pick when you feel like a change.

Winter cabbage
Soil They like a heavy loam.
Treatment See Spring cabbage.
Sowing Sow in seed beds in April and May.
Planting Plant two feet (61 cm) apart in rows two feet (61 cm) apart in midsummer.
After care Hoe regularly. Don't bother to top-dress.
Harvesting Where winters are not too severe leave them in the ground until you want them. Where there's lots of snow and ice, cut in autumn and clamp or make sauerkraut.

Red cabbage
Treat the same as Winter cabbage. Pickle or cook in oil and vinegar with spices. Cook it for some time because it is tough stuff.

CARROTS
Use Carrots have more vitamin A than anything else we are likely to grow, and in World War II it was put about that the uncanny success of British night fighter pilots was due to their huge consumption of carrots which helped them see in the dark. In fact, it was all due to radar, which the Germans knew nothing about. Carrots store well through the winter and are a most useful source of good food for the self-supporter. They can be eaten raw in salads or cooked with absolutely anything.

Soil Carrots like a deep, well-cultivated sandy loam. They grow well in very light soil, almost sand in fact.
Treatment Like most roots they fork if planted in soil which has recently been heavily manured with muck or compost, although in fact well-matured compost doesn't seem to affect them so much. Shakespeare compared Man to a forked carrot. So don't plant them after fresh muck. They don't like sour ground (a pH of about 6 is fine). The land must have been deeply dug and then worked down into a fine tilth.
Sowing There is no point in sowing carrots until the ground is dry and warm, say in the late spring. Sow very shallowly, as thinly as you can, and tamp down rows with the back of the rake afterwards. Some people sow a few radishes in with them to show where the rows are before the slower carrots emerge. Then they pull the radishes for eating when they are ready. Some people intercrop with onions, in the belief that the carrot fly are put off by the onions, and the onion fly are put off by the carrots.
After care If you sow in dry weather, it is good to water the rows to start germination. Hoe frequently and carefully so as not to damage the carrots, and hand-weed as well. Suffer not weeds to exist in your carrot rows. To get a heavy crop thin to about three inches (8 cm) apart, then harvest every other carrot so as to leave them six inches (15 cm) apart. This is best for big tough carrots for winter storing, but for summer and autumn use don't bother to thin at all. When you do thin try to do it when it is raining (to thwart the carrot fly), or if it's not raining sprinkle derris dust around the plants. After thinning draw the soil around the plants and then tamp down so the scent of bruised carrots will not attract the beastly carrot fly.
Harvesting Pull them young and tender whenever you feel like it. Lift the main crop with a fork before the first severe frost of winter, and store in sand in a cool place such as a root cellar. You can clamp (see p. 183) them but they sometimes go rotten in the clamp. Washed carrots won't keep at all whatever you do. They rot almost immediately.

CAULIFLOWER
Use Eat them in summer and autumn. Hearting broccoli are apt to take over in winter. Cauliflowers yield well, but you need skill and good land to grow them successfully. They are not a beginner's crop.

Soil They want deep, well-drained, well-cultivated soil, well manured, and with ample water. They won't grow on bad land or under bad conditions.

Treatment They must have non-acid conditions, like all brassica which means you must lime if necessary. A fortnight before planting fork on or harrow in a good dressing of fish manure or the like. They also need some potash.
Sowing They can be sown under cold glass in September or in a warm greenhouse in January or February. Sow outdoors in late spring. Plant two feet (61 cm) apart in rows two feet six (76 cm) apart.
Planting Autumn and winter sown plants go out in spring. Spring sown ones in summer.
After care Hoe of course. Make sure there is always plenty of moisture for they can't stand drought. Top-dress with nitrogen if you have any. Keep them moving, in other words, don't let them stop growing.
Harvesting Cut them when they are ready, early in the morning if possible. Don't boil them to death. They are nice boiled, then dipped in batter, fried and eaten cold.

CELERIAC
Use You can grate the big swollen roots and eat them raw. Or, you can peel and boil, or boil and then fry.

Sowing Sow, prick out and plant out just like white celery.
After care When you hoe draw

the soil away from the plants instead of earthing them up as you would for celery.
Harvesting Begin harvesting in autumn. Earth them up in the middle of November for protection against winter frost.

CELERY
White celery
Use It is said that celery is best after the first frost has been on it. If you are lucky it will keep going until a few weeks after Christmas as long as you ridge it well. It is a most delicious and useful winter vegetable whether eaten raw, as the blanched stems should be, or cooked in stews as the tops should be.

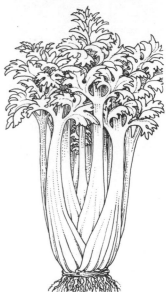

Soil It loves deep fertile soil, very moist but not swampy. The very best celery is grown in soil which is high in organic matter and retains moisture. Don't let the soil dry out.
Treatment Celery prefers acid to alkaline conditions, so never give it lime. It needs plenty of humus so dig in muck or well-rotted compost where it is going to grow.
Sowing Sow under glass at a temperature of between 60°F and 65°F (16°C and 19°C) in spring, or buy plants from a nursery. The seedlings must be kept moist. Spray them with water at least twice a day.
Planting Early summer is the usual time to plant. Plant very carefully a foot (30 cm) apart in trenches with muck underneath. Soak well with water.
After care You can grow catch-crops such as lettuce or radish on ridges between the furrows. When these catch-crops have been harvested, earth up the celery. Cut off the side shoots. Then hold the plants in a tight bunch and earth

up so only the tops of the leaves are above the new ridges. Always keep ground moist. Never let it dry out. To prevent leaf blight spray with Bordeaux Mixture (see p. 87) once or twice as you would spuds. If you want to extend the eating season in the winter protect the plants with straw, bracken, cloches, or what you will. Or you can heel them into dry ground in a protected position if you fear very hard frost. It makes harvesting difficult.

Harvesting Dig them out whenever you want them and eat them fresh.

Self blanching celery

You can grow this on the flat, in the same conditions as ordinary or white celery (see above). But you don't need to earth it up. It gets used before the white celery and must be finished before hard frosts begin as it is not frost-hardy. It is not as good to eat as white celery, but is a good standby in the autumn before white celery is ready.

CHICORY

Use Chicory makes good winter salading.

Sowing Sow the Witloof type in early summer in a fine tilth, and thin to a foot (30 cm) apart in rows 18 inches (46 cm) apart.

After care Cut down to just above the crown in November. Lift and plant in pots and keep in the dark at 50°F (10°C) or thereabouts. They will then shoot.

Harvesting Break the shoots off just before you need them. They should grow again every four weeks or so. Keep picking.

CORN SALAD

Use If you like eating salad in the winter this is an ideal crop for you.

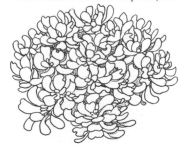

It produces leaves like tender young lettuce leaves.

Sowing Sow in drills one foot (30 cm) apart in late summer.

Harvesting Cut it when the plant is short with just three or four leaves. Don't let it get too lanky.

CUCUMBERS AND GHERKINS

Use Ridge cucumbers and gherkins, both of which are fine pickled, can be grown out of doors. Frame cucumbers, which are better looking and better tasting when fresh, are grown in frames or under cloches. A heated greenhouse is even better because you will get your cucumbers earlier.

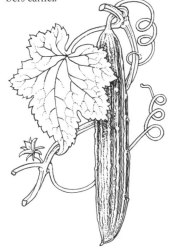

Soil Cucumbers will grow on light soil if it has plenty of manure in it. They must have plenty of moisture, and they don't like acid soil.

Treatment Dig plenty of mulch in during the previous autumn.

Sowing Frame cucumbers can be sown, under cover, in early spring. It is ideal if you can start them off in a heated greenhouse, keeping the temperature at about 60°F (16°C). Outdoor types can't be sown until early summer unless they are protected for the first month. In wet climates plant six seeds of an outdoor variety on a small hill, four inches (10 cm) high and later thin out to the three best plants on each hill. In dry climates use the same technique, but plant in a small depression that has had plenty of muck or compost dug below it the previous autumn.

Planting Outdoor cucumbers just continue to grow where you plant them. Frame cucumbers can be hardened off in early summer. If you grow cucumbers in a greenhouse, pot them in peat pots as they grow big enough to handle, then plant them, pot and all, in the greenhouse soil when they are

about to outgrow the pot. Always water them with warm water, keep the greenhouse humid and well ventilated.

After care They must have plenty of water and never be allowed to get dry. It helps to soak muck in the water. Ridge cucumbers should have all the male flowers pinched off them, so that the female flowers which produce the cucumbers don't get fertilized. If they do the fruit will be bitter. And ridge cucumbers should also have the growing points nipped out when the plant has seven true leaves.

Harvesting Pick them regularly while they are young and they will go on cropping. Pickle the last lot before the first frosts.

ENDIVES

Use A vegetable which can be eaten in winter instead of lettuce, in summer to complement it.

Sowing Sow in mid summer and put cloches over in late summer. Whitewash the cloches so as to keep out the light and the endives will blanch and make good winter salading. Blanching also helps to reduce the bitter flavour. For summer endives sow in the open from spring onwards and eat, green, in salads.

FRENCH BEANS AND DRIED BEANS

Use Haricots are ripe French beans that have been dried for winter use. Butter beans and Lima

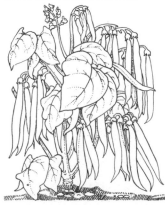

beans are specifically for drying and using in the winter. For vegetarians such dried beans are really necessary, because they are about the only source of protein readily available to them in winter time. French beans can be eaten green, pods and all, just like runner beans.

Soil They all like lightish well-drained, warm soil. It's no good trying to grow them in heavy clay or on sour land.

Treatment Like all the legumes, they grow best after a heavily mucked crop. Lime well if necessary.

Sowing Sow in early summer in a temperate climate. They are all very frost-tender, and will not thrive if sown in cold damp ground. Sow in a wide drill, about two inches (5 cm) deep, in two staggered rows, so the beans are about six inches (15 cm) apart.

After care Hoe well, and draw the soil around the plants. Dwarf varieties don't need sticking but high varieties do. Any arrangement of sticks, or wire and string supported on poles, will do.

Harvesting If the beans are for drying for the winter let them get quite ripe, then pull the plants intact and hang them upside down from the roof of an airy shed. Thresh them as required. If you are eating them green pull them and pull again. The secret of having plenty of them, young and fresh, is to keep on picking.

KALE

Use Kale is very hardy and therefore an excellent winter green standby. It will grow in cold and wet climates where there is little other greenstuff in winter and early spring. In the highlands of Scotland the "kale-yard" has often been the only source of greenstuff in winter.

Soil Kale is not at all fussy, but the richer the soil the better the crop.

Treatment See Spring cabbage.

Sowing Sow during late April and

early May in colder climes and in early April in warmer ones.

Planting It is a good idea to sow the seed *in situ* and not transplant it, but thin it instead. But you can transplant it if you need the land.

After care See Spring Cabbage.

Harvesting Leave kale until you really need it, that is after the Brussels sprouts have rotted, the cabbages are finished, the slugs have had the rest of the celery, and the ground is two-feet deep in snow and only your kale plants stand above it like ship-wrecked schooners.

LEEK

Use In cold wet areas this is one of the most useful plants, for it stands the winter and provides good food and vitamins in the months when perhaps little else has survived except kale. Onions are hard to grow and to keep, but leeks are an easy substitute. The Welsh are very sensible to have this excellent plant as an emblem and not some silly inedible flower or a damned thistle.

Soil Leeks grow on pretty well any soil as long as it is not waterlogged.

Treatment Heavy manuring is advantageous. Most people plant leeks out on land from which early potatoes have been harvested and which has been heavily mucked for that purpose. If you can't lift your earlies before mid summer however, this is too late. You must plant on other ground, which should be well dug and manured.

Sowing Sow the seed in the general seed bed, an inch (2 cm) deep in rows a foot (30 cm) apart, in spring.

Planting The traditional way to

plant leeks is to chop the bottoms off the roots and the tops off the leaves of the little plants, and just drop the plants in small holes and leave them. If you do this they grow and make leeks, but I have come to believe that this is a silly idea, and it is better not to mutilate the plants and also better to plant them properly. Why not try both methods and compare them? Draw drills three inches (8 cm) deep with a hand-hoe or a wheel-hoe and plant the leeks five inches (13 cm) apart in the furrows. Make a biggish hole for each leek and plant carefully making sure that the little roots are not doubled up. Don't press down as you would onions. Just water them in and this will wash a little loose earth into the hole round the roots.

After care Hoe them of course and ridge them, raising the ridges from time to time so as to blanch the lower parts of the stems.

Harvesting Leave them until you really need them and then, towards the end of the winter, dig them out and "heel them in" on another small piece of ground. Heeling in means opening a slot in the ground with a spade, putting the leeks in quite thickly, and heeling the earth back on their roots. They won't grow any more like this, but they will keep alive and fresh until you need them. They are very hardy and don't mind frost.

LETTUCE

Use Lettuce is the firm base of salads throughout all the fair months of the year, and with a little glass protection we can even have them through the winter if we feel we must. They are *not* a brassica so we needn't worry about club-root. Try growing different types of lettuce – some are much crisper than others.

Soil They like good soil, but will grow on most soil, especially if it

is richly manured. Lettuce likes it cool and will stand shade but will not grow well near trees. They like a moist climate.

Treatment Dig in well rotted muck or compost for summer lettuce, but not for winter, as winter lettuce doesn't like too much fresh manure: it gets botrytis. Work down to a fine seed bed.

Winter lettuce

Sowing and planting Sow about an inch (2 cm) deep in late summer and then expect to protect them with cloches or something over the winter. Of course in very cold climates winter lettuce is *out*. You can sow winter lettuce in seed beds with the intention of planting them out in early spring to get an early crop. And of course, you can get lettuces all winter in a heated greenhouse.

Summer lettuce

Sowing and planting Sow thinly starting in the spring with a foot and half (46 cm) between rows. Thin the plants out to over a foot apart, and transplant the thinnings elsewhere because they transplant easily. Don't sow too much at one time, but keep on sowing throughout the summer.

After care Hoe and hoe and water whenever necessary. Keep eating.

MARROWS, SQUASHES AND PUMPKINS

Use They can be kept for the winter, and are rich in vitamins and very nutritious.

Soil Nothing is better for these than to grow them on an old muck-heap, and that is what we often do. They love a heavy soil.

Treatment If you don't plant on a muck heap dig in plenty of muck or compost in the autumn.

Sowing Sow seeds *in situ* in late spring under cloches or, better still, under upturned jam jars. Other-

wise sow in soil blocks or peat pots under glass. Harden plants off gradually in early summer, by propping the jam jars up in the day, for example, and putting them down again at night. Remove the glass, or plant the potted plants out in the open, a few weeks later. Plant three seeds to a station and have the stations six feet (1.8 m) apart because these things like to straggle.

After care Hoe of course, water when necessary, mulch if you can and beware of slugs.

Harvesting Keep cutting them when they are young and tender and you will get more. Young marrows, or courgettes, are particularly good. In late summer leave some to ripen, and store them out of the frost in a cool place, preferably hung up in a net. In southern Africa, where you don't get too much frost, pumpkins are thrown up on corrugated iron roofs and left there all winter. They dry out in the winter sun, become delicious and form the chief winter vegetable of that part of the world.

MELONS

Use Melons grow outdoors in warm climates, and can be grown outdoors in cool climates as long as you start them off under cloches after the last frost. But they are best grown under protective frames in cooler climates.

Treatment Treat them exactly like cucumbers, but don't remove the male flowers. Plant them on small hills six feet (1.8 m) apart.

ONIONS

Use Good food is inconceivable without onions.

Soil They like medium loam well drained, deeply dug and richly composted. Onions are a demanding plant.

Treatment The soil must not be acid, so if necessary lime it in the autumn. Dig deeply in the autumn and incorporate manure or compost. Get it down to a fine tilth in the spring and then get it really firm, because firm soil is a necessity for onions to grow well.

Sowing You can sow in mid-summer, and leave in the seed bed until spring. Or you can sow in early spring, or as early as the ground is dry enough to walk on without it caking. Sow very shallowly, very thinly in rows ten inches (25 cm) apart, if you intend to thin the onions and grow them *in situ*. But you can have the rows much closer together if you intend to plant them all out. Rake the seed in very lightly and firm the soil with the head of the rake.

Planting Plant very firmly in firm soil, but don't plant too deeply. Plant summer sown seedlings in early spring – whenever the soil is dry enough. Inter-rowing with carrots is said to help against onion fly, and I believe inter-rowing with parsley is even better.

After care Growing onions means a fight against weeds which seem to love onions, and the onions have no defence against them from broad shading leaves as many crops have. Now I know that some people say onions will grow well in a mass of weeds, but my experience is that you must keep them free of weeds in the early months of their growth. It is true that if large annual weeds grow among them for, say, the last month they may still grow into good onions. I like to keep them weed-free and mulch them well with pulled-out weeds in their later stages. If you are growing onions *in situ* in the seed-bed, single them to about four inches (10 cm) apart. If you have sown very thinly you might like to try not thinning at all.

You will get smaller onions but they will keep better.

Harvesting When the tops begin to droop bend them all over to the ground. This is said to start the onions ripening, and possibly it also stops them growing up and going to seed. After a few days pull the onions and lay them down on bare soil or, better still, on a wire netting frame to keep them clear of the ground. Turn them occasionally. The more hot sun that falls on them the better. Before the autumn string them and hang them up, or hang them in net bags, or lay them on wire netting in a cool and draughty place. The air must be able to get between them. They don't mind some frost, but can't stand lack of ventilation.

Shallots
Sow the bulbs in late winter and you get lots of little onions that grow around the first bulb next summer. You can then go on picking until autumn. Keep some of the best bulbs to plant next year.

Tree onions
These onions are perennial so once you have planted them they will grow year after year. Each year, when the plant grows, little onions will form at the tips of the stems. When this happens you must support the weight of the plant on sticks. Plant six inches (15 cm) apart in rows 18 inches (46 cm) apart. You can use the onions that form underground as well as those on the leaf tips.

Pickling onions
These like poor soil. Broadcast the seed in spring and lightly rake it in. Hand weed but don't thin. Pull and pickle when ready.

Salad onions
Sow these like ordinary onions in late summer and again if you like in early spring. Don't thin, and pick to eat as required.

Onion sets
These are the lazy man's way of planting onions. Sets are immature bulbs, with their growth arrested by heat treatment. Plant them early in the spring very firmly, and re-plant any the birds pull out. Then treat them like ordinary onions. They are much easier to grow.

PARSNIPS
Use Parsnips make the best of the root wines, and, properly cooked and not just boiled to death, are a magnificent vegetable, very rich in vitamins A, B and C.

Soil They grow on any soil provided it is deep and not too stony. As with all root vegetables, don't use fresh manure.

Treatment They like potash, and the ground must be deeply dug. If you want to grow really big ones make a hole with a fold pritch, or steel bar, and fill the hole with peat and compost, or a potting compost, and sow on this.

Sowing Drill an inch (2.5 cm) deep and fourteen inches (36cm) apart, in early spring, or as soon as the land is open and dry enough. They take a long time to grow so sow some radish with them, as these declare themselves first and enable you to side-hoe.

After care You can intercrop with lettuces for one lettuce crop. Then hoe and keep clean.

Harvesting Leave them in the ground as long as you like. They are far better after they have been frosted. If you want them during hard frost, when it would be difficult to dig them out, pull them before the frost and leave them in a heap outside or in a shed. You can boil them in stews, but they are far better baked around a joint in fat, or partly boiled and then fried in slices. There are old boys in Worcestershire who devote half their gardens to rhubarb and half to parsnips. And the whole lot of both crops go to make wine!

PEAS
Use Eaten green, peas are delicious and extremely nutritious. Allowed to dry they can be kept through the winter and cooked like lentils. It is better to have fresh green peas in their season, and only then, so that you come to them every year with a fresh and unjaded palate. Freezing them is a bore.

Soil They like a medium loam but will grow on most soils. Like all legumes (and brassica) they don't like acid ground. They like to be kept moist.

Treatment If you want a bumper crop dig a trench in the autumn, fill it with muck, compost, or any old thing so long as it's organic, and bury it. Lime the soil well. Plant in what is left of the trench in the spring. But this is very laborious. Put your peas in after your spuds and your land should be well mucked already.

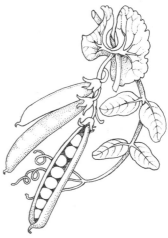

Sowing I personally sow peas thick in a little trench dug about three inches (8cm) deep with a hoe. And I eat a hell of a lot of peas. Plant each pea two or three inches (5-8cm) from its neighbour. Cover and firm the soil over the peas. It helps a lot to have soaked the peas for two or three days first to get them germinating so they sprout early. Also swill your seed in paraffin to deter mice. Birds too are a menace; wire pea-guards are an answer, and so is a good cat. You can sow some round-seeded peas in November in mild climates, and some more in February. For this the land must be light and dry. Of course if you cloche it it helps. You will thus get very early pickings, but for most of your crop sow from mid-March onwards in successional sowings right into July. For your last sowings use, paradoxically, "early" varieties. They will ripen quickly before the frosts cut them down.

After care Hoe until the pea vines themselves smother the weeds. And mulch does wonders with peas for it keeps the ground cool and moist, which is just what peas like.

Harvesting Pick them young to eat raw in salads, and then when the pods are tighter packed, pick for cooking. Keep picking as hard as you like, and if you have more than you can eat green, let them ripen on the vines and harvest properly. In other words, pull the vines when they are dead ripe (but before the autumn) and hang them up in the breeze but out of the rain. Thresh them in due course, stow them in jars, and eat them in soup.

PEPPERS

Use The peppers we can grow have nothing to do with real pepper, which is grown on vines in Malabar and marketed entirely by a strange lost race called the White Jews who have a monopoly of the trade.

Sowing and planting Sow seed indoors in early spring, and plant out in the garden on well-mucked ground at least a fortnight after the last possible frost, under cloches if you have them in cold climates. Plant two feet (60cm) apart in rows three feet (91cm) apart. After the ground has really warmed up, mulch. Peppers need moisture but not too much or they will die off. So in a wet climate plant them on the tops of ridges.
Harvesting Harvest them when they are green or leave them to turn red.

POTATOES

Use Quite simply one can live on them. They are one of the best storable sources of energy we can grow, and are our chief source of vitamin C during the winter.

Soil Potatoes like good strong soil. They will grow in clayey loam, love peat and are one of the few crops that not only tolerate but like acid soil. If you lime before planting they will get scabby. They want plenty of muck.
Treatment Better to dig deeply in the autumn and dig again in the spring, this time making ridges and furrows. They don't want a fine tilth but they want a deep one. Throw as much muck or compost as you can spare into the furrows before planting. Plant the spuds straight on top of it.
Planting Put your first earlies in when other people in your locality do, or a fortnight earlier under cloches or transparent plastic. The slightest touch of frost on the leaves blasts them and they have to start growing all over again. If you want early potatoes chit your seed potatoes, that is lay your early seed in trays, on shelves, or on old egg trays, in the light and not in the frost. 40°F to 50°F (5°C to 10°C) is right. When you plant them be careful not to knock off all the shoots. Leave two on each tuber. Don't chit the main crop. Bung them straight in in the late spring, but not before. Plant earlies only about three inches (8cm) deep, a foot (30cm) apart in rows eighteen inches apart. Plant main crop eighteen inches (46cm) apart in rows eighteen inches apart, but plant them about five inches (13cm) deep.
After care As soon as leaves show, earth up. In other words bank earth lightly over the potatoes. Three weeks later earth up some more, and with main crop earth up again in another couple of weeks. Hoe between the rows. Spray with Bordeaux Mixture (see p. 87) when the weather gets warm and muggy to prevent blight.
Harvesting If you have plenty of early potatoes in, don't deny yourself a feed or two when they are quite tiny: why should you? Then go on digging earlies until they are finished. If you have second earlies go on to them. Your main crop will then take over for immediate eating, but don't lift the bulk of the main crop until the haulms (tops) have completely withered away. Then fork them out carefully and let them lie on the ground for a day and a half to set their skins (more than two days might start them going green in which case they become poisonous). Then clamp them, or put them in a root store in the dark. They must never be allowed to be affected by frost or they will go bad.

RADISHES

Use Radishes grow just anywhere. Add them to salads for extra flavour, crunchiness and colour.

Sowing Sow the large seeds in drills and pick them when they are ripe after about six weeks. They are brassicas, but grow so quickly that they don't get, or perpetuate, club-root. Put in successional sowings all through the spring and summer so as to have a constant supply of tender young ones. Don't let them get old and go to seed.

RHUBARB

Use Rhubarb is a perennial, and once you have planted it, or inherited it, you have got it for good.

Soil Pretty well any soil is fine.
Treatment Put on plenty of muck.
Planting Buy or cadge crowns and plant them in late autumn. Leave three feet (91cm) between plants and four feet (1.2m) between rows and put some nitrogenous fertilizer on top to turn it into a self-activating compost heap. Put upturned pots or buckets over some of the plants in spring to force them on early.
After care Cover the beds with deep straw in autumn.

Harvesting Pull what you want when the stems are thick and tall. Leave what common sense will suggest, so as not to rob the plants too much.

RUNNER BEANS

Use These come later than the drying beans described earlier. They yield very heavily, are tougher and have a coarser, and I think better, flavour. They need more care in planting and must have tall sticks. Salted they are a great standby for the winter.

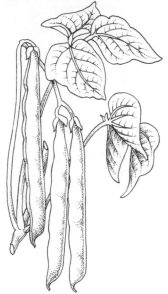

Soil They like good rich deep soil.
Treatment Double dig a deep ditch in early spring and incorporate plenty of compost or muck in the bottom of it. If you have comfrey leaves dig them in, because they are rich in potash which all beans like. As they come in your bean break you will already have limed the ground, if you had to, the previous autumn.
Sowing Sow them in the early summer in a wide but shallow trench two inches (5cm) deep in two staggered rows with the seeds nine inches (23cm) apart. Leave at least five feet (1.5m) between stands of beans. Put in tall sticks early enough for the beans to get a good start. Otherwise you can pinch the growing tops out and let the vines straggle on the ground, but you won't get much of a crop and in my opinion it's a poor way of growing these magnificent climbing plants which can be about the most beautiful and productive things in your garden.
After care Hoe of course and keep well watered in dry seasons. When they start to flower make sure they have plenty of water.

Mulch with compost if you can, and spray the flowers with water occasionally because this "sets" the flowers in the absence of rain.
Harvesting Just keep on picking. If you can't cope with the supply, and you probably can't because they crop like hell, just pick anyway. String the beans, slice them (you can buy a small gadget for this), and store them in salt (see p. 182). Pick them and give them to the pigs rather than let them get old and tough. Keep some though to get ripe for seed for next year.

SOYA BEANS
Use Soya beans have been grown in Asia for centuries. They came to the West less than 200 years ago – and are now proving to be a very worthwhile crop to grow in warm areas because of their high protein value. They do need a long, warm growing season though – at least 100 days. They can be eaten green like peas or the beans can be left to ripen and then dried for use all through the winter. The beans can be ground into flour.

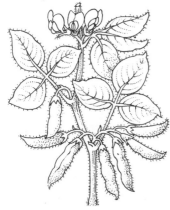

Preparation Dig the ground in autumn and add plenty of lime.
Sowing Sow in the late spring about an inch (2.5cm) deep, three inches (8cm) apart in rows two feet (61cm) away from each other.
Harvesting Pick the beans for eating green when they are young, certainly before they turn yellow. It is easier to remove the beans from the pods if they are boiled for a few minutes first. If the beans are for drying or for flour, leave them on the plants to ripen but they must be picked before the pods burst and release the beans. Judge this carefully but be guided by the colour of the stems on the plant – they should still be green.

SPINACH
Use There are several kinds of spinach, but treat them all as just spinach. There is New Zealand spinach, spinach beet, perpetual spinach, seakale beet.
Soil Like nearly everything else spinach likes a good rich loam, so give it as much muck as you can. It will do well on clay, but is apt to run to seed on sandy land unless you give it plenty of muck.

Sowing Sow an inch (2.5 cm) deep in drills a foot (30cm) apart. Later thin the plants in their rows to six inches (15 cm) apart.
After care Hoe, mulch and water during the summer.
Harvesting Pick the leaves when they are young and green, taking only a few from each plant leaving the smaller ones to grow bigger. Don't boil spinach. Wash it in water and put the wet leaves in a saucepan and heat over a fire. When you harvest seakale beet pull off the stems as well as the leaves. Eat the stems like asparagus.

SWEDES AND TURNIPS
Use Swedes and turnips can be eaten young and tender in the summer and autumn and clamped for winter use. Turnips will survive in the ground until severe frosts begin, maybe till Christmas in temperate climates. Swedes are much hardier and will live in the ground all winter. All the same it is handier to pull them and clamp them so you have them where you need them. They are cruciferous, which means they are subject to club-root, and should therefore be part of the brassica break so that this disease is not perpetuated. You want to leave the longest possible gap between crops that are prone to club-root. Kohl-rabi is much like turnip and is grown in the same way.
Soil Light fertile loam is best. Keep it well-drained, but not too dry. But turnips, particularly your main crop for storing, will grow on most soils.

Treatment In heavy rainfall areas, say over 35 inches (89cm) a year, it is a good thing to grow turnips and swedes on the tops of ridges to aid drainage. So ridge up your land with a ridging plough, or on a small scale with a spade, and drill on the ridges. If you want to grow on the flat just treat the land as you would for spring cabbages (see p. 147).
Sowing Very early sowing can be done in the early spring or a week or two before the last probable frosts, but you can sow turnips and swedes right up until August. Sow the seed shallowly in drills about nine inches (23cm) apart. Cover and press down.
After care Beware the flea-beetle. These are little jumpers that nibble tiny holes in the leaves. You can kill them by dusting with an insecticide, or you can trap them with a special little two-wheeled arrangement. The sticky underside of a board goes along just over the plants and a wire brushes the plants. The beetles jump and get stuck to the board. It sounds silly but it works. Thin to four inches (10cm) apart in the rows while they are still quite small. Hoe at least twice again afterwards.
Harvesting Eat them when they are ready (after about two months), or leave until early winter and pull, top, and clamp them.

SWEET CORN
Use Sweet corn is maize that has not been allowed to get ripe. The seeds are still fairly soft and slightly milky, and the carbohydrate is mostly in the form of sugar, which is soluble and can therefore move about the growing plant. As the cobs mature or when they are picked, the sugar changes to starch. It will grow in the hottest climates, and in temperate climates if you grow hardy varieties.

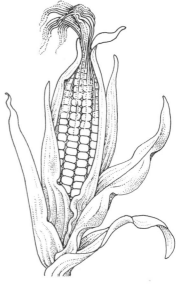

Soil Sweet corn will grow in most good well-drained soils, but it is a greedy feeder, likes plenty of muck, and a pH of about 6.5.
Sowing A long growing season is essential but sweet corn can't stand frost, so if we plant it a week or two before the last likely frost under upturned jam jars, or little tents of plastic, or cloches, so much the better. In warm climates you can sow it straight out in the open in early summer, but if your summers are a long time coming you would do better to sow it in peat pots indoors in late spring and then plant it out. Sow the seed an inch (2.5 cm) deep, fifteen inches (28 cm) apart in rows two and a half feet (76cm) apart. And try to sow in blocks, nothing narrower than four rows for example, because maize is wind-pollinated, and if it is sown in long thin lines many plants will not get pollinated.
Planting If you have grown it in pots plant it out very carefully, because it doesn't like being disturbed anyway. Plant out when it is about five inches (13cm) high and preferably plant peat pot and all. Water well after planting, but it is a lot better if you can sow them in their final position.
After care Hoe and top dress with nitrogen about a month after planting if your soil is not as rich as it should be, to keep the plants growing. Apparently the

Vegetables

Amerindians used to bury a dead fish under each plant. This is a very good idea, for the nitrogen would become available just when it was needed. I know a vet who gave all the dogs he "put down" to a fruit farmer who buried them under his newly planted apple trees for the same reason.

Harvesting Break the cobs off in the milky stage after the tassel has begun to wither and turn brown. To test, pull the leaves off part of a cob and press your thumb nail into the grain. It should be milky. They say you can walk down the garden to pick your corn, but you must run back to cook it; it must be dead fresh. This is because the sugar starts turning into starch as soon as you pick it and it loses flavour. If you have too many cobs, you can dry them in the way described on p. 182.

The straw makes good feed for cows, litter for pigs, or material for the compost heap, and it is a valuable crop for this reason alone.

SWEET POTATOES
Use Sweet potatoes can be your staple food in a dry warm climate, but you won't get much of a crop in a damp cool environment. They are very frost-tender.

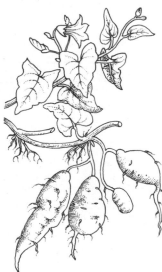

Soil They grow in sand, or sandy loam, and they don't like rich soil.
Treatment Just dig deeply. You needn't add anything.
Planting Plant tubers just like potatoes (if you are sure they haven't been sprayed with a growth-inhibitor). Plant them 16 inches (41cm) apart in rows 2 feet 6 inches (76cm) apart. Don't plant them anywhere in the world until two weeks after the last frost.
After care Just hoe.
Harvesting Dig them up very

carefully at least a fortnight before the first frost. Cure them by laying them carefully on hay and leaving them out in the sun for about ten days. They don't go green because they are no relation of real potatoes. Turn them from time to time. If there isn't enough sun keep them somewhere with 90 percent humidity between 80°F (27°C) and 90°F (32°C) for ten days. Store them packed lightly in straw in an airy place at not less than 50°F (10°C).

TOMATOES
Outdoor tomatoes
Use Outdoor tomatoes are a dicey business in any cold wet climate. What they need is a warm dry ripening season in late summer, and that is what, where I live, they don't get. But green tomatoes make famous chutney and if you store them well they sometimes get ripe in store, although they never taste like sun-warmed fruit picked off the vine and eaten straightaway. But if you can grow them they are an enormously valuable crop for bottling to keep your family healthy during the dark days of winter. They really are bottled sunshine.

Soil The soil *must* be well-drained, and in a sunny but sheltered position in cold climates.
Treatment I ridge the land in the autumn, put well-rotted compost or muck in the trenches in early spring, split the ridges over it and then plant the tomatoes on the new ridges.
Sowing The most luxurious tomatoes I ever saw growing were on the overspill of a sewage works, which leads one to think that it would be better to eat the seed before we plant it. But failing such extreme measures sow thinly under glass in John Innes seed compost, or in any equivalent seed compost, including the kind you make yourself. If you sow in the late spring

in a temperate climate the plants will grow even if you have no heat in your greenhouse, but if you do have a little heat so much the better. If you have no heat put thick newspapers over the seedlings at night to keep them warm. 55°F (12°C) is right. Water diligently with luke-warm water but not too much. Don't drown them. Or you can sow direct, *in situ*, a week or two later, under cloches in warmer climates, or just out of doors in hot climates.

Planting Most people plant twice. First, when they have three to four true tomato-type leaves they plant in either soil blocks, or peat pots, or in compost in small flowerpots. These pots can be put into cold frames and the plants gradually hardened off. Then plant out in the first fine warm weather in early summer. Plant very carefully, retaining as much of the compost on the roots as you can, and plant a little deeper than they were before. Plant on the mucked ridges described above. Give each plant a tall stake for support as it grows bigger and heavier.

After care Hoeing and mulching, within reason, help, and with low-fruiting varieties it is common sense to put clean straw on the ground to protect the fruit. Pick out all side-shoots. These are little shoots that grow between the fruiting branches and the main stem, rather as if you had another little arm growing out of your arm-pit.

You cannot pamper tomatoes too much. Water them whenever they need it. Many gardeners soak muck in the water so that they feed the plants as they water them. As they grow taller tie them carefully to the stakes with raffia or string. Spray them with Bordeaux Mixture to protect them from potato blight. (The tomato is so closely related to the potato that it is almost the same plant.) Don't touch them with tobacco-stained hands, because you can convey tobacco virus disease to them. (The poisonous tobacco plant is also closely related to the tomato.) Allow the plants to set about four trusses. To ripen tomatoes in dull climates it is often advantageous to lay them down flat on clean straw and place cloches over them. Some people pull leaves off "to let the sun get to the fruit". I don't think this is worth it.

Harvesting Homegrown tomatoes are so good to eat (immeasurably better than bought tomatoes that are bred for "a long shelf life" and not for flavour) that

you will not be able to stop eating them as they ripen. But try to bottle as many as you can. We wallow in vitamins in the summer: it is for the winter and the hungry gap that we need them.

Indoor tomatoes
Use If your greenhouse is heated you can sow seed in early winter and get ripe tomatoes in spring. If you don't want to eat them all you can sell them at a good price.
Sowing If you have an adequately heated greenhouse, sow seed in November at a temperature of 70°F (21°C). Never let it fall below 60°F (16°C) during the winter. If you can't raise a temperature of 70°F (21°C), sow seed in February and keep the temperature at 60°F (16°C). Sow in compost made of two parts sifted loam, one part leaf-mould and a little sand. Cover with glass to prevent evaporation. Keep them moist.
Planting When the plants have formed two rough leaves pot the plants singly in 5 inch (13cm) pots. Use the same compost as before but add some well rotted muck. When the first truss of flowers is formed, move the plants into much larger pots (about twelve inches or 30cm in diameter) or into the greenhouse soil.
After care Treat greenhouse tomatoes in the same way as outdoor tomatoes, but you can let them set up to ten trusses.
Harvesting Begin picking the tomatoes as soon as they are red. This will be much earlier in the year than outdoor tomatoes.

WATERCRESS
Use Watercress is one of the richest sources of vitamin C likely to come your way. It makes a superb salad, or it can be cooked.

Sowing Sow seed or rooted cuttings in a damp shady spot in late spring and midsummer. Dig the soil deeply and work in some peat if you can get it. Rake the bed, flood it and sow thickly when the water has drained away. You can grow it in an unpolluted stream.

Herbs

Herbs are a very cheap and easy way of improving the flavour of food; they also make it more digestible and do you good at the same time. In ancient times they were valued as much for their healing properties as for their culinary ones. The coming of the Industrial society saw a decline in the use of herbs, and until recently only parsley, mint and – in enlightened circles – horseradish were being much used in the North American and British kitchen. Now, the revival of a flourishing international cuisine has once more made people eager to experiment with a variety of new tastes. Consequently, growing fresh herbs to add natural enhancement to food is becoming an increasingly attractive proposition for everyone. Even people without gardens can grow them in pots.

A drift of borage or a sea of thyme look splendid from the kitchen window. There is really no reason why herbs should not take the place of inedible flowers in beds near the house instead of being relegated to an inaccessible patch at the back of the garden. But unless you are planning to become a herbalist it is better to concentrate on a few herbs that will be useful to you rather than cultivate scores of varieties, most of which you will neglect.

Herbs divide fairly straightforwardly into two groups: perennial and annual, with just the odd biennial to complicate matters. Most herbs prefer a light, well-drained soil and plenty of sun, although a few prefer the shade. All respond to constant picking.

Drying herbs

You dry herbs in order to keep the colour and aroma of a fresh herb in a dried one. It is a delicate operation as it requires both speed and care, but most herbs can be dried and stored.

As a general rule harvest the leaves and stems just before the plant flowers, on the morning of a fine hot day after the dew has gone. If you are going to preserve the herbs take them to a drying rack immediately. Do not over-handle them. They bruise easily, and every minute you waste means the loss of more volatile oils. These are what give herbs their flavour and quality.

Tie the herbs in small bunches and hang them in an airy place. Ideally you dry them at a temperature between 70°F and 80°F (21°C and 27°C), in the strongest possible draught of air. You can leave them hanging up indefinitely, but they will collect the dust. A better thing to do is to rub leaves off the stem when they are quite dry and brittle (but you hope still green), crumble them up and store in sealed glass or pottery jars in the dark. If the air is too damp to get them dry, lay them in a cool oven at 110°F (44°C) on sheets of paper overnight. Or you can hang them in a solar drier (see p. 214) which is ideal for drying herbs, but in that case watch the temperature by using a thermometer.

Below I describe some of the herbs that the self-supporter might find most useful for flavouring his food or fortifying his spirit or, even, banishing his ailments.

ANGELICA
Angelica archangelica
Biennial

Uses Angelica was once thought to cure the plague. The scented leaves make a fine tisane. The roots and stems can be candied or they can be crystallized.
Soil Angelica needs a rich, moist soil and a shady position.
Sowing Seeds should be absolutely fresh or they won't germinate. Plant in midsummer immediately they are ripe, in drills one inch (2.5 cm) deep.

Planting Transplant seedlings or young plants in the autumn and thin to 6 inches (15 cm) the first year, 2 feet (61 cm) the following year. In the third year distance them 5 feet (1.5 m) apart. They grow very tall and their leaves are spreading.
Harvesting Leaves should be cut in early summer while they are still a good colour. Stalks and leaves are best picked in late spring or they become too hard for candying. Roots should be dug up in the first year in the autumn before they get too woody. Wash thoroughly, then plait and dry as quickly as possible.

ANISE
Pimpinella anisum
Annual

Uses Anise has valuable digestive properties. The fragrant seeds can be used to impart a slight licorice flavour to breads, cheeses and puddings.
Soil A moderately rich and fairly dry soil is best.
Sowing Sow *in situ* in late spring, and thin later on to 8 inches (20 cm) apart. Take care when thinning, as the herb is fragile and easily upset.
Harvesting The seeds will mature the first year after 120 days, as long as they are exposed to full sun. Harvest when the seedheads turn grey-brown, and thresh them when they have dried out thoroughly.

BALM
Melissa officinalis
Perennial

Uses The leaves impart a fresh lemony flavour to soups and summer drinks.
Soil Balm likes a fairly rich, moist soil in a sunny, sheltered spot. If it is too shady, the aroma will be stifled; if too dry, the leaves will turn yellow.
Sowing Grows easily from seed which it self-sows profusely. Sow in spring or early summer in a cold frame. It should germinate in 3-4 weeks. Prick out and plant in the garden when 4 inches (10cm) high. Or sow the seed in your garden in midsummer and plant seedlings out in the early summer of the following year.
Planting Keep 10 inches (25cm) between the rows and 12 inches (30cm) between the plants. Balm is susceptible to frost, so protect your plants by earthing them up or giving them a light cover of manure, peat or leafmould.
Harvesting Don't expect too much the first year. Harvest just before the buds flower, and then again in the autumn. Balm bruises easily, so keep your hands off it as much as possible. Dry in the dark with plenty of ventilation, then store in stoppered jars in the dark. The temperature should never go beyond 100°F (38°C) or it will lose its flavour.

Herbs

BASIL
Ocimum basilicum
Annual

Uses A fine pungent herb, basil is superb in sausages, spaghetti, and stuffed tomatoes.
Soil Basil needs dry, light, well-drained soil and a sunny, sheltered position.
Sowing A hardy perennial in hot countries, basil is a delicate plant in colder climes where it has to be grown annually from seed. Sow indoors in early summer.
Planting Seedlings should not be planted until the soil is warm. Plant 8 inches (20 cm) apart in rows a foot (30 cm) apart.
Harvesting Basil needs plenty of water to keep the leaves succulent. The leaves can be picked off as soon as they unfurl. Cut down for drying in late summer or early autumn. Basil needs a longer drying time than most herbs; it is also very sensitive to light and heat, and it bruises easily – so handle as little as possible.

BAY
Laurus nobilis
Evergreen

Uses Once used to crown poets in ancient Greece, bay leaves are now more often used in casseroles.

Soil Bay is amenable to any reasonable soil. Give it shelter from harsh winds; it will grow in the shade, though it likes the sun. Intense frost will kill it; in colder climates bay is almost always grown in tubs so that it can be moved indoors in winter.
Planting It propagates rapidly from hardwood cuttings of half-ripened shoots. Don't let it dry out; feed manure occasionally.
Harvesting The leaves can either be dried (at a low temperature, which helps retain their natural colour) or picked all year fresh.

BORAGE
Borago officinalis
Annual

Uses Tradition has it that borage will stimulate the mind and fortify the spirit. Add a sprig or two to your wine and you will certainly notice a difference. The blue flowers can be used raw to garnish salads, and the leaves can be chopped into soups and stews.
Soil Borage needs sun and a well-drained loamy or sandy soil.
Sowing Seed is best sown in spring in drills 1 inch (2.5 cm) deep, 3 feet (91 cm) apart, 3 seeds to a station. Later, thin to 1 plant per station. Seeds will germinate early and thereafter sow themselves and need only to be kept weeded.
Harvesting Leaves are ready for use in approximately 8 weeks and only the young leaves should be picked. The herb is ready for harvesting as soon as it flowers, but it needs quick-drying at a low temperature.

BURNET
Poterium sanguisorba
Perennial

Uses Young tender burnet leaves lend a cucumber flavour to iced drinks or salads. They provide the perfect accompaniment to cream or cottage cheese. The dried leaves make a good burnet vinegar.
Soil It grows well in dry, light, well-limed soil.

Sowing Sow from seed in early spring and thin to 12 inches (30 cm) apart. You can also grow burnet from cuttings. Full sun is essential; seed should be sown annually if a constant supply of fresh leaves is required.

Harvesting The plant is hardy in most climates. Pick young leaves frequently for salads, or for drying.

CARAWAY
Carum carvi
Biennial

Uses As well as using caraway seed for cakes and breads, sprinkle the ground seeds on liver or roast pork, or cook them with goulash and sauerkraut. Leaves can go into salads, and the roots make a good vegetable if you boil them and serve them like parsnips.
Soil Caraway likes a fertile clay loam and a sheltered position. It is winter-hardy, and thrives in cool temperate climates.
Sowing Sow from seed in mid-summer, and it will flower and seed the following year. Protect flower stalks from the wind, to prevent the seedheads shattering before the seed is ripe.
Harvesting Cut off the flower heads as the seed turns brown, and dry the seed in an airy place before threshing.

CHAMOMILE
Matricaria chamomilla
Annual

Uses Sometimes used in flower borders, this herb is grown chiefly

for medicinal purposes. Chamomile tea is a cleansing aid to digestion, and an infusion of two teaspoons of flowers to a cup of boiling water makes a splendid gargle, or a soothing cure for toothache.

Soil Any good garden soil with full sun suits chamomile admirably.
Sowing Sow the very fine seeds mixed with sand or wood-ash, on a humid day in early spring. Thin later to 9 inches (22 cm) apart. The seeds self-sow easily. Watering is advisable during germination.
Harvesting Flowers appear and are ready for picking eight weeks after sowing. Pick often but only on sunny days when the oil content of the flowers is highest. Try not to touch the flowers too much.

CHERVIL
Anthriscus cerefolium
Biennial

Uses Chervil is famed for the flavouring it imparts to soups and sauces. It is well worth growing. Use it as a garnish, or make that classic dish – chervil soup.
Soil Chervil will grow in most soils but it will not thrive in a heavy, badly-drained soil.
Sowing Sow from seed in early spring out of doors and in the greenhouse at over 45°F (7°C) all winter. Sow in drills 1 foot (30 cm) apart. After that it will self-sow easily. Chervil does not transplant well so sow where you want it to grow. Seedlings should be thinned out when 2-3 inches (5-8 cm) high. Keep beds weeded and moist.
Harvesting You can eat chervil 6-8 weeks after sowing. Always pick leaves from the outside to enable it to go on growing from the centre.

Don't allow it to flower – it takes away the flavour. Chervil is a difficult herb to dry, needing a constant low temperature but as it is available fresh all year this should be no problem.

CHIVES
Allium schoenoprasum
Perennial

Uses Chives add an onion flavour with a green fresh difference to salads, soups or any savoury dish. Snip into scrambled eggs and cream cheese. The bulbs can be picked like small onions.
Soil Chives like a warm, shady position, and will grow in almost any soil, but they must have humidity. So plant them near a pond or water tank if you can.
Sowing Sow from seed in spring in drills 1 foot (30 cm) apart. Chives will thrive on doses of strong humus, and then need careful, frequent watering.
Harvesting Chives are ready for cutting about 5 weeks after spring planting. Plants sown in a greenhouse in winter at 80°F (27°C) will be ready in 2 weeks. Cut close to the ground.

CORIANDER
Coriandum sativum
Annual

Uses An important ingredient in Indian cooking, coriander can be grown successfully in cold coun-

tries. Use the seeds crushed or whole in curried meats or stuffed vegetables; add some to marmalade to make an exotic change. Seeds are sometimes sugar-coated and eaten as sweets.
Soil Coriander needs a sunny, well drained site in fairly rich soil.
Sowing Sow in late spring in drills a foot (30 cm) apart, and thin seedlings to 6 inches (15 cm). They will grow rapidly to about 2 feet (61 cm).
Harvesting Cut the seedheads when the pods are ripe, and allow the seeds to dry thoroughly before using, as they will taste bitter if they are still green. Thresh and store in the usual way.

DILL
Anethum graveolens
Annual

Uses The name comes from the Norse "dilla" meaning to lull to sleep, and the seeds were once called "meeting house" seeds for they were taken to church to be nibbled during endless sermons. While dill seed is the soporific ingredient in gripe-water, the herb can enliven your cooking. It is good with fish, roast chicken, vegetables and chopped up raw into salads and sauces.
Soil Dill needs a well-drained medium soil in a sunny spot.
Sowing Sow consecutively through late spring and early summer in rows 1 foot (30 cm) apart and later thin to 9 inches (23 cm). Keep plants well watered.
Harvesting Leaves can be used from 6 weeks to 2 months after planting. Cut dill for drying when 1 foot (30 cm) high, before the plant flowers. For pickling seed, cut when flower and seed are on the head at the same time. If seeds are wanted for sowing or flavouring leave longer until they turn brown. Seedheads should be dried and then shaken or threshed. Never dry the leaves in a temperature higher than blood heat or you will cook them and they will lose their strong flavour.

FENNEL
Foeniculum vulgare
Perennial

Uses Fennel's sharp-sweet flavour is specially suited to the oilier sea fish. Chop the leaves in sauces, salad dressings and marinades. The broad base can be sliced into salads or cooked whole with a cheese sauce. The seeds can be put into sausages, bread or apple pie.
Soil Fennel needs sun, a rich, chalky soil, and plenty of moisture.
Sowing Seeds should be sown in spring in stations of 3-4 seeds 18 inches (46 cm) apart. If you want to get seed you will have to sow earlier under glass and in heat. If propagated by division, lift the roots in spring, divide and replant 1 foot (30 cm) apart in rows 15 inches (38 cm) apart.
Harvesting Leaves can be used through the summer months and seedheads are ready for drying in the autumn. Harvest the seeds when they are still light green and dry in a very low temperature, never in direct sunlight. Lay in thin layers and move often as they sweat. Harvest the whole fennel when it takes on a grey-brown hue.

GARLIC
Allium sativum
Perennial

Uses Garlic is the basis of good health and good cookery. Unhappy are the nations who have to do without it. Use it liberally and use it often. Take no notice of foolish injunctions to "rub a suspicion" round the salad bowl. Chop a clove or two and put it in the salad.
Soil Garlic needs a rich soil, plenty of sun, and a certain amount of moisture. If your soil is light, enrich it with manure.

Planting Plant individual cloves in spring just like onion sets to a depth of 2 inches (5 cm), 6 inches (15 cm) apart. They will be ready for eating in the autumn. Plant again then and you will have garlic all year round.

Harvesting When the leaves have died down, lift the crop. Allow to dry in the sun a few days, then plait and hang in bunches under cover in a dry, airy room.

HORSERADISH
Cochlearia armoracia
Perennial

Uses Shred finely and use as it is or mix into a paste either with oil and a little vinegar, or grated apples and cream. Horseradish sauce is traditional with roast beef; it is also good with smoked trout and ham.
Soil It needs a rich, moist soil and a fairly shady position.
Sowing Horseradish grows furiously and spreads large tap roots with equal abandon. So give it maximum space. Plant the roots in early spring. Dig trenches 2-3 feet (61-91 cm) deep, throw about 15 inches (38 cm) of topsoil in the bottom, dig in a layer of good compost on top of this and fill with the rest of the soil. Take 3-inch (8 cm) pieces of root, plant

roughly 1 foot (30 cm) apart. And keep it weeded. Seed can also be sown in early spring and plants thinned to 1 foot (30 cm) apart.
Harvesting Roots are ready for eating 9 months after planting. Use the larger ones in your kitchen and the smaller roots for replanting.

HYSSOP
Hyssopus officinalis
Perennial

Uses Mentioned in the Bible for its purgative properties, monks now use hyssop to make green Chartreuse. You can use sprigs of it in salads, or chop it into soups and stews. Its slightly minty flavour is pleasant in fruit pies. I like it with fat mackerel. But use it sparingly.
Soil Hyssop prefers light, well-limed soil and a sunny plot.
Sowing Hyssop grows easily from seed and often self-sows. It can also be propagated by division, from cuttings taken either in the spring before flowering or in the autumn after it. Sow from seed in drills ¼ inch (0.5 cm) deep, and plant out seedlings 2 feet (61 cm) apart when 6 inches (15 cm) high.
Harvesting Cut back the tops of the plants often to keep leaves young and tender. Cut for drying just before flowering.

MARJORAM (POT)
Origanum onites
Perennial

Uses Pot marjoram has less flavour than sweet marjoram; use it in sausages and stuffings.
Soil It prefers a dry, light soil, and it needs sun.

Sowing Grow it from seed in spring in shallow ½ inch (1 cm) drills 8 inches (20 cm) apart. When the seedlings are big enough to handle transplant to 1 foot (30 cm) apart. Alternatively grow it under glass from cuttings taken in the early summer, and plant out later, allowing 2 feet (61 cm) between plants and between rows.
Harvesting Harvest as for sweet marjoram. Pot marjoram seeds ripen in late summer or early autumn. Cultivated pot marjoram can last for years.

MARJORAM (SWEET)
Origanum majorana
Annual

Uses Sweet marjoram lends a spicy flavour to sausages, and to game and poultry stuffings.
Soil It needs a medium rich soil, plenty of compost and a warm, sheltered spot.
Sowing Sow sweet marjoram in pots under glass in early spring and plant out in early summer 1 foot (30 cm) apart.
Harvesting Leaves and flowers are best collected just before the bud opens towards the end of summer. Dry in thin layers, at temperatures not over 100°F (38°C).

MARJORAM (WILD)
Origanum vulgare
Perennial

Uses Wild marjoram (oregano) turns up in many spicy dishes, which incorporate its overpowering flavour with ease. In delicate dishes use it in moderation.
Soil It needs a warm dry place to grow, and prefers a chalky or gravelly soil.
Sowing Sow from seed in early

spring. The distance between plants should be as much as 20 inches (51 cm); if you sow in drills you should thin to 8-12 inches (20-30 cm). Like pot marjoram, it can be grown from cuttings.
Harvesting Harvest as for sweet marjoram. Seeds ripen in early autumn.

MINT
Mentha sp.
Perennial

Uses There are several kinds of mint, with different properties and flavours, but they can be treated together. For mint sauce use Bowles mint rather than garden mint if you want a stronger flavour. A few sprigs of peppermint make a fine tisane. Mint added to any fruit dish or drink peps it up.
Soil Mint has a rampant root system and is best planted away from all other herbs. Grow mint in the sun and it will have a fuller flavour, but it needs a moist, rich soil and plenty of water.
Sowing Plant in autumn or spring from roots or runners. Lay horizontally in drills 2 inches (5 cm) deep, 1 foot (30 cm) apart. Hoe frequently during the first weeks and compost liberally.
Harvesting Mint for drying should be harvested at the beginning of the flowering season (midsummer), but fresh leaves can be cut any time. Frequent cutting helps the plant to grow. Don't cut for drying in damp, rainy weather, for the leaves will only blacken and go mouldy. Keep peppermint leaves *whole* when drying for tea. Rub them and they will have a totally different taste.

NASTURTIUM
Tropaeolum major or *minus*
Annual

Uses The round, hot-flavoured leaves are delicious tossed in rice salads. They are a healthy alternative to pepper for people who like spicy food. The flowers are good with cream cheese. The young green seeds can be pickled and used like capers. They are excellent with roast mutton.
Soil Given a light, sandy soil and plenty of sun, nasturtiums will grow almost anywhere. Plants grown for leaves need a ground rich in compost.
Sowing Sow the seeds *in situ* in late spring. If they are planted near other plants, they are said to protect them from pests.
Harvesting The highest vitamin content is found in the leaves before they flower in midsummer, so harvest then. Chop or dry, then rub or shred. The leaves dry well, but the flowers should always be eaten fresh.

PARSLEY
Carum petroselinum
Biennial

Uses There are several varieties of parsley, but all are rich in vitamin C, iron and organic salts. Chop it up into tiny pieces and use lavishly as a garnish.
Soil Parsley needs rich soil with a fine tilth.
Sowing Sow parsley fresh every year as it runs to seed. Sow in early spring and later in midsummer at a distance of 8-12 inches (20-30 cm) in drills ½ inch (1 cm) deep. Cover thinly and water well, especially during the 5-8 week germination period. When seedlings are 1 inch (2.5 cm) high, thin to 3 inches (8 cm) and finally to 8 inches (20 cm) when mature. Keep it well watered.
Curly parsley can often be sown three times a year: in early spring sow in a border, on open ground in early summer, and in a sheltered spot in midsummer.
Harvesting Pick a few leaves at a time. Bunches should not be picked until the stem is 8 inches (20 cm) high. Pick for drying during the summer and dry quickly. Plain parsley is the only herb requiring a high drying temperature; it must be crisp and brittle before you start rubbing it.

ROSEMARY
Rosmarinus officinalis
Perennial

Uses This evergreen shrub was thought by the Greeks to stimulate the mind. We use it to stimulate meat, fish and game dishes.
Soil Rosemary can grow to well over 5 feet (1.5 m). It likes a light, dry soil in a sheltered position, and it needs plenty of lime.
Sowing Sow seeds in early spring in shallow drills 6 inches (15 cm) apart. Transplant seedlings to a nursery bed when they are a few inches high, keeping 6 inches (15 cm) distance between plants, and finally plant out 3 feet (91 cm) apart. Cut in midsummer so shoots have a chance to harden off before winter sets in. Then cover the soil over the roots with leafmould and sacking for the winter.
Harvesting Leaves can be picked from the second year on, at any time of the year, although late summer is the best time for drying purposes. Rosemary flowers should be picked just before they are in full bloom.

SAGE
Salvia officinalis
Perennial

Uses Although now better known for its presence in stuffings, sage was for centuries regarded as one of the most universal healing remedies. Narrow-leaved sage is better for cooking, while broad-leaved sage is much more suitable for drying.

Soil Sage grows to around 2 feet (61 cm) and needs a light, dry chalky soil. It makes a good border plant and loves the sun.
Sowing
Narrow-leaved sage Sow seed in late spring, in humid soil and cover lightly. Germination takes 10-14 days. Transplant seedlings 15-20 inches (38-50 cm) apart in the early summer.
Broad-leaved sage is always propagated from cuttings taken in very late spring. When rooted, plant out 15-20 inches (38-50 cm) apart in rows 2 feet (61 cm) apart.
Harvesting Second year plants are richer in oils and give a better harvest. Broad-leaved sage is best cut in midsummer and again a month later to prevent it becoming too woody. Don't expect it ever to flower in a temperate climate. Cut narrow-leaved sage in early autumn. Sage leaves are tough and need a longer drying time than most herbs.

SAVORY (SUMMER)
Satureja hortensia
Annual

Uses Summer savory is known as the "bean-herb" and brings out the innate taste of all beans.
Soil A bushy plant growing about 12 inches (30 cm) high, it flourishes best in a fairly rich, humid soil, without compost.
Sowing Sow in late spring or early summer, in rows 1 foot (30 cm) apart. Thin seedlings to 6 inches (15 cm). You will get two cuts from this sowing, one in midsummer and another, smaller one in autumn.
Harvesting Cut shoots for drying shortly before flowering occurs (from midsummer through to autumn). Harvest seeds as soon as they are brown.

SAVORY (WINTER)
Satureja montana
Perennial

Uses Winter savory has a strong flavour and goes well with sausages, baked fish or lamb.
Soil Winter savory makes an ideal herb garden hedge, prefers a chalky, well-drained soil and plenty of sun.
Sowing Winter savory is germinated by light, so don't cover the seed. Sow in late summer in drills 12-15 inches (30-38 cm) apart, or propagate by cuttings in spring, planted out 2 feet (61 cm) apart. Plants will continue to grow healthily year after year in the same place.
Harvesting Cut shoots and tips from early summer of the second year onwards. Cut before flowering to get oils at their peak.

SORREL
Rumex acetosa
Perennial

Uses Pick young leaves and eat them raw or cook like spinach. Sorrel's acid taste combines well with rich stews and fish. Sorrel soup is a speciality of France.
Soil Sorrel needs a light, rich soil in a sheltered, sunny spot.
Planting The herb is best propagated by division of roots in spring or autumn. Plant out 15 inches (38 cm) apart. When the plant flowers in early summer, cut it back to prevent it from going to seed.
Harvesting Pick 3-4 months after planting when it has 4 or 5 leaves. Harvest shoots and tips for drying in the early summer before flowering starts.

TARRAGON
Artemisia dracunculus
Perennial

Uses An important cooking herb, tarragon is a classic for shellfish, and is also delicious with chicken and buttered vegetables (especially courgettes). The young leaves are fine in salads.
Soil Drainage is important if you are to grow tarragon well. Slightly sloping stony ground is ideal.

Planting Tarragon is another sun-loving herb and the roots will spread out about 4 feet (1.2 cm) so give it growing room. The best way to establish is to buy plants from a nursery and plant out 2 feet (61 cm) apart after the last frost of winter. Pull underground runners away from the main plant for propagation in late spring. Transplant cuttings either in spring or autumn.

Harvesting Fresh leaves can be picked continually all summer long and this will encourage new ones to grow. Harvest the leaves for drying at the beginning of the flowering period.

THYME
Thymus vulgaris
Perennial

Uses Garden thyme is a good herb to put in the pan with any roast meat, or to use in stews and stuffings. It should not be used too freely as it can drown other tastes.
Soil Thyme thrives in a dry, well-drained position, with light soil.
Planting Seeds can be sown in late spring ¼ inch (0.5 cm) drills 2 feet (61 cm) apart, but the herb is generally grown from cuttings taken in early summer. Side shoots can be layered in spring. Transplant the rooted cuttings or layers 12 inches (30 cm) apart in rows 2 feet (61 cm) apart. Keep beds well watered and free from weeds.
Harvesting In the first year only one cutting should be made. Two cuttings can be taken from the second year on, the first in early summer, just before flowering, the second in midsummer. Don't cut stems from the base of the plant, cut shoots about 6 inches (15 cm) long. Trim the plant after flowering to prevent it growing leggy.

Food from the Garden
Vegetables through the Year

Exactly the same principle of crop rotation applies to the garden as to field crops, but in the garden there are two main considerations to take into account: you want the biggest possible gap (at least three years) between brassica crops to prevent club-root disease building up, and the biggest possible gap between potato crops to guard against eelworm. You should also take into account that potatoes don't like freshly limed ground, which makes them scabby, whereas beans and peas do. Brassica prefer limed ground, but after the lime has been in it a few months. The root crops don't like land too freshly mucked or dunged.

You can pander to the needs of all these plants if you adopt a four year rotation something like this: Manure the land heavily and sow potatoes. After the potatoes are lifted, lime the land heavily and the next year sow peas and beans. Once the peas and beans are lifted, set out brassica immediately from their seed bed or their "holding-bed" (see below). The brassica will all have been eaten by the next spring and it will be time to put in what I call mixed crops. These will be onions, tomatoes, lettuce, radishes, sweet corn, and all the gourd tribe (marrows, squash, courgettes, pumpkins, cucumbers). Follow these with root crops such as carrots, parsnips, beet and celery. (Mixed crops and root crops can be very interchangeable.) Don't include turnips or swedes which suffer from club-root and therefore must go in the brassica rotation, if you aren't already growing them on a field scale which suits them better. Then back to spuds again, which is where we started.

This suggested rotation will suit you if you garden in a temperate climate with a fairly open winter. (Snow doesn't hurt unless it is extremely deep, but intense frost stops you having anything growing outside in the winter at all.) Probably no-one would stick to this rotation, or any other, slavishly. I know that there are idiosyncrasies in it, but I also know that it works. For example, I cram the brassica break in after the peas and beans, and clear the land of brassica the subsequent spring: this may be crowding things a bit, but two main crops are being produced in one year. Now to do this (and personally I find it a very good thing to do) you must sow your brassica seed in a seed bed, preferably not on any of your four main growing plots at all but in a fifth plot which is for other things such as perennials. Then you

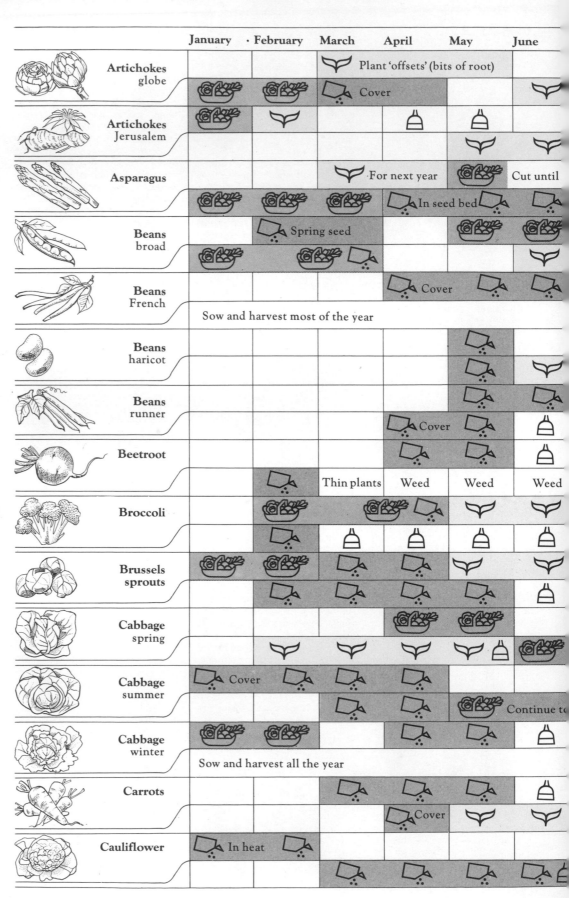

	January	February	March	April	May	June
Artichokes globe			Plant 'offsets' (bits of root)			
			Cover			
Artichokes Jerusalem						
Asparagus			For next year		Cut until	
Beans broad			In seed bed			
		Spring seed				
Beans French				Cover		
Beans haricot	Sow and harvest most of the year					
Beans runner						
Beetroot				Cover		
Broccoli		Thin plants	Weed	Weed	Weed	
Brussels sprouts						
Cabbage spring						
Cabbage summer		Cover			Continue to	
Cabbage winter						
Carrots	Sow and harvest all the year			Cover		
Cauliflower	In heat					

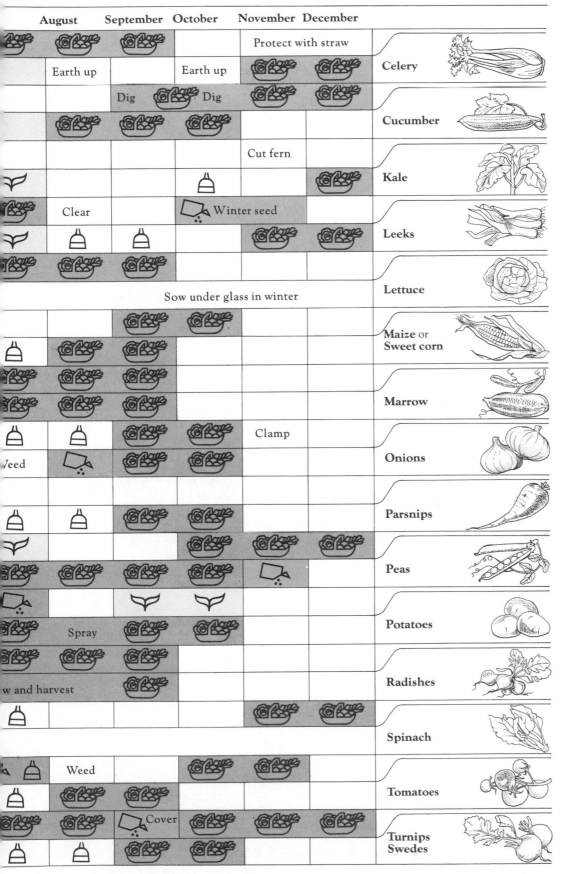

	August	September	October	November	December	
	Harvest	Harvest	Harvest	Protect with straw		**Celery**
	Earth up		Earth up	Harvest	Harvest	
		Dig	Dig	Harvest		**Cucumber**
	Harvest	Harvest	Harvest			
			Cut fern			
	Plant out		Hoe		Harvest	**Kale**
		Clear	Winter seed			
	Plant out	Hoe	Hoe	Harvest		**Leeks**
	Harvest	Harvest	Harvest			
			Sow under glass in winter			**Lettuce**
			Dig	Dig		
	Hoe	Harvest	Harvest			**Maize or Sweet corn**
	Harvest	Harvest	Harvest			
	Harvest	Harvest	Harvest			**Marrow**
	Hoe	Hoe	Harvest	Clamp		
	Weed	Sow	Harvest			**Onions**
	Harvest	Harvest	Harvest			
	Hoe	Hoe	Harvest	Harvest		**Parsnips**
	Plant out			Harvest	Harvest	Harvest
	Harvest	Harvest	Harvest	Sow		**Peas**
	Sow	Plant out	Plant out			
	Harvest	Spray	Harvest	Harvest		**Potatoes**
	Harvest	Harvest	Harvest			
	Sow and harvest		Harvest			**Radishes**
	Hoe			Harvest	Harvest	**Spinach**
	Hoe, Weed	Weed		Harvest	Harvest	
	Hoe	Harvest	Harvest			**Tomatoes**
	Harvest	Cover	Harvest	Harvest	Harvest	
	Hoe	Hoe	Harvest	Harvest		**Turnips Swedes**

must plant out the little plants from your crowded seed bed to a "holding bed". This is a piece of clean, good land, in which these small brassica plants can find room to grow and develop, for it will be late in the summer before many of them can go in after the just-harvested peas and beans, and it would be fatal to leave them crammed in their original seed bed until that late. So cramming five main crops into four years requires a holding-bed as well as a seed bed.

We can then look upon such quick-growing things as lettuces, radishes, and early peas (which are actually best sown late) as catch-crops, ready to be dropped in wherever there is a spare bit of ground.

Perhaps you think that radishes are brassica and therefore should only go in the brassica break? Well, we pull and eat ours so young that they don't have time to get and perpetuate club-root. But don't leave them in to get too old and go to seed, or they will spread this rather nasty disease.

There are plenty of other rotations, one of which might suit you best, but provided you keep brassica crops three years away from each other, you won't go far wrong.

Climate of course is all-important, and for the seasonal plans on the following pages I have taken as the norm a temperate climate, which will support brassica out of doors all winter but which will not allow us to grow sub-tropical, or even Mediterranean plants out of doors at all. In a climate with no winter frosts we could get three or four crops a year, provided we had enough rain, or enough water for irrigation. In climates too cold for winter greens outside we would have to devote the summer to one plot of brassica for storage during the winter. But it goes without saying that the reader must make allowances for climatic differences.

A vegetable calendar
The chart shows the sowing, planting out, hoeing and harvesting times for vegetables that you might grow in a temperate climate. But check with your neighbours first; the climate where you live could make as much as a month's difference.

Key:

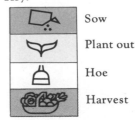

	Sow
	Plant out
	Hoe
	Harvest

Winter

Winter is a time for building and repairing, for felling timber and converting it, for laying hedges, digging drains and ditches, building fences and stone walls. If the soil in the garden is heavy clay, it is best to keep off it as much as possible, because digging or working such soil in winter only does harm to it. On lighter land the same inhibition does not apply. In cold climates the land may be deep under snow anyway, and all the crops that have been harvested will be safe in clamp or root cellar, or stored away in jars or bottles, crocks and barrels. The good husbandman should start the winter feeling that his labours have secured him a store of good and varied food, to keep him and his family through the dark months, and provide hospitality for his friends too. So for the self-supporter winter is also a time for feasting.

Greenhouse and perennials
In the greenhouse, it is time to clear winter lettuce, and the enriched soil that grew tomatoes last year goes out to the garden, with fresh soil barrowed in and mixed with compost. Tomato and cucumber seed are sown in the heat of the greenhouse. "Hot beds" can be built up in the cold frames. Mature compost is emptied on to the land intended for potatoes. Any remaining compost then goes into an empty bin to aerate it, and a new compost heap is begun. Perennial plants protected from the winter cold by straw and seaweed, are resting, preparing for their spurt of growth in the spring.

Plot A
This plot will have been very heavily mucked after the potatoes were lifted last autumn. A small proportion of it may well be winter-sown broad beans this year, if the winter is mild. The rest will go under winter rye or another winter green crop, which will stop the loss of nitrogen, and keep it ready to dig in as early as the land is dry enough to work in the spring. The plot was limed last autumn, after the spuds had been lifted, and this will benefit the peas and beans that are to follow and also the brassica crop which will come after them. A small part of this bed will have been planted with spring cabbage plants last autumn, and there will be a bed of leeks, which will be ready to pull.

Sow cucumber and
tomato seeds

Make hot bed with compost

Begin new compost heap

Pull leeks

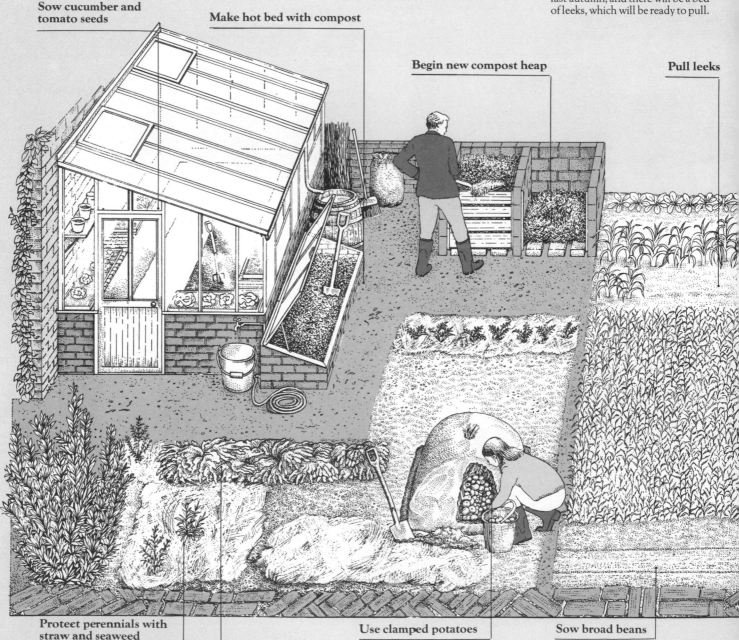

Proteet perennials with
straw and seaweed

Use clamped potatoes

Sow broad beans

Plot B

This plot should be full of big brassica plants: Brussels sprouts, hearting broccoli ("winter cauliflower"), big hard-hearted winter cabbage, kale, red cabbage, and any other brassica plant that can weather the winter. There may well be a few rows of swedes if these haven't already been harvested and clamped. Turnips must be in the clamp or root cellar by now, for they can't stand the winter as swedes can. This plot will provide most of the greenstuff during the winter, helped by the leeks in plot A. In temperate climates, this helps to avoid much complicated canning and bottling. Shallots are planted out, as this plot becomes the "miscellaneous" break next summer.

Plot C

This plot is under green manure such as rye or some other winter crop. Last year it bore the miscellaneous, short-lived crops. As soon as the land is dry enough to work, the green manure can be forked into the ground, so that it can begin to rot down. There is no hurry, because this plot is going to be "roots" this year, and most of these will not have to be planted out very early.

Plot D

This plot is fallow, or else under green manure, although if the roots were harvested late last year, there may not have been time to sow any green manure. It is time to barrow out compost or muck for the future crop of spuds. If barrowing is done in heavy frost, it is easier to push the barrow. It also does the ground less damage. There may be a row of celery left undug, and this can be remedied as the winter progresses.

Fruit plot

The fruit trees only need spraying with a winter wash if pests have afflicted them badly. Two-and-a-half pounds (1.1 kg) of caustic soda dissolved in ten gallons (45.5 litres) of water was the old-fashioned remedy, but these days most people buy proprietary winter washes. After the middle of February fruit trees, gooseberries, and other bushes are pruned. The blackcurrants may well have been pruned in the autumn. Muck or compost is barrowed and dumped around trees and bushes, and the ground between soft fruit bushes is forked lightly. All prunings should be burned.

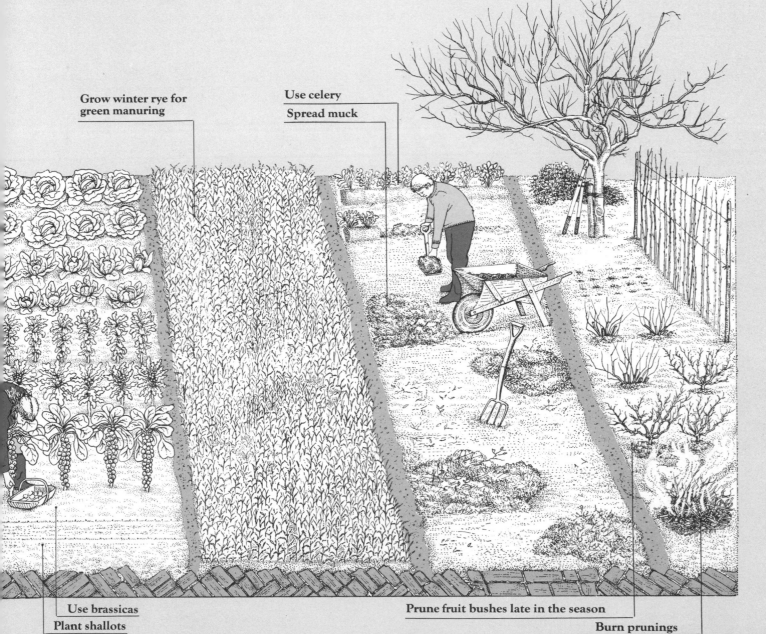

Spray and prune fruit trees if necessary

Grow winter rye for green manuring

Use celery

Spread muck

Use brassicas

Plant shallots

Prune fruit bushes late in the season

Burn prunings

Food from the Garden

Spring

There is so much to do in spring that it is difficult to get going fast enough. For a start, the green manure crops are turned in (a rotovator is quite good for this), the seed beds prepared and seed sown. But it is no good being in too much of a hurry to sow seeds, because they can't grow in half-frozen ground, and wet ground is cold ground. It is better to sow a week or two later, in dry warm soil, than earlier, in wet cold soil. Some things, like parsnips, need a very long growing season, and can be put in early. Some others are best started off early, but under glass. Cloches are a great help at this time of year, to warm the soil for early sowing. In March I have a big sheet of transparent plastic over February-planted early potatoes. The soil under it feels warm to the touch, while the soil outside is freezing.

Greenhouse and perennials
In a heated greenhouse, sweet corn is sown in peat pots and green peppers in seed boxes. As the tomato and cucumber plants become big enough they can be planted out in pots or greenhouse soil. Cucumbers can be sown in the hot bed. In the herb garden it is time to lift, divide, and replant perennial herbs such as mint, sage and thyme, if they need it. The seaweed covering should be removed from the asparagus bed, and the seaweed put in the compost heap. Rhubarb is forced under dark cover. Globe artichokes should be progressing well. Seeds are sown in the seed bed ready for planting out later: onion, all broccoli, cabbage, kale, cauliflower, Brussels sprouts and leeks. Lettuce can also be sown in the seed bed if there is a shortage of space in the main garden and lettuce plants are wanted ready for replanting later when there is room.

Plot A
The leeks are cleared and eaten as the spring advances. The winter-sown broad beans will be growing well, but if there aren't enough of them spring-sown varieties may be planted early in the season, when early peas will also go in. After this, peas will be sown in succession as the year advances. However many are grown, there will never be enough! Early turnips, soya beans and swedes should go in this plot, which will be brassica next winter. The row of spring cabbage will do for fresh greens, and will get eaten as spring advances.

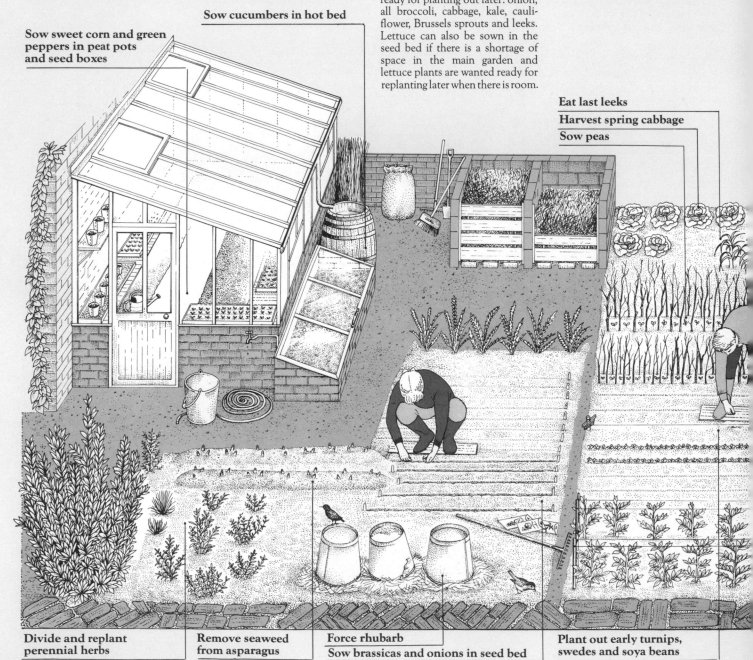

Sow sweet corn and green peppers in peat pots and seed boxes

Sow cucumbers in hot bed

Eat last leeks

Harvest spring cabbage

Sow peas

Divide and replant perennial herbs

Remove seaweed from asparagus

Force rhubarb

Sow brassicas and onions in seed bed

Plant out early turnips, swedes and soya beans

164

Plot B

Spring is more of a hungry-gap than winter, but the late hardy brassica, together with the leeks, tide things over. The brassica are nearly finished, but maybe a few Brussels sprouts are still standing, with some kale, some sprouting broccoli, and perhaps a few hearting broccoli. As the plants are finished, they must be pulled out, the stems smashed with an axe and then put on the compost heap. The shallots should be growing well.

Plot C

By now the winter rye sown last year as a green manure crop should be dug in, to make way for the roots to be sown later in the year. The only root crop sown early on is parsnip, but as spring progresses onion seed and carrots are sown in the bed. It is time to plant out onion sets and autumn-sown onions. If there is no garlic in the herb garden, it must be put out here early in spring. As spring turns into early summer more and more crops go into this root break bed.

Plot D

A row of early potatoes could be growing under cloches or transparent plastic. These will have been planted towards the end of February in mild climates, or late March in severer ones. The main crop won't go in until mid-April. The earlies get planted shallowly but the main crop go in deep furrows, both with ample muck or compost. They are ridged up as they grow.

Fruit plot

Prune gooseberries early in the season. Some people set out strawberry plants in March or April. The ground around soft fruit such as blackcurrants, gooseberries and raspberries should be kept hoed and cultivated to prevent grass from growing. Insect pests are to be avoided and something must be done about them if they attack. Grease-bands put around fruit trees will catch crawlies climbing up. It is important not to spray insecticides on flowering trees, as they kill the beneficent bee.

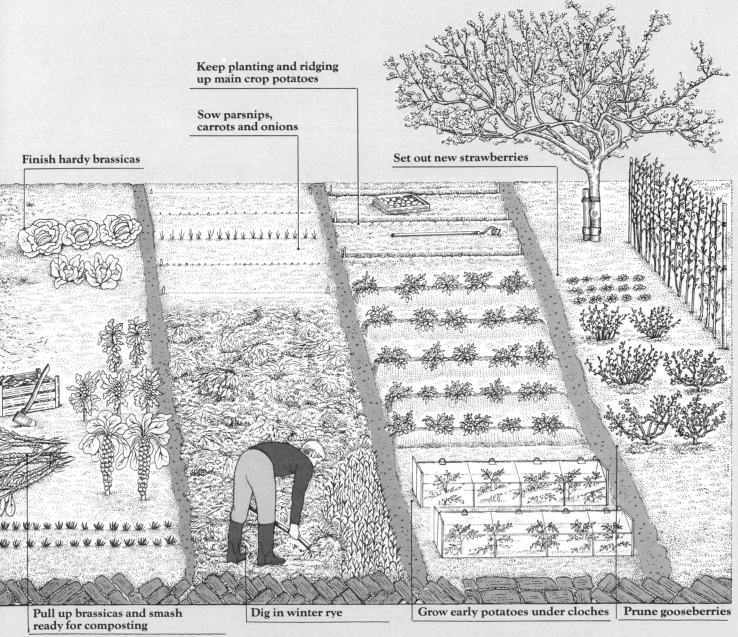

Keep planting and ridging up main crop potatoes

Sow parsnips, carrots and onions

Finish hardy brassicas

Set out new strawberries

Pull up brassicas and smash ready for composting

Dig in winter rye

Grow early potatoes under cloches

Prune gooseberries

Early Summer

Successional planting must go on unabated with many crops during April, May and June. A constant supply of fresh peas, lettuces, radishes and French beans can be maintained by planting these short-lived plants little and often. Fresh young turnips should be available all summer too. Hoeing should never be neglected during the early summer, as this is the time when the weeds are raring to get a foothold along with everything else. If they are allowed to get away with it, the crops will be miserable or non-existent. Onions and carrots must be meticulously hand-weeded. If some radish seed is sown along with the parsnips, radishes will be clearly visible before the slow-growing parsnips have declared themselves, and can be side-hoed with safety.

Greenhouse and perennials

Asparagus can be cut and eaten until the end of June, when it must be abandoned and allowed to grow. Herbs will thrive on frequent pickings. Artichokes are growing fast. The seed bed is kept weeded and if flea-beetle appear on brassica seedlings, they can be dusted with derris or pyrethrum dust. The ventilation in the greenhouse must be carefully adjusted. The top glass should be lightly shaded with whitewash. A good airing is vital during the day, but cold air must be kept out at night. The air is kept humid by spraying the floor and plants. Tomato plants are fed with water in which muck has been soaked, and as small cucumbers begin to develop they too are fed. Brassica plants are pricked out into a holding bed. The lids on cucumber frames should be propped open. Forcing of rhubarb continues.

Plot A

Peas are sown in succession and given sticks to twine around as they need it. More turnips and swedes can be sown. May, or June in later districts, is the time to sow out French and runner beans on previously prepared, well-composted beds. These need regular weeding and watering; all these legumes want frequent watering in a dry season. It is time to harvest broad beans, and if there had been any signs of black-fly earlier the tops of the broad beans should have been snapped off immediately and cooked. As soon as they are finished cut them down and sow French beans in their place.

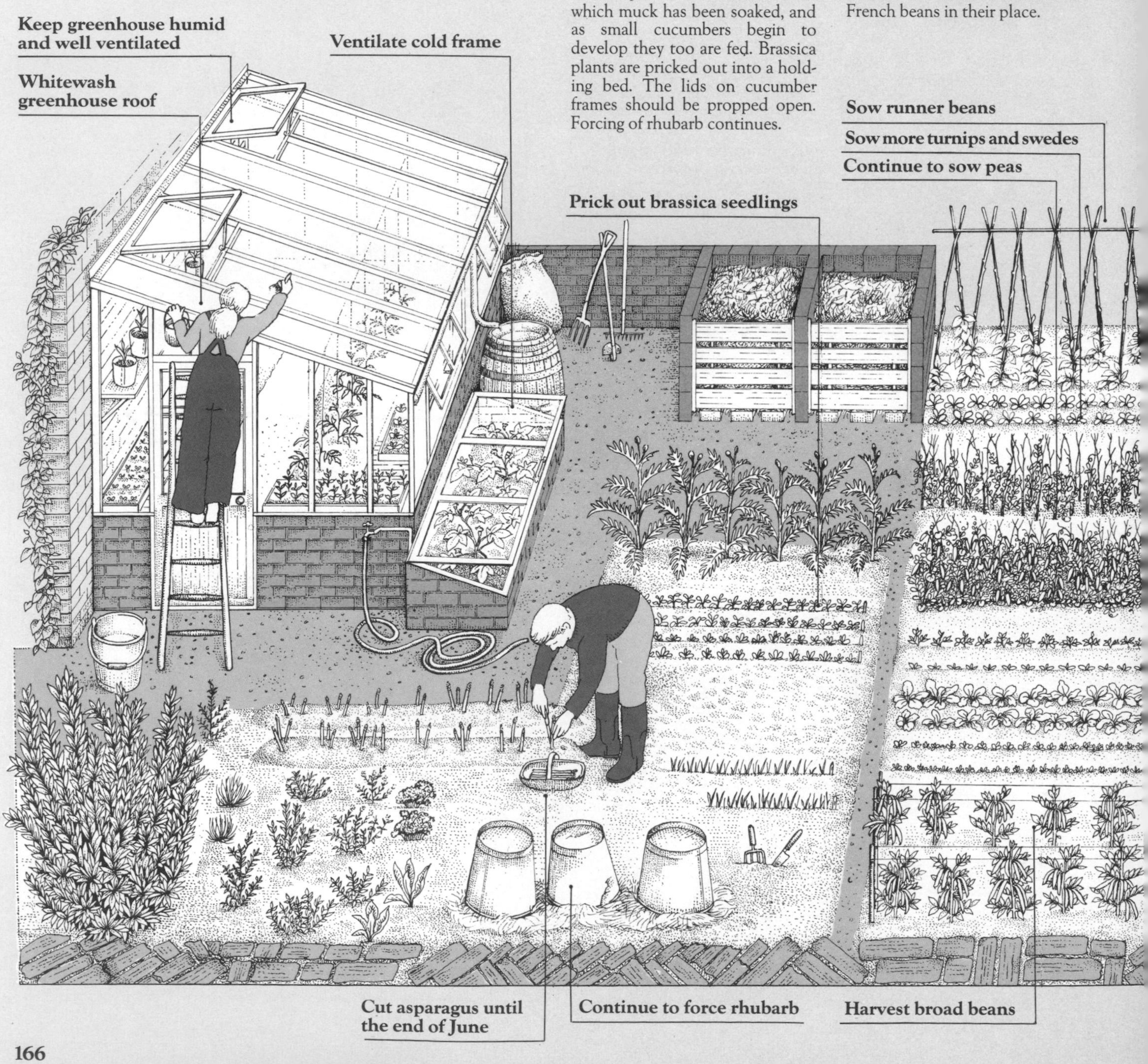

Keep greenhouse humid and well ventilated

Ventilate cold frame

Whitewash greenhouse roof

Prick out brassica seedlings

Sow runner beans

Sow more turnips and swedes

Continue to sow peas

Cut asparagus until the end of June

Continue to force rhubarb

Harvest broad beans

Plot B

Now cleared of last winter's brassica, this plot becomes the new miscellaneous bed, for outdoor tomatoes, courgettes, melons, marrows, pumpkins, squashes, radishes, lettuce, ridge cucumbers, spinach and sweet corn. As all these things – some of them reared in greenhouse or cold frame – become ready, and the weather is warm enough, they are planted out, and should be watered and tended. A good mulch of well-rotted muck or compost, if it can be spared, will do them all good. It revives the soil, and shouldn't make next year's roots "fork" too much, if put on well in advance.

Plot C

Onions in the root break plot should be growing well and will need weeding and thinning. The carrots should be thinned if they are wanted for winter storing but not if intended for summer eating. The wily carrot fly must be avoided. Carrots should only be thinned when it is raining, otherwise paraffin, or some other strong-smelling stuff, must be sprinkled on the row after thinning. Parsnips are thinned and weeded. Endive and beet are sown. Celery should be planted out before the end of May in a previously prepared celery trench, and never allowed to dry out at all.

Plot D

The potatoes already planted should be earthed up as they grow. Very early morning, or late evening, is the best time to do this, because the leaves lie down and sprawl during the day and make earthing up difficult. Turnips can be sown to come up in the brassica break when the early potatoes are out. The trick of planting leeks after spuds have been lifted can only be done if the spuds are early ones. Earlies are being eaten by June, so leeks can be transplanted into the ground when it is clear.

Fruit plot

Nets go over strawberries and straw underneath them, and birds must be kept off other soft fruit too. Soft fruit such as gooseberries can now be picked, starting with the hard ones for cooking, so as to give the younger ones a chance. Insects and various blights must be kept at bay. The ground between soft fruit bushes is hoed, and a mulch of compost or anything else put on. It is vital on light land.

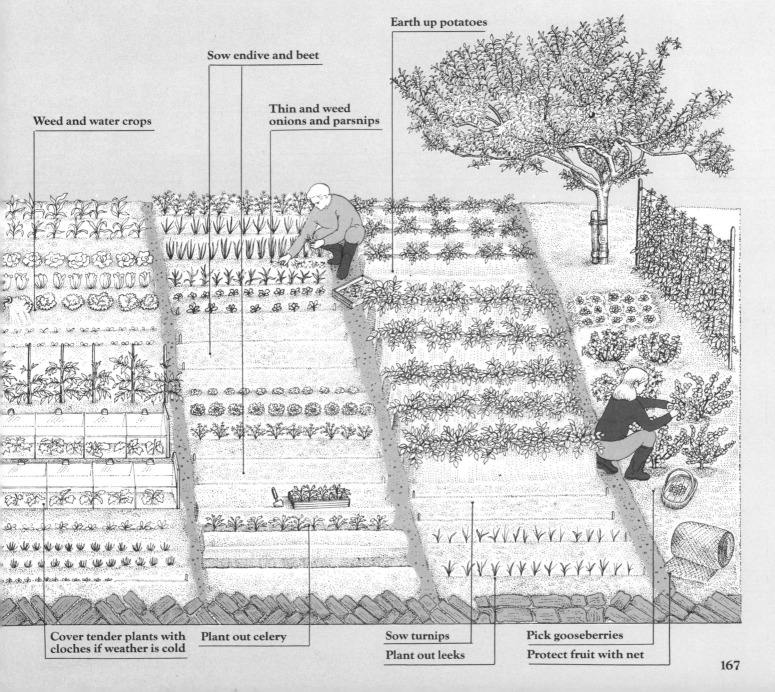

Earth up potatoes

Sow endive and beet

Thin and weed onions and parsnips

Weed and water crops

Cover tender plants with cloches if weather is cold

Plant out celery

Sow turnips

Plant out leeks

Pick gooseberries

Protect fruit with net

Late Summer

Earlier labour will now start bearing fruit in earnest. There is almost an *embarras de richesse* of harvest, and it is time to think of giving away, or trading, the surplus of many crops. The surplus of French or runner beans can be stored in salt, and the haricot beans and peas prepared for dry storage. As fast as peas and beans are harvested and cleared the space is filled with well-grown brassica plants. Fitting the main brassica crop in as a catch-crop after the peas and beans have been cleared is made possible by the use of the "holding-bed", which comes into its own this season. Brassica seems to benefit by the twice planting-out. Hand-weeding must go on incessantly, for weeds that are too big to hoe must be pulled out before they have time to seed: one year's seeding is seven years weeding.

Greenhouse and perennials

With the lid now taken off the cold frames, the cucumbers will run riot. Tomatoes, cucumbers and peppers in the greenhouse will be bearing, and will want watering and feeding. They now need plenty of ventilation. In the seed bed early spring cabbage seed can be sown. The herb and asparagus beds are kept weeded and the rhubarb needs to be regularly pulled. Soon the flowers of globe artichokes will be eaten; they should not be neglected, because uncut plants will not produce any more. But it is fun to leave a few to burst out in brilliant blue flowers and add to the scenery.

Plot A

The peas and beans are watered if they need it, and the flowers of runner beans sprayed with water every evening, to help the flowers set. Peas, French beans, and runner beans galore are now ready to be picked. So are the turnips. As each row passes its best, it must be ruthlessly cleared out of the way, and the space planted up with well-grown brassica plants from the holding bed. When the runner beans begin to yield, they must be picked and picked again and never allowed to get old and tough. A great many are salted for the dark days of the winter. The true countryman always bears the winter in mind; it is easy enough to get plenty to eat in July.

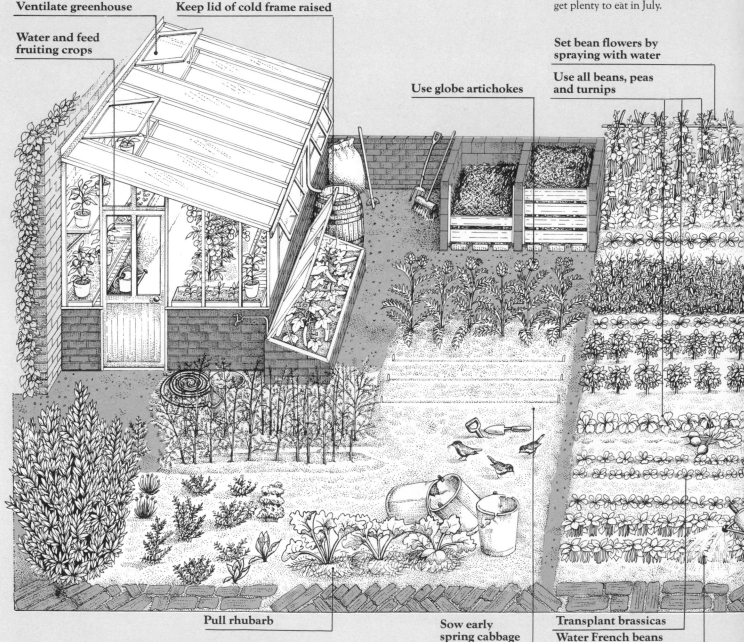

Ventilate greenhouse

Keep lid of cold frame raised

Water and feed fruiting crops

Set bean flowers by spraying with water

Use globe artichokes

Use all beans, peas and turnips

Pull rhubarb

Sow early spring cabbage

Transplant brassicas

Water French beans

Plot B

Any straggling vines of melons, pumpkins and squashes must be cropped. The tomatoes must be staked, side-shoots picked out, and the plants stopped when they have four trusses. They must be well watered if it is dry. In damp climates, it is a good idea to lay the tomatoes down at the end of August and put cloches over them so that more of them may ripen. Outdoor cucumbers are stopped before they get out of hand, and they must be picked hard and continuously so as not to get too big and bitter. All male flowers must be picked off. Lettuce should be eaten when ready, and not allowed to go to seed. Successional plantings of both lettuce and radishes continue. Sweet corn is now high, in a block to facilitate wind-pollination. The shallots can now be harvested.

Plot C

There is little to do now but hoe all root crops, keep weeds down and kill slugs. In fact, this is by far the best time of the year to clear all the weeds in the garden. Celery can be earthed up and sprayed with a Bordeaux Mixture in preference to leaf-spot. Start harvesting the onion tribe.

Plot D

By now the early potatoes are gradually being eaten, and the second lot started on if there are any. The main crop must not be lifted yet, but can be sprayed twice with Bordeaux Mixture, if blight is feared. Warm muggy weather is the enemy. The main crop must be well earthed up, but when the tops meet across the furrows it won't be possible or necessary to hoe any more, though the big annual weeds should still be hauled out. Turnips and leeks should be establishing themselves.

Fruit plot

Any superfluous suckers are cut out from the base of the raspberry plants. Immature apples are thinned where they are too thick on the tree (although the "June drop" may do this naturally) and fruit trees, particularly cordons and trained trees, are summer-pruned. Plums and soft fruit should be eaten now, while birds are eating the cherries. I think August is the time to plant a new strawberry bed, so root the strawberry runners in small sunken pots. Hoeing between soft fruits continues, it keeps the grass down and also gives the birds a chance to eat creepies.

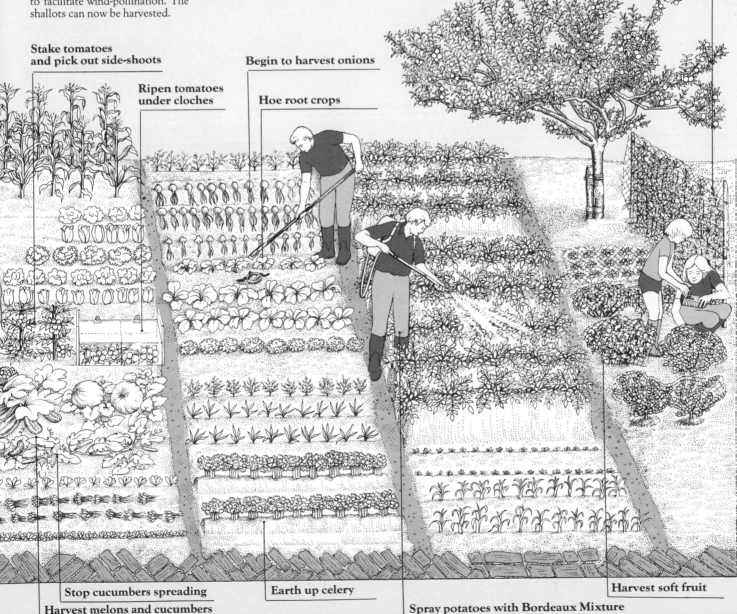

Thin apple crop

Remove raspberry suckers

Stake tomatoes and pick out side-shoots

Begin to harvest onions

Ripen tomatoes under cloches

Hoe root crops

Stop cucumbers spreading

Harvest melons and cucumbers

Earth up celery

Spray potatoes with Bordeaux Mixture

Harvest soft fruit

Autumn

Autumn is the season of mists and mellow fruitfulness according to Keats. It is also the real harvest time, when all the main crops have to be gathered in and stored for the winter. The good gardener will try to broadcast green manure seed wherever beds are left empty, although on very heavy soil old-fashioned gardeners are fond of leaving it "turned up rough" after digging so that frost can get at it. I prefer the green manure approach. After the first frost has touched celery and parsnips it is time to start eating them, and time to think of parsnip wine for Christmas (or the Christmas after next, as purists would have it).

Greenhouse and perennials
Frames and greenhouse can be sown with winter lettuce, spring cabbage and summer cauliflower. The last two will be planted out next spring. Asparagus ferns are cut down and composted, thus defying the asparagus beetle. Potatoes may well be clamped near the house, or put in the root cellar (or anywhere cold, dark and frost-proof). Globe artichokes are cut as long as there are any left. Then they are abandoned, except for a covering of straw, as they die down, to protect them against frost. It is a good idea now to cover the asparagus bed with seaweed, or manure, or both. All perennial crops want lavish manuring.

Plot A
Now it is time to clear away all the peas and beans, even the haricot beans, soya beans and any others intended for harvesting and drying for the winter. This bed will hold winter and spring brassica, planted late perhaps, but none the worse for that, as they have been growing away happily in their holding bed. The cabbages will benefit from the residual lime left by the peas and beans and the residue of the heavy manuring given to the previous spuds. When all weeds are suppressed it is a good idea to mulch the brassica with compost, but slugs must be kept down.

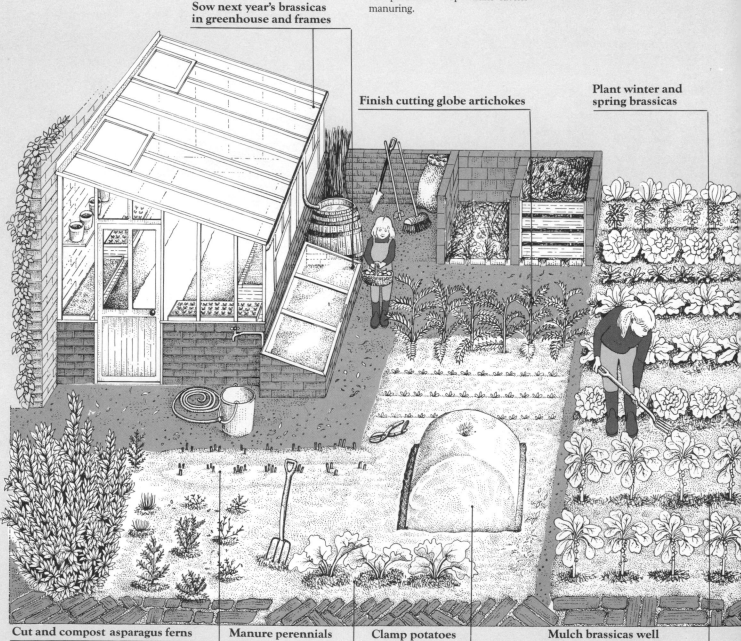

Sow next year's brassicas in greenhouse and frames

Finish cutting globe artichokes

Plant winter and spring brassicas

| Cut and compost asparagus ferns | Manure perennials | Clamp potatoes | Mulch brassicas well |

Plot B

All the plants in this bed (which are plants with a short growing season) will have been harvested. After the bed has been cleared, it should be lightly forked over, and winter rye planted for green manure. Unfortunately, it is not much good trying a clover for this as it is too late in the year; only a winter-growing crop like rye will work.

Plot C

Parsnips can stay in the ground indefinitely. Once earthed up, celery will also survive much of the winter. The rest of the roots are lifted in September and put safely in store. Red beet needs lifting carefully, as its roots bleed when damaged. As the land is cleared rye can be sown in it at least up until the end of September. This bed will be spuds next year, and manuring can now begin.

Plot D

The main crop of potatoes is lifted quite late, just before the first frosts are expected. This way, the tubers will harden in the ground and keep better, and if blight is present there is less chance of the spores being on the surface of the ground to infect the tubers when they are lifted. The spuds should lie drying out on the surface for a day or two, while their skins set. Then they are clamped or stored away. The leeks are earthed up and will be a great winter standby. As this plot will be the pea and bean break next year, broad beans are planted in October or September if you have hard winters.

Fruit plot

Runners are cut away from the strawberries, the ground cleared and given a good top-dressing of muck or compost. All fruit is harvested as it becomes ripe, then apples and pears are stored in a cool but not a frosty place, so that they don't touch each other. The old fruiting canes of raspberries are cut out, leaving the young wood, and blackcurrants are pruned in November or December. New fruit trees can be planted in November if the ground is not too wet. As tree leaves fall, rake them up and compost them, because they harbour troublesome pests.

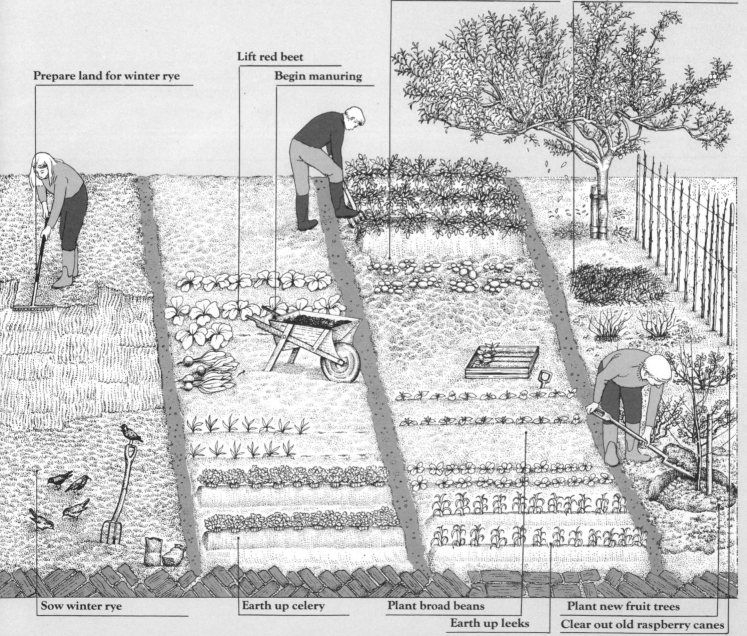

Lift main crop potatoes

Top-dress strawberries

Lift red beet

Begin manuring

Prepare land for winter rye

Sow winter rye

Earth up celery

Plant broad beans

Earth up leeks

Plant new fruit trees

Clear out old raspberry canes

The Greenhouse

A greenhouse can be a very basic thing; it can consist of a three foot (91 cm) high foundation of brick, concrete or stone, a wooden framework containing the glass (heavy glass is best), a door, and four ventilators (two at each end of the building, one high up and another low down). Inside you need staging for standing seed boxes on, and you should be able to remove this so that in the summer you can plant tomatoes in its place.

Unheated greenhouses

In countries where grapes and tomatoes will grow reliably out of doors I personally would not bother to have a greenhouse, but would spend the money on other things. But in cooler climates even an unheated greenhouse is enormously useful for starting off things like celery seed, sweet corn, early summer cabbage, and anything else you wish to get off to a flying start out of doors as soon as the frosts are over. You can also use it during the summer for growing that magnificent plant the tomato. Tomatoes are a most desirable crop for the self-supporter. They are expensive to buy, but easy to grow; they bottle well, and having a store of them makes all the difference between some possibly pretty dull food in the winter and *"la dolce vita"*. A couple of dozen large kilner jars filled with fine red tomatoes on the shelves come autumn are a fine sight and give us hope for the future.

And in summer your cold greenhouse may nurture such luxury crops as aubergines, melons, green peppers which turn into red ones if you leave them long enough, and of course cucumbers. The cucumbers you grow inside a greenhouse taste much better than frame or ridge cucumbers grown out of doors. And you can have lettuce nearly all the year round if you grow it in a greenhouse. In spite of this, a cold greenhouse will not help you much in the winter time, except by bringing along some early cabbage or some winter lettuce, or something that is pretty hardy anyway, because the temperature inside the greenhouse, when there is no winter sun, may go well below freezing point. So do not expect marvels. Remember the limitations.

Heated greenhouses

If you can just manage – by hook or by crook, by oil or electricity, or wood burning or coal – to keep the temperature of the air in your greenhouse above freezing all winter, and your greenhouse is big enough, you can have peaches, pears, nectarines, grapes, and most Mediterranean climate fruits every year in any climate.

If you want to heat your greenhouse, you can have water pipes running through it. The pipes should slope gently up from the boiler as far as they go, since the hot water will tend to rise and the cold to sink back to the boiler. At the highest point of the pipes there must be a bleeder-valve to let out air or steam that may collect. If the masonry inside the greenhouse is painted black, heat is absorbed during the day and let out during the night to allay the frost.

The self-supporter will like the idea of heating his greenhouse without buying fuel. This can be done with a Fachongle Furnace (see pp. 248-249), or possibly by water or wind-generated electricity. The former is likely to prove more reliable. Solar heating, properly used, has always been adequate to heat greenhouses in the warmer months of the year.

Greenhouse temperatures

In the winter the temperature should be about 40°F (4°C) at night. The sun should bring this to about 50°F (10°C) on bright days. The day temperature should not be allowed to get too high, but it must not be kept down by admitting freezing air into the place, as this will inevitably kill tender plants. So cool the air by letting the boiler fire go out, but get it going

A lean-to greenhouse
This greenhouse is a practical way of getting such things as lemons, peppers, grapes and tomatoes off to a flying start in a temperate climate.

again in the afternoon so that the temperature can be kept up at night. During the daytime in winter have the leeward top ventilator open. Then, as spring gets into its stride, open both top ventilators a little more. Eventually, open one of the bottom ones as well, but arrange for the cold air coming in through this to go over the hot pipes. In spring and summer sprinkle water on the floor occasionally to keep the air humid. It helps if you can arrange for the water from the roof of your house to go into a butt kept inside the greenhouse. This will be easier if you have a lean-to greenhouse.

Greenhouse soil

Greenhouse space, whether heated or not, is expensive, and it is therefore not practical to fill your greenhouse with any old

Upper ventilator

Black wall to absorb heat during the day and release it at night

Water kept at greenhouse temperature

Lower ventilator

soil. The better the soil in the greenhouse the better use you will be making of this expensive space. If you mix very good compost, good topsoil and sharp sand in equal parts, and add a scattering of ground rock phosphate and a little lime, you will have a very good soil for your greenhouse. You can put this soil in raised beds, or straight on to the existing soil of the greenhouse. The more you rotate crops inside the greenhouse the better, but if you are driven to growing the same crop year after year then you may have to remove the old, or spent, soil bodily and replace it with new. Tomatoes particularly can suffer from disease if grown too many years on the same soil.

Greenhouse crops

As to what to grow in the greenhouse, we are all guided in this by what we can grow and what we want. A cold greenhouse enables you to grow a slightly greater range, more reliably than you could outdoors. A hothouse enables you to grow practically anything that can be grown on earth. For my part the main uses of the greenhouse are: winter lettuce and other saladings; seed sowing in flats or seed boxes in the early spring of celery, tomatoes, peppers, melons, aubergines, sweet corn, cucumbers; and my greenhouse crop is tomatoes which go on all through the summer. I know you are supposed to be able to grow tomatoes outdoors in a temperate climate but you can't really, whereas a tiny greenhouse will produce a really impressive tonnage of ripe red tomatoes that can be eaten fresh until you are fed up with tomatoes. Then they can be bottled to provide marvellous food and flavouring right through the year. You simply cannot have too many tomatoes.

As for cucumbers, they can be grown out of doors (the ridge and frame varieties), but there is no reason why you should not grow a few in the tomato greenhouse too. The conditions are not ideal for them though: the true cucumber house is much hotter and more humid than the good tomato house. My advice is to keep your house to suit tomatoes and let the cucumbers take pot luck and do the best they can.

And then there is no harm, when you live too far north to grow grapes reliably out of doors, in having a big old vine growing up the back (north) wall of the greenhouse, trained under the roof so as to get the benefit of the sun without shading the precious tomato plants. A fan-trained peach tree, too, is a pleasing luxury in a fairly large greenhouse. And in countries with very cold winters it is quite useful to sow the seeds of temperate things like brassica in the greenhouse in the very early spring.

Whatever you do don't overcrowd your greenhouse. It is far better to grow plenty of one really useful crop, like tomatoes, in the summer, and another really useful crop, like lettuces, in the winter than to fill your greenhouse with innumerable exotic fruits and vegetables. Make all the use you can of hot beds under cold frames, cloches, jam jars and sheets of transparent plastic and the like, out of doors (see pp. 142-143).

Soft Fruit

It takes courage to plant top fruit trees knowing that you have many years to wait before you harvest any fruit, but unless you have one foot actually in the grave there is no excuse for not planting soft fruit. Soft fruit comes into bearing quickly enough: strawberries planted one summer will give you a big yield the next, and bush fruit does not take much longer. And soft fruit will give you, besides a lot of pleasure, a source of vitamins, easily storable, which will ensure the good health of you and your family.

By far the best soft fruit to plant, for my money, is blackcurrants. They are hardy, prolific, extremely nourishing – about the richest source of vitamin C and other vitamins you can grow – and easily preserved. With blackcurrants you can be sure of an ample source of delicious fruit right through the winter and hungry-gap. Bottled they taste nearly as good as fresh, and they very seldom seem to have a crop failure: in fact, in twenty years of growing them I have never known one.

White currants and redcurrants are not nearly as heavy yielding as blackcurrants. One might grow a few for the novelty, and for variety, but they won't really make much difference to whether you starve to death or not during the winter months. Raspberries are a good grow – they can be very prolific, and are fine for jam. They are also hardy and will thrive in wet and cold latitudes. Raspberries are far easier to grow than strawberries and really just as good to eat. They have a long picking season and children can be turned out to graze on them.

Blueberries and the many small berries of that ilk are grown by people who are hooked on their flavour. They are so laborious to pick in any quantity that they must be looked upon as a luxury. They are useful, though, in cold climates where lusher fruit will not grow.

BLACKBERRIES OR BRAMBLE FRUIT

Use I live in countryside where brambles are a blasted nuisance, and as we pick bushels of wild fruit from them, I wouldn't dream of planting blackberries. But cultivated brambles provide a heavier crop of bigger, sweeter fruit, and are very hardy. They also make good prickly hedges, although you may prefer a thornless variety.

Planting If you want a hedge of tame blackberries make sure the ground is completely clear of

perennial weeds such as couch grass. Dig in muck or some phosphatic manure, or both, then plant small plants every six feet (1.8 m). Each plant must have a bit of stem and a bit of root and each stem and root should have been shortened

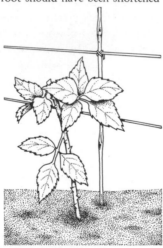

to about half its length. Provide them with a wire fence and they will climb along it. In fact they will spread at an amazing rate, so keep a close eye on where they are growing.
Pruning If you inherit wild brambles, and want to improve them for fruiting, cut the big patches into blocks by clearing rides, or paths, through them. Cut a lot of the dead wood from the bushes, clip the long straggling runners and fling in some phosphatic manure if you really want to make a meal of it.
After care Keep the rides clear, and you will greatly improve both the yield of that bramble patch and the ease of picking the fruit. Do not forget to watch for stray shoots growing up nearby.

BLACKCURRANTS

Use Blackcurrants are by far the most important soft fruit you can grow. They are the richest in vitamin C, and make the best wine of all the fruits.

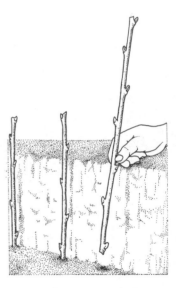

Soil They thrive on a cool and rather heavy soil, even on clay.
Preparation of soil The land should be limed the previous autumn if it is under about pH6. Get rid of any perennial weeds and dig in plenty of muck.
Planting Take your cuttings from existing bushes in late autumn. Do this in the ordinary course of pruning and remove the tops and bottoms with a very sharp knife. Cuttings should be about ten inches (25 cm) long. The lower cut should be just below a joint. Make a slot in the soil with a spade, put a little sand in the bottom and if you

are a perfectionist, stick the cuttings into it with about a foot (30 cm) between each. Cover them with leaves or compost as protection against the frost heaving the soil up during the first winter. Nurserymen in cold climates make the cuttings from prunings in November, tie them in bundles and heel them in until March. Then they plant them as described above. Next November lift the young rooted plants carefully and plant them one foot (30 cm) apart in rows 18 inches (46 cm) apart. At the end of the second year, lift them and transfer them to their permanent quarters, six feet (1.8 m) apart. Don't plant them too deeply.
Pruning Blackcurrants, unlike red or white currants, fruit on new wood, so, if you can, cut out all the wood that was fruited on last year. But you will often find that you are faced with a long old branch with a new branch growing on the end of it, so you will end up retaining

some of the old wood. Do not worry.
After care Give them plenty of muck every winter and keep the ground clear of grass and weeds.
Pests "Big-bud" is the worst pest. This is caused by a mite, and causes swollen buds. Pick off all such buds and burn them. Another disease they can get is "reversion" when the leaves go a weird shape like nettle leaves. Pull these bushes right out and burn them, so the disease doesn't spread to other plants.
Harvesting Some very lazy people commit the awful atrocity of cutting the fruiting branches off, taking them indoors, and stripping the berries off there! Well of course, it is easier to sit at the kitchen table and pick berries off a branch than to stoop or kneel out in the garden, and you kill two birds with one stone because you should prune out those already-fruited branches that winter anyway. I know people who do it, and it seems to work. But I have never been able to bring myself to do it, because I know that there is still a lot of "nourishment" in that green branch, which will go down to the roots as winter comes on, and I feel it is a crime to cut it off before this happens.

BLUEBERRIES
Use Blueberries aren't much good in warm climates, but people living in cold northern regions should consider them very seriously, for they are basically mountain fruit.

Planting Blueberries prefer acid soil to alkaline, so don't put lime on them. They stand up to intense cold and like a rather shallow water table so their roots are near the water. They can't grow in a swamp unless on a hummock. They will grow well on mountain peatland and prefer a pH value of about 4.5, which is very acid. Propagate from cuttings, or buy three-year-old

plants, and plant them six feet (1.8 m) away from one another.

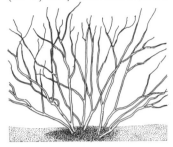
Before pruning

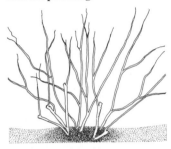
After pruning

Pruning When the plant is four years old (the first year after planting three-year-olds), cut out most of the flower clusters and cut away the suckers, the shoots that come up from the roots. Do this for two years. Then limit the suckers to two or three for each bush. From then on cut away old wood from time to time. Don't pick the berries until they come off very easily, or they will have little taste.

CRANBERRIES
Use These fruits are most commonly used to make cranberry sauce which is traditionally eaten with turkey. They will only grow under carefully controlled conditions and for this reason they are rarely grown in gardens.
Soil Cranberries grow in very acid soil. They must be well drained yet well watered in summer, and then flooded in winter.
Planting Cuttings can be planted

in spring in a three inch (8 cm) layer of sand on top of peat.
Harvesting After three years of weeding, watering, and protecting, the plants may begin to fruit. The fruits are hand-picked.

GOOSEBERRIES
Use Gooseberries are a very useful source of winter vitamins, and they bottle and cook well. You can't have too many of them, and for my part these and blackcurrants and raspberries are the only bush fruit really worth bothering about.

Soil They like a good deep loam, but you can improve clay for them by digging sand in, and you can improve sand by digging clay in, and you can improve all soils by heavy mucking.
Propagation Just like blackcurrants (see above), except that you rub out, with your fingers, all the lower buds on the cutting leaving only four at the top. They also layer well – peg a low branch to

the ground and it will root. Cut it off and plant it.
Pruning Prune hard the first year or two to achieve a cup-shaped bush (open in the middle, but with no branches straggling down). Then shorten the stems to three or four inches every winter, cutting out all old branches that don't fruit

any more. Always keep the middle open so you can get your hand in to pick the fruit. But never prune gooseberries in frosty weather.
After care Muck or compost mulch every year. Bullfinches will destroy every bud during the winter if they can, so build a fruit cage if you have to. Leave the cage open in the summer until the fruit can form in order to let goody birds in to eat the pests, but close it in the winter to keep baddy birds from eating the buds. The bullfinch plague in England and other places is due to game-keepers. They have destroyed all the predators, like owls and hawks, and small birds have now become a pest.
Diseases A horrible aphis sometimes lives inside gooseberry leaves and makes them curl up. Pick the curled leaves off and burn them. American gooseberry mildew can be sprayed with two ounces (56 g) of potassium sulphide dissolved in five gallons (23 litres) of water. You can recognize it by a white felt-like growth over leaves and fruit.
Harvesting Just pick them when they are ready. You will find them good for bottling or for wine.

GRAPES
Use Grapes don't mind how cold the winter is, provided the summer is warm enough and there is enough sunshine. They will grow as far north as Suffolk, England. I grew ninety outdoor vines there and got plenty of grapes. The pheasants ate all the grapes, but I ate all the pheasants, so that was all right.

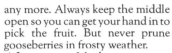

Soil Grapes need a very well-drained, warm soil, rich in humus, and they want plenty of sun and air. A south-facing hillside is fine. A pH of 6 is good, so you may have to lime. They can also be grown in a greenhouse and left to climb all over the place.
Propagation They grow well from

Soft Fruit

cuttings. Plant rooted cuttings out in lines six feet (1.8 m) apart in cold climates, and maybe more in warm. Grapes will fruit better in cold climates if you keep the vines small, and near the ground.

Pruning Have two horizontal wires, one a foot (30 cm) from the ground and the other two-foot six (76 cm). Vines fruit on this year's wood, so you can always prune last year's off provided you leave two or three buds which will produce this year's shoots. In cold damp climates, don't be too ambitious, leave three shoots to grow. One is a spare in case something happens to one of the others, and you cut it off when the other two are established.

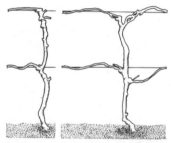

Train the two you leave in the same direction along the two wires by tying them. In warmer climes, leave five shoots. Train four along the wires, two each way, and keep one spare. Prune in late winter. Cut the shoots off after they have made about six buds.

After care Mulch heavily every year with compost. Keep down weeds, and spray with Bordeaux Mixture (see p. 87) in June.

Harvesting Cut the bunches off with secateurs. Never tear them off roughly.

RASPBERRIES AND LOGANBERRIES

Use Both taste excellent with fresh cream, and store well as jam.

Soil They like a heavy, moist soil and will thrive in cold northern regions better than most soft fruit. They tolerate shade and a northern aspect. Get rid of all perennial weeds and muck very heavily. They are greedy feeders of muck and will thrive if you give them plenty.

Propagation Either buy young plants from a nursery, raise them from layers, or just dig them out from the ground near existing raspberries.

Planting Plant them quite shallow, two feet (61 cm) apart, in rows five feet (1.5 m) apart. Establish a fence for them to climb up, or to contain them. I just have three pairs of horizontal wires and make

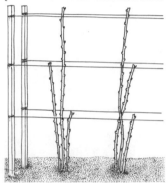

sure the canes grow between these, but some people tie them to the wires to give the canes extra support and to keep them neater.

Pruning Let them grow, but don't let the first shoots flower – cut them down before they do that. The second generation of canes will fruit. Cut the canes out after they have fruited, and just keep three new canes to fruit next year. Cut out all the weak canes. As the years go on leave more canes to grow, up to about a dozen. Suppress suckers, or dig them up to plant elsewhere. Cut the tips at different levels because they fruit at the tips and you want fruit at all levels on the plant.

RED AND WHITE CURRANTS

Use These are nothing like as useful as blackcurrants, but I grow them for fun. They are good for making jelly.

Planting Propagate from cuttings just the same as you would with blackcurrants (see p. 174).

Pruning They fruit, not on the leaders, like blackcurrants, but on spurs like apples. So cut back the

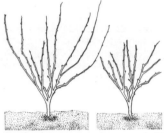

first leaders, or new shoots, to half their length the first winter. Then cut all the main leaders back to half their length, and cut out all subsidiary leaders to within half an inch (1 cm) of where they spring. Fruiting spurs will form at these points. In fact, keep as much older fruiting wood as possible, while cutting out much of the new wood.

After care Otherwise treat them just the same as blackcurrants. They don't get "big-bud" or "reversion".

STRAWBERRIES

Use This fruit is a very good source of vitamin C, rashes in some small children, and income for homesteaders. Strawberries are very labour-intensive, but they yield about the highest income per acre of anything you can grow. If you grow different strains you can have strawberries all summer.

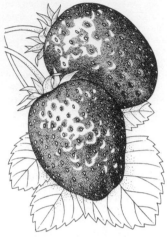

Soil They are a woodland plant so they need tons of muck and slightly acid soil: no lime.

Propagation Strawberries make runners which root, and you can dig these out of the ground. Or you

can make the runners root in little buried flower-pots with compost in them. Then when they are rooted you can cut the runners, remove the pots, and plant them out.

Planting Put little plants in during August and then transplant them a foot (30 cm) apart in rows eighteen inches (46 cm) apart. Don't plant them deep and spread the roots out shallow.

After care Hoe and weed constantly or your bed will become a mess, and mulch heavily with peat, if you have it, or compost. Beware of slugs. If you haven't any peat, put straw below the plants to keep the berries clean. If you get botrytis (grey mould), dust with flowers of sulphur.

Harvesting It is best to let them fruit for three years, then scrap them. Establish a new bed every year for a constant supply.

Tree Fruit

Happy is the homesteader who inherits a holding which has plenty of established fruit trees. Unfortunately farms that have previously been tenanted almost never have any. Why should a tenant plant trees on another man's land? So it often happens that the newcomer finds no fruit at all, and has to wait several years before he picks even a solitary apple. The only thing you can do is plant fruit as soon as possible.

Plant: some standard or half-standard hard fruit trees; some espalier or cordon hard fruit trees (especially if your space is limited), or else dwarfed trees which generally yield a much heavier crop much more quickly than full-size trees; and some soft fruit. The latter will give you fruit in three years, or less if you plant two-year old bushes. The big standards, or half-standards, will eventually give you a great bulk of fruit, possibly for the rest of your life, and provide you with enough apples for cidermaking. So, to reap your reward quickly, put them in as soon as you possibly can.

However, if you have a very small garden you had better not grow too much top fruit (that is fruit grown on large trees) because trees take up a lot of space and sterilize the ground underneath them for some distance by drying out the soil, extracting nutriments from it, and shading it from the sun.

When you site your orchard you must consider drainage. This is very important because no fruit trees will thrive with their feet in water. Air drainage is vital too. Frost runs downhill and therefore a basin is a "frost pocket". Thus you don't want a hedge below a sloping orchard because this will impede the flow of cold air downhill, creating frost which will impair the quality of your soil. Apples, pears, plums and the rest need good soil.

APPLES

Use Apples are quite simply the most useful fruit of all for cool and temperate climates. By having both early and late varieties, and long-keeping varieties, you can have prime apples *nearly* all the year, with maybe a little gap in summer when you have plenty of soft fruit anyway. A raw apple a day can be one of the most valuable items of your diet.

Soil They like good deep loam but will grow in most soils with plenty of muck. They don't do well on acid soil so you might have to lime. Land must be well drained and not in a frost pocket.

Preparation Cultivate well and get rid of all perennial weeds. Dig holes bigger than the tree-roots are likely to be, and if you can get it, throw some lime builder's rubble in the bottom of the hole (and plant a dead dog down there too if you have one).

Planting If you buy trees from a nursery get them to prune them before they send them. Three year-old trees are usual, but if you take immense care with the planting you can have an almost ready-made orchard by planting even seven-year-old trees. Planting trees is covered in detail on p. 180.

Varieties There are at least a thousand varieties in Europe alone so I cannot begin to deal with them here. Get local advice on the best varieties to grow in your area, and make absolutely sure that varieties that need other varieties to pollinate them have their mates nearby. Otherwise they will remain fruitless old maids.

Pruning Pruning is of vital importance if you want large fruit, but don't prune until the middle of February (to guard against rot spores). If your apples are "tip-bearers", and you must find this out from the nursery, the only pruning you should do is cut out some main branches, and in fact cut out the odd complete branch to keep the tree open and not too densely crowded.

But most other apples you will have to prune more scientifically. Cut all "leaders" (leaders are the long shoots which you want to leave to form new branches) to a third of their length, and cut to about half an inch beyond an outward-facing bud. This is because the last bud you leave will turn into a branch next year and you want the branches to grow outwards, away from the centre of the tree. Try to aim for a cup-shaped tree, open in the middle with four or five nicely-shaped main branches growing out from the trunk at about 45°. Don't let it get too crowded with minor branches. So for the first year or two remove all young shoots that are not required for leaders to create the final shape of the tree. Cut them off half an inch (1 cm) from where they join the trunk.

Then the aim should be to encourage fruiting spurs and discourage too much non-fruiting wood. If you cut off young shoots within half an inch (1 cm) of their base a fruiting spur will probably grow in their place. So, on each small branch, cut the middle, or main, leader back to half its length but cut all the subsidiaries back to within half an inch (1 cm) of their bases so that they will form additional fruiting spurs.

Prune lightly in mid summer too. Don't prune leaders, but cut all subsidiary shoots that have grown that year down to within about four inches (10 cm) of their base.

In later years you may have too many fruiting spurs. In this case you must cut some out. And if a tree bears a lot of small fruit one year and none the next thin the flowers out. If, during a good year, your tree appears to be supporting an excessive amount of fruit, thin out some of the tiny apples to make sure that the fruit left grows to a good size.

Pruning is very complicated and I would recommend that you find yourself an experienced adviser.

After care Try to keep the ground directly around your trees free of weeds and grass; annual heavy mulching with whatever waste vegetable matter you have, plus muck or compost, helps this. However, don't put too much highly nitrogenous compost on. Pigeon and chicken dung are out for apples. They cause too much rank growth and not enough apples. Grass the space in between the trees if you don't want to intercrop with something else, but above all keep the grass close-mown all summer and don't remove the cut grass. Leave it there to rot and for the worms to pull down.

Don't start spraying until you are hurt. If you obey all the books you read you will swamp your trees with deadly poisons (some growers spray a dozen times a year, drenching trees, fruit, and soil with persistent toxins) and you will kill all the predators, the insects and arachnids that feed on your insect-enemies, as well as your enemies themselves. If you don't spray at all you will probably be all right.

If you get "canker" (rotting patches on the branches) cut out all dead wood and paint the affected areas with white lead paint. If you get "scab" (brownish scabs on the apples) carefully collect all fallen leaves, pruned branches and so on and burn them every year. Spray with Bordeaux Mixture (see p. 87), but add half as much again of water as you would for potatoes. Spray just before the flower petals look as if they're going to open and again just after the flower petals drop. If you get "apple sawfly" (maggots that bore into the apples) spray with quassia, which kills the maggots but not the predators.

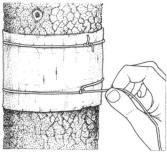

Grease-banding really is a good old safeguard against many horrid things. Just stick bands of greasy material around the tree above the ground. Many nasty things try to climb up the trunk and get stuck in the grease. I believe keeping a few hens under fruit trees is good, because the birds scrap out a lot of wicked insects. Planting buckwheat near fruit trees is said to be good, for it attracts beneficial hover-flies. But you may well find you need do nothing to protect your trees, and you still get good apples.

CITRUS FRUIT

Use If I could only grow one citrus fruit tree – in other words if I only had room for one tree in a greenhouse – I would grow a lemon, because you could not hope to produce a significant amount of oranges off one tree whereas one lemon tree would keep a family in lemons, and without lemons a good cook is lost. You can, of course, grow oranges or lemons in tubs, kept indoors in the winter and put outside in the sunshine in summer, but you will get very little fruit like this.

Soil and climate Citrus fruit will grow well outdoors in subtropical climates. Lemons are slightly more frost tender than oranges: 30°F (−1°C) will kill the young fruit and 26°F (−3°C) may kill the tree. Oranges will put up with a degree or two colder. The best soil is sandy loam, pH between 5.5 and 6.2, and good drainage is essential.
Planting Plant like any other top fruit trees (see p. 180).
After care Keep the ground constantly moist for several weeks after planting. After the second year, if you are using irrigation, they should have at least 20 gallons (90 litres) of water a month. They don't need much pruning except for rootstock suckers and diseased or injured wood. They like plenty of compost mulch, but keep it from touching the trunk's foot – if you do not, foot-rot may result.
Harvesting Citrus fruits are harvested during the winter and can be left on the trees quite safely for

many months. So obviously it is best to leave them on the tree until you want them and then pick them while fresh.

CHERRIES

Use Two distinct species of cherry (*Prunus avium* and *Prunus cerasus*) have given rise to the many varieties now cultivated. The former are sweet, the latter sour, but hybrid breeds are common. The vitamin content of the fruit is high, and cherry juice has been used to help relieve sufferers from acute arthritis.

Soil and climate Successful cultivation of cherries depends more on a favourable climate than on any other single factor. An unexpected late frost will kill the crop without fail. Good water and air drainage is crucial. On well-drained soil trees can send their roots down as far as 6 feet (1.8m), at which depth they are not in danger of suddenly drying out. Sweet cherries like a dry friable loam; sour cherries prefer a clay soil which is more retentive of moisture.
Planting Cherries are best planted in autumn, and the first buds will appear early in spring. A thick mulch applied soon after planting protects the tree.
After care Cherry trees bear their crop early in the season, so if a good mulch is maintained, moisture other than natural spring and winter rain will not be necessary. A young cherry tree should be trained in a way that creates a central trunk with branches coming

from it all the way up, not an open cup-shaped tree, which will bear less fruit. The birds will get all your cherries if you just grow them in the open so the answer is to grow them up a wall where they can be protected by a hanging net. Or else don't have so many birds.

If they get "die-back" (branches that are dying from the tips) prune the dead wood away and burn it. If they get "leaf-curl" spray with Burgundy Mixture (see p. 87) before the leaves open in spring.
Harvesting Picking cherries with their stems is not simple, for it is easy to damage the fruiting twigs. The smallholder with the single tree may find it easier to pick his cherries without stems, although the fruit must then be used at once before any bacteria have time to enter through the break in the skin. The longer the fruit is allowed to hang when ripe the sweeter the juice will become.

FIGS

Use The ancient Greeks called figs the Fruit of the Philosophers and all one can add to this is that the philosophers must have had very good taste, for fresh figs, sunwarmed, are a unique experience.

Soil and climate They are truly a Mediterranean fruit but will bear fruit out of doors in cooler climates, including England and many parts of the northern USA. In such climates the Brown Turkey fig is the only one to grow. They are best grown against a south facing wall, and in rainy and fertile land their roots should be confined in some way. A box a cubic yard in size is ideal. The walls should be concrete and the floor should be soil with broken stone on it. The reason for this is that figs grown unconfined in moist and fertile places put on too much leaf and branch growth and not enough fruit. An eccentric parson of my acquaintance confines the roots of his fig trees with tomb stones of the long deceased.

The fig will thrive in most soils, but a light or sandy loam is held to

be best. In fact the fig is very much a fruit of poor soils.
Planting Figs grow well from cuttings. Take two to three year old wood of under an inch (2.5 cm) in diameter in winter, cut to ten inch (25 cm) lengths, plant almost completely buried in the soil and keep moist. In places where figs grow well a fig tree can do with about 20 feet (6 m) of space. In colder climates fan-train up against a wall.
After care Figs need little pruning unless fan-trained. If their roots are not enclosed and they do not fruit, root-prune them severely. An interesting thing about some figs, particularly the Smyrna fig, is that they can only be fertilized by a certain very slim wasp (*Blastophaga psenes*) which can crawl into the fig's neck. The fig is not a fruit, but a piece of hollow stem which has both male and female fruits inside it. When the Smyrna fig was taken to America it was not understood why it would not fruit until it was discovered the fig wasp was needed, and these were imported in a certain wild fig called the Caprifig. The Brown Turkey fig which is the one to grow in northern climates does not need *Blastophaga* to fertilize it.

Figs can be dried, and make a very nutritious and easily stored food for the winter.

OLIVES

Use Where you can grow it the olive is the most valuable tree imaginable, for it produces quite simply the best edible oil in the world besides the most delicious and nutritious fruit. In fact one could live on good bread, olives, and wine, and many people have done so. Olives and the locust bean tree are among the most desirable trees you can grow, for they draw their sustenance from the deep subsoil, and allow inter-cropping with grass or other smaller herbage. This is true three-dimensional farming, which may well be the subsistence farming of the future.

Soil and climate Olives suffer damage at 18°F (−8°C) and very severe damage at 10°F (−12°C) so they are not suitable for cold climates. But they don't worry about late frosts above these temperatures because their flowers don't come until late spring or early summer when such frosts will not occur. They will not grow at altitudes over 800 metres unless they are very near the sea, but near the sea they suffer from "fumagine" (a sooty mould disease). If you can match these conditions grow them on a slope if you can, because they cannot stand having their roots in stagnant water. On the credit side they will put up with practically any soil at all. If on sandy soil in a semi-desert climate they will survive with as little as 8 inches (20 cm) of rain annually. In clay soils further north they will need 20 inches (50 cm) or over. The best soil of all for olives is sandy soil interspersed with clay layers. They need rain in the summer period, and if there is none you must irrigate profusely and regularly.

Propagation If you take cuttings in late summer and plant them in a mist propagator you can grow trees from these. There are three ways you can do it: you can plant small cuttings of $\frac{3}{4}$ to $1\frac{1}{2}$ inches (2 to 4 cm) diameter and 10 to 12 inches (25 to 30 cm) long vertically in the ground; you can plant larger cuttings $1\frac{1}{2}$ inches by 10 inches (4 cm by 25 cm) below the ground horizontally; or you can plant root cuttings (taken from a tree growing on its own roots of course, not from one grafted on a wild olive root stock) either in a bed or in the position you want your new tree.

Professionals grow trees from seed, then graft them on wild olive stocks, but this is a very tricky business. If you are going to grow olives on any scale you should plant about 250 trees to the acre. Plant them any time between late autumn and early spring. Trees may begin to produce at five or six years old, be producing heavily at ten to fifteen years and go on for a hundred. Mature trees will give from 90 to 150 lbs (40-70 kgs) of fruit and about 18 pints (10 litres) of olive oil.

After care Olives must be heavily pruned, but this is a complicated job which must be learnt from someone with experience. Alternatively, you can find a professional who will come and prune your trees.

Harvesting You can harvest from the end of November right on through the winter. If you are going to eat your olives you must carefully pick them by hand. If you want them for oil you should shake them down into a sheet.

PEACHES AND APRICOTS

Use Peaches and apricots are perhaps most appreciated in temperate climates where they are not so easy to grow. Increasingly they are found frozen or tinned, so it is worth growing them fresh.

Soil and climate Paradoxically peaches and apricots need both heat and cold. If they don't get cold in winter, say 40°F (4°C) or below, they don't have their winter sleep and exhaust themselves. On the other hand one late frost after flowering will wipe the crop out and they need real heat and sunshine in summer. Most of the people who were going to make a fortune growing outdoor peaches in England after the war have given it up. They like light soil, sandy or gravelly loam.

Planting The fruit is best planted in spring except in climates where the winters are exceptionally mild.

After care Prune right back when you transplant the tree. Prune sensibly in the early stages to shape the tree, and nip out half the fruit if it is too crowded. If they get leaf-curl disease spray with Burgundy

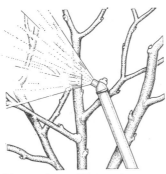

Mixture (see p. 87) in early spring, just before the buds swell.

Harvesting Peaches and apricots are ripe when all green in the skin gives way to yellow. Be careful not to bruise the fruit when picking, as once bruised they degenerate very rapidly. You can store them for up to two weeks.

PEARS

Treat almost exactly the same as apples. Pears like a more sheltered spot than apples and are not quite so hardy. Plant a succession of varieties. Give copious top dressings of manure, but see that it doesn't touch the stem, or roots will grow out from the scion instead of the stock. Incidentally – if you graft pear scions on wild hawthorn bushes they will grow and produce pears! And remember pears won't keep as well as apples do.

PLUMS

Use A number of very different species are all known as plums. They range from sweet dessert plums to tart damsons exclusively used for jam. Prunes are varieties of plum which have so much natural sugar that they do not ferment while drying out with the pit still inside the fruit.

Varieties Plums are not always self-pollinating, so you must make sure that the varieties you plant are capable of pollinating each other or you won't get any fruit. If you only want to plant one tree, find out if any of your neighbours have plum trees and choose a variety which can be pollinated by any of them.

Pruning Don't prune plums for the first three years you have them and then don't prune them until early summer or disease might get into them. Then take out any over-

crowded branches, and if the tree is too luxurious shorten leaders to a foot (30 cm) and side-shoots to six inches (15 cm). This will slow them down and make them fruit. Always in early summer cut out any "die-back" (branches that are dying from

the tips) and paint the wound with paint. Never prune plums in winter.

After care "Silverleaf disease" is a bad disease of plums. If you get it the leaves will turn silver and the insides of the twigs brown. Cut off

the twigs and branches until you get into clean wood, and – an old

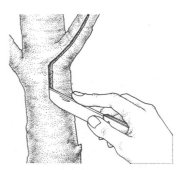

remedy – slit the bark with a knife right from the cut you have made down the trunk to the ground. Of course burn all affected parts to prevent the disease spreading.

Harvesting Plums for preserving can be picked as soon as a bloom appears on the skin, but if they are to be eaten fresh they should be left to hang for longer. Their flavour is best when they look and feel over-soft.

Caring for Fruit Trees

Planting

All fruit trees are planted in the same way. It is best to plant during the winter months when the sap is not moving around the tree. Normally you would buy three-year-old trees to plant from a nursery, but get the nursery to prune them before they deliver them.

However, if you take enormous care with the planting, you can have almost an "instant orchard" by planting even seven-year-old trees. But these trees would be considerably more expensive, and you really need to know what you are doing when you plant them. You would have to put a bag around the root ball to keep the soil in, dig right below and all around the roots, plant with immense care, and keep watered for a month. But I would recommend anyone inexperienced in orchard growing to buy three-year-old trees. The techniques of planting are illustrated below.

Grafting

If you buy trees from a nursery they will already be grafted: cuttings from the fruit tree that you think you are buying will have been grafted on to another kind of tree. The latter will be some hardy, near-wild variety: for example it will be a crab if the fruit tree is an apple. Thus you have the advantage of a hardy variety for the all-important root and trunk, and a highly-bred, high-yielding variety for the fruit. Very few amateur gardeners do much grafting, but there is no reason why they shouldn't, as it is easy enough.

It is no good grafting on to an old diseased tree, or one that is prone to, or has had, canker (rot in the bark or wood). A very useful exercise is the top-grafting of old established fruit trees, which are of a poor variety, or are neglected, badly pruned, otherwise inefficient, and in need of reviving. The growing tree you graft on to is called the stock, and the tree you graft on top of it is called the scion. Scions can be made from winter cuttings. Heel in the cuttings (plant them in a cool place) after you have cut them off an existing healthy young tree of the type you fancy, just as if they were ordinary cuttings. Then, in spring, cut all the branches of the old tree you wish to revive down to about a foot from their point of union with the trunk, for top-grafting. Trim the edges of the saw cut with a super-sharp knife, and go about grafting your scions on to each branch.

There are several methods of grafting, according to what sort of branch you are grafting on, but the principle is always the same, and involves bringing the cambium (under-bark) layers of stock and scion into close contact. It is in this layer just under the bark that growth and union of tissue start.

Apples and pears are easily grafted; grafting plums is much more difficult because grafting lets in silver-leaf disease. So don't graft plums unless you have to, and then only with great care. You can, by the way, graft pears on to white thorn or may trees, and get pears! If we had the time and energy we could do this all along our hedges.

Planting a tree

When planting out a tree or a bush put yourself in its place. Consider the shock to the roots, accept that the tree is delicate and treat it accordingly. Start by digging a hole much bigger than the root ball of the tree.

Drive a stake into the bottom of the hole before you put the tree in. You train the tree up the stake. Then put the tree in and prune off any broken roots or very long ones.

You will of course only be transplanting the tree in winter when it is dormant, but even so minimize the shock. Put a heap of rich loam in the middle of the hole and spread the roots round it. Make sure that you plant the tree at the same depth as it was before. Sift in more loam round the roots with your fingers, and rub the soil gently into them. Continue filling the hole until the roots are in close contact with the soil.

As the tree grows it will need a good supply of nutriments below it. So the soil under the tree and all round it must be firm; if the soil caves away under the roots and leaves a cavity, the tree will die. You should firm each layer of soil as you plant, making sure it is broken up finely. When you have installed the roots to your satisfaction (and the tree's), throw more soil in on top and stamp gently but firmly.

Do not stamp heavily as this will tear delicate roots. When the hole is completely filled in, and the soil heaped up a little, you can stamp harder. The stake ensures that no movement disturbs the roots of the tree once growth begins.

A tree must have moisture after it has been replanted. So water it well, and then put a good thick mulch of organic matter on the soil around the tree to conserve the moisture.

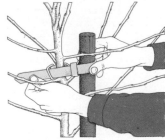

Tie the tree to the stake with a plastic strap and buckle. You can then adjust this when the trunk thickens.

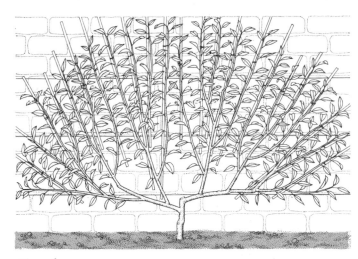

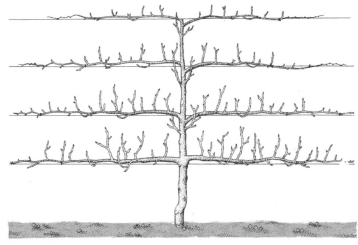

Tree shapes

Train your young fruit trees into a variety of decorative shapes. This can save space, and in some cases can considerably increase yields.

Fans

Train a "maiden" (a single-stemmed, one-year-old tree) along a wall or fence, with the help of canes tied to wires 6 in (15 cm) apart (above).

Cordons

Train a young fruit tree up a fence at an acute angle, and limit it to one stem and no long laterals (right).

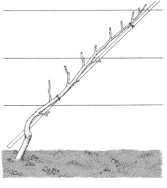

Whip grafting

This is a form of grafting which is used when the stock and the scion are approximately the same size. The stock is the branch on to which you graft the scion; the scion is a shoot that you have cut in winter, and then "heeled in" to a cool place until needed for grafting.

Prepare the scion by making a cut just behind a bud at the lower end of the scion so that it slopes away to nothing at the base. The cut might be two inches (5 cm) long. Near the top of this cut make another small one upwards, without removing any wood, so that a small tongue is formed. Cut the tip off the scion leaving from three to five buds. Now make cuts on top of the stock branch to correspond with those you have made in the scion.

Fit scion to stock, slipping one tongue down behind the other. The two cambium layers must be in contact with each other.

Tie the two parts together with raffia (cotton will do) and cover the whole joint with grafting wax.

Espaliers

Stretch horizontal wires one foot (30 cm) apart between posts. Train the central stem vertically upwards, and the lateral shoots at 90°, tying them to canes fastened to the wires.

Dwarf pyramids

The advantages of dwarf trees are that they take up less space than full-size stock, but their fruit yields are as heavy. Restrict the growth of a young tree to 7 feet (2.1 m). Keep side shoots short. Dwarf trees fruit earlier, but do not live as long as full-size stock.

Budding

This method of grafting is much used by rose-growers, although it can also be done with fruit trees. In summer select a strong healthy scion about a foot long and put it in water.

Cut a T-shaped slit along the back of your stock.

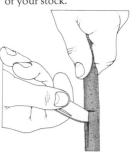

Peel back the two flaps of bark formed by the cut.

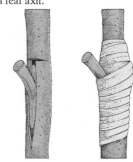

Take your scion out of water and slice out a shield-shaped piece of bark which contains a bud within a leaf axil.

Insert the shield into the T-shaped cut. Remove any of the shield sticking out above the T-shaped cut, and put back the flaps on each side. Bind with raffia or tape after insertion. As the bud grows you can cut off any stock above the bud-graft.

Storing Fruit & Vegetables

VEGETABLES
Clamping

Clamping is the process of making a pyramidical pile of potatoes or any other root, covering this with a good layer of straw or bracken or any dry litter, and then covering this with a layer of earth about six inches (15 cm) thick. The earth must be beaten flat with the back of a spade. In order to allow air circulation there should be small tunnels along the bottom of the clamp where the straw has been allowed to protrude through the earth, and small chimneys along the top. Water should be kept out by the trench you have dug to get the earth for the covering, but beware of thieving, destructive rats.

All potatoes and roots can be clamped. The advantage of this is that if there is blight in your spuds, or any other root disease, you don't get a build-up of the organisms as you would in a permanent building. In intensely cold winters and in severely cold climates clamping may not be possible – no clamp would stop the frost, and potatoes cannot stand much frost or they will rot. In these conditions they must be stored inside, ideally in a cellar although any frost-proof building will do.

Burying in sand

Carrots are traditionally laid down in dry sand, each root separate from the others, and stored in a frost-proof place. Lift them gently, trying not to damage them with the fork. If you wash them before storage they will just rot, and there's an end to it. They can be clamped in larger quantities, but don't expect them to last too long. There are few things more ugly than tons of slimy, putrescent, carrots. Beetroot and sweet potatoes can also be stored in this way.

Heeling in

Jerusalem artichokes, celery and leeks are generally best left in the ground until required, but if you fear hard frost, heel them into dry ground nearer the house where they will derive some protection from harsh weather.

Hanging in nets

All manifold squashes, such as marrows or pumpkins, should be stored away from frost. They will keep best if hung in nets, although they can be stored on shelves, if turned occasionally.

Stringing

It is a very good idea to string onions with baler or binder twine. Then hang them in a cool airy place. In many peasant communities the tradition is to hang them against the wall under the eaves of the house. Onions don't mind ordinary frost but must be dried thoroughly and not kept in a warm place. Warmth makes them sprout and go bad. Dry them in the sun on wire netting or on the ground. If it rains they should be in the wind, but under cover.

Drying

Beans and peas should be dried and stored away in great quantities every autumn. When they are thoroughly dried, threshed and winnowed, store them in crocks, barrels, bins or other mouse-proof places.

Mushrooms and most fungi can be treated in the same way as apples (see below), but they dry out at an ideal temperature of 120°F (50°C). Crumble them afterwards into a powder and store them in closed jars. The powder is marvellous for flavouring soups, stews, and so on.

Sweet corn is excellent dried: it really is a thing worth having. Boil it well on the cob, dry the cobs in a slow oven overnight, cut the kernels off the cobs and store them in closed jars. When you want to eat them just boil them.

FRUIT
Wrapping and shelving

As a rule the early-maturing varieties of apples and pears will not store well. So eat them as you pick them, and store only late-ripening varieties. Leave these on the trees as long as possible and only pick them when they are so ripe that they come off if you lift them gently. Pick them and lay them carefully in a basket. Then spread them out gently in an airy place to let them dry overnight. Next day store them in a dark, well-ventilated place at a temperature of 35°-40°F (2°-4°C). Pears like it very slightly warmer.

Ideally each fruit should be wrapped individually in paper to isolate any moulds or bacteria. Only perfect fruit can qualify for storing. So disqualify any with bruises, cuts, or missing stalks. It is better if the floor of the store is earth, stone or concrete, so you can throw water on it occasionally to keep the air moist. Storing fruit in a hot dry attic is simply giving the pigs a treat.

Apples may well keep until spring. Pears have a critical moment when they reach utter perfection. This lasts a few days. If they are not eaten then, they go sleepy and should be given to the pigs. So gourmets need to be very selective.

Drying

If you are afraid your stored apples won't keep long enough, you can happily dry them. Core them, slice thinly, string up the slices, and hang over a stove, or in a solar-heated drier (see p. 214), at a temperature somewhere around 150°F (65°C) for five hours. When they are crisp and dry put them into an airtight container and store in a cool place.

Prunes can be made of plums or damsons, and are rich in vitamin A. Plunge your plums in a lye, made of 1 oz (28g) caustic soda dissolved in a gallon (4.5 litres) of water, for a few minutes. This softens the skins. Then wash them very thoroughly in cold water. Dry them on trays over a stove, or in a solar drier, at 120°F (50°C) at first, raising it gradually to 160°F (71°C); it must be raised gradually or the plums will burst. Keep them in this heat for two days. When you want to use them soak them first in water for twelve hours.

Clamping

Clamping is a method of protecting root crops in the open, where diseases do not build up as they can in a cellar. But no clamp keeps out hard frost, so in very cold winters you must store indoors.

When you pick potatoes for clamping you should let them dry for 2 or 3 hours first. Prepare the clamp by putting a layer of straw on the ground.

Heap the potatoes (or other root crop) up on top of the straw in the shape of a pyramid so that when it is finished, rain will drain off.

Cover with a layer of straw or bracken. Allow a period for sweating before covering with earth.

Cover with a layer of earth five or six inches (13-15 cm) thick. Beat the earth flat with the back of a spade.

Make sure that bits of straw protrude from the clamp to admit some air to the crop inside.

Other storing methods

Late-ripening apples last all winter if you keep them in a cool dark place, but be sure that they aren't touching each other. Preferably wrap each one in paper. Hang marrows and pumpkins in nets; store beetroot and carrots in dry sand so that the roots don't touch. Keep all these safe from frost. If leeks, celery and artichokes are exposed to frost in the open, "heel" them into dry, sheltered ground.

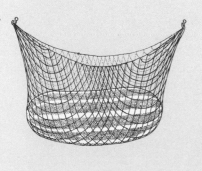
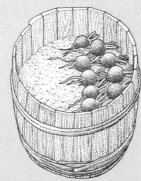

Stringing onions

You can store onions on trays with slats, on polythene netting, or on a wooden stand. But the ideal way of keeping them is to string them up in a cool place with access to plenty of air. Before you store your onions, always remember to dry them thoroughly first, either by leaving them on the ground in the sun, or covered but in the wind if it is wet.

Make sure that all the onions you want to string have long stalks. Start by knotting four of them firmly together.

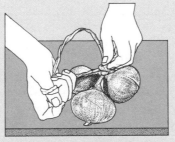

Plait the knotted stalks round the end of a long piece of string so that the onions hang evenly when you hold them up.

Add onions one by one to the original four. Twist their stalks and knot them tightly round the string.

Continue adding individual onions to the growing bunch, ensuring that each one is securely tied on, and that the bunch does not become unbalanced.

Hang the string up when you decide that your bunch is complete. The onions should keep indefinitely.

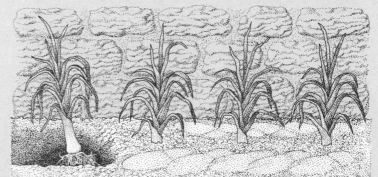

Preserving

The harvest season is short for most things, although in a temperate climate it is possible to pick fresh green things every day of the year. The urge to prolong unnaturally the season of every mortal thing, by embalming them in deep-freezes and the like, should be resisted. Few things can equal the pleasure of coming fresh to new green peas at the beginning of their season after six months of pea-abstinence. The palate, jaded and corrupted by months of frozen peas, or quick-dried peas masquerading as fresh garden peas, does not find this fierce pleasure. True dried peas, cooked as pease pudding, or put in soups and stews, are quite another thing. They are a traditional time-honoured way of preserving plant protein for the winter months, and eating them all winter does not jade the palate for the fresh garden pea experience every June.

At the same time there is, potentially, a vitamin shortage in the dark winters, and those dark cold days should be enlivened by nice tastes and odours besides that of salt bacon. So the self-supporter will wish to preserve certain things, preferably by a process which improves their natural flavour, such as bottling, pickling, chutneying or wine-making. There is nothing more encouraging in autumn than the sight of shelves heavily laden with full jars and crocks. More than anything they give you the feeling that you are likely to survive the winter. This may sound like a contradiction but it isn't. You cannot improve any food by deep-freezing, but you actually improve fruit and vegetables by making them into chutney, jam and the like. Freezing meat is another matter: unless you are very hungry you cannot eat a bullock before it goes bad. In more sensible times people killed meat and shared it. Now the whole principle of sharing with neighbours is forgotten and the cold of the deep-freeze has replaced the warmth of neighbourly relations.

Wine

Wine-making, like beer-making (see pp. 70-73), turns sugar into alcohol. Some fruits, such as grapes grown in a warm climate, have so much natural sugar in them that you don't have to add any. But many of the things you can make wine of are low on sugar. So you will have to add sugar if you want alcohol of a decent strength. And remember that weak wine won't keep: it just goes bad. Some "wine" described in books of wine recipes is simply sugar-water fermented and flavoured with some substance. Most flower wines (see p. 192) are made like this and people even make "wine" of tea-leaves – that sugarless substance!

Fruit wines have their own sugar, though generally not enough, so you must add some. The same goes for root wines. Parsnip, which is by far the best, has quite a lot of sugar. What country wines do is to preserve and even enhance the flavour and bouquet of the things they are made of. They cheer us up in the dark days of winter and are very good for us too.

Chutneys and pickles

You make both chutneys and pickles by flavouring fruit or vegetables, or a combination of both, with spices and preserving them in vinegar. The methods of preserving, however, do not resemble each other (see pp. 188-189).

Chutneys are fruits or vegetables which have been cooked in vinegar, often heavily spiced and sweetened. They are cooked until all excess liquid has evaporated, leaving a thick pulp, the consistency of jam. The flavour is mellow. Pickles are put down whole or in large chunks in vinegar, but not heated in it. Anything which is to be pickled must not have too much moisture in it. So sometimes moisture must be drawn out first with salt. The resulting flavour is full and sharp.

Both chutneys and pickles are an excellent way of preserving things for the winter and of enhancing their taste as well. They are delicious with cold meats and meat pies, and also offset the taste of curries or cheeses.

Ketchups and similar sauces are strained juices of fruits or vegetables spiced and cooked in vinegar. These too, if well made, can give a lift to plain food.

Bottling

The principle of bottling is very simple. Food is put in jars, the jars and their contents are heated to a temperature which is maintained long enough to ensure that all bacteria, moulds and viruses are destroyed; at this point the jars are completely sealed to prevent any further pathogens from getting in, and then allowed to cool. Thus the contents of the jars are sterilized by heat, and safe from attack by putrefactive organisms (see pp. 186-187).

The same principle applies to tinning, or canning, except that the product is preserved in an unattractive steel box. It is also a process that the self-supporter will find considerably less easy than bottling.

Fruit bottles very well. Vegetables are far more difficult, because they are low on acid, and acid makes food preservation easier. My own feeling about the bottling of vegetables is – don't do it. What with salted runner beans, sauerkraut, clamped or cellared roots or cabbages, and, in all but arctic climates, quite a selection of the things that will grow and can be picked fresh out of doors all winter, there is no need for the rather tasteless, soggy matter that vegetables become when they have been bottled.

On the other hand tomatoes, which aren't strictly speaking a vegetable, are a very good thing to bottle indeed. They give a lift to otherwise dull winter dishes like nothing else can. They are easy to bottle, you can grow a big surplus during their short growing season, they are rich in vitamins and they taste delicious.

Fruits of the year
It is autumn, and you have a surfeit of all the crops you have been gathering through the summer. What more fulfilling than to bottle, pickle and preserve in all possible ways for the dark days of winter ahead?

Food from the Garden

Bottling

Glass jars for bottling must have airtight tops, capable of supporting a vacuum, and arranged so that no metal comes into contact with the contents of the jar. If you examine the common "Kilner" jar, or any of its rivals, you will find quite a cunning arrangement ensuring that the above requirements are met. A rubber ring compressed by a metal screw-cap forms an airtight seal, and only the glass disc inside the screw-cap comes into contact with the jar's contents. Kilner and other proprietary jars need the metal parts smearing with vaseline to prevent them rusting, both when in use and when stored away. Keep the rubber rings in the dark, for light perishes rubber.

To bottle you also need a container in which jars can be boiled. If you buy one it should have a false bottom, so that the jars are not too close to the source of heat. Alternatively, put a piece of board in the bottom, or else just a folded towel. When bottling fruit pack the jars as tightly as you can; tapping the base of the jar on the table helps to settle the fruit, and drives air bubbles out.

BOTTLING FRUIT
Cold water bath method

Put the fruit into jars of cold brine or syrup and put the jars in cold water. Take an hour to bring water to 130°F (54°C), then another half hour to raise it to the temperature given on the chart below.

Oven method

Fill the jars, not putting any syrup or brine in them yet, and covering them with loose saucers only. Put them in a low oven at 250°F (121°C). Leave them for the time given in the chart, take out and top up with fruit from a spare jar that has undergone the same process, then fill up with boiling brine or syrup, screw on the tops, and leave to cool.

Hot water bath method

If you have no thermometer, and no oven, use the hot water method. Fill packed jars with hot syrup or brine, put the lids on loosely, lower into warm water, bring to the boil, then simmer for the length of time shown on the chart.

For fruit other than tomatoes, use a syrup of sugar and water if you wish. Water alone will do, and if you pack the fruit tightly you won't need much. But if the fruit is sour a weak syrup does help.

BOTTLING VEGETABLES

I strongly advise against the bottling of vegetables, but if you insist upon doing it you must heat in a pressure-cooker, as boiling at atmospheric pressure is not enough to make it safe. Sweet corn can be bottled (although I prefer the oven drying method I described on p. 182): husk your corn, remove the silk, wash well, and cut the corn off the cob with a knife. If you force the cob on to a nail sticking up from a board at an angle you will have it steady for slicing. This will leave a little of each grain on the cob, but that's all the better for the pigs. Pack the corn in the jar to within an inch of the top, add half a teaspoonful of salt to each pint of corn, fill up to half an inch from the top with boiling water, put the lid on loosely and heat in a pressure-cooker at 240°F (115°C), at ten pounds pressure, for an hour. Remove the jars from the cooker and seal.

Salting runner beans

Use a pound (0.5kg) of salt to three pounds (1.4kg) of beans. Try to get "dairy" salt or block salt but vacuum salt will do. Put a layer of salt in the bottom of a crock, a layer of stringed and sliced beans (tender young French beans do not need much slicing, whereas runners always do) on top, another layer of salt, and so on. Press down tightly. Add more layers daily. When you have enough, or there are no more, cover the crock with an airtight cover and leave in a cool place. The beans will be drowned in their own brine so do not remove it. To use, wash some beans in water and then soak them for no more than two hours.

	Cold water bath		Hot water bath		Slow oven	
Basic method	Take 90 minutes to bring water from cold to required temperature. Then follow instructions given below.		Start at 100°F (39°C) taking 25-30 minutes to reach required temperature of 190°F (88°C). Follow instructions.		Preheat to 250°F (121°C). Leave bottles according to times given below.	
Liquid in bottles	Put cold syrup or water in before processing.		Put hot liquid at 140°F (60°C) in before processing. For tomatoes, liquid is optional.		Add boiling liquid at end of processing.	
	Temperature	Time	Temperature	Time	Temperature	Time
Soft fruit Blackberries, raspberries, currants etc. and apple slices.	165°F (74°C)	10 mins	190°F (88°C)	2 mins	250°F (121°C)	45-55 mins
Stone fruit Cherries, plums etc.	180°F (83°C)	15 mins	190°F (88°C)	10 mins	Heat oven to 300°F (149°C) and put hot syrup in before processing them.	40-50 mins
Citrus fruit						
Tomatoes	190°F (88°C)	30 mins	190°F (88°C)	40 mins	250°F (121°C)	80-100 mins
Purées and tight packs	Allow 5-10 mins longer than times shown above and raise temperature a little.					

Bottling tomatoes

Jars of bottled tomatoes on your shelves in winter are a cheering sight. They are easy to bottle, and it even improves their flavour.

Remove the green tomato stalks, and nick the skins with a knife.

Put the tomatoes in a bowl and pour over boiling water. Leave until the skins have loosened.

Drain and cover with cold water. Don't leave them very long as they soon go soggy.

With a sharp knife peel off the skins carefully so that the tomatoes retain their shape and do not loose any juice.

Make up a brine by mixing half an ounce (14 g) of salt to a quart (1.1 litres) of water.

Pack tomatoes in jars very tightly. Push large fruit into place with the handle of a wooden spoon.

If sterilizing in water, fill the jars with brine, cover with sealing discs and screw lids on loosely; if in the oven, add brine after.

Put jars in a pan of water, or stand on newspaper in the oven. Cook.

When cool, try lifting bottle by disc only. The vacuum should hold.

Making sauerkraut

You can clamp the hearting cabbages you harvest in late autumn, but, if greens are scarce, sauerkraut is a noble winter standby.

Shred hard white cabbage hearts finely, and estimate ½ oz (14 g) salt for each 1 lb (0.5 kg) of cabbage.

Pack layers of shredded cabbage into a stone crock or wooden tub; sprinkle salt between the layers.

Spread one big cabbage leaf across the top, put a cloth over it, and cover that with a plate.

Weight down and leave in the warm. In 3 weeks put it in jars and sterilize as described opposite.

Making Pickles & Chutneys

Pickles and chutney are another way of preserving produce. They add flavour to cold meats, meat pies, cheeses and curries. The principle of both involves flavouring fruit and vegetables with spices, and then storing them in vinegar.

Ideally you would make your own vinegar and I describe how to do this on p. 196. But if you cannot do this, and have to buy it, you should note that there are vinegars of different strength, cost and flavour. Distilled or fortified vinegar is much the strongest (it is also the most expensive). Wine vinegar is the strongest natural vinegar, and more expensive than cider or malt vinegar. Remember that vinegar leaves its flavour in chutney, and even more so in pickles, so if you want to have the best-tasting accompaniments to your cold pies, you may find yourself paying for your vinegar. And the best-flavoured vinegar is wine. However, when you make chutney much of the liquid is evaporated during the cooking, so a malt vinegar may prove to be a more economic proposition.

PICKLES

The vinegar is first steeped with spices and sometimes cooked with sugar, to improve and mellow its sharpness. To make a spiced vinegar suitable for a variety of pickles, you can add any spices you like. Ground spices make vinegar go cloudy, so if you want the pickle to be attractively presented, and clearly recognizable, you should use whole spices.

The ideal way of making spiced vinegar is to steep all the spices in cold vinegar for a couple of months, after which time the liquid is ready to be strained and used. Since this is not always practicable, what follows is a speeded-up version. For 2 pints of vinegar take 2-3 oz (56-84 g) of spices and tie them in a little muslin bag. Include:

a piece of cinnamon bark
slivers of mace
some allspice
6-7 cloves
6-7 peppercorns
½ teaspoon mustard seed

If you like the flavour of garlic, or of any particular herb, add it. If you like a hot taste add chilli, ginger or more mustard.

Now put the vinegar and spices into a jug or heatproof jar which can be covered with a lid or a plate. Stand it in a panful of water. Bring the water to the boil, then take it off the heat. Leave the whole thing to cool down for two hours, by which time the spices should have thoroughly flavoured the vinegar. Remove the little bag and the vinegar is ready to use.

You can pickle fish, eggs, fruit, and vegetables, and you can pickle them whole or in pieces. Moist vegetables and fish are usually salted first. This draws out some of their water. Crisp pickles like cucumbers, beetroot, cabbage and onion are put straight into cold vinegar. Others like plums, tomatoes and pears are cooked till soft in spiced vinegar, which is then reduced to a syrupy consistency before finishing. When adding sugar to sweet pickle, use white sugar – it keeps the pickle clear and light.

Pickle jars need close sealing to prevent evaporation, and the vinegar must not come into direct contact with metal lids.

You should eat all pickles within six months; after this they are likely to soften.

Pickled eggs

Hard boil as many new-laid eggs as you like: you need about a quart (1.1 litres) of vinegar for every dozen. Shell them. Pack them in jars and cover them with spiced vinegar. Add a few pieces of chilli if you like. Close tightly and begin to eat after one month.

Pickled onions

Choose small button onions. Don't skin them at once, but soak them in a brine of salt and water using four ounces (114 g) of salt to each quart (1.1 litres) of water. After 12 hours skin them. Put them in a fresh brine for two to three days, with a plate on top so that they stay submerged. Then drain and pack in jars or bottles with spiced vinegar. A little sugar added to the vinegar helps the flavour. They are good to eat after two or three months.

Pickled apples

This is a sweet pickle. Use small apples (crab apples are good). For two pounds (0.9 kg) of apples use two pounds (0.9 kg) of sugar and one pint (0.6 litres) of spiced vinegar.

Cook the sugar and vinegar until the sugar is just dissolved. Prick the apples all over, using the prongs of a carving fork. If they are too big for the jar cut them in half. Simmer in the vinegar/sugar mixture until they are soft but not falling apart. Put them gently in jars. Reduce the syrup to half a pint (0.3 litres) by boiling. Pour it hot over the apples, but not so hot that it cracks the glass.

CHUTNEYS

Chutney is a concoction of almost any fruit or vegetable you like, flavoured with spices and cooked with vinegar to a thick jam-like consistency. Soft, over-ripe fruit and vegetables are suitable, as they turn into pulp quickly.

Possible ingredients for chutney are marrows, pumpkins, swedes, turnips, peppers, onions, beetroot, carrots, celery, aubergines, mangoes, tomatoes, apples, rhubarb, black-berries, pears, bananas, lemons, damsons, gooseberries, plums, dried fruit, peaches, elderberries, cranberries, oranges and grapefruit.

The herbs and spices can be any of these: bay leaves, chilli, cumin, coriander, cardamom, cinnamon, cloves, ginger, allspice, peppercorns, mustard seed, horseradish, paprika, cayenne, juniper and garlic.

It is best to mince vegetables or fruit for chutney finely and then cook them slowly for a long time to evaporate the liquid. Sugar plays a large part in chutney. Most chutneys go dark as they are cooked, so if you want an even darker one use brown sugar. Black treacle is a possible alternative.

Making tomato chutney

The secret of good chutney is to use contrasting ingredients. In this particular case the spice and garlic offset the tomatoes and apple.

You need: 2 lbs (0.9 kg) tomatoes, 2 onions, 1 cooking apple, raisins, 2 cloves garlic, ½ oz (14 g) fresh ginger, 2 oz (56 g) brown sugar, ½ pt (0.3 litres) vinegar, salt and some spices.

Skin the onions, peel and core the apple. Then chop them up finely.

Simmer the onion in a small pan with a little water. Add the apple and the raisins, and cook gently until they soften.

Skin the tomatoes, then chop them up roughly into chunks.

Crush the garlic and fresh ginger in a pestle and mortar with salt. If you are using dried ginger instead, add ¼ oz (7 g) to the bag of spices.

Tie up in a little muslin bag: 1 crushed bay leaf, 2-3 crushed dried chillies, ½ teaspoon mustard seed, 4-5 cloves; add cardamoms, cinnamon, coriander, peppercorns as you wish.

Tie the muslin bag to the handle of a large saucepan, so as not to lose it in the chutney.

Pour the softened ingredients into the pan, then everything else.

Cook on a low heat for an hour or so, until the mixture thickens so that when you draw a spoon through it you can see the pan.

Pot at once in hot clean jars. Seal and label.

Cooking chutney

Use aluminium, stainless steel or enamelled pans. Copper, brass or iron pans are not suitable as vinegar eats into them.

Simmer hard ingredients such as apple and onion in a little water before mixing with softer ingredients such as marrow or tomato, and before adding salt, sugar and vinegar, which tend to harden fruit or vegetables.

Put whole herbs and spices in a muslin bag, which you can tie to the handle of the pan so that you don't lose it in the chutney. If you prefer to use powdered spices they can be added loose to the other ingredients. Crush garlic and fresh ginger in a pestle and mortar before adding to chutney. Soak dried fruit in water before cooking it.

Use sufficient vinegar just to cover the ingredients. Cook until the consistency is of thick jam, and there is no free liquid. Be careful it doesn't burn towards the end. Stir well while it cooks. Pot while still hot, in clean hot jars, cover, label and store in a cool, dark place.

Storing chutney

Chutney improves with keeping, so store it in glass jars. Make sure they are tightly sealed or the vinegar will evaporate, leaving an unappetising dry shrunken mess. Cellophane papers such as are sold for jam covers are not suitable. I use twist-on metal caps from old jam or pickle jars. Check that the metal from the lid is well lacquered or protected with a waxed cardboard disc, otherwise the vinegar will corrode the metal. You can also use synthetic skins, or waxed paper circles underneath a greaseproof paper tie-on cover. Cover the jars with a cloth that has been dipped in melted candle-wax.

Making Jams & Syrups

Jams and conserves of all kinds are a very useful way of preserving fruit. Usually the fruit is cooked first without any sugar, to soften it and to release the pectin, which is what makes it set. Sugar is added next, and the whole thing boiled rapidly until setting point is reached. As long as jams are properly made, well covered, and kept in a cool, dry place, they keep for ages.

Fruit should be under rather than over-ripe, and clean. Bruises on damaged fruit don't matter as long as they are cut out. It is important to weigh the fruit before you begin cooking, otherwise you don't know how much sugar to add. Don't add more water than necessary to cook the fruit. The sugar should be preserving sugar as this dissolves fastest. Brown sugars are OK but bear in mind that they add a flavour of their own and in some cases are damp, therefore adjust the weight.

Some fruit has more acid and pectin in it than others. Fruit which is low in acid or pectin usually needs extra acid or pectin added to it (see below).

In general, jam-making goes like this: clean, sort and prepare fruit. Weigh it. Cook it with sufficient water to make it tender. Put it in a large wide pan, and when it is boiling add the required amount of sugar. Stir until all the sugar is dissolved. Bring to a rapid boil. Don't stir. Test from time to time to see if setting point (see below) is reached. Stop cooking when it is, allow to cool a little so that pieces of fruit will not float to the top of the jam in the jars. Fill hot clean jars to the brim with jam: cover, seal, label.

Testing for pectin

Put into a little glass a teaspoonful of strained cooled fruit juice from the cooked fruit, before you add the sugar. Add three teaspoons methylated spirits, and shake together. Wait a minute. Pour the mixture out into another glass. If the fruit juice has formed one solid blob, the pectin is good. If it is several blobs, it is not so good, so add less sugar. If it is all fluid, it is useless, in which case boil fruit again. Even add commercial pectin at a pinch.

Testing for set

Put a little jam from the pan on a saucer to cool. If the surface wrinkles when you push it with your finger, it is done. Examine the drips from the spoon: if a constant stream flows, it is no good; if large thick blobs form, it is OK. The temperature of the boiling jam should reach 222°F (105°C). It is best to use all or at least two of these methods to be absolutely sure your jam is ready.

Potted fruits or conserves do not keep as long as jam, but because they are only cooked briefly the flavours are very fresh. It is not so necessary to worry about pectin with conserves, so you can make them with low pectin fruit like raspberries, strawberries, blackberries and rhubarb. Note that there is more sugar per pound in conserves.

Damson or plum jam

Much of the pectin in plums is found in the stones, so if you can, extract the stones first, crack some of them and tie the kernels in a little bag. If this is difficult, never mind; they will float to the top when the jam cooks and you can skim them off with a slotted spoon at the end. You will need:

6 lbs (2.7kg) damsons or plums
6½ lbs (3.0kg) sugar
½ pint (0.3 litres) water

Wash the plums, cut them in half. Simmer with the water until tender. Add the sugar, stirring until dissolved, then boil hard until setting point. Remove floating stones, or if you put kernels in a bag, remove the bag. Leave the jam to cool a little before potting so that the fruit will not rise to the top of the jars. Pot, seal and label.

Raspberry conserve

4 lbs (1.8kg) raspberries
5 lbs (2.3kg) sugar

You can use damaged but not mouldy fruit. Warm the sugar in a bowl in a low oven. Butter a large pan, put in the fruit and cook over a very low heat. As the fruit begins to give up its juice and bubble slowly add the warm sugar. Beat hard until the sugar is quite dissolved. It should remain a lovely bright colour and taste of fresh raspberries. It should be quite thick. Pot and cover in the usual way, but examine for mould after a few months.

Another way is to put sugar and raspberries in layers in a large bowl. Leave overnight, and bring just to the boil next day, before potting.

Lemon curd

This is not a jam, but a good way of using up eggs.

4 oz (114g) butter
1 lb (0.9kg) sugar
4 eggs
3-4 lemons depending on size and juiciness

Grate the rind from the lemons, squeeze out their juice. Put rind, juice, butter and sugar into a small pan and heat until the butter melts and the sugar just dissolves. Let it cool. Beat up the eggs. Put them in a bowl which will just fit over a saucepan of simmering water, and stir in the juice. Beat over the saucepan of water, or use a double boiler, until the mixture thickens to curd consistency. Pot and cover.

Lemon curd doesn't keep long, so use it up quickly. Don't make too much at a time.

Richer curds can be made using eight egg yolks instead of four eggs. Variations include using oranges or tangerines instead of lemons. Use less sugar for sweeter fruit.

Lemon and carrot marmalade

8 oz (228g) thinly sliced lemon
8 oz (228g) shredded carrot
2 pints (1.1 litres) water
1 lb (0.9kg) sugar

Mix the lemon, the carrot and the water. Cover and allow to stand overnight. Cook in a covered saucepan, bring to the boil, then simmer for about half an hour, or until tender. Then add sugar, and simmer until it completely dissolves; boil rapidly until setting point. Try a little on a cold plate to see if it jells; it may take 15-30 minutes. Pour into clean, warm jars, cover with waxed paper and seal.

The flavour of carrot and lemon is very fresh and fairly sweet. Eat within three months.

Making fruit butters and cheeses

Fruit butters and cheeses are jams made from puréed or sieved fruit. Butters are softer than cheeses. Cheeses, if firm enough, can be turned out of their moulds as little "shapes".

Three fruit marmalade

Make this from oranges, lemons, and grapefruit as a substitute for Seville orange marmalade.

Squeeze out the juice from eight oranges, two lemons and two grapefruit. Strain it and save the pips.

Shred the peel coarsely or finely, depending on how thick you like your marmalade.

Tie the pips in a bag, and soak with the peel and juice for a day in 10 pts (5.7 litres) water. Boil for 2 hrs.

Test for pectin by adding 3 teaspoons meths to 1 of juice. Shake. The juice should solidify.

Remove the bag of pips from the pan. Boil the mixture, add 7 lbs (3.1 kg) sugar, stir until dissolved. Cook until it sets.

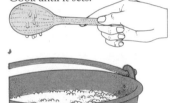

Let some marmalade drip from a spoon. If it falls in thick flakes it is properly set.

Or cool a little on a saucer. It is done if the surface creases when touched.

Put into hot clean jars, cover with greaseproof paper and cellophane, seal and label. Start eating it as soon as you like.

They are delicious eaten as puddings with cream or even spread on bread.

Blackberry and apple cheese

You will need equal amounts of blackberries and apples. Wash the apples but don't bother to peel or core them. Cut them up roughly. Pick over the blackberries, wash them if they are dusty. Put both fruits into a pan, just cover with water and stew, stirring occasionally, until the apples have gone mushy. Sieve the cooked fruit. You should have a fairly thick pulp. Weigh it. Add one pound (0.9kg) sugar to each pound of pulp. Boil together. Stir all the time, as this burns easily. When it thickens enough for you to see the bottom of the pan as you draw the spoon across it, it is done. Pot and cover like jam. It sets quite firmly, like cheese, and will last for ages.

Making jellies

Jellies are simply jams which have had all the solids strained from the cooked fruit. When the juice is boiled up with sugar it forms jelly which can be used in the same way as jam.

Blackberry and apple jelly

This recipe will suit any high-pectin fruit, such as crab apples, redcurrants, citrus fruits, quinces, gooseberries, sloes, damsons, and rowanberries. You can also experiment with mixtures of fruits. Cook them separately if one needs more cooking than the other.

Proceed as for blackberry and apple cheese to the point where the fruit is cooked and soft. Then strain the juice through a cloth. Don't succumb to the temptation of squeezing it to speed it up or the finished jelly will be cloudy. Measure the juice and add one pound (0.9kg) sugar to each pint (0.6 litres) of juice. Cook until setting point is reached and pot and label in usual way.

If you are very economically minded you can stew up the residue of fruit in the jelly bag with more water, then either extract more juice or make a fruit cheese by sieving it. Follow the instructions given above if you want to do this.

Fruit syrups

Fruit syrups are made in the same way as fruit jellies, though you don't need to add so much sugar to syrups. To prevent spoiling by fermentation (when you would be on the way to making wine) you have to sterilize syrups and keep them well sealed. They make very refreshing drinks and milk shakes in summer, or you can use them as sauces for puddings and cereals.

Extract the juice from any unsweetened cooked fruit you fancy, as for jelly, or, if you wish, extract it by pressing then straining. Measure the amount and then add about one pound (0.9kg) sugar per pint of juice. Heat it until the sugar is just dissolved – no more or it will start to set like jelly. Let it cool. Sterilize the bottles and their lids, preferably the screw-cap sort, by immersing in boiling water for 15 minutes. Drain, then fill with syrup. Screw up tightly then unscrew by half a turn, so that the heating syrup will be able to expand (leave a one inch or 2.5cm gap at the top of each bottle).

Stand the bottles in a pan deep enough for the water to come up to their tops. If possible use a pan like a pressure-cooker, that has a false bottom. Bring slowly to the boil and keep boiling for 20 to 30 minutes. Take out the bottles and screw the lids on tightly as soon as they are cool enough. If you are doubtful about the tightness of the seal, coat with melted candle wax.

Making Wine

Books about home-made wine-making have rolled off the presses in their regiments these last few years, each one blinding us with science more effectively than the last. You really only need to remember a few essentials:

You are unlikely to get more than three pounds (1.4 kg) of sugar to ferment in a gallon (4.5 litres) of water, so keep to approximately this ratio if you want strong wine.

You must keep all wine-making equipment scrupulously clean. Use boiling water whenever possible.

You must ferment at the temperature most favourable to vital yeasts.

You must give your special cultivated yeast every help and an unfair advantage over the wild yeasts and other organisms that might ruin your brew.

You must keep all contaminants out of your wine, especially vinegar flies, those little midges that hang round rotting fruit, carrying the bugs that turn wine to vinegar.

You must "rack", or pour off, the wine from the lees and sediments before the latter spoil its flavour.

You must allow the wine to settle and clear in the cool after the yeast has done its work.

Finally, having safely bottled your wine, you must try to keep your mitts off it for a year with red wine, if you can, and at least three months with white.

Strict cleanliness is essential in wine-making, for wine is made by a living organism (yeast) and if other living organisms (wild yeasts or other moulds or bacteria) get into the act either the tame yeasts that you want to use for your wine cannot do their job, or you get putrefaction, bad tastes and odours.

Equipment

You need jars, barrels, or bottles for fermentation. You need fermentation locks (if you can get them). The purpose of these is to allow the gases produced by fermentation to escape while keeping out air, which is always germ-laden, and vinegar flies. Many a gallon of fine wine has been made without a fermentation lock and with just a plug of cotton wool stuffed in the neck of the vessel. Many a gallon of wine has been ruined this way too. A fermentation lock is a very useful thing. A thermometer is not to be despised. You also need a flexible tube – rubber or plastic – for "racking" or syphoning, a funnel or two, and bottles or flagons for the final bottling of the wine. A corking gun is very good for driving in corks, which have to be driven in dead tight or air gets in and the wine goes bad. Polythene sealers are quite a good substitute for corks if you do not want to invest in a corking gun.

Materials

You will need yeast. Old fashioned country wine makers, including myself, have used all kinds of yeasts – bread yeasts and beer yeasts and so on – but undoubtedly it is best to buy wine yeasts from a shop. For very good and strong results some people use yeast nutrients, also bought from a shop. Acid is another thing you may have to add. Lemons will provide this, as will citric acid which you can buy. Tannin too can be bought, but tea or apples – particularly crab apples – will provide it. The reader may say that it is not being self-sufficient to buy all this stuff from a shop. True, but I would say that a trivial expenditure on this sort of thing is necessary if you are going to make a great deal of fine wine.

GRAPE WINE

There is no wine like grape wine. Red grape wine is made by fermenting the grapeskins in with the wine. White wine is made by taking the skins out. White wine is often made with red or black grapes, for all grapes are white inside. It is easier to make red or rosé wine than white because the tannin in the skins helps the "must" (wine-to-be) to ferment better, and the quicker it ferments the less chance there is of bad organisms getting to work.

Crushing

Crush your grapes any way you like. Personally I could not drink wine if I had seen somebody treading it with his bare feet, so I would use some sort of pestle and mortar for this job. If you want to make white wine, press the broken grapes in a press (a car jack will do), having first wrapped them in strong calico "cheeses", which I describe on p. 196. In the case of red or rosé press in the same way, but then add a proportion of the skins to the wine. The more you add the deeper the red of the wine but, in cold climates at any rate, the deeper red ones may contain too much tannin and will be a little bitter as a result. Now in real wine-growing climates (where you will not be reading instructions like this anyway since your neighbours will initiate you), you don't need to add any sugar. In less sunny climates add between four and six pounds (1.8-2.7kg) of sugar to every ten gallons (45.5 litres) of wine. If there has been a hot season and the grapes are sweet you need less, if a bad season, more.

Fermenting

Let the juices and skins ferment in a vat. Grapes have their own yeasts in the "bloom" on their skins but you had better add a wine yeast culture bought from a shop if you can get one. Warm a bottle of the must (juice) to 75°F (24°C), dump the yeast culture into it, and stand it in a warm place with some cotton wool in the neck. Meanwhile try to get your main body of must to 75°F (24°C). When the "starter", or culture in the bottle, has started to fizz pour it into the main body. If you keep the temperature at about 75°F (24°C) fermentation will be so active that there is no danger of air getting to the must, for the carbon dioxide given off will prevent this. Don't let the temperature rise above 80°F (27°C) or some of your good yeast will be killed. Don't let it fall below 70°F (21°C) if you can help

Wine-making equipment

*Don't attempt to make your own wine without arming yourself beforehand
with plenty of containers, to hold the must at each of its many stages. Bottles
are only the end of a long fermentation process, during which you will at least
need jugs and jars, and quite possibly vats and barrels too.*

Key
1 Corking gun
2 Jug
3 Bottle
4 Sieve
5 Bottle brush
6 Funnel
7 Hydrometer
8 Measuring cylinder
9 Plastic or rubber syphon
10 Earthenware vessel
11 Barrel and tapped vat
12 Fermentation jar and lock
13 Cork and plastic sealer

it, or your yeast will get sleepy and foreign yeasts will have
the advantage. At all times keep the skins stirred into the
must. They will float on top, so don't let them form a dry
floating crust.

Racking

When the first violent fermentation has ceased, rack off the
must, squeeze the juice out of the skins so as not to waste
it, and pour the juice into a barrel or carboy, so that the
must fills it completely. Do not leave an air space above it.
Let the temperature fall now to ordinary room temperature
of about 60°F (16°C). When you think most of the
sediment has sunk to the bottom, rack the wine into another
container. At this stage people in continental climates
often put wine out of doors in winter so that it almost
freezes, as this hastens the settling down of sediment. Rack
it again. After another month or two bottle it in the way I will
now describe.

Bottling

Bottles must be completely cleaned and then sterilized. It
is no good "sterilizing" anything with dirt in it; the dirt must
first be removed. Sterilize by heating slowly so as not to
crack the bottles, in an oven if you like; then pour in boiling
water, or put in cold water and slowly bring to the boil
and boil for five minutes. Hang the bottles upside down
immediately to let them drain and stop dust floating down
into them. Either use as soon as they are cool or cork until
you want them. Boil the corks before you use them and
wang them in with a special corker. Store bottled wine on
its side so as to keep the corks wet. If they dry out they will
shrink, and air and vinegar-bacillus will get in. Store wine
in the dark, at a cool even temperature. A cellar is ideal.

COUNTRY WINES

Overleaf are some recipes for "country wines" that work,
as I know from long experience. I would not put anybody off

Making Wine

"scientific wine-making", which is reliable and produces good wines, but country people all over Europe and North America have used the sort of recipes I give for centuries, and very seldom have failures; indeed their wines are very good. One point worth noting is that the larger the bulk of wine you make, the less likely you are to have a failure. My old friends in a Worcestershire village who all brew rhubarb wine in the summer and parsnip in the winter, in batches of sixty gallons (273 litres) stored in huge cider barrels, have never known what a failure is. Their wives cry in vain for them to grow something else in their gardens, but their wine is superb.

Flower wines

Pour a gallon (4.5 litres) of boiling water over an equivalent quantity of whatever flowers you wish to use, cool, and press the water from the flowers. Add four pounds (1.8kg) of sugar, half a pound (228g) of raisins (optional), and the juice of three lemons. As the flowers don't give much nutriment for the yeast, and sugar alone is not enough for it, add some yeast nutriment if you have some. A tablespoon of nutriment to a gallon of wine is about right. Then, when the temperature has fallen to 75°F (24°C), add yeast. A bought wine yeast is best. Put the wine in a vessel with a fermentation lock, and leave it to ferment. Rack off and bottle when ready. I have made wines from broom flowers, gorse flowers, elderflower (superb), cowslip, dandelion, and I have drunk good rose wine.

MEAD

To supply what in your estimation is about three pounds (1.4kg) of honey to a gallon (4.5 litres) of water you want comb cappings, odd bits of "wild comb" that you can't put through the extractor, and perhaps some pure honey stolen from the main storage pot when your wife isn't looking. Melt the honey in the water and ferment. Honey is deficient in acid, so put the juice of two or three lemons in a gallon, or some citric acid. Mead also likes some tannin to feed the yeast, so some crushed crab apples are a good idea. I have heard of people putting tea in mead. I once dumped some rose hip syrup that the children decided they didn't like into my mead, which wasn't fermenting very well, and it started to ferment like blazes. Mead goes on fermenting for a long time, so don't hurry it, and if you can leave it in a bottle for a few years so much the better. But can you? Here are some wine recipes to try for yourself:

Rhubarb wine

15 lbs (6.8kg) rhubarb
2½ lbs (1.1kg) sugar
1 gallon (4.5 litres) water
yeast

Chop up the rhubarb, pour boiling water over it, and mash. Don't boil it any further. Leave it to soak until the next day, strain off your liquor and press the "fruit" to get as much out as you can. Stir in the sugar and bung in the yeast. Leave it to ferment, then rack it and bottle it.

Nettle wine

4 lbs (1.8kg) nettle tips
4 lemons
2 lbs (0.9kg) sugar (preferably brown)
1 oz (28g) cream of tartar
2 gallons (9.0 litres) water
1 tablespoon dried yeast or brewer's yeast

Put nettles and cut-up lemons in the water and boil for twenty minutes. Strain liquor out and add cream of tartar and sugar. When cool enough add yeast and ferment for three days in a warm place. Then let it settle for a couple of days in a cooler place before bottling in screw-top bottles. You can drink it in a week and it doesn't keep long. It is extremely pleasant and refreshing. If you add some ginger to it, it is even better.

Parsnip wine

4 lbs (1.8kg) parsnips
3 lbs (1.4kg) sugar
1 gallon (4.5 litres) water
some lemons or citric acid
yeast

Cut the parsnips up and boil them without letting them get too soft. They should just be easily prickable with a fork. Boil a couple of lemons up with them if you have them. Strain off the liquor, and while it is still hot, stir in the sugar, so that it dissolves. Put in some lemon juice or citric acid, and some raisins if you like. The purpose of the lemon juice or citric acid is to give the yeast enough acidity to feed on, as parsnips are low in acid. Put everything in a vessel, wait until the temperature drops to blood heat, then add your yeast and allow to ferment. Like all other wine, ferment under a fermentation lock, or put a wodge of cotton wool in the neck of the vessel, to keep the vinegar flies out and let out the carbon dioxide. Rack it well a couple of times and then keep it as long as you can lay your hands off it.

Elderberry wine

6 lbs (2.7kg) elderberries
3 lbs (1.4kg) sugar
1 gallon (4.5 litres) water
2 oz (56g) citric acid or lemon juice
yeast

You are supposed to get all the berries off the stalks, but I have shoved in stalks and all and it has made no difference. After all, if you can save a lot of work by departing from slavish convention why not do so? Pour the boiling water on, mash hard with a potato masher, cover and leave to soak for 24 hours. Put the sugar and yeast in and leave it alone. The longer you leave it the better. When it has finished fermenting rack it into bottles or other containers, so as to leave the sediment behind. You do this with all wines.

The above recipe can be applied to any wine that is made from berries or currants.

Elderflower "champagne"

This is nothing like champagne of course but it is a very refreshing summer drink and it does not have to be kept long before you can drink it.

12 heads of elderflowers (in full bloom and scent, picked on a hot day)
1½ lbs (0.7kg) sugar (white sugar is less obtrusive than brown in such a
  delicate drink)
1 lemon
2 tablespoons wine vinegar

Put blooms in a bowl with the juice of the lemon. Cut up the rind of the lemon and put that in (minus the white pith). Add the sugar, vinegar, a gallon (4.5 litres) of water and leave for 24 hours. Strain liquor into screw-top bottles, cork up and leave for a fortnight. Don't add yeast – the weak yeasts on the flowers are enough. Drink before three weeks old.

Making rose hip wine

The principle of wine-making does not vary much according to the main ingredient. The addition of a wine yeast to your brew starts off the fermentation process which can take as long as three months.

Take 3 quarts (3.4 litres) of rose hips, clean them and chop them up finely. Crush with a wooden spoon or mallet.

Put the crushed hips into a deep bowl and pour 1½ gallons (6.8 litres) of boiling water over them. If you like you can add the rind and juice of an orange.

Add 2 lbs (0.9 kg) of sugar to the brew, and heat it to 75°F (24°C)

Stir in a teaspoon of fresh yeast. You can put this first into a bottle of "starter", which you add to the brew when it starts fermenting. Add one teaspoon of citric acid and half a teaspoon of tannin.

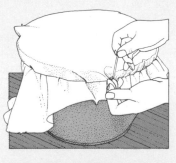

Cover the must to keep out vinegar flies and all other contaminants. Leave for 24 hours.

Strain the must from the hips through a sieve or muslin cloth. For even clearer must use both these methods.

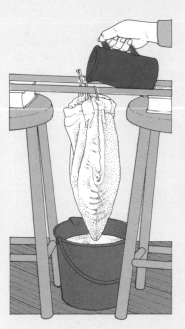

Or you can strain through a jelly bag, suspended from two stools. Don't press it, or it will go cloudy.

Strain the must into fermentation jars. Use a funnel. Keep at a temperature of 75°F (24°C).

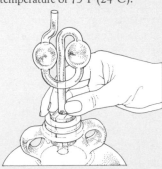

The fermentation lock keeps air out but allows gases to escape.

When fermentation stops rack the wine off the lees into bottles. Use a rubber or a plastic tube for this.

If you have no tube, use a hand jug and a funnel. Leave an inch (2.5 cm) at the top for corks when filling the bottles.

A corking gun is excellent for driving corks in tight, but a wooden mallet will do. Date, label, and leave for a year.

Making Cider & Vinegar

CIDER

Cider should be made from a mixture of apples. The ideal mixture is rich in acid, tannin and sugar, so a good combination mixes very sweet apples with very sour ones, perhaps with some crab apples thrown in to provide the tannin. Cider can be made with unripe apples but it is never very successful. Ideally the apples should be picked ripe and then allowed to lie in heaps for two or three days until they begin to soften a little. A few bad or bruised apples in the press don't seem to affect the quality of the cider at all. Apples vary greatly in juice content, so it is not possible to tell exactly how much cider you will get from a given number of apples. As a rough estimate, 10-14 lbs of apples make one gallon (4.5 litres).

Crushing

You then crush the apples. Traditionally this was done by a horse or an ox pulling a huge round stone round a circular stone trough. You can crush apples in a cider mill, which is an expensive item to buy, or you can just use any hard object, such as a wooden mallet, as long as it is not metal. Crushing is an arduous task. I did have one friend who used to put his apples through a horizontal mangle, which reduced them to pulp very effectively. Put the juice in a fermenting vat and wrap the pulp in hessian or coarse cloth to form "cheeses". Pile the "cheeses" in a press one on top of the other and press to extract the juice. After one pressing rearrange the "cheeses" and press again. The pressed pulp can be fed, in strict moderation, to pigs or cattle.

Fermenting

Traditionally the juice is put in large vats, which are great hooped wooden structures. Commercial ones are enormous and hold thousands of gallons, but the self-supporter who might make ten gallons at a time will find an ordinary wooden barrel or an earthenware crock perfectly adequate. No yeast or other additive is put in: the stuff just ferments, and there are stories of farmers putting lumps of beef in to add strength, and having them simply eaten up by the potent cider. As all the sugar in the apples ferments out to alcohol the cider is terribly sharp, and is known as "rough" in cider circles. Only a hardened rough cider drinker can drink it without a shudder going down his spine.

If you want to speed up the fermentation process, you can add a culture of wine yeast when you have extracted the juice from the pulp. This should work faster than the wild yeasts, which may or may not be man enough for the job. If you want a sweet cider rack the fermenting cider off its lees (syphon it off without disturbing the sediment) and add roughly six pounds (2.7 kg) of sugar per ten gallons (45.5 litres); then, allow it to ferment once more and in about a week rack it again. If you want to bottle it and have sparkling cider, it is best to try bottling a small quantity first. Fill a screw-topped flagon half full, screw it up, and put it in a warm place. After six hours open it. If it is filled with gas, and has thrown a heavy deposit, the cider is not ready for bottling. It is only safe to bottle when you find just a little fizz of gas given off, and no heavy sediment thrown.

Cider improves with keeping, so you shouldn't drink this autumn's cider until next summer.

VINEGAR

Vinegar is wine, beer or cider, in which the alcohol has been turned into acetic acid by a species of bacteria. This bacillus can only operate in the presence of oxygen, so you can protect your wines, beers and ciders from turning to vinegar by keeping them from the air. Yeast produces carbon dioxide in large quantities, and this expels the air from the vessel that the beverage is stored in. But yeast cannot operate in more than a certain strength of alcohol, so fermentation ceases when so much sugar has been converted into alcohol that the yeast is killed or inhibited by its own action. This is the moment when the vinegar-forming bacillus, *Acetobacter*, gets active, and the moment when your beverages need protecting most rigorously from fresh air and bacterial infection.

But if you want to make vinegar, then you must take your wine, beer, or cider, and expose it to the air as much as possible. If you just leave it in an open barrel it will turn into vinegar in a few weeks. But it is better to speed up the process, as smells from the surrounding atmosphere might give the vinegar a taste, and hostile bacteria have time to attack. To hasten the process, take a barrelful of beech shavings. Beech is traditional but any shavings will do as long as they do not come from a very resinous tree. Soak them well in a good vinegar of the type you are trying to make. Then put a per-forated wooden plate in the barrel over the shavings and pour your wine, beer or vinegar on to this plate. The liquid will then drip slowly through the holes, which must be very small, mere pin-holes. The liquid drips slowly through the shavings, thus being well exposed to both air and *Acetobacter*, and at the bottom it is drawn off through a cock. Leave it then in an open cask and it will turn into vinegar within a week.

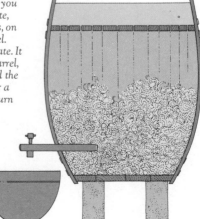

Making vinegar
First soak a barrelful of beech shavings in vinegar of the sort you are making. Put a wooden plate, perforated with pin-sized holes, on top of the shavings in the barrel. Pour your alcohol on to the plate. It will drip slowly through the barrel, and be well exposed to air and the vinegar-forming bacillus. After a week in an open cask, it will turn into vinegar.

Food from the Wild

"A man may fish with the worm that
hath eat of a king, and eat of the fish that
hath fed of that worm."

SHAKESPEARE

Game

Man should be a husbandman, not a bandit. We have no right to slaughter other animals just for fun or to assuage our blood-lust. Nor have we the right to deplete the stock of any species of animal so that it becomes scarce or extinct. Yet we have a part to play in maintaining the balance of nature and if we fail to play it nature will very rightly shrug her shoulders and shake us off.

If man plays his proper part in husbanding nature he not only helps to maintain a proper balance, he also supplements his diet with good food (wild meat is a far better source of protein than the meat of domesticated animals), and he protects his crops. The true husbandman will accept his responsibility in this matter. He will also accept responsibility in the way he hunts his game. It is unforgivable to wound an animal instead of killing it outright, so don't go shooting until you are a good shot. And never take a shot unless you are absolutely certain of a kill.

Guns

A shotgun is a smooth bore tube which fires a charge of shot. Shot always used to be made of lead but it is now agreed that lead should never be used for this purpose. The main reason is that the lead is gradually polluting the environment. Always buy cartridges using shot of other metals.

The sizes of shot are numbered according to what number of individual pellets it takes to make up an ounce (28 g): thus no. 1 shot is very big (it is used, wrongfully in my opinion, for roe deer), no. 3 is about right for wild geese, no. 5 for duck, and no. 6 for pheasants, rabbits and small game, while nos. 8 and 9 are used for snipe or woodcock. 8 or 9 for snipe or woodcock.

Shotguns are graded according to the size of their bore (size of their barrel). The bore depends on the number of lead balls in a pound (0.5 kg) that exactly fit a barrel. Thus the barrel of a twelve bore takes twelve balls to fit it, making up a pound. The twelve bore is by far the commonest size all over the world now and is a good all-purpose gun. Sixteen and twenty bores are sometimes found: they hit as hard as a twelve but have a smaller "pattern" (area covered by the shot at a given distance from the barrel). They are light and handy but to use one well you must be a good shot. The "four-ten" (.410 inch) is commonly used to start children off. Ten and eight bores are heavy guns used for wildfowling, particularly for geese and wild duck. The four bore, almost extinct now, is a very heavy gun indeed, used for firing at mobs of birds on estuaries; the giant "punt guns" of yore could be "half-crown" bore (the barrel the size of the old British half-crown) or even larger, and would fire up to two pounds (0.9 kg) of shot.

In Europe the double-barrelled shotgun is common; in America pump action semi-automatics are usual, or else fully self-loading automatics. It is all a matter of what people think is "sporting". Cartridges are loaded with nitro-powder, which is smokeless and reliable, but some people load their own brass-cased cartridges (with an apparatus bought from a gun shop) and thus save a lot of money. Modern cartridges are fired by a percussion cap (small brass cap containing fulminate of mercury) pressed into the base of the cartridge.

The old muzzle loading guns, which are very good but need a longer time to load, used percussion caps put into a hole in the breach of the barrel and hit by the hammer. Before that invention they had flint locks: a hammer with a piece of flint in it came down and struck a steel pad, sending a spark down into some gunpowder in a pan which communicated with the charge inside the barrel. There was a slight delay when you fired one of these and some uncertainty as to whether it would go off at all. But muzzle loaders could be very effective weapons and may very well come back one day. It is perfectly possible to fire a ball from a shotgun, but common sense will tell you that it must not be larger than the smallest part of the barrel, otherwise you will kill, not the quarry, but yourself. A ball, however, is not very accurate over more than a few score yards. To achieve great accuracy with firearms it was found necessary to make the projectile spin, so as to cancel any irregularities in it and give it a gyroscopic effect. Muzzle-loading rifles are possible, but slow to load.

A rifle has a series of spiral grooves cut down inside the barrel, and a single bullet of soft metal, or coated with soft metal. When the bullet is propelled out of the chamber of the gun into the barrel, the metal around it conforms to the shape of the spirals and this gives the bullet a spin. Without this spin the bullet will not travel accurately but will invariably veer off to one side or another. The "two-two" (.22 inch bore) is common all over the world and is perfect for small game such as rabbits, hares, small deer or buck, and birds, or vermin such as foxes, crows and other marauders. Its ammunition is cheap, light and small, and the rifle is very effective up to several hundred yards. I have shot kudu, reed-buck, and various other big game with a two-two, and have never once merely wounded one of them or failed to kill it; but then I would never use a two-two for such a purpose unless I was very close and quite sure of my target.

For larger game, however, larger rifles are really much better. Seven millimetre is a very common size (the 7 mm Mauser has always been, in my opinion, the best small sporting rifle in the world; the 6.5 mm Manlicher is as good ballistically but has an inferior magazine). The 9 mm is fine for thick-skinned game. I used a .404 inch bolt-action rifle in Africa; it gave me a certain sense of security when being charged by a buffalo but by God it kicked.

Rabbits

Rabbits are temporarily being controlled in Europe by myxomatosis, a disease that originally came from America, where it is epizootic among the cottontails and does them very little harm, whereas European rabbits had no resistance to it. So at the moment they should be "given law" (spared, in hunters' parlance). When they come back in strength they must be well controlled, or they will become the all-pervading menace they once were, when no forester could

Hares and rabbits
Rabbits in plenty should play a large part in the self-supporter's diet. Hares are not as easy to find, but make a wonderful winter meal.

Deer
If deer are not protected where you live make the most of your hunting and live on venison for weeks.

Game birds
Many of the smaller game birds are protected now, but the self-sufficient person can still enrich his table with wild duck, roast pheasant and the occasional festive goose.

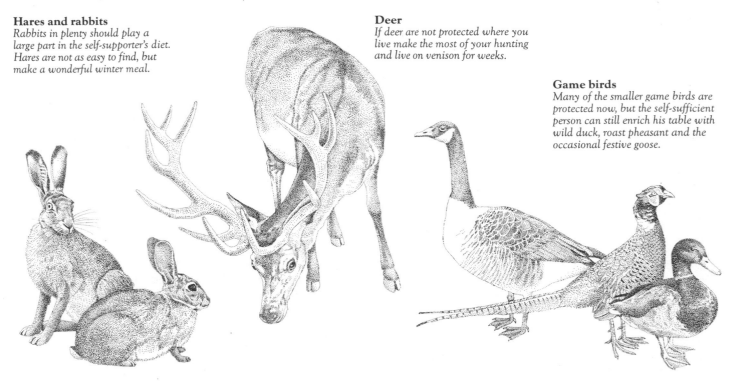

plant a tree without enormous expense on extermination and rabbit-proof fencing, and when twenty-five percent of the crops in many areas went down the rabbits' throats. In any case they are also very good food.

The most humane way of taking rabbits (along with most other small animals and birds) is to shoot them either with a shotgun or a two-two rifle. Very early in the morning is the best time to "walk-up" rabbits with a shotgun, or to lie in wait for them with a two-two.

Long-netting is perhaps the second best way of killing rabbits. It is humane, quiet, cheap (no expenditure on cartridges) and properly done it can be very efficient. You set up the net between the rabbits' grazing ground and their burrows in the day time at your leisure. Keep it folded up out of the way where the rabbits can get underneath it, with a release string to let it drop when you pull it. You then go along at night, when the rabbits are out in the field grazing, and the net is between the grazing ground and the rabbit warren. You pull the string, down comes the net, your accomplice gets behind the rabbits, makes a noise; they all run off into the net, get tangled, whereupon you kill them. If you are netting on land where it is better for you to remain inconspicuous, you creep out after dark, get between the grazing rabbits and their burrows in absolute silence, set up the net quickly (not folded up) and then get the rabbits chased into the net. I used to do this on heavily game-keepered land with an accomplice who was deaf. This made it very difficult to communicate without alarming the whole countryside. I have had a dozen rabbits with one setting of a long net.

Snaring is an effective way of getting a rabbit for the pot if you really need one and have no other way, but I don't like it for it is somewhat cruel, in spite of the fact that a rabbit generally strangles itself very quickly in a snare. Brass picture wire is good for rabbit snares: unravel it and use three strands or so. It is advisable to buy a snare first and copy it. The best places for snares are rabbit runs, entrances to burrows, or holes in fences.

Ferreting is a good way of controlling rabbits. Furthermore it is great fun. Keep ferrets in a hutch, keep them clean, feed them sparingly on fresh meat, and handle them often to keep them tame. Use deliberate steady movements when handling them, as they will sometimes bite your hand, thinking that you are giving them a piece of meat.

You can work ferrets loose, on a line, or with a bell. Only a reliable ferret can be worked loose; an unreliable one may kill a rabbit down the hole and "lay up" with it. A line ferret has a collar round her neck with a long line on it. The disadvantage of this is that the line may get snagged around a tree root far down a burrow, in which case you will have a lot of digging to do. We used to work them loose but keep one "liner" in reserve. If a ferret did lay up we would send the liner down and then dig along the line and thus find the errant ferret. The point of a bell is that the ferret wearing a bell scares the rabbits out without being able to kill them; also, if the ferret does lay up, you can hear the bell and dig him out. Probably the best thing is just to use loose ferrets and trust to luck.

There are ways and means of recapturing a ferret if he lays up. The best is probably a box trap, with a dead rabbit inside it, and a trap-door, so that when the ferret goes in the door shuts behind him. Anyone with some ingenuity can devise one of these.

Game

Rabbits "bolted" by the ferret are best caught in purse nets. These are simply small bags of nets staked around the entrances to the holes. You can shoot the rabbits with shotguns as they bolt, but this has the disadvantage that the noise of the guns makes the rabbits still down the holes shy of bolting. Purse nets are far and away the best method. On a larger scale a warren can be ringed with long nets and the rabbits driven out by the ferrets and chased into the long nets by dogs.

When you have caught your rabbits you must kill them. I have already described how to do this on page 123. "Hulk" or "paunch" rabbits as soon as you catch them: this means removing its guts. A countryman can hulk a rabbit without using a knife: he uses the rabbit's own sharp claw instead.

Hares

Hares can be snared, but it takes practice to know where to put the snare. If you examine a hare's run you will see where the hare commonly lands after each leap. Put the snare just before this spot. Purse nets can be set over gaps in fences or hedges where hares are known to go and the hare can be chased in by a dog. A good lurcher will run a hare down and kill it, but it has got to be a good lurcher, for the hare runs at enormous speed. You can train lurchers to keep out of sight, and never to come near you if a stranger is anywhere about.

When you have caught your hares, hang them for at least a week, because hares, unlike rabbits, are game. Only after hanging should you hulk and skin the hare. This is an evil-smelling job, but persevere. Hares make a wonderful meal.

Snaring
Place a wire snare in a rabbit or hare run; the animal is caught by getting his head stuck in the wire ring, which tightens and traps him. Snaring is an effective method, but a cruel one.

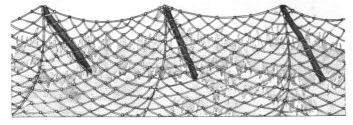

Long-netting
Position your net between burrows and grazing grounds. Erect it folded up, and pull the release string while the rabbits are feeding. Startle them back towards the warren, and they will get caught in the net.

Game birds

Pheasants and partridge can legally be shot on your own land, always assuming that the previous owner did not reserve the right to shoot them when he sold the land. If there seem to be no pheasants actually on your own land, there is nothing to stop you attracting them from your next door neighbour's land. Pheasants are incapable of resisting Jerusalem artichokes, and about a quarter of an acre of these will bring the birds flocking from far and wide. Buckwheat and sunflowers are also superb crops for attracting pheasants' attention. Maize and kale are also useful.

It is of course unforgivable to take a hen bird from off the nest, and, if ever this should chance to happen, as an honourable poacher you would of course take the eggs and hatch them out under a chicken hen. Chicken hens never seem to mind whose eggs they sit on when they are broody.

Pigeons are best shot over decoys, which are model pigeons. Place them on a pigeon feeding ground: under an oak with plenty of acorns dropping from it is ideal, but your cabbages will do. Conceal yourself well – pigeons have gimlet eyes – and shoot them as they swoop in. If you have no decoys shoot a few and set them up as decoys on forked twigs. Always face your decoys up-wind.

Wild ducks can be lured to decoys too. They are magnificent food, and, unlike the domestic duck, should be hung as game. I stopped shooting wild geese when I discovered that they mate for life. Most other game birds are fine delicacies, but they are now almost all protected; the rarer the delicacy the more unlikely you are to be eating them legally.

Big game

Deer, antelope and other big game are often shot in Europe with the shotgun. This, to my mind, is quite wrong, for deer undoubtedly get away with shotgun pellets inside them. The rifle is the only weapon for the humane killing of deer, unless you are really expert with the cross-bow or the bow and arrow. An effective way of shooting deer or antelope is at night with a "balala light". A balala light (the word is African) is a light with a powerful beam and you strap it to your forehead. The heavy battery is carried on your belt. The beam illuminates both the quarry and the sights of your rifle. The advantage of shooting at night is that the game are generally quietly grazing, not expecting danger, and you can often walk right up to them; somehow, shooting down the beam of a light, it seems impossible to miss. In any case you get nothing but very close shots. I have shot hundreds of buck in Africa in this manner (they were our only source of meat) and never missed, or only wounded, a single one. The method is against the law in many countries, and as long as shooting is looked upon as "sport" this will be so. When it is looked upon, as it should be looked upon, as "work" – a legitimate way of harvesting a crop of meat – then such silly laws will be changed.

Shooting in the daytime is a matter of walking very quietly up or across wind if possible, keeping calm and cool, not

Skinning a rabbit

Once you have killed your rabbit, you will need to prepare him for the pot. Before you skin him you must "paunch" him: that is, remove the guts. Skinning is not difficult; you will find that the skin comes away from the flesh very easily. And if the thought of preparing the animal still appals you, just brace yourself and think hard of rabbit pie.

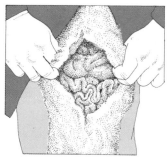

Prise open the belly to expose the guts and remove them. "Paunching" is now complete.

Invert the skin and fur, so that the flesh of first one hind leg, then the other, is exposed.

Expose the front legs and cut away the last tendon joined on to them.

Hold the rabbit between your knees by its head, so that its tail hangs free and its belly faces upwards. Cut a hole in its belly.

Cut off all four paws of the rabbit with a sharp knife.

The hind quarters are now free from all skin and fur, and now is the moment to cut off the tail.

Pull the skin over the rabbit's neck and cut off its head.

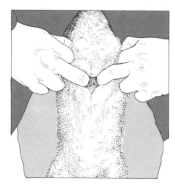

Pull the skin apart at the cut, and insert two fingers into the hole.

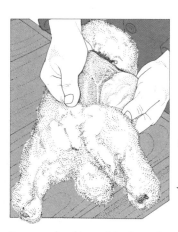

Separate the skin and fur from the flesh of the rabbit, at the belly.

Hold the hind legs in one hand and pull the skin down to the front legs.

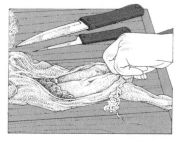

Split the hind legs from the belly and cut out the anal passage. Then place your knife in the rabbit's breast, and remove the "lights" and heart. You must also remove the gall from the liver.

getting puffed or out of breath, observing closely, and seeing the game before they see you. Shooting deer or wild pig in northern woods is best done by sitting in a hide up a tree near a pool or some likely grazing place.

If you do just wound a buck or a deer sit down and rest for at least half an hour. Don't follow the blood spore immediately. If you do, the animal, on the alert, will hear you before you see him and get up and run away. Leave him for half an hour and he will lie down, get stiff – he is losing blood all the time – and probably go to sleep. When you then walk quietly up you will see him before he sees you and get another shot in. You will almost never kill a wounded buck if you follow the blood spore immediately.

Hanging game

Most game should be "hung", that is hung up in a cool airy larder for some time before eating. Hang game birds up by the neck, not the feet as with tame birds. The reason for this is so the guts do not press against the meat of the breast. Do not gut the birds then. In the winter in a northern climate it is all right to hang a pheasant, or a wild duck for as much as ten days. At the end of this period pluck them and gut them. Game birds hung up with their feathers on look pretty, but, if you just want them to eat, it is quite a good plan to pluck them when you shoot them there and then (always assuming that you are not on somebody else's land), because the feathers come out easily when the birds are still warm.

Fish & Sea Foods

The self-supporter ought to make the most of any opportunity he gets, and fish should figure at the forefront of his healthy, varied, natural diet. The "sport" of angling, in my opinion, is a complete waste of time. Catching fish, weighing them and throwing them back does no one any good. Many anglers hold the misguided belief that freshwater fish are inedible or unpleasant, but this is quite untrue. Freshwater fish make wonderful food. People should be encouraged to take or farm freshwater fish for food. The methods I describe are not necessarily legal in every country, but all I can say is that they ought to be.

FRESHWATER FISH

Trout Plenty of people catch trout with their bare hands by "tickling". You lean over a bank and very gently introduce your hand into a cavity underneath it, waggling your fingers in a tickling movement as you do so. When you feel a fish with the tips of your fingers you just gently tickle its belly for a minute; then grab it and fling it on the bank. "Groping" is another method: wade along in a shallow stream, walking upstream, and grope with your hand under rocks, grabbing any fish you find there. You are quite liable to get bitten by an eel while you are doing it, though.

Pike "Snaring" was a method much used in East Anglia when I was a boy. You have a wire snare hanging from a stick, and when you see a large pike hanging in the water, as pike do, you very carefully insert the snare in front of him and let it work slowly back to his point of balance. When you think it is there you haul him out. If the wire does just touch him as you work it over him he thinks it is a stick because it is going downstream.

Salmon You can "gaff" salmon. To gaff a salmon first locate him; you will find him resting in a pool or under an overhanging tree. You then take the head of a gaff, which can be made from a big cod hook, out of your pocket, cut a light stick from a bush, and lash the gaff on to the stick. You have a lanyard (light cord) running from the eye of the gaff to your wrist where it is tied round. You drag the gaff into the fish and then just let go of the stick. The line unwinds from the stick which falls away, and you haul the fish in with the line. If you try to haul him in with the stick he may well pull you in.

Eel Sensible people, among whom I include the Dutch and the Danes, account the eel the best fish there is, and indeed if you have ever eaten well-smoked *gerookte palling* in Holland you must agree. You can take eels in "grigs" or "eel-hives": these are conical or square baskets made of osiers, wire netting or small mesh fish netting on a frame, with an admission funnel like a very small lobster pot. Bait this with fresh fish or meat; whatever people say eels don't like bad fish. Fresh meat or fresh chicken guts in a gunny sack, with the neck of the sack tied tight, and some stones inside it to sink it, will catch eels.

"Babbing" for eels is a good way of catching them. Get a bunch of worms as big as your fist, thread wool yarn through them, tie them in a bunch, and lower them into shallow water on the end of a string, which is tied to a stick. After a while haul the "bab" gently out and eels may be found hanging to it, their teeth entangled in the yarn. Pull the bunch over your boat, or over the bank, and give it a shake. I have caught a hundredweight of eels this way in an afternoon.

I have not discussed conventional angling with rod and line, for this is done more as a sport than for food production, although good anglers can sometimes get a lot of food this way too. But the fresh waters should be farmed for fish just as the land is farmed for crops and animals. To reserve fish solely for sport is an indulgence that a hungry world cannot afford: they should be cropped, harvested and conserved, and looked upon as a source of good food. If we have some fun catching them as well, then so much the better. I discuss the techniques of fish farming on p. 246.

SEA FISH
Catching pelagic fish
From the point of view of the person who wishes to catch sea water fish, they fall into two groups: pelagic and demersal. The former swim freely about the seas, independent of the bottom. The latter are confined to the bottom. Obviously the means of taking them are quite different.

Hooks and feathers Sometimes you can catch hundredweights in a few hours when hooking for pelagic fish. Mackerel in particular can be caught productively in this way, though traditionally they were caught by a last. This was a piece of skin, about two inches (5 cm) long, cut from near the tail of a mackerel you had already caught. The method was to move along at about two knots dragging the last on a hook astern. Then somebody discovered the "feathers". With this new invention you have perhaps a dozen hooks, on snoods (short branch lines), tied to a line with a weight on it. Each hook has a white or coloured feather whipped to the shank (though almost anything will do: bits of white plastic, or shiny tin). You lower the tackle from a stationary boat, find the depth at which the mackerel are biting, and plunge the feathers up and down with a motion of your arm.

Don't waste time trying to catch mackerel when there aren't any. Wait until other people report them in good quantities, and then go and hit them hard. Often one day's fishing, salted, will give you enough to last you a year. The rest of the time forget about it. Time is of great importance to the self-supporter, and he can't afford to waste it.

Drift net Herring cannot be caught on a hook. Unlike mackerel they don't hunt other fish, but live on small fauna in the plankton, so their mouths are too small for hooks. They are traditionally caught with a drift net. This fine net hangs down vertically in the water suspended from a float-line, which is a line with corks or plastic floats all along it. You can let it drop to any depth you like by hanging it on longer or shorter pendants. The whole net must have positive buoyancy. It will catch more at night, and a fine night is the best time for catching herring. "Shoot" (to shoot, in fishing terms, means to put into the water) the net from a boat and hang on to one end of it for an hour or two, letting both boat and net drift with the tide. Cast off occasionally and row along the net, and just lift a few yards of it to see if there are any fish. If a shoal hits the net haul it in. Don't bother to try getting the fish out of the net into the boat, just pay the net down into the stern of the boat and go back to port. Then unload the net and shake the fish out into a piece of canvas, laid on the beach. Drift nets will take any pelagic fish if the mesh is the right size: mackerel, sprats, pilchards, salmon, sea-trout and many other fish are all taken in drift nets.

Catching demersal fish

Trawl net Bottom fish can be taken by a trawl net. There are basically two sorts: the beam trawl and the otter trawl. The beam trawl is a net bag with its mouth held open by a beam which is supported on two "heads" which are like the runners of a sled. The otter trawl has two "otter boards" holding its mouth open: they swim through the water like kites, holding the trawl mouth open as they do so. Probably for the self-supporter with a small boat the beam is best, although many would dispute this. You need considerable power to haul a trawl, particularly an otter trawl which takes a certain minimum speed to keep the otter boards working. A small beam trawl can be hauled by sail alone, especially if you work down-tide. Often the tide is enough to pull the net. Always trawl down-tide anyway, as the fish face up-tide. A small-meshed beam trawl also takes shrimps.

Tangle net This is a recent invention made possible by very strong, thin, man-made fibre. It is a very light, large-meshed net which sinks to the bottom of the sea, where some of its width is supported by a submerged cork line and the rest just lies in a heap on the bottom. Anything that walks or swims near the bottom is taken by it, getting inextricably tangled, and then you have the lovely job of clearing the net! That is the disadvantage, for the net is hell to clear and always gets badly torn, so that you have to repair it. But it catches a lot of fish and will take crabs and lobster along with everything else.

Shore seine net This is another of the long wall nets. You keep one end of it on the beach while the other end is taken out in a boat which goes round in a half circle, coming back to the beach again. Both ends of the net are then pulled in and any fish that were caught are dragged up on to the beach.

Nylon drift net You can also catch salmon with nylon drift nets as they run up river from the sea. These should be mist green monofilament, six meshes deep, with meshes $5\frac{1}{4}$ inches (13 cm) apart for medium fish and $5\frac{1}{2}$ inches (14 cm) for large. Four inches (10 cm) is fine for sea-trout. These monofilament nets are so invisible that you can fish for salmon by day with them as well as by night. Your only trouble (apart from any stray fishery-law enforcement officers!) may be seals, which pursue the fish into the nets and tear the latter to shreds.

Long-line You can shoot this from a boat. The line can have

Hooks, lines and sinkers
1 *Parlour pot, a type of lobster pot.* 2 *Bab, a tied bunch of worms for eels.* 3 *Feathers, weighted line with snoods.* 4 *Feather (detail).* 5 *Barbless hook, for removing hook from fish.* 6 *Last, a piece of shiny skin.* 7 *Lug-worm bait.* 8 *Treble hook for pike.* 9 *Hook for cod.* 10 *Hook for dabs.*

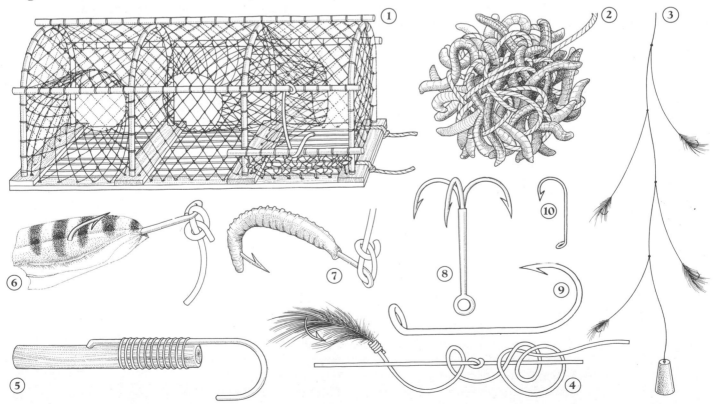

any number of hooks on it, each one in a snood, and each one baited. Coil the line down carefully in a basket, or tin bath, or plastic tub. As you coil the line down lay each hook in order over the side of the receptacle, next to the following hook in the line. The snoods are long enough to allow this. Bait each hook. Then go up-tide from where you wish to shoot the line, throw out one anchor, and let the line whip overboard as the tide drives it inexorably down-tide. The baited hooks should fly over in their turn. Have a short piece of stick in your hand to help them do this if they are reluctant. If you get in a "fangle" let the whole line go over; don't try to unfangle it or you get a hook in your hand as sure as fate. If you work carefully and keep cool it should go over clear. When you get to the other end throw over the other anchor and the buoy and that is that. Come back next day and haul against the tide, using oars or engine or the wind to carry the boat along at the right speed.

The size of hooks will depend entirely on the kind of fish you hope to catch. Size 6 or 8 hooks are fine for dabs, plaice and so on, while size 4/0 to 8/0 may be needed for conger-eel, or large cod. Conger are a fish very apt to be caught on long lines: I once helped catch half a ton in a night. Mind you, there were twelve hundred hooks. For such large fish, particularly conger, it is an advantage to have a swivel on each snood, so that the hook can turn as the conger turns.

Getting a hook out of the throat of a large fish is very easy when you know how to do it. You need a small barbless hook securely attached to a handle. Get the hand-hook, as I shall call it, in the bite of the fish-hook, and yank the fish-hook out with the hand-hook, holding the snood firmly with your other hand so as to keep the two hooks engaged. You should carry a "priest" (small wooden club, traditionally of box-wood). It is so called because it administers the last rites, and is more humane than letting fish drown to death in air which is what happens otherwise.

Hand-line Only in certain circumstances is hand-lining for bottom fish productive. Those lines of hopefuls who lean endlessly on the rails of piers spend far more on bait and tackle than they take home in fish. Only bother to hand-line on the bottom when you know there are fish there. At certain times of the year you can sometimes find a good mark for whiting, or codling, that makes hand-lining more than just a way of passing the time. Enquire and observe closely what locals do before wasting a lot of time.

THE SEASHORE

You do not need a boat to benefit from the riches of the sea. A visit to the seashore provides ample opportunity to accumulate edible sea creatures of various sorts. Obviously the man who takes some equipment with him will be better off than the one who takes a casual stroll, but a very little know-how means that anyone can return after a walk along the seashore with the makings of a snack if not a full meal.

A man without a boat may catch fish quite effectively with a beach long-line. Go down to the bottom of a beach at low tide and lay a long-line (as described earlier) along the sand near the sea. As the tide comes back demersal fish will follow the water, intent on helping themselves to such small beach animals as emerge from the sand to go about their business when it is covered. You will catch some fish, perhaps not many; you will be lucky to get a fish every twenty hooks, but after all one fish is a meal and better than no fish at all. If you really want to practise this fishery effectively put down a lot of hooks; a hundred is not too many.

The long-line must be anchored by a heavy weight at each end and should have a pennant (branch line) on it with a buoy on top so as to make it easy to recover. Remember here that the tide is not the same every day. About the time of every full moon and about the time of every new moon there is a spring tide, when the water goes both higher and lower than in neap tides, which occur at half-moon periods. Even these spring tides vary: some come up much higher and go down much lower than others. So you may lay your line out at the bottom of the beach on one tide only to find that the tide does not go out far enough to uncover it next day. If you have a buoy on a pennant you will be able to wade out and recover your line.

As for bait, nearly everywhere on sandy beaches you will find the reliable "lug-worm". This can be dug out at low water with a spade or fork. There is a trick to this, and if you do not know it you will not find many. The lug-worm throws up a worm-shaped cast of sand. Do not dig under this. Instead, look for a small hole which should be a foot away from the cast. This is the worm's blow-hole. Dig there, dig fast, throw the sand out quickly, and you will get your lug-worm.

Other forms of bait are limpets, mussels, slices of herring or mackerel, whelks and hermit crab tails. Limpets must be knocked off the rocks with a hammer by surprise; once you have warned them of your intentions they cling on – well – like limpets, and you can only get them off by smashing them to pieces. Mussels are somewhat soft and some people tie them on to the hook with a piece of cotton.

Shellfish

Mussels Pick these as low on the rocks as you can get at low tide, preferably below the lowest tide mark although this is not always possible. They must be alive: if they are firmly closed it is a sign that they are. They must not be taken from water in which there can possibly be any pollution from sewage as they are natural filters and will filter any bacteria out of the water and keep it in themselves. The advice commonly given to cook them only long enough to make them open their shells is extremely dangerous: all mussels should be boiled or steamed for at least twenty minutes otherwise food poisoning can take place. What you do with them after that does not matter.

Cockles Rake these out of the sand with a steel rake. You soon get good at spotting where they are under the sand which has a different look somehow. It is often greyer than the surrounding area. Then rake them into small hand-nets and wash the sand out of them in shallow water. It is much easier to harvest cockles on the sand flats when shallow water still lingers over the sand. Boil or steam them for twenty minutes.

Razor fish These betray themselves by squirting water out of the holes in the sand in which they live. They do this when you tread on the sand nearby. They live very low down on the beach, right down where the sand is only uncovered at low spring tides. If you walk backwards over the sand you will see the spurts of water after you have passed. The best way to get them is with a razor spear. This is a pointed iron rod with small barbs near the point. You push it gently down the hole and the razor fish closes on it and is pulled out. Another method is to dump a handful of salt on the hole. This makes the razor fish stick out and you grab it.

Limpets Limpets are only just edible. If you are hungry enough you can eat them raw (provided you are sure they are unpolluted) but they are much better cooked and they make quite good soup.

Oysters You should only eat oysters raw if you are sure they are unpolluted. But they are delicious cooked and much safer to eat then. To open an oyster hold it in a cloth in your left hand and plunge a short stiff blade into the hinged end. You can cheat by popping them in a hot oven (400°F or 204°C) for not more than four minutes, but if you intend to eat them raw this is desecration.

Clams Clams are dug out of sand and are traditionally baked in the United States on hot stones in a sand pit. Dig a pit, put large stones in the bottom, and keep a fire going on them for three or four hours. Put some seaweed over the stones, and clams on top of it along with sweet corn or anything else you fancy. Add more seaweed, chuck some seawater over all of it, cover with a tarpaulin, and let the lot steam until the clams begin to open.

Winkles These can be picked up in small rock pools at low tide. Boil them for a quarter of an hour in water. Pick them out with a pin, sprinkle them with vinegar and eat with bread and butter. They are pretty dull.

Whelks Whelks are a deep water shellfish and are caught in pots like lobster pots but smaller. Salt herring or mackerel make a good bait. Boil them for half an hour, or steam them. They taste rather like wet leather.

Plants and creatures of the seashore
1 *Razor* 2 *Common whelk* 3 *Common limpet* 4 *Edible cockle* 5 *Common oyster* 6 *Common mussel* 7 *Common winkle* 8 *Edible crab* 9 *Lobster* 10 *Brown shrimp* 11 *Purple laver* 12 *Sea lettuce* 13 *Dulse*

Fish & Sea Foods

Lobsters and crabs These are normally caught in pots, which are cages with funnels into them so that the shellfish can get in but not out. The pots can be made of willow, steel mesh or wire netting. A more sophisticated pot is the "parlour pot" which is longer than the usual pot with an entrance hall at each end and then net funnels into the "parlour" which is in the middle. If you have to leave pots out for long because of bad weather the parlour pot is good, because the lobsters, on finding themselves confined in the entrance halls, try to get out, get into the parlour, and wait there. Meanwhile the bait is not eaten and attracts more lobsters.

When trawling you may catch hermit crabs. If fishermen do not want the tails of these for bait they normally throw them overboard. This is nonsense as the tails, boiled, are delicious. Spider crabs, too, are delicious to eat.

Seaweeds

Many seaweeds are edible, but there are two plants that are excellent to eat: laver weed (*Porphyra umbilicalis*) and samphire (*Salicornia europaea*).

Laver weed has thin, translucent purple fronds and grows on rocks on the beach. To cook it you soak it for a few hours in fresh water, dry it in a slow oven and powder it in a mortar. Then boil it for four hours, changing the water. Drain it and dry it and you have made laver bread, the stuff that the South Wales coal miners used to think was good for their chests. Eat it with bacon for breakfast. You can just wash laver weed well and boil it for several hours in water in a double saucepan. Beat this up with lemon or orange, and a little butter or oil and it makes a good sauce for mutton.

The other really valuable seaweed, samphire, is not really a seaweed at all. It looks like a miniature cactus growing below high-tide mark, and can be eaten on the spot raw as it is (provided the estuary is not polluted). It can be boiled and served like asparagus with butter but if you eat it like this you must draw the flesh off between your teeth leaving the rough fibres behind. Samphire also makes a most magnificent pickle. To pickle, fill a jar with it, add peppercorns and a grated horse-radish, if you like, then pour into the jar a boiling mixture of dry cider and vinegar in equal quantities, or else just vinegar.

Some of the other more delicate seaweeds, such as sea lettuce (*Ulva lactuca*) and dulse (*Rhodymenia palmata*) can be treated in the same way as laver weed.

Sea-kale is also edible but it is really a perennial vegetable. It is native to the sandy shores of the North Sea, Atlantic and Mediterranean, but it can be cultivated in the garden where it should be treated like rhubarb. The leaf shoots of sea-kale are blanched and eaten like asparagus, and you can cultivate it in any cool or temperate climate which is similar, to some extent, to its seashore origin.

SMOKING AND PRESERVING FISH

Eel To smoke eel, gut the fish but do not skin them. Wash them and lay them in dry salt for twelve hours, then hang them on sticks and dip them in boiling water for a few seconds. This makes the fish open out. Smoke over an open fire at 140°F (60°C) for from two to four hours according to what size they are. Eat them like that, don't cook them. They are probably the most delicious food known to mankind.

Salmon To smoke salmon, fillet the fish and remove the ribs. This is difficult, but you can trim the flesh away a little so that you can see the ribs and pull them out with a pair of pincers. String through the shoulders and carefully score the thickest part of the head end of the fish so the salt can get in. Lie the fish on a layer of fine salt, put half an inch of salt on the thick end and taper the salt off to nothing at the tail end. Leave the fish in salt for 12 hours for a 1½ to 2 pound (0.7 – 0.9 kg) fillet, 18 hours for a 3 to 4 pound (1.4 – 1.8 kg) fillet, and 24 hours for a fillet over 4 pounds (1.8 kg). If the underlying flesh still feels soft at the end of the given period leave the fish a little longer in the salt. Then wash the salt well out, and smoke the fish for 24 hours at 70°F (21°C) in heavy smoke, and for 12 hours at 80°F (27°C) in lighter smoke. Olive oil rubbed on the fish during the cooking is a good idea.

Neither smoked eel nor smoked salmon will keep indefinitely. To deep freeze them should be an indictable offence, although to deep freeze the fresh fish and then thaw and smoke them is pardonable. Plenty of other fish, both fresh water and salt, can be smoked to advantage. The above methods are known as "cook-smoking", as opposed to the "cold-smoking" that produces kippers (and bacon).

Kippers To make kippers, split your herrings, mackerel or pilchards down the back, running your knife alongside the backbone. Soak in 70 to 80 percent brine for an hour or two, then smoke for 6 hours at 85°F (30°C). The harder you smoke them the longer they will keep but even that is not very long.

Bloaters To make bloaters, do not head or gut your fish. Leave them buried in dry salt overnight, and smoke them for four hours at 80°F (27°C). I merely leave them in the big open chimney over a wood fire. Then if I come in hungry late at night, I pull a few down, lay them on the hot ashes for a few minutes, and eat them.

Salting pelagic fish

To salt herrings, mackerel, pilchards and other pelagic fish, gut the fish and bury them, in barrels or crocks, in dry salt. You can soak the salt out when you want to eat them, and cook them with plenty of boiled potatoes as the West Highlanders do; but the longer they have been in salt the longer you have to soak them, and this often amounts to forty-eight hours. And then they are still not very nice, at least not for soft southerners. Pickled herring is far more pleasant to eat.

Pickling herring

To pickle herring soak the salt herring (or mackerel or whatever) for twenty-four hours, and lay it in vinegar for at least a

Making rollmops

Rollmop herrings prepared at home are both cheap and delicious.

Remove your salted herrings from their crock. Gut and decapitate them, and soak them in water for 24 hours to draw out the salt.

Slit the fish very carefully down the belly.

Lay the fish on its opened belly. Press very hard and firmly along the backbone of the herring with your knuckles or thumbs to ease the ribs away from the flesh. This process flattens the fish further.

Draw out the ribs and backbone of the fish. You will probably find that you have to cut the bone away from the tail with a knife.

Cut the fish in half lengthways down the middle.

Lay one or two pieces of peeled and chopped onion across the middle of the fish; then roll it up tightly, starting from the wide end. Tuck in peppercorns and a chilli as well if you like.

Take a sharpened matchstick or a skewer, and pierce the centre of each fish to hold the onion in place.

Pack the rollmops tightly into a jar, and fill the jar with spiced vinegar. Ease the fish from the sides of the jar with a wooden spoon to let out air bubbles.

week, with onions, peppercorns, a chilli or two and any other spice you fancy. It is best to split the fish first. To split it cut the head off, lay the fish on its opened belly and press very hard along the backbone with your knuckles. This draws the ribs out, and you can then pull most of them out along with the backbone. If you really want to go to town make "rollmops" (see illustration).

Salting demersal fish

You can also salt cod and other demersal thick white fish. Split the bigger fish down the belly and rip out all of the backbone except the tail, which you keep as a handle. Pile them up with dry salt between each layer. Leave them for fifteen days if the fish are large, a week if small, letting the brine drain away. Then expose them to dry on racks in the wind and sun, but not in rain.

Preserving small fish

To preserve sprats, anchovies and other small oily fish, first soak the fish in 80 percent brine for fifteen minutes. Stick a sharpened stick through their gills and hang them while still wet, in smoke at 90°F (32°C) for half an hour and then 180°F (83°C) for half an hour. You can eat them like this. Or you can put them in sterilized jars and cover them with olive oil or vegetable oil, sterilize them by heating them for half an hour, and seal. They then keep for a long time and taste absolutely delicious.

The Dutch way of eating salt herring or mackerel is to soak the fish in fresh water overnight, then slice them into very thin slices. Soak them in vinegar for an hour, smoke them in dense hot smoke for half an hour, and pack them in olive oil. They keep for a couple of months in cool weather and taste marvellous when you come to eat them.

Potting mackerel

During the annual mackerel campaign I generally pot mackerel, thus copying the fishermen of north Norfolk. Cut the fish up into sections about two inches (5 cm) long and drop them into vinegar with onions, spices and all the rest of it. A chilli or two always helps on these occasions, as do bay leaves which are traditional. Put the earthenware crock, with the fish and brine inside it, into a slow oven overnight. In the morning cover the pot with grease-proof paper or something similar and put it away in a cool cupboard. Potted fish are an excellent standby, to be eaten just as they are, cold, say late at night when you come home from the pub.

Plants, Nuts & Berries

There are innumerable wild foods that you can find growing in the woods and fields and hedgerows, but my advice would always be: find out what the local people consider good to eat in your locality and eat that. An enormous number of "weeds" can be eaten, so can all kinds of seeds, and of course a great many wild fruits, berries, nuts and fungi.

With fungi you really must know which ones are safe and for this you need either a knowledgeable friend or the advice of local people. Beside the common field mushroom a few fungi that are delicious to eat and easy to identify are: Shaggy ink cap (try it boiled lightly in milk), Giant puff ball, Parasol, Shaggy parasol, Horse mushroom, Cep, Boletus (several species), Morel and Chanterelle.

More "weeds" can be eaten than are a positive pleasure to eat, but a few that are excellent are: Nettles, Fat hen and Good king henry. Treat all three exactly as you would spinach: pick them in the spring when they are young and tender, cover with a lid and boil. Some other wild substitutes for green vegetables are: Shepherd's purse, Yarrow, Ground elder and Lungwort. Common mallow can be puréed and turned into a good soup; Chickweed can be cooked and eaten like spinach or used in salads; Jack-by-the-hedge is a mild substitute for garlic. You will find many other varieties in your locality, and don't forget the dandelion – delicious raw in a salad. But use it sparingly.

Of the edible nuts, walnut is the king in temperate climates. After picking, leave the nuts for some weeks until the husks come off easily, then dry them well. You can pick hazel nuts green when they are nice to eat but won't keep, or you can pick them ripe and bury them, shells and all, in dry salt. Sweet chestnuts are magnificent food. Pick them when they ripen in autumn. Shell the prickly covers off

them, and store in a dry place. Of course the finest way to eat them is to roast them in the embers of a fire, but prick them first to stop them exploding. Raw they are bitter. Puréed they taste marvellous, and turkey is unthinkable without chestnut stuffing. Beech nuts are tasty but fiddly to eat; better to crush them in a mill, put the pulp in cloth bags and press it. It yields a fine oil. Ash keys make quite good pickle; boil them well and pickle in vinegar.

Among the wild fruits the elderberry is perhaps the most versatile. The berries can be used for cooking in a number of ways. Mixed with any other fruit they improve the flavour; boiled in spiced vinegar they make an excellent relish or sauce which will keep well, if properly bottled when hot. The berries also make an excellent wine as do the flowers (see pp. 192-195), and the flowers add flavour to cooked gooseberries and also gooseberry jam. If you find blueberries, or bilberries in the wild, do not ignore them: they make a wonderful pie. And if you find cranberries you can preserve them but their flavour is nowhere better captured than in a fresh cranberry sauce. Mulberries and rowan berries make very good jam. And do not forget juniper berries, which can impart an agreeably tart flavour to all savoury dishes.

Sloes make marvellous fruit wine. Take half a pound (228g) of sloes, prick them all over with a fork, and half fill a bottle with them. Add an equal quantity of sugar, fill the bottle with gin, and in a few months you will have a liqueur as fine as you can buy.

Crab apples vie with sloes for the title of the sourest fruit. Some of their bitterness is caused by tannin, in which they are rich, and one of their good uses is as an additive to tannin-poor wine. Mead ferments better if you put crab apple juice in it, but the best use for crab apples is jelly.

Fruit
1 *Elderberries*
2 *Juniper berries*
3 *Sloe berries*
4 *Rowan berries*
5 *Mulberries*
6 *Crab apple*
7 *Bilberries*

Nuts
8 *Sweet chestnuts*
9 *Beech nuts*
10 *Ash keys*
11 *Walnuts*
12 *Hazelnuts*

Fungi
13 *Field mushrooms*
14 *Chanterelle*
15 *Shaggy ink cap*

Weeds
16 *Shepherd's purse*
17 *Nettle*
18 *Dandelion*

Natural Energy

"Take care, your worship, those things over
there are not giants but windmills."
CERVANTES

Saving Energy

THE ALTERNATIVES

Throughout this book I have advocated an integrated approach to the land: the encouragement of organic beneficial interaction of soil, crops and animals. When considering energy we must adopt this same approach. We should look upon our holding of land as having a certain energy potential that we can use for our own good purposes, and we should aim to make our holding autonomous in this respect, as we have aimed to make it for food. There is something wrong about burning coal to heat water on a hot sunny day, or burning oil to warm a house when there is a fast flowing stream next to it. Or, for that matter, using mains electricity to drive a mill or a power loom, when there is potential wind or water power nearby.

Water power is most available in hilly, rainy countries and wind power in flat lands, but wind power should never be used where water power is available. The simple reason for this is that the wind is fickle while water is relatively reliable and consistent. Where there is hot sun it is ridiculous not to use it. It is obviously unproductive to feed cold water into your water boiler when the corrugated iron roof over your shed is so hot you can't hold your hand on it.

A characteristic of natural sources of energy is that they lend themselves much more to small scale use than to large scale exploitation. For example more energy can be got out of a given river more cheaply by tapping it with a hundred small dams and waterwheels right down its length, than by building one enormous dam and driving one set of huge turbines. The wind's energy can be tapped, but only by a myriad of small windmills: not by some gigantic wind-equivalent of a power station. Every house in a city could have a solar roof, and derive a great part of its energy requirements from it, but a solar collector big enough to supply a city belongs to the realms of fantasy. Scattered farmsteads can easily make their own methane gas, but to cart muck from a hundred farms to some central station,

Heat loss
A house built in the traditional way loses vast amounts of heat through **1** *the roof,* **2** *doors,* **3** *windows,* **4** *the floor,* **5** *outside walls. Use a*

combination of the methods illustrated and, as shown in the diagram (left), you will find that you can save as much as two thirds of the annual domestic energy

requirement. Fire is still the cheapest way of producing heat where and when you need it. But an open fire wastes as much as 90 percent of its energy, so controls are essential.

| 1 | 2 | 3 | 4 | 5 | Heat used |

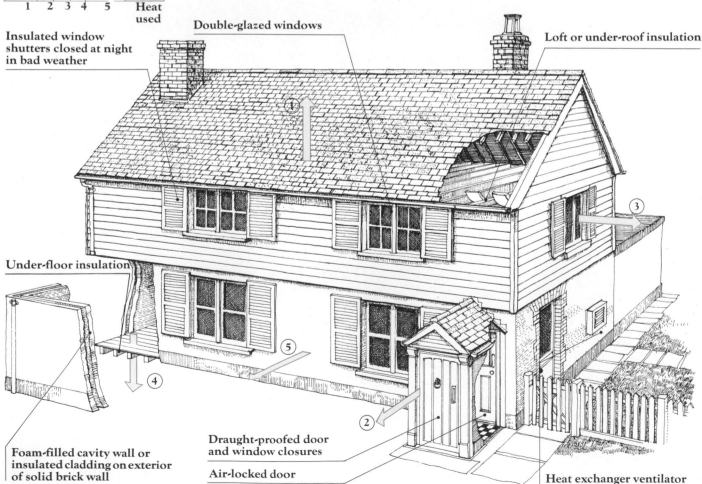

Insulated window shutters closed at night in bad weather

Double-glazed windows

Loft or under-roof insulation

Under-floor insulation

Foam-filled cavity wall or insulated cladding on exterior of solid brick wall

Draught-proofed door and window closures

Air-locked door

Heat exchanger ventilator

make gas from it and then redistribute it would be madly uneconomical. So these "alternative energy devices" commend themselves especially to the self supporter.

Now it may well be that it is better for the self-supporter to combine several sources of energy instead of concentrating on just one. For example, you could have a big wood-burning furnace (see p. 248) that does the cooking for a large number of people, and heats water for dairy, kitchen, butchery, bathroom and laundry. If you preheated the water that went into it with solar panels on the roof, you would need less wood to heat more water. Then if you had a methane plant to utilize animal and human waste and used the methane to bring the hot water from the furnace to steam-heat, for sterilizing dairy equipment, better still. Then you could use a pumping windmill to pump up water from the clear, pure well below your holding, instead of having to use the very slightly polluted water from the hill above. And what about lighting your buildings using the stream that runs nearby to drive a small turbine? All these things are possible, would be fairly cheap, and would pay for themselves by saving on energy brought in from outside.

SAVING ENERGY

There is little point devising elaborate systems for getting heat from natural sources until you have plugged the leaks in the systems you have already got.

For keeping heat in a house there is nothing to beat very thick walls of cob, stone, *pise* or brickwork with small windows and a thatched roof. The thin cavity walls of modern brick or concrete block housing only insulate well if plastic foam or some other insulating material is put between the walls and laid on the joists in the roof. The big "picture windows" beloved of modern architects are terrible heat-losers. Double glazing may help but it is very expensive. The country man, working out of doors for most of the day as people were designed to do, wants to feel, when he does go indoors, that he *is* indoors, he gets plenty of "view" when he is out in it and is part of the view himself. Therefore, for country housing, big windows are a mistake.

Huge chimneys, very romantic and fine when there are simply tons of good dry firewood, send most of their heat up to heat the sky. In a world short of fuel they are inexcusable. Long straggly houses are also great heat-wasters. A compact shape is more desirable. A round building will lose less heat than a square one, because it has a smaller surface area in comparison with its volume. A square building is obviously better than an oblong one. It is always best to have your primary heat source in the middle of the building rather than against an outside wall.

Most insulation nowadays is achieved with high-technology products, and these are very expensive. What we can do is search for cheaper and more natural materials. Wherever the cork oak will grow it should be grown, for it provides an excellent insulator and in large quantities.

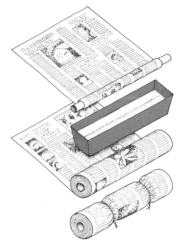

Using up newspaper
Most wood stoves and ranges will burn almost anything combustible. You can turn old newspapers into useful "logs" by wrapping them tightly round a length of wood and soaking the centre of the "log" in old oil or fat. Dead wood and all other inflammable rubbish provide additional free fuel supplies which can be saved and stored during summer and autumn for use in winter. A large old fashioned, cast iron range can supply the major source of domestic heat as well as being used for cooking meals. You can feed any methane from a waste fermentation unit or digester straight into the grate through a copper or stainless steel burner pipe.

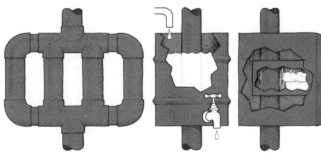

Making a heat exchanger
You can make your own heat exchanger. One way is to have an open water container, as shown, to provide a ready source of warm water. Alternatively, install a "doughnut" arrangement which will increase the surface area of the flue pipe and so transfer more heat to the air inside the house. You can even build an oven. One word of caution to the self-supporter building his own heat exchanger: any system which transports flue gases must be completely leakproof, as stove fumes contain carbon monoxide and can kill in certain circumstances. Your system should be made from heavy gauge steel; thin sheets of steel will quickly corrode through.

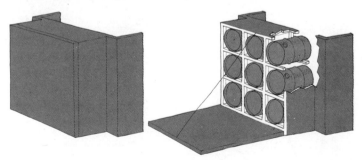

Heat storage
Most of the domestic energy-saving schemes on this page can be fitted or adapted to any conventional house. If you are building a new house from scratch, consider introducing large heat storage reservoirs. Being able to store heat is especially valuable if you use solar collectors or windmills as energy sources. The illustration above shows a combined solar collector and heat store. This consists of water-filled oil barrels painted black behind a glass panel. An insulated cover lies open on the ground: it reflects sunlight on to the glass during the day and can be hinged up to lock the heat in at night. The whole structure forms the south wall of the house. You can use rocks to store heat, by circulating hot air from a solar collector through them during the day to warm them, and then circulating air from the house through them at night, when the rocks will release stored heat back into the air and so prevent the temperature of the house from dropping too far.

Power from Water

Parakrama Bahu, King of Ceylon, or Sri Lanka, in the seventh century, decreed that not one drop of water that fell on his island should reach the sea: all should be used for agriculture. In wetter climes, where irrigation is not so necessary, the inhabitants would do well to take the same attitude, but change the objective a little: "let not one river or stream or rivulet reach the sea without yielding its energy potential".

Water power is completely free, completely non-polluting, and always self-renewing. Unlike wind it is steady and reliable, although of course there may be seasonal variations but even these tend to be consistent. Like wind, it is generally at its strongest in the colder months, and is therefore at its greatest strength when we most need it.

The primitive water wheels that have stood the test of centuries are not to be despised, and for many uses are better than more sophisticated devices. For slow-flowing streams with plenty of water the "undershot wheel" is appropriate. With this you can take in the whole of quite a large stream, and thus exploit a river with a low head but large volume. Your wheel will be slow-turning, but if you use it for a direct drive to slow-turning machinery, a corn mill for example, this is an advantage. It is a common mistake of "alternative energy freaks" to think that all power should first be converted to electricity and then converted back to power again. Energy loss is enormous in so doing.

It may be worth your while to install a more sophisticated water engine than a water wheel, particularly if you want to generate electricity with your water power, for this requires high speeds to which more complex water engines are well suited. For small heads – from as low as a yard (91 cm) to up to 20 feet (6.1 m) – the propeller turbine is very good. As you get over 12 feet (3.6 m) you may prefer a Banki turbine.

Water wheel (overshot)
The oldest method of using water power, the overshot water wheel (right) is up to 70% efficient. The water goes over the top, filling the buckets round its rim. Water wheels like this turn quite slowly but with considerable force, making them best suited for driving mill-stones (as shown) or other heavy, slow-speed equipment. Depending on flow rate, power from this wheel might be anything from five to twenty horsepower (4-16 kw).

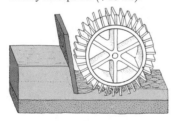

Water wheel (undershot)
Undershot wheels are less efficient than overshot, but are used when there is insufficient head of water for it to fall over the wheel. They can produce from two to five hp (1½ – 3 kw).

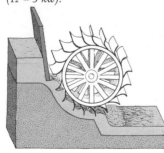

Breast wheel (undershot)
An undershot wheel with straight blades is up to 30% efficient; fitting curved blades increases this to 60%. A breast wheel makes twice the power from the same source.

Water power

To calculate the available water power of a stream measure the flow rate of the water, and multiply it successively by the density ($62.4 lb/ft^3$), the head of water, and the efficiency of the turbine or water wheel you will be using – e.g. in a hilly area the flow rate might be $\frac{1}{2} ft^3$ water per sec. This flow falling 40 ft through an 80% efficient Pelton wheel would give:

$$\frac{1}{2} \times 62.4 \times 40 \times \frac{80}{100} = 998 \frac{ft/lb}{sec}$$

$$\frac{998}{550 \, (1 \, hp)} = 1.8 \, horsepower.$$

If used for generating electricity, 60% of the turbine's power might be converted into electrical power: i.e. in this example 60% of $1.8 = 1.08$ hp and as 1 hp = 746 watts, this is the equivalent of 805 watts.

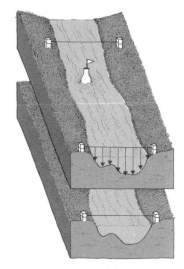

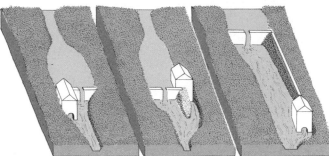

Positioning and types of dam

In order to build up a head of water and control its flow, it is often necessary to build a dam or a weir (above) across the main stream, usually at a narrow point or where there are rapids. A head race or leat, dug along a contour above the stream, will create enough head for a water wheel or turbine to function. A dam can be a pile of rocks in a stream, although wooden dams (below right) or combined wood and earth-fill ones (right) are effective.

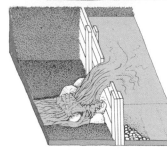

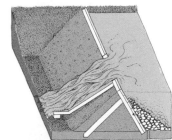

Flow rate

Water power depends primarily on the flow rate and available head of water. The flow rate of a stream therefore needs to be measured, as well as its fall, to predict the available power. A simple method is to find a length of the stream that is straight and has as constant a cross-section as possible. The cross-section of flow is estimated by taking soundings at regular intervals across it (below left) and calculating the average depth: area equals average depth times width. This should be repeated at several points to arrive at an average cross-sectional area for the chosen length. A sealed bottle (top left) is then timed as it drifts along the middle of the chosen section. Flow rate for the stream will be around 75% of the speed of the bottle times the average cross-sectional area of that length of stream. An example of a water power calculation using flow rate is given in the caption, left.

Hydroelectric power

If you are fortunate enough to have a stream available for use, one of its most valuable capabilities is the production of a free and continuous supply of electricity. It is inadvisable to use a water wheel to run a generator because this turns so slowly that an enormous step-up ratio of gears or belts and pulleys is needed to arrive at the required generator speed. Small turbines turn much faster and need little more than a pair of pulleys and vee belts to connect them to a generator. They are less expensive to build because their smaller size means they need much less steel, and they are also slightly more efficient than water wheels. There are many different types of turbine. The Pelton wheel turbine (top right) is for high head applications where the fall is 40 ft (12 m) or more, and is up to 80% efficient. A special nozzle directs the water at high speed against a set of spoon-shaped deflector buckets set around the periphery of the turbine wheel. The Banki turbine (centre right) is for medium head, up to 65% efficient and best suited to a fall of 15 – 40 ft (4.5 – 12 m). Again a special nozzle directs water into the periphery of a spool-like wheel with curved blades. The propeller turbine (bottom right), up to 75% efficient, operates best on heads of under 20 ft (6 m), right down to 6 ft (1.8 m). It is the best substitute for a water wheel on an old mill site. In principle it is merely a propeller in a pipe. To obtain reasonable efficiency, the water must be given a spin opposite to that of the propeller. This is best done by running it through a spiral volute before entering the draft-tube containing the propeller.

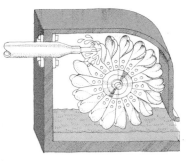

Pelton wheel

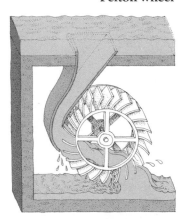

Banki turbine

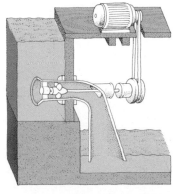

Propeller turbine

Heat from the Sun

The most practical solar collector is a wood, for woodland can collect the sun's rays from vast areas, and, properly managed, can continually convert them into energy, while to cover a few square yards with a man-made solar collector costs a lot of effort and money. But if collecting and storing the sun's heat can be done relatively easily and cheaply, as it usually can on the roof of an existing house or wall, then, if nothing more, solar energy can be used to reinforce other sources of energy. The drawback is that in cold climates we want heat in the winter and we get it in the summer, but if

the winter gap is filled in with wind or water power (both at their best in the winter) a consistent system can be evolved.

The practical choices open in temperate climates are:
1 Heating water by letting it trickle over a black-painted corrugated roof under a transparent covering which turns the roof into a heat collector. You will have to buy your transparent covering and a pump to circulate the water. All the same this will allow you to collect the sun over a large area.
2 Heating water with black-painted pipes behind transparent material. This has the advantage that there is no obscuration

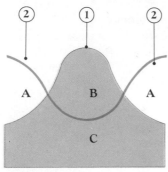

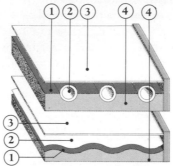

Solar energy
Solar energy **1** *is most abundant in midsummer while our heating requirements* **2** *are greatest in midwinter. Most solar collectors provide more heat than we need in summer* **B** *and less than we need in winter* **A**. *The productive use of solar energy* **C** *reaches peaks in spring and autumn. Received energy per day per m² might be 4 or 5 kw hrs in summer, and ½ to 1 kw hr in winter in a temperate climate.*

Flat-plate solar collectors
Most solar energy collectors use a black surface **1** *to absorb the sun's radiation and produce heat. You transfer the heat into a hot water tank, or to heat space, by passing water, or air in some cases, through pipes or channels* **2** *behind the absorbing surface. A glass or plastic covering* **3** *prevents heat loss from the front of the collector, while insulation* **4** *prevents it from the rear and sides.*

Heating air: the Trombe wall
Named after Professor Trombe, this is a clever method for making use of solar energy in winter. The Professor perfected the wall high up in the Pyrenees, where the sun shines quite often in winter, albeit weakly. You use a vertical double-glazed plate glass window **1** *which faces south, and allow a black-painted wall* **2** *behind it to catch and trap the sun's heat. When you require heat inside*

the house you open ventilators **3**, **4** *and these allow warm air to circulate between the glass and the wall. An over-hanging roof* **5** *prevents the high summer sun from striking the glass and also protects the building from getting overheated. An alternative to the Trombe wall is a glass-covered extension to your house, in other words a conservatory. This will warm the house if properly ventilated.*

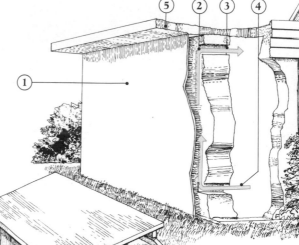

A solar still
This shallow concrete basin, painted black or tarred **1** *contains a few inches of polluted water. A heavy-gauge polythene tent* **2** *encloses this, and condensation runs down the inside surface of the tent into a pair of collecting gutters* **3**. *The condensation is pure distilled water which you can syphon off. Hold down the plastic sheeting by heavy wooden battens* **4** *and close the cover ends rather like a ridge tent. You can replenish the polluted water through a hose* **5**.

Solar drier
An inclined, glazed, flat-plate solar air heater admits air through an adjustable flap **1**. *The air heats up as it crosses over a blackened absorber surface* **2**, *because the heat is trapped by glass panels* **3**. *The heated air rises through a bed of rocks* **4** *and then through a series of gratings which hold the produce to be dried. A flap* **5** *under the overhanging roof allows the air supply to be adjusted or closed off. The rock bed heats up in the course of the day and continues releasing a measure of warmth to the crop after sunset, thereby preventing condensation from occurring. There is a door in the back of the unit to allow crops to be added or removed.*

**Heating water:
the trickle roof**
Provide a large surface area for a solar water heater by having water trickle down a blackened, corrugated, aluminium roof behind an area of glazing. Insulation behind the aluminium prevents overheating of the roof space and keeps most of the heat in the water. A small pump drives the water

round the system whenever a sensor on the roof tells a control-box that the roof temperature is higher than that of the water in the copper immersion heater. This system is not ideal, but it is cheap enough to make it worth converting an entire south-facing roof.

by misting-up and you don't need a circulatory pump because hot water rises. But it is expensive to cover large areas.

3 Solar stills: these are arrangements for using the heat of the sun directly for distilling water or other liquids.

4 Solar driers: these can be used for drying fruit, grain, vegetables, malt and many other things.

5 Solar hot air heaters: these provide extra heat for a greenhouse.

6 Solar-heated walls: such as the Trombe Wall, these store heat during the day and release it during the night.

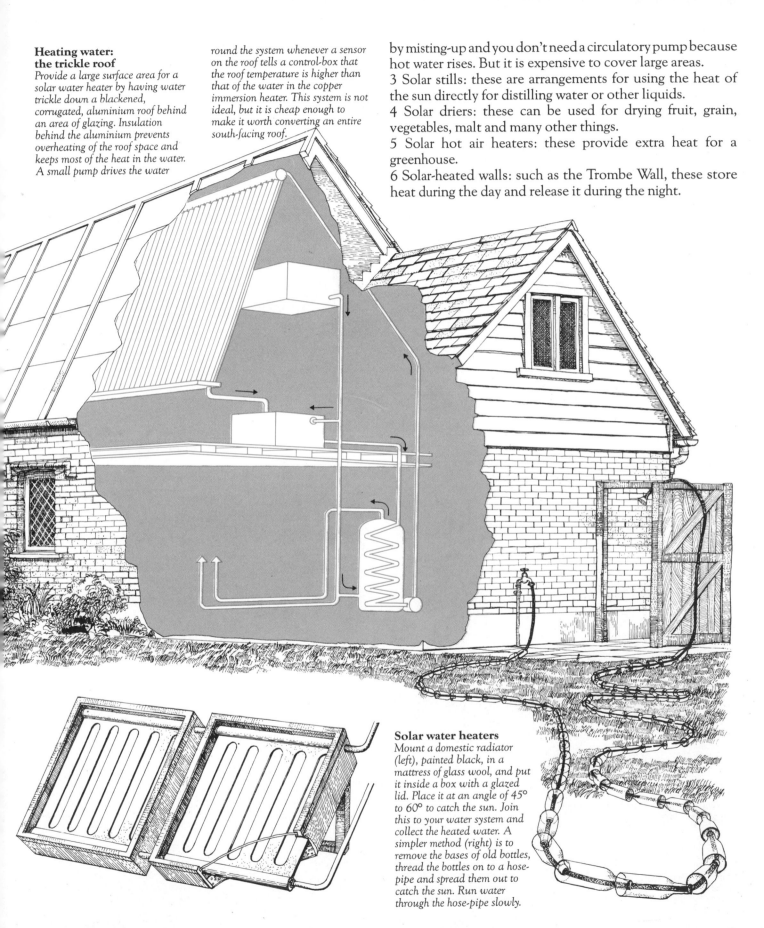

Solar water heaters
Mount a domestic radiator (left), painted black, in a mattress of glass wool, and put it inside a box with a glazed lid. Place it at an angle of 45° to 60° to catch the sun. Join this to your water system and collect the heated water. A simpler method (right) is to remove the bases of old bottles, thread the bottles on to a hose-pipe and spread them out to catch the sun. Run water through the hose-pipe slowly.

Power from the Wind

The common factory built steel pumping windmill, seen in thousands in all lands where water has to be pumped up from deep boreholes, is one of the most effective devices ever conceived by Man. Many an old steel "wind pump" has been turning away, for thirty or forty years, never failing in its job. Such machines will pump water comfortably from a thousand feet (304 m) and work in very little wind at all. The tail vane is arranged on a pivot so that they can turn themselves sideways on to the wind in a storm.

Wind power has followed the same trend as water power in that low-powered but high-speed devices are now wanted for driving dynamos to produce electricity. But the wind, of course is completely unpredictable, and so you must either accept that you cannot use a machine in calm weather, or in severe gales, or you must be able to store electricity and that is very expensive. However, if you can use the power when it is available, say for grinding corn, or store it, as heat for example, the total wind energy available over a period of time tends to be fairly constant.

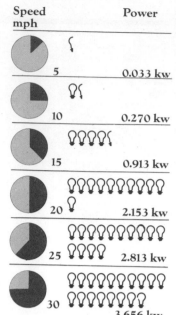

Speed mph	Power
5	0.033 kw
10	0.270 kw
15	0.913 kw
20	2.153 kw
25	2.813 kw
30	3.656 kw

How much power?
The main problem in harnessing wind is that it carries very little power when it blows lightly, but offers an embarrassing surfeit in a gale. The power of wind is proportional to its velocity cubed: in other words, if the wind speed doubles its power potential rises eight-fold. This means that a fairly large windmill is needed if useful amounts of power are to be extracted from a light breeze, and that the windmill must be protected from storm damage by having a hinged tail-vane which can swing the wind-rotor out of the wind. Or it can have removable sails or blades which can be made to twist into a "feathered" position where they act as air brakes to slow the rotor. The diagram shows how many 100 watt lightbulbs a 15 ft (4.5 m) diameter electricity-generating windmill is capable of powering.

This is a variation on a Mediterranean sail windmill. Used for irrigation water pumping by market-gardeners on Crete it is readily improvised.

This typical all-metal windmill is used for pumping water. A swinging tail-vane turns it out of the wind in a storm. Many abandoned, pre-war ones can still be renovated.

In this German water-pumping windmill, the rotor runs in the lee of the tubular steel tower; weights at the blade roots swing the blades into a feathered position in strong winds.

This electricity-generating windmill needs only three aerodynamically profiled blades. The machine trickle-charges a bank of batteries to supply low-powered appliances.

To be self-sufficient in electricity

Wind power is hard to win and store, so you should always use wind-generated electricity sparingly. Never use it for heating appliances. In order to exploit wind power you must have an average wind speed of at least 9 mph, with no lengthy periods of low winds; even so you will need battery storage to cover up to 20 consecutive days of calm. Apart from an electricity-generating windmill, you need a voltage regulator and a cut-out to prevent the battery from overcharging. Total battery storage capacity needs to be: 20 × average current needed in amps (watts ÷ volts) × average usage time in hours per day, measured in amp hours. Standard domestic electric appliances requiring 220 volts a.c. can be driven from a bank of 12 volt (d.c.) batteries by an electronic invertor. Alternatively low voltage appliances may be used directly. A typical 2 kw, commercially manufactured windmill will often generate at 110 volts d.c. to charge a bank of low voltage batteries, wired in series. You might get 5000 kw hrs annually from a 2 kw windmill. 1 kw is equal to one unit of electricity.

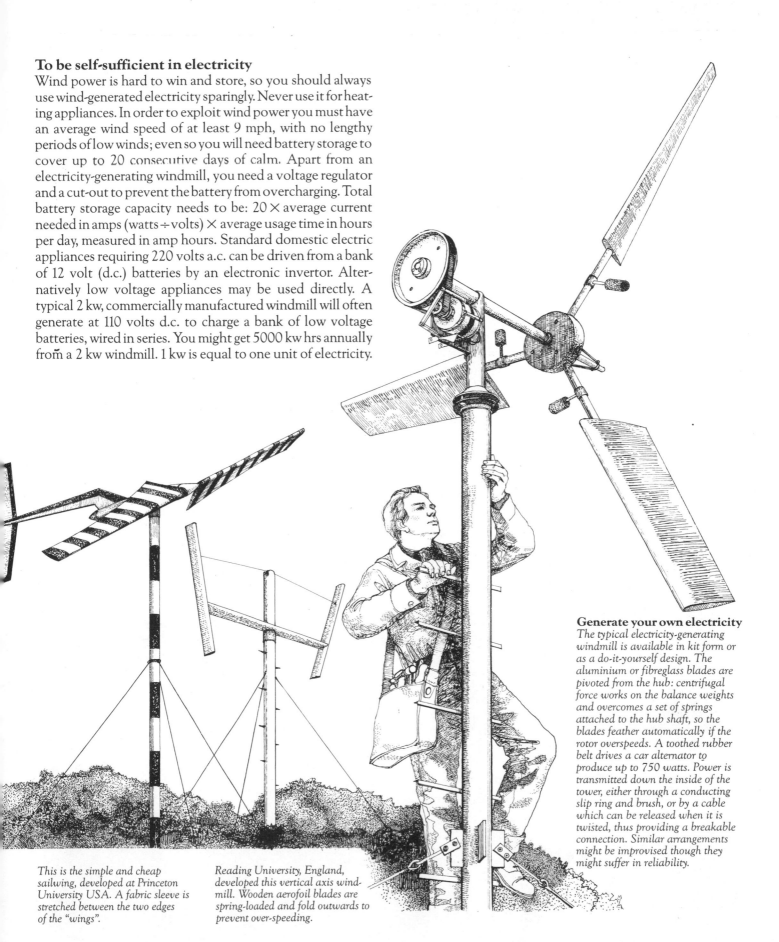

Generate your own electricity
The typical electricity-generating windmill is available in kit form or as a do-it-yourself design. The aluminium or fibreglass blades are pivoted from the hub: centrifugal force works on the balance weights and overcomes a set of springs attached to the hub shaft, so the blades feather automatically if the rotor overspeeds. A toothed rubber belt drives a car alternator to produce up to 750 watts. Power is transmitted down the inside of the tower, either through a conducting slip ring and brush, or by a cable which can be released when it is twisted, thus providing a breakable connection. Similar arrangements might be improvised though they might suffer in reliability.

This is the simple and cheap sailwing, developed at Princeton University USA. A fabric sleeve is stretched between the two edges of the "wings".

Reading University, England, developed this vertical axis windmill. Wooden aerofoil blades are spring-loaded and fold outwards to prevent over-speeding.

Fuel from Waste

The attitude that has grown up in the Western world that all so-called "waste" from the body, human or otherwise, is something to be got rid of at all costs and very quickly, becomes harder to sustain as our planet's fossil fuel comes into shorter supply. If we can take the dung of animals or men, extract inflammable gas from it in quantities that make the effort worthwhile, and still have a valuable manure left over to return to the land, we are doing very well.

Methane is a gas which is produced by the anaerobic fermentation of organic matter: in other words allowing organic matter to decay in the absence of oxygen. It is claimed that after the gas has been produced the resultant sludge is a better manure than it was before, for some of the nitrogen which might have been lost as ammonia is now in a fixed form which will be used by plants. As the methane gas itself is quite as good a fuel as natural gas (in fact it is the same thing) and is non-toxic and safe, methane production from farm and human wastes seems very worthwhile.

Methane is made with a methane digester which is fine for animal wastes but there is a limit to the amount of bulky vegetable matter that you can put into it. This precludes filling it with either tons and tons of straw or with the large quantities of valuable manure that result from the traditional practice (well proven) of bedding animals with straw. The spent sludge from the digester is itself an excellent manure, but my own feeling is that, rather than dump it straight from the digester on to the land, it should flow on to straw or other waste vegetable matter. There it will undergo further, this time aerobic, fermentation, and at the same time activate the bacteria which will break down the tough cellulose content of the litter.

Human being
1 ft³
600 BTU

Chicken
½ ft³
300 BTU

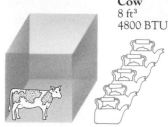

Cow
8 ft³
4800 BTU

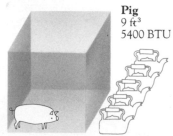

Pig
9 ft³
5400 BTU

How much gas?
The diagram above shows the amount of gas produced by the waste of different animals in a day. The gas is sufficient to boil the number of kettles shown.

The methane digester
The process shown below involves the digestion of organic wastes by bacterial action in a sealed container from which all air is excluded. Animal manure mixed to a slurry with water is added to a holding tank 1 daily. The input is fed into the digester by gravity when a valve 2 is opened. The stirrer 3 has an airtight joint where it enters the digester and prevents scum building up. The tank is well insulated with straw or similar material 4 as the process only works effectively at temperatures close to blood heat. Each fresh addition causes an equivalent amount of digester sludge to overflow into the slurry collector 6. The digestion process takes from about 14 to 35 days depending on the temperature of the digester, so the daily input should vary from 1/14 to 1/35 of a digester volume to achieve the desired "retention time". The gas bubbles up through the slurry into space 5, and is syphoned along a delivery line 7 to the gas holder 8. An important safety precaution is a brass or copper fine mesh flame trap at the entry to the delivery pipe to protect the gas holder if air gets into the line and causes a burn-back. The gas produced, called bio-gas, is a mixture of about 60% methane (the inflammable fuel component) and 40% carbon dioxide which is inert but harmless. The digested sludge makes a valuable fertilizer, being rich in nitrogen and trace elements.

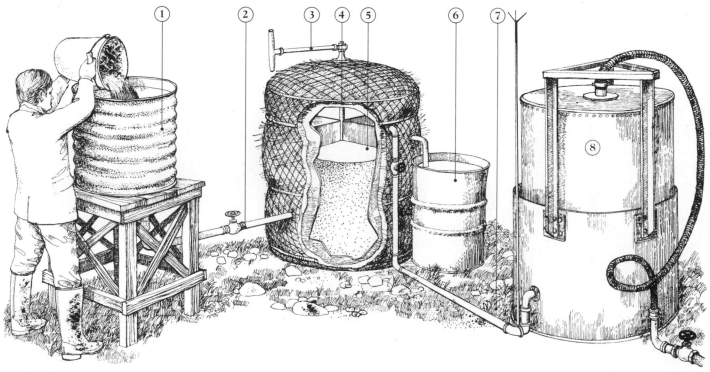

Crafts & Skills

"Whatsoever thy hand findeth to do,
do it with thy might."
ECCLESIASTES

Basketry

You can go for a walk in the country with no other equipment than a sharp knife and come back with a basket. One-year shoots of willow, lilac, elm, lime, poplar, hazel, or young ash, can all be used for the tougher rods that radiate outwards from the centre of the bottom of the basket, and vines, creepers or brambles like blackberry, snowberry, honeysuckle, dogwood and clematis can be used for the "weavers", as the more pliable, horizontal, members are called. But if you can find, or grow, osiers, which are one-year-old canes of those special straight-caned willows that are grown for basketry, you are off to a flying start. Use osiers or other tough shoots for hard basketry.

Hard basketry

To make a basket you must first form the "slath", which is the bottom. Do this by making a cross from six or eight strong rods interlocked at right angles, and weaving round their ends with a long weaver (see illustration).

Then you shove in your stakes, which are the vertical rods on which you weave the weavers right up to the top. When you reach the top you have got to finish the basket off, in other words make a border. There are two main patterns: the "trac" border (see illustration) and the "three-rod" border.

Finally you have to make the handle. This is done with a "bow", a long osier which makes the core, and one or more very long and supple weavers (see illustration).

Soft basketry

Baskets can be made from reeds, rushes, sedges and grasses. Rushes and sedges are best, being soft and pithy, and very tough and long lasting. They should be cut in midsummer. The best way to cut them is to wade in shallow water pushing a punt, cut the plants as low as possible with a sickle and lay them carefully in the punt so they keep parallel and don't bend. Dry rushes for about three weeks, in the shade if you can because the sun bleaches them which spoils their appearance. Then bundle them and tie in "bolts", traditionally with a strap 45 inches (1.14 m) long.

Before you use dried rushes wet them well and wrap them in a blanket for a few hours to soften. Then make long ropes of plaited rushes, taking three rushes at a time and plaiting them. Avoid having them all come to an end at the same time so that you can feed another rush in as one comes to an end. Mats are made by simply coiling plaits up and holding the coil in place with waxed thread. To make a basket make a flat coil and when you get to the "chine", or bottom corner, continue the coil up at whatever angle you like until you get to the border. A handle is best made by sewing a rush rope right round underneath the basket.

The basketmaker
You can make baskets out of reeds, creepers, osiers, and tree shoots. You can make "trugs", as opposite, out of wood. By mastering a craft you gain two important things: immense satisfaction and a commodity for trading.

Making a hard basket
You need three different types of rod: eight short stout rods for the "slath", or base; a number of strong but bendy rods for your side stakes; and some weavers, the long thin whippy rods which hold the basket together. Side stakes are generally about eight inches (20 cm) longer than the intended height of the basket. Weavers can be any length, but they should be at least long enough to go round the basket once. They come in varying thicknesses.

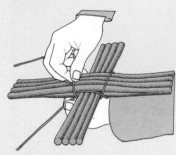

Soak all your rods for an hour before using them. Cut eight rods for your slath, and cut slits in four of them. Poke the other four through to form a cross. Take a weaver about four feet long and tie tightly round the cross three times and tuck the ends in.

Loop a weaver round one rod, and "pair" by weaving with both its ends. Pair until the base is the right size.

Cut the ends of the base rods.

Shove in 31 side stakes, one each side of every rod, with one gap.

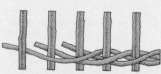

Start the sides with three rounds of "waling" (above). Take three weavers, hold them behind three adjacent stakes and weave round two stakes at a time.

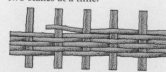

"Rand" up the side of the basket (above). Use long weavers and weave in front and behind each stake. Begin and end weavers behind a stake.

Finish off with three rows of waling and then make a trac border (above) by bending the stakes over.

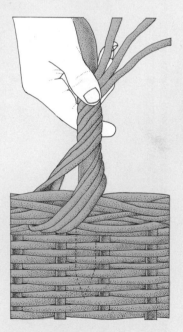

For the handle take a good thick base rod, sharpen both ends and poke them well down into the top waling on both sides of the basket. Take three thin weavers and loop them under the waling on one side. Plait them round the rod, and when you reach the other side poke the end well into the waling.

Crafts & Skills

Pottery

Clay is very often overlain with earth, and so you may be walking on it, or even living on it, without knowing it is there. Prospect where a cutting has been made, or a well, or anything that exposes the subsoil. If it looks like clay, and when wetted becomes plastic and sticky, it is clay.

Testing clay

Once you have found it you have got to find out if it is any good. It probably isn't. Wet some down to a plastic state and then allow it to dry out. If it has a noticeable scum, usually a whitish stain, on its surface after it has dried, it contains undesirable alkali and probably isn't worth using. Drop a sample of the clay into a beaker containing a 50 percent solution of hydrochloric acid. If it fizzes forget it. Too much lime. If the clay looks dark brown or black and is very sticky then there is too much humus. Clay very near the surface may be like this, but there is often better clay underneath.

To test for plasticity, which is important, make some clay into a stick the size of a pencil and see if you can bend it into a ring an inch in diameter without it breaking. If you can it is good clay.

If there is too much sand in your clay it may be hard to mould or throw on the wheel. If this is so mix a fatter, less gritty, clay with your sandy clay and try that. You can screen sand out of clay, but it is a laborious job and probably not worth it.

Mixing and screening

If you want to mix it with other clay, or screen it, you must mix it with water to a pretty sloppy liquid. Throw the clay into a tank full of water (don't pour the water on the clay) and mix. You can do this by hand, or with a paddle, or in a "blunger", which is a special machine for the job, or in an ordinary washing machine. The semi-liquid clay is then called "slip". The slip can be poured through a screen, to screen it. Use a 60 mesh to the inch screen for ordinary earthenware and a 100 mesh for porcelain or china. If you want to mix two or more clays make slip of them all and then mix them up in that condition.

The next job is getting the water out of the clay again. An easy method is to let your slip sit in a barrel or tank for a few days until the clay all sinks to the bottom. Then you siphon the water off, much as a winemaker racks his wine. There is a machine called a filterpress which will then extract the rest of the water, but if you haven't got one you can place the slip in bowls of unglazed earthenware and leave these in a draughty place. The absorbent earthenware draws the water out of the clay. The water is then dried off by the air, and after a few days the clay is fit to work.

Preparing clay

If you are very lucky, you may well find a clay that you don't have to combine with anything else, or screen, and all you have to do is dig it up and let it weather, or age. All clay is better aged even if only for a fortnight, because bacteria do good things to it. Then you must mix it with water and "pug" it, which means you must tread it well with your feet. Finally you must "wedge" it. This is the process of pushing the clay away from you on a board, pulling it towards you, rolling it, cutting it up and recombining it: in fact giving it a thorough kneading just as you knead bread.

Shaping pots

There are many ways of shaping a pot. Almost certainly pottery was discovered because baskets used to be plastered with clay to make them hold water. One day a basket got burnt and the clay became hard and durable. This was the first pot made with a mould. Simple ways of making pots by "pinching", "coiling" and with "slabs" are described overleaf.

The potter's wheel

The invention of the potter's wheel was the great break-through, and there is really no substitute for it. You "throw" a lump of clay on the wheel, "centring" it plum in the middle of the wheel by pressure from both hands as the wheel revolves. Then you shape it with pressure from your hands, fingers, tools and so on. Remove the pot from the wheel: usually you cut it off with a piece of wire. Set it aside to dry. Then replace it on the wheel by sticking it with a little water, and "turn" it, that is spin it round and smooth off the rough edges with a steel cutting tool. Turn it twice: once with the pot the right way up, and again with it upside down.

Making a wheel

In primitive countries they still use wooden cart, or wagon, wheels as potter's wheels, and if you can get hold of one you can do this too. You mount the wheel horizontally near the ground, ideally on a short section of its original axle. Make a hole in the side of the wheel towards one edge or in a spoke if it has them. To use it you squat by the side of the wheel, put a stick in the hole and set the wheel turning. Because the wheel is very heavy it goes on turning by its own momentum and your hands are then free to throw a pot or two.

A more sophisticated potter's wheel can be made by casting a reinforced concrete wheel, say 28 inches (71cm) in diameter and 3½ inches (9cm) high with a 1 inch (2.5cm) diameter steel shaft about 30 inches (76cm) long through it. The bottom of the shaft should protrude a couple of inches and steel reinforcing bars should be welded radiating from the shaft so as to be embedded in the concrete. This is not the wheel you throw on, but one you kick to make the throwing wheel revolve. Then build a table high wooden frame which has a bearing let into it to house the top bearing of the shaft, and a thrust bearing at the bottom to take the bottom of the shaft. The frame should also include a seat for you to sit on, and a table to place clay. Fix the concrete wheel and shaft into the frame. And now you must fix on your throwing wheel. Weld (see p. 238) or braze a wheel-head, say a foot (30cm) in diameter and a ¼ to ½ inch (0.7cm to 1.2cm) thick, to the top of a steel hub (a short piece of water pipe will do). Put this on top of the shaft and weld, or braze, it on. To use your wheel just sit on the seat and kick the concrete wheel round with your foot. Being heavy it has plenty of momentum.

Firing

Firing is necessary to harden the clay. With most glazed ware there are two firings: the "biscuit firing" which is just the clay and not the glaze, and the "glost firing," which is the biscuit ware dipped in the liquid glaze and fired again.

You can fire pots to flower-pot hardness in a large bonfire, although you cannot, of course, glaze them like this. Lay a thick circle of seasoned firewood on the ground, lay your ware in the middle, build a big cone of wood over it, and light. Pull the pots out of the ashes when they are cooled.

Traditional kilns are "updraught" kilns (see illustration) and you can build one yourself if you can lay bricks. "Down-draught" kilns are a more recent development and a little more difficult to build. The kiln is arranged so that the heat from the fire is sucked down through the pots before it is allowed to rise up the chimney. Much higher temperatures can be achieved using this method.

Temperature can be a matter of experience, or can be measured with "pyrometers" or "cones." Cones are little pyramids of different kinds of clay mixture which are placed in the kiln and which tell us the temperature by keeling over when they get to a certain heat. You can buy them very cheaply, but if you plan to use them remember to build some sort of a peep-hole in your kiln so you can see them.

Glazing

Most glaze is a mixture of silica, a "flux" which is generally an oxide of some metal (like rust), and alumina which is clay. China clay is the most usual form of alumina in glazes. The silica melts and solidifies on cooling to form a coating of glass on the ware. The flux helps the fusion, lowers the melting point of the silica, and provides colour. The alumina gives the glaze viscosity so that it does not all run down the side of the pot when you put it in the kiln.

Anybody can make their own glazes. You must grind the components down fine, either with a pestle and mortar or in a ball mill. The latter is a slowly revolving cylinder which you fill with flint pebbles and whatever material you want to grind. You can make a raw glaze from 31 parts washing soda (the flux–sodium is a metal); 10.5 parts whiting; 12 parts flint (the silica); 55.5 parts feldspar. Grind this, mix it and pass it through a 100 mesh to the inch (2.5cm) lawn, which is a piece of fine linen. There are hundreds of glazes and the best thing you can do is get a book on the subject and experiment with a few.

Before shaping your pot

Let newly-dug clay age for at least a fortnight. Then pug it to get the air out. The easiest way is to mix it with water and trample on it.

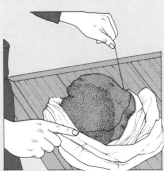

Use a wire to cut a workable lump from your store of pug.

Wedge the lump to make it a soft

homogeneous mass, free of air bubbles and foreign bodies like bits of stone and grit. You can wedge in the same way as you would knead dough for bread. Roll the clay towards you with both hands, twist it sideways and push it down into itself. Press out air bubbles and pick out bits of dirt. If you are mixing two clays wedge until your clay is one uniform colour.

After shaping your pot

Most glazes are applied after the first firing in the kiln, the biscuit firing. The commonest method is to dip your pot in a soup of powdered glaze and water, but it takes practice to avoid finger marks. You can pour glaze so that it flows over the pot. You can spray it, or paint it on with a brush.

A solid fuel updraught kiln

You can get kilns which use electricity, gas or oil, but a solid fuel kiln can be equally efficient, and you can build it yourself out of ordinary bricks. Updraught kilns are the simplest. You have your fire box at the bottom. If you burn wood you can do it on the ground, but coal and coke should be burned on steel firebars so that the ash can drop through. Build your pot chamber directly above the fire, by supporting a system of shelves made of firebrick on steel firebars. Include a peephole so you can watch your pots progress. And as long as you build the whole structure firmly the chimney can be directly over the pot chamber.

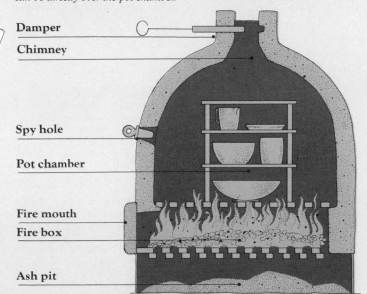

Damper

Chimney

Spy hole

Pot chamber

Fire mouth

Fire box

Ash pit

Pottery

Making pots by hand

Before you begin to throw pots on the wheel you need a thorough knowledge of clay itself: what happens to it when it is pulled about, when it dries, when it is fired and so on. This vital knowledge is best gained by shaping some pots by hand before you ever try the wheel. Many potters prefer to work by hand because they can create irregular shapes instead of being limited to those formed by the wheel.

Coil pots

You can make coil pots with no other tools than your fingers simply by rolling out long sausages of clay and coiling them into whatever shapes you want. Obviously each turn of the coil has to be pressed hard against its neighbour, and the sides of the pot have to be painstakingly smoothed. If you use a lot of care and patience your pot can have as fine a finish as anything thrown on a wheel. If you use a few simple tools (see illustrations) your job will be a lot easier.

Shaping a coil pot

A turntable is a great help. Instead of inching your coil round the pot, you can hold the coil still and turn the pot round. Begin with a ball of clay and flatten it to form a base half an inch (1 cm) thick. Smooth the surface of the base with a knife and cut it to a perfect circle by holding the knife still and revolving the turntable. If you have not got a turntable make the base on a plate and cut round to form a circle. Use a modelling tool to give the base "tooth," which means roughen it so that the coil above has something to cling to.

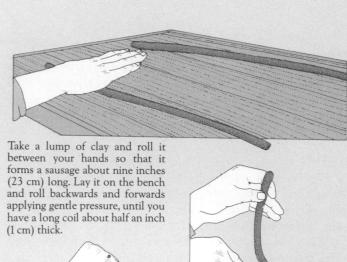

Take a lump of clay and roll it between your hands so that it forms a sausage about nine inches (23 cm) long. Lay it on the bench and roll backwards and forwards applying gentle pressure, until you have a long coil about half an inch (1 cm) thick.

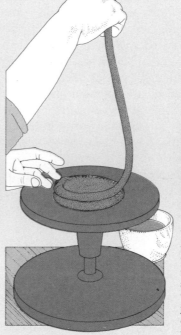

Make up some slurry, a mixture of clay and water. Brush some round the edge of the base with a toothbrush to make the coil stick. Lower the coil on and press down with your fingers on the inside and outside.

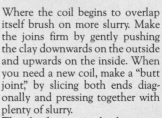

Where the coil begins to overlap itself brush on more slurry. Make the joins firm by gently pushing the clay downwards on the outside and upwards on the inside. When you need a new coil, make a "butt joint," by slicing both ends diagonally and pressing together with plenty of slurry.

The finish is completely up to you. If you like the corrugated look leave the outside as it is, but it is worth smoothing the inside a bit to make it easy to clean. You can smooth outside and inside to near perfection with a flat piece of wood.

Slab pots

"Slabbing", as the cognoscenti like to call it, is the best way to make angular pots with flat surfaces, particularly boxes and trays. You need a coarse grained clay if your pots are to be of any size, say more than six inches (15 cm) in any dimension. All you need is two battens and a rolling pin to make a slab from which you cut the parts of your pot. If you want to make slab pots with sides which are not rectangular you can cut a set of patterns in paper, and use them to cut up your slab.

Building a rectangular slab pot
Cover your bench with fabric to stop the clay sticking: an old sack is ideal. Put a large lump of clay on the sack and wallop it with your fist to flatten it out. Take two battens of whatever thickness you want your slab to be (half an inch or 1 cm is average but allow for shrinkage). Lay them either side of your clay so that your rolling pin can rest across them, and roll the clay into a slab of the right thickness.

Cut out the base and the four sides using the battens, or a ruler and set square. Now you must leave the pieces until they have dried leather hard. Turn them over as they dry, otherwise one side will shrink more than the other. Roughen the edges of the base with a modelling tool.

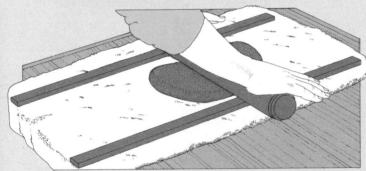

Coat the edges with slurry, and stick on the sides in whichever order seems intelligent. Use slurry to secure the vertical joins as well. If your pot is a large one, reinforce the inside corners with coils of clay pressed in with slurry. Trim and smooth ready for firing.

Pinch pots

Pinch pots can be made entirely by hand, although a knife and a turntable help create a neater finish. Similar to the pinch pot is what I call the "thumped pot". You get a thick plank, carve a concave shape in it, lay your clay in this and thump it with your fist. Thump it out thin, keep turning it round and shaping it, and you will make a pot.

Keep your thumb in there and slowly rotate the ball with the hand that is holding it. Gradually widen the hole made by your thumb by pinching the clay (as shown right) but press your thumb in deeper at the same time. Push evenly with your thumb and fingers as you turn the pot, and apply less pressure as the wall of the pot gets thinner. When you have finished pinching the pot and it feels quite smooth, put it on a turntable, turn it round slowly and trim the rim with a knife (as shown below right). Allow the pot to dry out thoroughly, glaze it and fire it in the normal way.

Hold the ball in one hand and make a hole with the thumb of the other hand. Don't put your thumb in too far at first.

Making a pinch pot
Roll a small lump of clay into a smooth ball between your hands.

Spinning Wool & Cotton

WOOL

Wool should be selected (or sheep should be selected) for the job to be done. Different breeds of sheep give wool of varying lengths of "staple" or fibre. Long staple wool is better than short for the hand spinner. Rough hairy wool is fine for tweeds and rugs: soft silky wool for soft fabrics like dress material. There are no hard and fast rules though.

To turn raw wool straight from the sheep into yarn ready for weaving you usually begin by "teasing" (see illustration) to straighten the wool out and get rid of dust, burrs and other rubbish. Then you card (see illustration) to create "rollags", which are rolls of well-combed wool ready for spinning. Spinning (see illustrations) is done with a spindle, a hedgehog or a spinning wheel, and whichever it is the principle is the same: to stretch and twist the straight fibres of wool from your rollags to make lengths of yarn ready for weaving or knitting. The subtle feature of a spinning wheel is that the endless twine which acts as a driving band goes over two pulleys of different sizes. This means that the bobbin and the flyer which the pulleys drive, revolve at different speeds. The flyer is therefore able to lay the yarn, as it is spun, on the bobbin at the right tension.

Roving

A self-supporting friend of mine wears the most flamboyant garments, very warm and good looking and he makes them entirely from wool, with no other tools but five sticks and a needle. He spins them on one stick and weaves them on the other four. Now it is possible to spin wool without carding it first. Instead you have to "rove" it, which can be done with the hands alone. Take some teased wool in your left hand, release a little of it between your finger and thumb, and pull it out in a continuous rope with your right hand, but not pulling so hard that you break or disengage the rope. This is not as easy as it sounds and it needs practice. When you have so pulled out all the wool, bend it double and do the whole operation again. Bend it double again (sometimes you might like to triple it) and go on doing this until you are satisfied that it is fairly parallel and well teased-out. This is now a "roving" and you can spin it direct.

Types of yarn

For weaving you generally use single-ply wool. The warp yarn should be fairly tightly spun: the weft yarn less so. If you intend to knit with the yarn, double it. To do this put two full

Preparing raw wool

You can turn a fleece into spun wool with just a spindle, but it is easier to use cards, and a hedgehog, or spinning wheel.

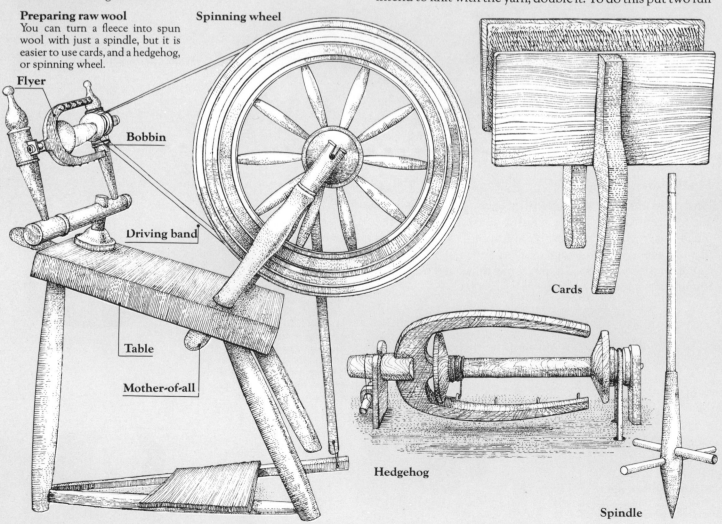

Flyer

Spinning wheel

Bobbin

Driving band

Table

Mother-of-all

Cards

Hedgehog

Spindle

bobbins on a "lazy kate", which is simply a skewer held horizontally at each end (two upright pegs will do just as well), put the ends of the two yarns together, feed them into the spindle on your spinning wheel just as if you were going to spin, put them round the flyer (see illustration), tie them to the spindle, and then turn the wheel backwards, or from right to left. This will make two-ply wool. If you want three-ply do the same thing with three bobbins.

COTTON

Cotton is often "willowed" before being carded. In the west this generally means being put in a string hammock and beaten with whippy willow rods. The vibrations fluff out and clean the cotton very effectively. It is then carded just like wool, but it cards much more easily, the cotton staples being much shorter.

Spin it as if it were wool, but keep your hands much closer together, treadle more quickly, and don't hold the cotton back too much with the left thumb and finger or it will kink. Angora hair, if you can get it, is delightful stuff and can be treated just like cotton. It makes amazingly soft yarn, much softer than most wool.

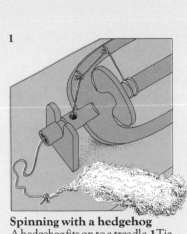

Spinning with a hedgehog

A hedgehog fits on to a treadle. **1** Tie a string round the bobbin, loop over first two hooks, poke through and tie to your rollag. **2** Treadle, and pull unspun wool from your left hand with your right. **3** When you have a good length of spun wool, stop treadling, move the string on to the next hook, hold the outer bracket still and treadle. The spun yarn will be drawn on to the bobbin.

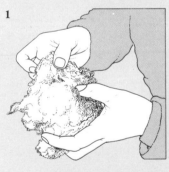

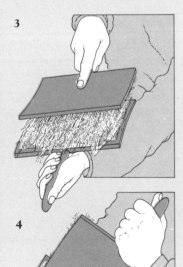
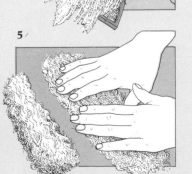

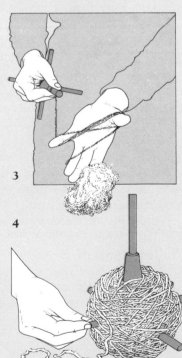

Teasing and carding

1 To tease take raw wool and pull out small pieces. **2** Lay teased locks evenly over your left card. **3** Stroke the left card with the right until the fibres are well combed. **4** Transfer fibres from left card to right. Comb and transfer about five times. **5** Get all the wool on one card and roll it off. Make a rollag, by rolling between the card backs or on a table.

Spinning with a spindle

1 Tie some spun yarn to your spindle, take a turn round the handle and tie to your rollag. **2** Spin the spindle. Pull unspun wool out between forefinger and thumb of your left hand. **3** When the spindle reaches ground, haul it up wrapping the newly spun wool round your fingers. Transfer the spun wool back to the spindle. Spin another length of wool. **4** Pull out the dowels to release your wool.

Dyeing & Weaving

DYEING

Stock dyeing is best for the self-supporter, that is dyeing the fibre in the skein before it is woven. It is easier thus to get an even distribution of colour.

Natural dyes will generally only dye natural materials: they will not dye nylon and the other synthetics. But the right natural vegetable dyes, used with the correct "mordants", will dye any natural fabric with good and fast colours. (Mordants are chemicals which bite into the fabric and give the dye something to fix on.) Although aniline dyes, which are derived from coal tars and other strange chemical substances can get close to natural colours they can never quite make it. But if you want very brilliant colours, then you will probably need artificial dyes.

Some plant-derived dyes don't need a mordant, but most do. The mordants that you should be able to make for yourself or come by very readily are vinegar, caustic soda and ammonia. To get a greater range of colours you need substances like cream of tartar, alum, chrome (potassium dichromate), tin (stannous chloride), and iron (ferrous sulphate). Alum is the most useful one, and if that is the only one you have, you can still do a lot of dyeing.

To mordant with alum heat 4 gallons (18 litres) of water, dissolve 4 oz (114 g) of alum and 1 oz (28 g) of cream of tartar in a little water and then add it to the 4 gallons (18 litres). Immerse 1 lb (0.5 kg) of clean, scoured (washed), dried wool in the form of a skein and simmer for an hour, stirring occasionally. Lift the wool out and press gently.

To prepare your vegetable dye cut up your vegetable matter into small pieces, let it stand in cold water overnight and boil it for an hour. Then add more water if necessary. You will need four gallons (18 litres) of dye for a pound (0.5 kg) of wool. Drop wetted, mordanted wool into the dye all at once. The dye should be warm. If it isn't, heat it. Leave the wool in for an hour, stirring occasionally very gently. Then take it out and drain.

A few materials that make strong colour are listed below, but the field is open to endless experiments.

Yellow Bark of ash, elder, brickthorn, apple, pear and cherry; leaves and shoots of broom and gorse; privet leaves; onion skins (not very fast in sunlight though); marigold flowers; golden-rod; Lombardy poplar leaves; lily-of-the-valley leaves; bog myrtle leaves; dyers' chamomile; spindle tree seeds; pine cones (reddish yellow); barberry roots and stems (no mordant required).

Green Purging buckthorn berries; heather leaf tips; privet berries (a bluish green); bracken leaves; spindle tree seeds boiled in alum; elder leaves.

Brown Walnut roots, leaves or husks of shells (no mordant required); slow or blackthorn bark (reddish-brown); boiled juniper berries.

Red Spindle tree seed vessels; blood root.

Black Oak bark, which will dye purple if mixed with tin (stannous chloride). Oak galls make ink.

Purple Bilberries are much used for tweeds in the Highlands of Scotland and are a fine dye (no mordant required); willow roots.

Violet Wild marjoram.

Orange Lungs of oak, *Sticta pulmonacea* (no mordant required).

Magenta Lichen makes a magenta on the first dye and other colours as you enter successive dye-lots into the same dye. When the dye seems quite exhausted freshen it with vinegar and you will get a rosy tan.

BLEACHING

Fabrics can be bleached by soaking them in sour milk and laying them in the sun. A mixture of chlorine and slaked lime also bleaches and is good for flax and cotton. Wool and silk can be bleached with fumes of sulphur. Simply hang the skeins over burning sulphur in an enclosed space.

WEAVING

Weaving on a good hand loom is a magnificent accomplishment, and if you can do it you have made a big step towards true self-sufficiency. Once you have the loom, and are proficient, you can achieve a considerable output of very good cloth. Machine-woven cloth does not compare with hand-woven, nor have machines yet been devised that can even imitate the hands of the weaver.

Fasten four sticks in a square frame shape, tie lots of threads over them all parallel with each other (the "warp"), and haul another thread (the "weft") through the threads of the warp with a needle or sharpened stick, going over one and under the next thread of the warp and so on. Then bring the needle back with another thread on it, going over the ones you went under before. Keep on doing this and in no time you will see your cloth appear.

If you need to make cloth seriously you will soon find yourself inventing ingenious devices to make your task easier and your cloth better. Firstly you will devise a comb (see illustration) to poke between each pair of threads in the warp and beat the threads of the weft together so that the weave is not too loose. You will have invented the ancestor of the "reed".

Then you will find that it is tedious to go on threading the weft through with a needle and so you will invent an arrangement of two sets of strings, with loops in their middles, hanging from sticks, and you will thread each thread of the warp through the loop in one of these strings, each alternate thread going to a different set of strings from its neighbours. You will have invented the "heddle". You will lift each set of heddles alternately, on a frame called the "harness" and it will leave a space called the "shed" between the two lots of threads. You will be able to throw your needle through the shed so that you can criss-cross, or weave, the threads without having to pick through each individual warp thread with your needle.

The square weaver

The simplest loom is the 5-inch (13 cm) "square weaver". It makes 4-inch (10 cm) squares of cloth which can be sewn together as patchwork. String the warp as shown below and weave the weft with a 5-inch (13 cm) needle. Design your own patterns on graph paper (right): on black squares the weft goes under, on white squares it goes over.

Pattern with plain weave **Simple checks** **Diagonal weave**

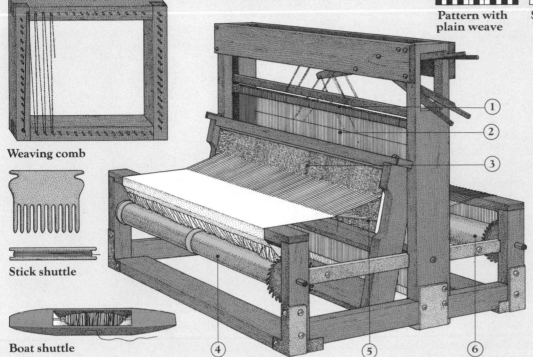

Weaving comb

Stick shuttle

Boat shuttle

Warping frame

The four harness table loom

A table loom takes up much less space than a floor loom and does all the same things. It is a little slower because the harnesses are operated with handles instead of pedals.

Key
1 Harness	4 Cloth beam
2 Heddles	5 Shed
3 Reed	6 Warp beam

Next you will find it a nuisance having to attach a new weft thread to your needle each time. So you will carve notches at either end of a stick and wind the thread round it in such a way that the stick can turn and release, or pay out, the yarn.

You will have invented the "stick shuttle" (see illustration). As you get more inventive you may invent the "boat shuttle" (see illustration), into which you can drop a reel of thread, ready wound. You will soon find that, with all your new gadgets, you quickly come to the end of your weaving frame and only have a small piece of cloth, so you will invent a roller at each end of your loom, one for rolling the threads of the warp on, the other for rolling the newly woven cloth on. This time you will have invented the "warp beam", or "warp roller" (see illustration), and the "cloth beam", or "cloth roller" (see illustration).

You will find lifting the alternate harnesses up to form your shed a nuisance, so you will connect the harnesses up to some foot pedals with an elaborate arrangement of strings. You will have invented "treadles", with "marches" or "lamms" above them to transmit the motion to the harnesses.

Then, if your life depends on weaving an awful lot of cloth, you will devise a sling device worked by a handle, which will fling the shuttle backwards and forwards through the warp without your having to touch it. By this time, you will have invented the "flying shuttle" and, believe it or not, you will be getting dangerously near the Industrial Revolution.

Now, when you come to thread your new patent loom up with the warp threads you will find that it is so difficult that you nearly go mad, so you invent a revolving spool, a "warping mill", to wind the threads of the warp around, or else a rack, a warping frame (see illustration), with pegs that serve the same purpose.

Finally you will realize that by having four harnesses instead of two you can greatly vary the pattern formed by the warp, for you can lift different combinations of warp threads. And by having two or more shuttles, with different coloured weft thread in them, you can alter the pattern in other ways.

But to learn to weave you simply must get somebody who knows how to do it to teach you: you cannot learn it out of a book, although a good book on weaving will help you.

FINISHING CLOTH

"Fulling" partially felts cloth and makes it denser and stronger. You do it by beating the cloth in water. Try putting it in the bath and stamping on it hard. If you add "fuller's earth" you will fill up the pores of the cloth.

"Raising" is done by picking the surface of the cloth, traditionally with "teazles", which are the heads of large thistles. You can often find them growing wild, or you can cultivate them yourself. The effect of raising is to give the cloth a fluffy surface.

Spinning Flax

Flax is the most durable of all the fibres available to us. Man-made fibres haven't been invented long enough yet to know whether they will outlast flax: my guess is they won't, for quite good-looking pieces of flax linen have been dug up in Egyptian pyramids and my corlene rope won't last two years.

The crop is harvested before the seed ripens which is a pity because it means losing the oil the seeds would ultimately produce. It is pulled, not cut, then tied in sheaves and stacked.

Preparing raw flax

Flax must first be "rippled" which means pulling the heads through a row of nails with their heads filed to points. This removes the unripe seeds, which make a marvellous stockfood. Then flax is "retted" which really means rotted. Lay it in stagnant water for two or three weeks, until the fibrous sheaf separates easily from the central woody portion. You can ret in running water but it takes much longer, or you can spread your flax on grass for about six weeks and let the dew do the job. After retting dry the flax carefully.

Then you must "scutch" which is the process of breaking the stems of the flax. Do this by beating the flax on a table with a broad wooden blade, or with a special "scutcher".

"Hackling" is the next step, and consists of dragging the flax across a bed of nails to remove the "tow", which is all the short fibres, and leave the "line" which is the long ones. The tow can be used for caulking deck seams on boats, or stuffing mattresses, or it can be carded and spun to make a rather coarse and heavy yarn. The line can be spun to make linen thread.

To spin (you don't card line) you have to dress the line on a "distaff" which is simply a vertical stick, or small pole, which can be stuck into a hole in a spinning wheel.

Dressing a distaff

Dressing a flax distaff needs considerable skill. Put an apron on (if you don't happen to be wearing your long bombazine skirt), tie a string round your waist leaving the two ends a few inches long, and sit down. Take a handful of line, such as falls naturally away from the larger bundle, and tie round one end of it carefully with the two ends of the string round your waist and secure with a reef knot. Cut the two loose ends of the string. Lay the flax out full length on your lap with the knotted end towards you. Hold the bundle with your left hand at the end furthest from you, pull a few fibres away from the main bundle with your right hand, and lay them on your right knee. Pull some more fibres away and lay them next to the first few. Go on doing this until you have made a thin, fine fan of flax on your lap. Remember that the end nearest to you is tied fast. Now grab the main bundle in your right hand and reverse the process, laying a second fan from left to right on top of the first fan but be sure to pull from the same part of the main bundle. Go on doing this, alternating hands and directions, until all the flax of the bundle

Dressing line on a distaff
Before it can be spun, line must be dressed on a distaff so that the fibres are separated out. You take a handful of line and tie it at one end with string which you have first wound round your waist. Sit down and carefully spread out a series of fans of fibre on your lap, one on top of the other. Cut the knot, lay the distaff on one edge and roll up the fans. Stand the distaff in its hole and tie with ribbon.

has been laid out, in criss-crossing fan shapes, one on top of the other. As you work try to criss-cross the fibres, otherwise they will not pull out properly when you come to spin.

Now cut the string, take it away and slightly loosen the top end of the bundle where it was tied. Then lay the distaff on one edge of the fan, with its top where the knotted string was. Wind the fan up on the distaff, winding very tightly at the end nearest you but keeping the flax very loose at the bottom of the distaff. Then put the distaff, with the flax fan round it, upright into its hole and tie the middle of a ribbon tightly round the top. Then criss-cross the two ends of the ribbon downwards round the cone of flax until you reach the bottom. Tie the two ends in a bow.

Spinning flax

Take the yarn that you have already tied into the bobbin of the wheel and catch it in the flax at the bottom end of the distaff. Spin. Have a bowl of water by you and keep wetting your fingers so as to wet the flax. Use your left hand to stop the spin from going up into the distaff, and your right to clear knots and pull out thick threads. If you have done your dressing operation right the line should steadily feed itself through the thumb and finger of your left hand into the spinning thread. Turn your distaff as required, and, when you have cleared the distaff as far as the bow in the ribbon, untie the latter and tie it further up to expose more fibres. Keep doing this until you come to the very top of the distaff and the last few fibres.

Curing & Tanning

Animal skins become hard, like boards, when they have been pulled off the carcass and dried for some time, and then they are good for practically nothing. Early on, mankind found two ways to overcome this disadvantage: mechanical methods which produce rawhide, and chemical methods which produce leather.

To make rawhide you must take hide straight off the animal and begin working it before it gets hard. In this way you will break down the fibres which set to make it hard and it will remain permanently soft. A great deal of working is needed. Eskimo ladies, we are told, do it by chewing the hide. Undoubtedly chewing, and working between the hands, for long enough (probably pretty constantly for about a week) will do the trick.

Curing

I use a method which is part mechanical and part chemical to cure sheep-skins, fox skins, and especially rabbit skins, which come up beautifully. The end product is a cross between rawhide and leather.

Wash your animal skin well in warm water and then rinse it in a weak borax solution. Then soak it in a solution of sulphuric acid made by mixing 1 lb (0.5 kg) of salt with 1 gallon (4.5 litres) of water and pouring in $\frac{1}{2}$ ounce (14 g) of concentrated sulphuric acid. Don't throw the water onto the acid or you may lose your eyes and spoil your beauty.

After three days and nights take the skin out and rinse it in water and then in a weak borax solution. If you put it in the washing machine and let it churn about for an hour or two so much the better (after you have washed the acid out of it of course). Next hang it up and let it half dry.

Take it down and rub oil or fat into the flesh side and work it. Scrape it and pull it about. Pulling it with both hands backwards and forwards over the back of a chair is a good method.

Leave it hanging over a chair and pull it about every time you go past. Rub more fat in from time to time. It will become quite soft and as good as tanned leather.

Tanning

Tanning with tannin is a purely chemical method, and the end product is leather. It takes half a ton of good oak bark to yield a hundredweight (50.8 kg) of tannin, and this will cure two hundredweight (101 kg) of fresh hides. Wattle, elder, birch, willow, spruce, larch and hemlock also contain tannin. The bark must be milled: that is pounded up small and soaked in water. The hides must be steeped in the resulting solution for, from four months in the case of small hides, to a year in the case of big ones. For really perfect results it is best to soak hides in a weak solution at first, putting them in increasing strengths as the months go by.

A fool-proof method is to soak the hides in a weakish solution for say a month, and then to lay them in a pit or tank with a thick layer of bark between each skin. Then just cover the pile with water. Leave like this for at least six months.

A quick way of tanning a skin is the "bag method". You make a bag out of a skin (or take the skin off whole). Hang the bag up, and fill it with tannin solution. After a week or two the hide should be tanned.

To get the hair off skins, lay them in a paste made of lime and water for three weeks, or in a lime-sulphide paste for a day. De-lime by washing in a weak vinegar solution.

Sewing leather

Sewing leather is as easy as sewing cloth: all you need are a few large needles (sailmaker's needles are fine), an awl for making holes in the leather and some strong waxed thread. Any thread dragged through a lump of beeswax is waxed thread. For stitches see illustrations.

Stitching leather

You need an awl to make holes, strong needles and tough waxed thread. The strongest stitch is the opposing stitch. Put a needle on each end of a long thread. Push one needle through the first hole and pull half the thread through. From then on push both needles through each hole, but from opposite directions. The blanket stitch and the crossover stitch are both good for light leather.

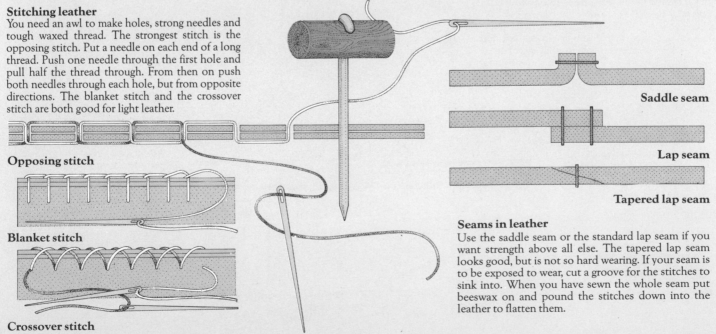

Opposing stitch

Blanket stitch

Crossover stitch

Saddle seam

Lap seam

Tapered lap seam

Seams in leather

Use the saddle seam or the standard lap seam if you want strength above all else. The tapered lap seam looks good, but is not so hard wearing. If your seam is to be exposed to wear, cut a groove for the stitches to sink into. When you have sewn the whole seam put beeswax on and pound the stitches down into the leather to flatten them.

Making Bricks & Tiles

If you can help it, don't *buy* clay to make home-made bricks. Instead try the different clays on your land and in your locality. You are quite likely to find one that makes a good brick, and save yourself a lot of money.

When you have found it dig the clay and puddle it. You can do this by laying the clay in a pit, wetting it, and trampling it for an hour or two with your feet. This method works very well, but any way of well working the clay with water will do. Then, when the clay is of the right consistency, solid but malleable, you can make bricks using the method illustrated.

Drying and firing bricks

In countries with a rainless dry season the easiest way to dry bricks is to lay them out in rows on level sand and just leave them. In rainier climes they must be under cover, and are usually piled up about six courses high, criss-cross to leave spaces for the air to circulate.

Bricks must dry for anything from a week to a month according to the climate, and then they must be fired. To fire bricks you must build a clamp, which is basically a rectangular pile, at least the size of a small room, made of bricks criss-crossed so as to leave cavities between them. There are two ways of using the clamp. One is to leave fireplaces sufficiently large to contain fair-sized wood fires at roughly three foot (91cm) intervals on the two long sides of the clamp. Then you plaster the whole clamp with clay except for some small chimneys at the top of the leeward side, and light fires in the fireplaces on the windward side.

If the wind changes block up the fireplaces on the new leeward side, open up the fireplaces on the new windward side, and use them. The fireplaces can be rough arches of already burnt, or half-burnt, bricks, or false arches made by stepping bricks. After firing for a week let the fires go out and allow the clamp to cool. Open up, pull out the well-fired bricks, and keep the half-fired ones to be fired again.

The other method, which I think is easier and better, does not require fireplaces. Instead you fill the gaps between the bricks with charcoal (coal, anthracite or coke will do). The clamp can be smaller, seven feet (2.2 m) high by any width or length you like. Plaster the whole clamp with mud except for a hole at the bottom on the windward side and a hole at the top on the leeward side. Light a small wood fire in the hole on the windward side and go away and forget it. The charcoal will quickly catch. After five or six days, when it has cooled, open the clamp and take your bricks out. You get more completely fired than with the other method.

Tiles

Tiles can be made of the same clay as bricks, but it must be carefully puddled and mixed. They can be flat, or they can be pantiles, which have a convex and concave side, or they can be, as most Mediterranean tiles are, half-cylinders. In Spain and Italy the latter are commonly tapered, because, it is said, in Roman times they were moulded on a man's thigh. These can be, and often are, made by throwing a cylinder on a potter's wheel and splitting it in half before drying and firing. Any other tile must be made in a mould.

Fire tiles in the same clamp as bricks and build it in such a way that the bricks take the weight. Tiles are not strong. And don't forget they must have holes for nailing or pegging.

Brickmaking: the essential tools
Most important is the mould which you should make precisely the right size to allow for the shrinkage of your particular clay. Make it from jointed wood and, if you want it to last, put a steel pin secured with a bolt through each end. Make your bow by bending a length of hazel and stringing a wire across it. The cuckle is an excellent tool for moving large amounts of clay. Your sand tray should be deep enough to immerse the mould in. You need a knife for cleaning the mould and boards for drying bricks.

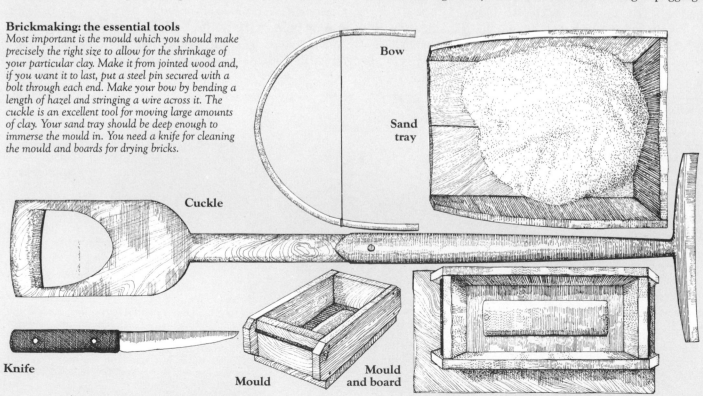

Bow

Sand tray

Cuckle

Knife

Mould

Mould and board

Making bricks in a mould

A lot of time and practice has determined that bricks should measure 9 inches (23 cm) by 4½ inches (11 cm) by 2¼ inches (5 cm). The length is double the width which is itself double the height. The whole is very convenient for a man's hand. Depending on your clay and how much it shrinks, your mould must be marginally bigger in all its dimensions. So experiment and make a mould to suit your clay.

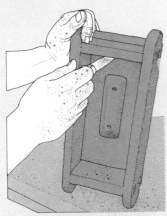

Clean the inside of your mould by scraping round with a knife.

Coat the inside of the mould with sand as you would a cake tin with flour, by dipping in sand and shaking.

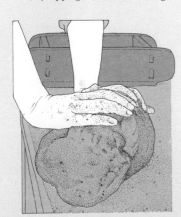

Take what you think is the right

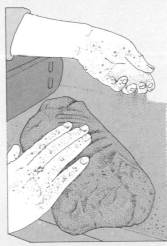

amount of clay and begin to form a "warp", a brick-sized lump.

Work warp into the right shape by rolling on a board. Sand the board and your hands to stop the clay sticking to them.

Gather the clay towards you (as shown above) roll the ends in and drop it with a spinning action so that it thuds on to the bench (as shown below). This is to knock out

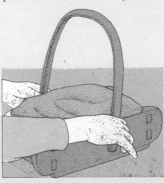

all the excess air.

Throw the warp hard into the mould so the clay spreads out towards the corners.

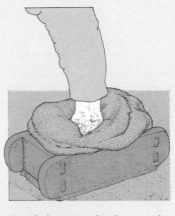

Punch down into the clay to push it into the corners and leave a hole in the middle.

Ram more clay into the hole and press down as hard as you can.

Cut off excess clay by running your bow across the top of the mould. Peel off severed clay and return it to your pile.

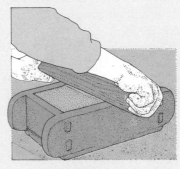

Dip a length of wood in water and use it to smooth over, or "strike", the top surface. Then sprinkle the top with sand.

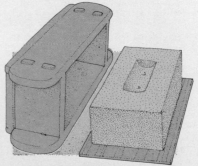

Pick up the mould and tap its corners against the bench until you see gaps on all sides of the clay.

Dry on a board for a month.

Working in Stone

Some stone, particularly granite, is awkward for building because it does not split easily in straight lines. Other stone, most sedimentary stone in fact, has been laid down in layers under water and therefore splits easily along horizontal lines, but they are not necessarily horizontal in the ground. The beds may have been tilted. Other stone still, which builders and quarrymen call freestone, splits easily both horizontally and vertically. This is what the builder is looking for and if he can find it he is a very lucky man. Much of the oolitic limestone from Britain's Jurassic sea is like this, and it gave rise to the superb school of vernacular building which stretches from Dorset to Lincolnshire: the huge quarries of Barnack in Northamptonshire having supplied much of the material for the great gothic churches and cathedrals of Eastern England. The Jurassic limestone of the Isle of Portland is a freestone *par excellence* as is Purbeck stone.

Freestone can often be split out with wedges instead of explosives. Holes are drilled in a line along the rock, the wedges are driven in, in sequence further and further until suddenly the rock splits along the line. If you are splitting off a big piece you can use "the plug and feathers". The feathers are two pieces of steel that you put down either side of a hole drilled in the rock. The plug is a wedge that you drive in between them. The advantage is that the feathers exert a more even pressure than the plug alone and so the rock splits evenly when it comes away from the parent rock.

Holes are driven in rock by a rock drill, which is a steel bit with an edge like a chisel sharpened at a very obtuse angle. You either hit the bit in with a hammer, turning it between each blow, or you drive it in with a percussion drill. You can drill the hardest rock in the world like this and in soft rock go quite quickly even with a hand hammer. Put water in the hole for lubrication, and get rid of the ground rock dust by splashing. Wrap a rag round the bit so you don't get splashed in the eye with rock paste.

You can break out, subdivide, and dress to rectangle, any rock, even the roughest and most intractable basalt or granite: the harder the rock the harder the work. You can build with uneven, undressed boulders, and fill the inevitable spaces with – well, just earth, or earth and lime, or in these decadent days concrete made with cement so the rats can't get in. But there will always be places where you need a solid, rectangular stone: doorsteps, lintels, hearth stones and other similar things.

Slate is a metamorphic rock, which means it is a sedimentary rock that has undergone great heat and pressure. The original layerings or laminations have been obliterated and others have developed more or less at right angles to the first. It cleaves easily along these. Generally there are faults or weaknesses in large masses of slate more or less at right angles to the laminations of the slate. These make it possible to break out large blocks without too much blasting. Slate is the very best roofing material, and thicker slabs are ideal for shelves in larders.

Handling the mason's tools

To prepare stone you need two types of chisel and hammer. The points and the edging-in chisel are given sharp, direct blows with a steel hammer. Claws and other chisels must be given softer blows so for these you use a wooden mallet.

Pointing

Hold the point at an angle and hit sharply with a steel hammer.

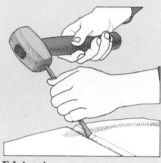

Edging-in

To help you control the edging-in chisel, place your thumb across it. Use small hard strokes keeping the chisel in position on the stone.

Cleaving a large block of stone

Mark round with a pencil. Drill and chisel deep V-shaped slots in the top and sides. Crowbar the block up and place a steel section below

Finishing a surface

Skim rhythmically with the claw or chisel: **1** place tool on surface; **2** hit firmly with mallet; **3** draw back tool and mallet together and repeat.

1

2

3

the future breaking point. Put steel wedges in the slots and hit in sequence with a steel hammer, listening to the ring of the stone. It dulls as the stone cleaves.

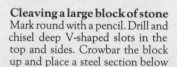

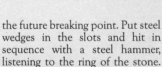

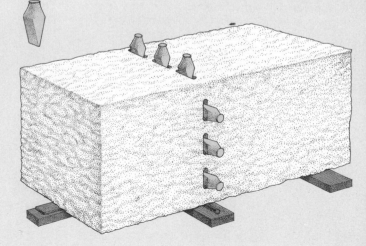

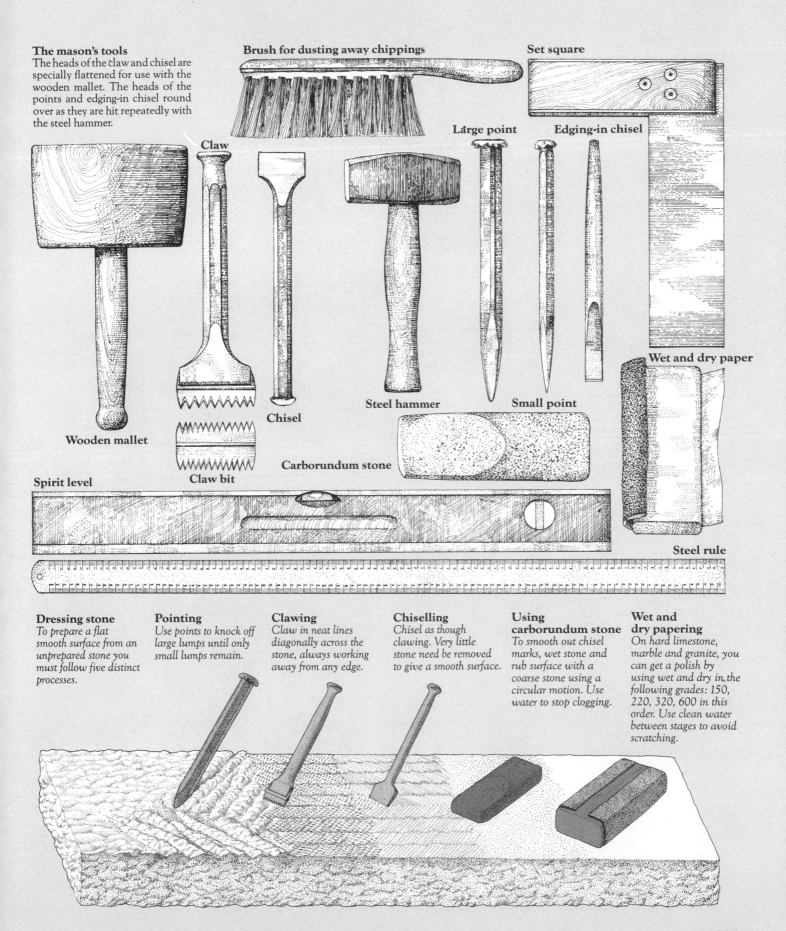

The mason's tools
The heads of the claw and chisel are specially flattened for use with the wooden mallet. The heads of the points and edging-in chisel round over as they are hit repeatedly with the steel hammer.

Brush for dusting away chippings

Set square

Claw

Large point

Edging-in chisel

Chisel

Steel hammer

Small point

Wooden mallet

Carborundum stone

Wet and dry paper

Spirit level

Claw bit

Steel rule

Dressing stone
To prepare a flat smooth surface from an unprepared stone you must follow five distinct processes.

Pointing
Use points to knock off large lumps until only small lumps remain.

Clawing
Claw in neat lines diagonally across the stone, always working away from any edge.

Chiselling
Chisel as though clawing. Very little stone need be removed to give a smooth surface.

Using carborundum stone
To smooth out chisel marks, wet stone and rub surface with a coarse stone using a circular motion. Use water to stop clogging.

Wet and dry papering
On hard limestone, marble and granite, you can get a polish by using wet and dry in the following grades: 150, 220, 320, 600 in this order. Use clean water between stages to avoid scratching.

Working in Stone

Masoning a block of stone

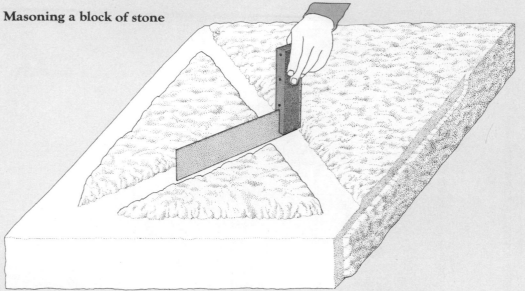

Cut two draughts. Join them up.

Remove islands. Make a diagonal.

Join to corners and remove islands.

Levelling and edging

To get a smooth surface on an uneven block you must establish "draughts" or "datum lines". Choose a rough plane for your proposed surface by eye. Then mason your first two "draughts", which are simply strips chiselled down to your chosen plane. Make them parallel to two edges of the block, so that they meet in a right angle in the corner. Next join their ends to form a triangle and, if your block is large, cut the triangle in half with a fourth draught. Then with point, claw and chisel remove the "islands" thus formed. Use straight edge and square continually to check levels. Repeat the process on

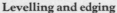

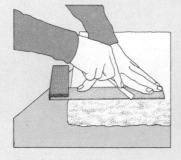

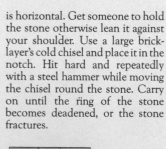

the other half of the surface.

To make a square edge use your edging-in chisel to inscribe a line on your top surface. If there is a border of rough stone round your top surface inscribe the line inside it.

Very carefully edge in along your inscribed line using an edging-in chisel and a steel hammer. Take off a narrow strip all the way along so that you are left with a clean, sharp edge on your block.

Then with point, claw and chisel – and be sure, always, to use them in that order (see previous page, bottom right) – remove the central island. And remember: always work away from the edge.

Coping stone

You "cleave" large stones (see previous page). You "cope", or split, smaller ones. You do this either when you want to take a small piece off a stone to make it exactly the right size, or when you want to split a stone into two or more pieces. Simply by coping you can make rough fence posts, corner stones, anchors for fences and so on.

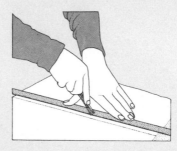

First use your edging-in chisel to inscribe two parallel lines ½ inch (1 cm) apart on all four sides of the

stone, around the proposed breaking point.

Again using your edging-in chisel, inscribe a V-shaped channel about ¾ inch (2 cm) deep between the lines on all four sides. A stone will always break at its weakest point, so be sure your stone has no flaw which will prove weaker than your inscribed notch.

Up-end the stone so that the notch

is horizontal. Get someone to hold the stone otherwise lean it against your shoulder. Use a large bricklayer's cold chisel and place it in the notch. Hit hard and repeatedly with a steel hammer while moving the chisel round the stone. Carry on until the ring of the stone becomes deadened, or the stone fractures.

Bricklayer's cold chisel

236

Pitching

Pitching is a method of removing stone from slabs of limestone or sandstone. You can use a special blunt-ended chisel called a pitcher, though in fact any blunt chisel will do the job.

As with coping inscribe two lines ½ inch (1 cm) either side of the proposed break on all four sides, and using your edging-in chisel cut a V-shaped notch approximately ¾ inch (2 cm) deep. Support the stone on the ground and lean it against your left shoulder. In this way all the shock waves go through the stone and not into the wall, or table or whatever you normally lean it against. It is vital that you get the chisel at the right angle (illustration right).

The angle for pitching

The pitcher or chisel should be held against the stone at slightly less than right angles, and given a hard blow. With limestone you will be able to pare off strips about 1 inch (2 cm) thick; with sandstone these will be 1½ inches (4 cm), or more. Knock off strips as necessary so that your last strip takes you into your notch. Then finish the edge off with ordinary masonry techniques.

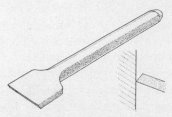

Cutting slate across the grain

Inscribe slate with two lines ½ inch (1 cm) apart. Then "stitch chisel", meaning drill a row of holes like perforations, between the lines with a ¼ inch (0.6 cm) tungsten masonry bit. Saw from hole to hole using a medium blade in a hacksaw. Smooth off the edges with a dreadnought file.

Stitch chiselling

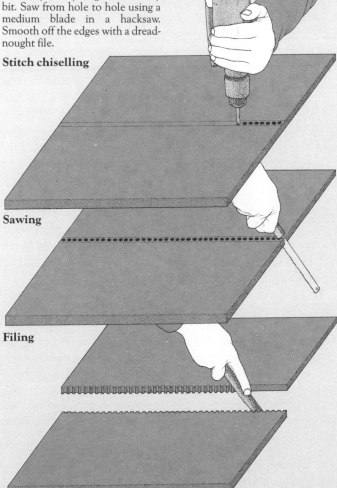

Sawing

Filing

Splitting a large slate slab

To split a large slab find the grain that seems nearest to dividing the slab in half. Give a sharp tap with a cold chisel against that grain half way along each side of the slab. When you have walloped it on the fourth side the slab should split easily in half.

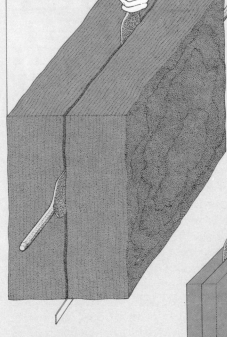

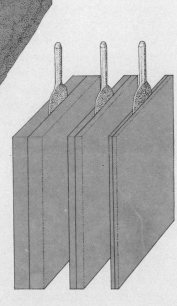

Making roof slates

Take a thick piece of slate between your knees, rest it on a steel profile on the floor, whack it with a cold chisel and watch it split. Put aside one half and split the other. Carry on doing this until you have two slates the right thickness. Then use up your pile of "halves".

Working in Metal

BLACKSMITHING

To learn to be a proper blacksmith should take seven years, but you can learn to bend, shape and weld wrought iron in a few hours. To do it well takes practice though, and you will ruin plenty of iron first. If you are planning to work with iron a lot you need equipment: a forge, an anvil, a bench with at least one good vice on it, and suitable hammers, and tongs. But I have done simple forge work by crawling about on my hands and knees in front of an Aga cooker, poking bits of iron into the firebox, and hammering them on the head of a sledge hammer laid on the ground. A little knowledge may be a dangerous thing but it helps sometimes.

Blacksmiths work with ferrous metal and there are many kinds. Wrought iron is the blacksmith's classic material. It is made from pig-iron (the stuff which runs out of the bottom of blast furnaces) by persistent heating and hammering. It has enormous advantages for blacksmithing: you can shape it, split it, weld it, in fact treat it as if it were clay or plasticine, provided you get it to the right temperature. When cold it is hard (but nothing like as hard as steel), tough and strong, ideal for much agricultural machinery, chains, shackles, split-links, and the iron components of carts, boats, and buildings. It does not corrode easily.

Malleable iron is only used for a few things, like the fingers of mowing machines, which have to be shaped when cold.

Cast iron is what it says it is: cast in moulds. It is extremely hard, but brittle. It will not stand hammering and it is no good for edge tools as the edge would just crumble off, but it does not corrode easily.

Steel comes in many forms and qualities. "Mild steel" is much used by blacksmiths nowadays because they cannot get wrought iron. It is nothing like so good because it is harder to work and it rusts easily.

For forging wrought iron you need an ordinary blacksmith's forge. This is a fire tray, or hearth, with a pipe, called a tuyere, or tue iron, which blows air into the fire. The tuyere commonly passes through a water bath before it reaches the fire so that it keeps cool enough not to burn away, but sometimes it simply passes through a massive piece of cast iron. Cast iron can stand great heat without melting or burning. The fire can be of coal, coke breeze or charcoal.

If you use coal or coke, clinker will form, and hamper your work. Let the clinker solidify and remove it. Keep the fire as small as possible by wetting the fuel around its centre, and place the work to be heated in the heart of the fire. Draw wet coal in sideways as needed: don't dump "green" coal on top of the fire. The blast can be provided by a bellows worked by hand, by an electric air pump, or by a vacuum cleaner turned the wrong way round so it blows instead of sucking but don't use more blast than you need.

Different jobs require different degrees of heat.

Blood red is for making fairly easy bends in mild steel.

Bright red is for making sharper bends in mild steel, or for punching holes and using the hot chisel in mild steel.

Bright yellow is the heat for most forging jobs in wrought iron, and for drawing down and upsetting (making thinner and making thicker) both wrought iron and mild steel. It is also right for driving holes in or hot chiselling heavy work (iron or steel more than an inch or 2 cm thick).

Slippery heat is just below full welding heat and is used for forging wrought iron and for welding mild steel if it proves difficult to weld it at a higher temperature. It takes speed and skill to weld steel at this heat.

Full welding heat is for welding wrought iron and most kinds of steel. When you reach it white sparks will be flung off the white hot metal making it look like a sparkler.

Snowball heat is the temperature for welding very good quality wrought iron, but it is too high for steel. If you go beyond snowball heat you will burn your metal.

Tempering

Tempering is the process of heating and then cooling metal to give it different degrees of hardness and brittleness. The general rule is that the higher you heat it and the quicker you cool it the harder it will be, but the more brittle. When tempering a steel cutting tool you harden it first, by heating it to somewhere between black and blood red and then plunging it into water. When you have done this you temper it by heating it again, dipping the cutting edge into water so as to cool it, then letting the colours creep down from the rest of it until exactly the right colour reaches the edge and then quenching it again.

Welding

To weld wrought iron or mild steel first get the metal to the right temperature. Then take the first piece out of the fire, knock the dirt off it and lay it face upwards on the anvil. Whip the other bit out, knock the dirt off it, lay it face downwards on the first bit and hit it in the middle of the weld with a hammer, hard. Keep on walloping it: on the flat if it is flat work, around the beak of the anvil if it is, say, a chain link. But all this has to be done very fast. If the weld hasn't taken put it in the fire again. If the centre has taken but not the outsides, fire again, or "take another heat" as blacksmiths say.

To weld anything harder than wrought iron more modern forms of welding must be used. From the point of view of the self-supporter these are oxy-acetylene and electric arc. Neither of these are as formidable as they sound: every gypsy scrap-dealer uses oxy-acetylene and many a farmer has his own small electric welding set and can use it too. But for either gas or electric welding always wear goggles or a mask. It is possible to blind yourself permanently if you gaze at an arc or a gas flame for more than a second or two, and it is very easy to do severe damage to your eyes.

Oxy-acetylene

Oxy-acetylene tackle consists of two pressure bottles, one of oxygen and the other of acetylene. The latter gas, in the presence of oxygen, gives off an intensely hot flame, and a flame, furthermore, that acts as a protection against oxidation for the hot metal before it cools. The two gases are brought together by pipes and then burnt at a nozzle. It is the inner flame that you must use – not the outer. The aim of the welder is to melt rod metal and use it to fuse two metal faces together, and also to fill in any spaces between them. Ideally the edges of the steel plates should be bevelled where they meet, and the space left filled with the rod metal.

There are two methods then of oxy-acetylene welding. One is "leftward", or "forward", welding. In this method the rod, which is made of metal of more or less the same type as the work to be welded, is held in the left hand and moved to the left while the torch is held in the right hand and follows the rod. The edges of the pieces of steel are pre-heated. Be careful not to keep the flame in one place too long, or the metal will be distorted. In "rightward", or "backward", welding the torch is moved to the right, and the rod follows it. Less rod metal is used with this method, and it is considered better than leftward welding particularly for joining larger pieces of steel, anything over ¼ inch (0.6 cm).

Electric arc

Electric arc welding is a simple matter of using a very high voltage to create a spark at the top of a rod. Held between the two surfaces to be welded the spark melts them and also the tip of the rod. The material to be welded must be earthed. You can buy quite cheap and simple a.c. welding sets that work off the mains, and also portable sets that have a small motor to generate current for them.

Sharpening tools

The principle of sharpening is that, if it is just a freshening up of the edge you want, you use a "whetstone", but if the tool has begun to lose shape then you put it on the "grindstone" first, grind it down to shape, and then hone it on the whetstone afterwards. Whetstones come either as slipstones, which are shaped to be held in the hand, or as oilstones which are mounted in a wooden box and used on a bench. Both should be oiled with thin oil when used. Grindstones are coarser and are frequently circular and mounted with a handle over a trough of water so that they can be kept wet.

Most sharpening stones that you can buy nowadays are artifical with carborundum embedded in them. They are undoubtedly better than anything except the best Arkansas stone, which is an almost pure quartz, grainless and hard.

You must grind your cutting tools at the right angle. This will be a compromise between the acute angle needed for easy cutting and the obtuser angle needed for strength. Thus a chisel to be whanged with a mallet must have a more obtuse edge than one to be used for delicate carving in the hand. You can buy a guide, or jig, to help set the angle.

Using your anvil
If you want to work seriously with metal you need an anvil. Most of your work will be done on the anvil's "face", the flat section at the top. You should use the "table", the short step down, for cutting or

chopping, because its surface is softer and will not suffer damage. The "beak", the long pointed bit, is for working anything that needs a curved edge. To flatten metal, or remove marks made by a hammer or other tool, you should hold hot metal on the face of your anvil with tongs, hold a flatter over it and whack it with a sledgehammer until you achieve the desired effect.

The hammer and pritchell
To make holes in any metal, and particularly in horseshoes, you should use a pritchell, which is a square-handled punch. Again use this on your anvil's face and hit it with a heavy blacksmith's Warrington pattern hammer (above), or with a ball pane hammer. If you need to make a large hole, do it over the round hole in the "tail wedge" of your anvil to avoid damaging the table underneath.
Some of your most important tools will be your pincers. You need them for bending metal, pulling out nails

and just holding things. The longer the handles, and the smaller the head, the greater the leverage.

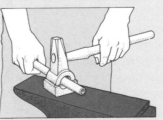

The top and bottom swage
The swages are for shaping circular rods from hot iron, or for bending rods or pipes. The bottom swage slots into the square "hardie hole" in the anvil's tail wedge.

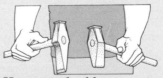

Hot sett and cold sett
The hot sett (left), with an edge sharpened to about 35 degrees, cuts hot metal. Place it on the metal and wallop with a sledgehammer. The cold sett (right), whose edge is about 60 degrees, will cut light iron or mild steel cold.

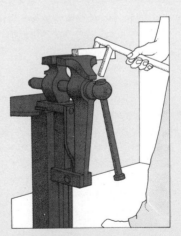

Leg vice and scroll wrench
The best vice for a smithy is a leg vice. It will stand up to heavy hammering because it is made of wrought iron, instead of the more normal cast iron, and some of the load is transferred through the leg to the floor. The front arm is held on a hinge and is opened by a spring. The leg vice is excellent for bending metal, because the leg will stand up to heavy levering. A scroll wrench has rounded jaws for pulling strip metal, especially wrought iron, into curves. Quite intricate designs can be made with it.

Building & Thatching

BUILDING

The cheapest way to construct a solid building is to use mud and thatch, and don't be put off by the way it sounds. Mud is rot-proof and fire-proof, and it keeps sound out and heat in pretty efficiently. Mud for building should be fairly free of organic matter, so dig it from well below the surface: from two to three feet (61-91 cm) is best. Save your humus-laden topsoil for growing things.

Your building should be simple, with large areas of unbroken wall, few and small windows, all loads well spread on timber plates, and no outward thrusting roofs.

An easy but effective method of building with mud is cob building. Cob is simply clayey or chalky mud, mixed with straw and laid in one foot (30cm) layers with a shovel and trowel. Each layer is laid at a different angle from the one below it so that there is a certain amount of binding. The wall should be at least 18 inches (46cm) thick, 24 inches (61cm) if your building is to be more than one storey. You cannot build very fast with this method, for each course has to dry out to some extent before the next one is laid on it. The resulting wall is only weatherproof if you keep "its head and its feet" dry. In other words give your building a good over-hanging roof and solid foundations using concrete if possible. And if you can, build a base wall of stone or brick, preferably with a damp proof course (slate is impervious to water and makes a good one), on top of your foundations up to ground level. The outside too, should be protected by cement rendering if possible: otherwise with a lime and sand mortar rendering, or at least a thick whitewash. Broken glass is sometimes embedded in the base of a cob wall to deter rats. Window sills must be protected by slate or other stone or concrete.

Rammed earth, or adobe, blocks are an improvement on cob because shrinkage takes place in the brick before the wall is built, you can make smoother surfaces and you can easily build cavity walls. The blocks are made by ramming a mud and straw mixture into wooden moulds. Dry them in the shade, so that they don't dry too quickly and crack. The earth should be, like brick earth, of just the right consistency for the job: that is a benign mixture of clay and sand. The higher the clay content the more straw you should add, up to 20 percent straw by volume.

African hut

To make an African hut dig a circular trench, stand straight wall-high poles in it so that they touch one another and stamp them in leaving a space for the door. You can have one section shorter than the others if you want a window. Then on the ground make a conical roof of what is basically giant thatched basket-work. Get some friends to help you lift the roof and lash it on to the circular wall. Plaster the pole wall with mud, preferably mixed with cow dung. If you rub the earth floor with cow dung and sweep it every day it will become as hard and clean as concrete.

Building with mud and thatch

You can build yourself a warm and solid house or barn mainly out of mud and straw. To make your building last you should build foundations. "Cyclopean concrete", which is large stones embedded in concrete, is effective and fairly cheap. On top of this build a stone or brick wall to just above ground level and top it with a damp course, ideally of slate. Walls can be built of "cob", which is mud mixed with straw. Make your wall at least 18 inches (45 cm) thick, and lay in "courses" one foot (30 cm) deep. Allow two or three weeks drying between courses. To keep rats out of your house you can set broken glass in the wall at ground level. Use slate sills and timber lintels for windows. Render the outside with cement or lime "rough cast", a lime and sand mixture. Apply two coats of pitch at the base to keep it dry. Top the wall with a timber wall plate and to this attach your tie beams, which run right across from wall to wall. Each beam carries a king post, which supports the ridge and the struts which in turn support the principals. The purlins run the length of the building from principal to principal and carry the rafters to which you nail the battens which will key your thatch. Secure the joints with suitable strong bolts and straps.

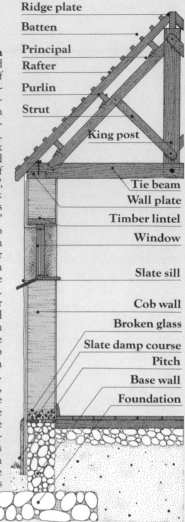

Ridge plate
Batten
Principal
Rafter
Purlin
Strut
King post
Tie beam
Wall plate
Timber lintel
Window
Slate sill
Cob wall
Broken glass
Slate damp course
Pitch
Base wall
Foundation

THATCHING

Phragmites communis, commonly called "Norfolk reed", is the best thatching material there is. A good roof of reed will last seventy years. A roof of "wheat reed" which is simply wheat straw that has not been broken in the threshing may well survive twenty or thirty years. Wheat straw that has been threshed and stored in a stack can be used for thatching ricks. To get it ready for thatching you "pull" it by hauling some down to the foot of the stack and throwing several buckets of water on it. Then you pull the wet straw in handfuls from the bottom of the heap. Because the straw is wet the handfuls come out straight with the straws all parallel to each other. Lay the straws in neat piles about six inches (15 cm) in diameter. Tie these with twine or straw rope to make your "yealms". The secret of thatching is that each layer should cover the fastenings that tie down the layer below it, so that no fastenings are visible or exposed to the weather. In practice this means that each layer must cover just over three quarters of the layer below it.

Ricks

Rick thatching is fairly easy and uses comparatively little material. You only need a coat of thatch two or three inches

Tools for thatching

*A shearing hook **1** and thatching shears **8** trim thatch, a rake **2** combs it, and a leggat **3** shapes it. A whimbel **4** is for making "bonds", the long twists of straw for tying yealms. Brortches **6** cut from hazel with a spar hook **5** hold the thatch down, and iron hooks **7** secure it to the rafters. Protective knee and hand pads **9** are essential.*

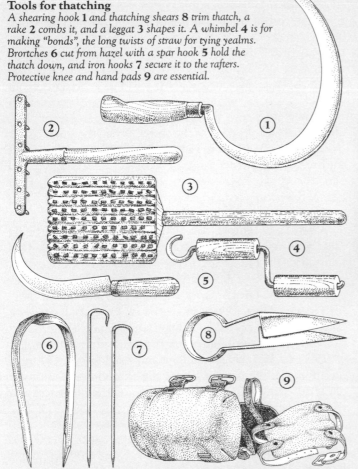

Thatching a roof

Always begin thatching at the eaves on the right hand side. Secure a short row of "yealms", straw bundles, to the roof with "sways", lengths of bendy hazel held to the rafters with iron hooks. Gather the straw together at the upper end of each yealm by pushing in a "brortch". Keep laying rows of yealms, each overlapping the one below, until you reach the ridge. Then move your ladder to the left and thatch another stretch of roof. Carry on like this until you have reached the ridge on both sides of the roof.

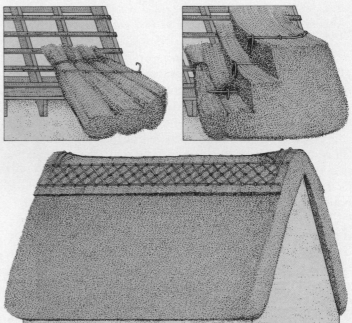

To thatch the ridge lay **a row of** yealms horizontally along it, and cover them with more yealms folded over the ridge and secured on both sides with sways, brortches and hooks. You can use hazel sways to decorate the roof.

(5-8 cm) thick to shed the rain. Lay the straw or reed, ears upwards, in a row along the eaves of the rick. Hold this first row down with one or two lengths of string and hold the string itself down with "brortches". These are two foot (61 cm) lengths of hazel or willow (I prefer hazel), twisted in the middle, bent into a hairpin shape and sharpened at both ends. Ram your brortches down over the string and bang them into the rick with a mallet, so that they hold the string down tight. Space the brortches at the intervals that common sense suggests (every thatcher has his own ideas). Now lay your next layer of straw so that it overlaps a little more than three quarters of the first layer and covers the strings. Peg this down too with string and brortches. Go on, layer after layer, until you get to the top.

You then have the problem of ridging. Make bundles of straw, about big enough to clasp in both hands, tie them tightly with string and lay them along the ridge of the rick. Then lay long straw over these bundles so that it overlaps the top layer of thatch on both sides of the ridge. String and brortch this down on both sides. Or, better still, use hazel or willow rods instead of string here, and brortch them down. Make a pretty criss-cross pattern if you like. Of course with a round rick you don't have a ridge, but a point, and this makes

the job much easier. It is a very simple matter to fashion a conical cap of straw and fasten it down with brortches.

Buildings

You can thatch a building with a comparatively thin layer of straw laid on, much as in rick thatching, pretty well parallel with the slope of the roof. This makes a watertight thatch provided the pitch is steep enough but in a wet climate it is unlikely to last more than two years.

Thick thatching is quite different (see illustration). The bundles of reed are laid on much nearer the horizontal, so that the coat of thatch is nearly, but not quite, as thick as the reed is long. Such a roof takes an enormous quantity of material, a lot of time, the right equipment and a great deal of skill. But if made of true reed, it will last a lifetime. It is completely noise-proof, very warm in winter and cool in summer: in fact it is, quite simply, the best insulation in the world.

If you are building a mudhouse or a barn, you can use rough, unsawn and unriven poles for the framework of the roof, and they don't have to be seasoned. Thatch is flexible and if the timber moves it does not matter. The timber will season naturally in the well-ventilated conditions of the thatched roof, and generally last at least as long as the thatch.

Working in Wood

Making a barrel

We take barrels for granted, and assume there will always be enough of them about for our purposes. Sadly there will not be, because there are practically no coopers left in the Western World and all the old sources of barrels are drying up. And for the self-supporter there is just nothing to take their place. We need them for beer, wine, salt fish, pickled meat, beans and other dried seeds: in fact for innumerable purposes. In my experience you just cannot have enough.

You cut an oak tree down, cut it into logs and rive (see p. 35) the logs into "billets", or rough planks (see illustration). Pile these up in stacks in the wood and cover them with leaves so that they dry slowly. You then cut the billets into "staves" with your axe and from these you make the barrel. After rough trimming with the axe you shape the staves with a drawknife and a "jigger" which hollows them out inside. The edges of the staves must be "shot" at exactly the right angle with a plane so that when they are pulled together they will fit perfectly. If you are making a "stout cask" (a heavy one) you must boil the staves: for a "slight cask" they must be soaked.

The two "heads", the ends of the barrel, are sawn out in three or four pieces with a bow saw and the pieces are dowelled together. A groove is cut right round the inside of the staves for each head to fit into. Rushes called "flags" are put in these grooves to make the joints watertight. The hoops can be iron, or wood. Yew wood is best for this. If you use wood you should put three rivetted hoops at each station, instead of a single iron one. You can make iron hoops by rivetting 1/10th inch (2 mm) mild steel in a circle, and taper them by hammering on one edge only with a hammer on an anvil.

Putting the barrel together is called "raising it up". The staves are balanced together with their top ends touching and their bottoms splayed out. The top head is put in and the "raising-up hoop", one of the "chime" hoops (see illustration), banged on to hold them. The "ash runner" (a piece of round

ash, steamed and bent into a circle with its ends rivetted together), is put on over this and banged down. The whole barrel is then put over a "cresset", which is an iron basket containing a fire. The fire softens the staves and makes it possible to bend them. Bang down the ash runner so that it forces the staves together. When you get it right down bang down a second runner half an inch (1.2 mm) smaller in diameter than the first. Bang down the quarter and "booge" runners (see illustration) for that end of the barrel. When the staves are as close as you can get them in this way turn the barrel over, off the fire, work the other chime hoop over the bottom end, and bang that down. In this way the staves are brought together. Before they come right together put in the other head. Then bang on the other quarter and booge runners.

When a new barrel is complete it must be pickled by being filled with concentrated brine and sodium carbonate. This neutralizes the tannic acid in the oak. Pickle it for three days, wash it out well and fill it with clear water for a day, wash it out again and fill it. Use the same process if you have a "sour cask" (one in which beer or wine has turned to vinegar). If you get a "stinker" (an old barrel that stinks) you can cure it by pickling as above, or by burning an ounce or two of sulphur in it or, if it is really bad, by taking a head out and shaving 1/8 inch (3 mm) off the inside. To take a head out bang hard on the chime hoop of the other end. Then knock the hoops off the end where you want to free the head.

Obviously making a barrel is a fantastically complicated job and unless you are prepared to take weeks over it and make several false starts you are well advised to watch, or get help from, a professional cooper.

Making a ladder

Uprights for ladders should be sawn out of a long, straight, clean-grained log ideally of ash, Scots pine, spruce or thuya. Rip the log in half with a rip-saw and rough saw the planks for the uprights from each half of the log. The uprights for any ladder should be from the same piece of wood split in half. They are, as it were, mirror-images of each other.

The rungs should be oak or hickory. They are riven, or split out with wedges, then placed on the spoke-shave horse and spoke-shaved down. Professional ladder-makers use a "stave block", which is like a large pencil sharpener, to shape the ends of the rungs but you can do it with a spoke-shave or even a draw-knife.

Traditionally the uprights are marked by flipping a taut string dipped in wax and lamp-black against them. This is quicker and better than trying to mark a pencil line on them with a ruler. Then rough-trim them with an axe or an adze and then plane. They should be rounded on one side and flat on the other. All ladders except thatchers' ladders are rounded only on the outside. Thatchers like their ladders rounded on the inside so that there are no sharp corners to annoy their knees.

Drill the holes for the rungs nine inches (23 cm) apart,

The parts of a barrel
Barrels are made from billets split from a tree trunk (top left), preferably an oak. Staves (bottom left) are shaped from billets with an axe and draw-knife and then hollowed with a jigger. The top and bottom, the heads 1, of the barrel are made from sawn billets held together with dowels. The barrel is secured with three pairs of hoops, the chimes 2, the quarters 3, and the booges 4. The wide point of the barrel is the pitch 5.

and drill them right through the upright. Lay one upright down, clamp it in place and drive rungs into every hole. They should stick out the other side. Lay the upright with rungs attached on its side and fit the other upright to it. Bang the two uprights tight on to the rungs, and then put an iron rod through at each end to hold the ladder together. Saw the ends of the rungs off where they stick out.

Making a lathe

A simple wooden foot-powered lathe can be made very easily, and although it works slowly it works as well as any other lathe for wood-turning. The "chair-bodgers" of the English woods worked them until very recent years.

Plant two wooden uprights in the ground, or if you live indoors attach them to the floor, about 3 feet (91 cm) apart. Six inch by four inch (15 cm x 10 cm) posts would be ideal. Nail a block of wood to each post, just at hand height and on a level with each other. Drill a hole in each block big enough to take the ends of the "stock," which is the piece of

wood to be turned. (You will have to whittle down the ends of this with a knife to make it small enough to fit the holes). Arrange a simple foot-pedal below. This can just be a piece of wood, held at one end by a pin which is supported on two short stakes.

Arrange a bendy horizontal pole of ash or other springy wood above the contraption, so that one end sticks out and can be bent up and down. You can use trees, stakes, or, if you are indoors, the rafters to support this pole. Tie a piece of rope, or rawhide, to the foot pedal, take one turn with it round the stock, tie the other end to the end of the whippy pole. Nail another piece of wood across the posts next to your stock to rest your chisel on, and you have a lathe. Depress the pedal and the stock turns one way, release it and the pole above your head straightens and turns it the other way. You only make your cut when it's turning the right way, of course.

Wood turning is skilled work (see illustrations). If you can, go and watch a skilled craftsman at work.

Turning a bowl on a lathe

These pictures show a bowl being turned on a simple lathe powered by electricity, but you can turn a bowl in the same way on a treadle lathe, or, rather laboriously, on a chair bodger's pole lathe (see above). If you use the latter you

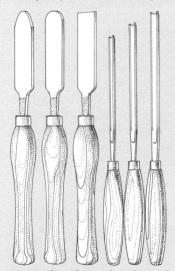

must replace the stock with a rod fixed to a chuck to which the bowl can be attached. For the heavy work of removing unwanted wood you need three gouges of differing thicknesses (above right), and for the more delicate shaping and smoothing you need scrapers (above left). Never press hard with any tool, particularly a gouge. If they stick you are in trouble. Keep your tools sharp. Factory-built lathes often have a revolving sharpener built on. Otherwise use an oilstone.

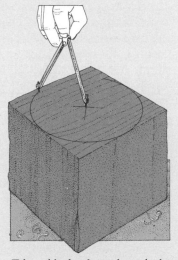

Take a block of wood, mark the centre with a cross and draw a circle with a compass slightly larger, say $\frac{1}{4}$ inch (6 mm), than the intended diameter of your bowl.

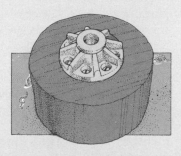

Cut roughly round your circle with a saw. Then establish the mid point for your chuck and screw it on evenly. Use short strong screws, because the base of your bowl must

needs be thicker than your screws are long. Your work will be ruined if you come down to a screw when shaping the inside.

Round off edges with a large gouge.

Shape the outside with a smaller gouge. Use the handrest and keep the gouge moving slowly along it.

Smooth off the outside with your scrapers. Then, keeping the bowl on the lathe, rub with sandpaper, which will give the wood a gloriously smooth finish.

Move the handrest so that you can work on the inside. The unbreakable rule for hollowing wood on a lathe is: begin at the outside and work towards the centre. Start with a gouge, then scrape with round-ended scrapers only, and finally sandpaper it smooth. Remove the chuck from the lathe, unscrew it and fill the holes with plastic wood. Polish the whole thing with beeswax and glue felt on the bottom.

Wells, Ponds & Fish Farming

SINKING A WELL

The easiest way of finding water is to drill a hole with a drilling machine, and if you can get hold of one it is well worth using it. But they are expensive, even to hire, and all they really save is time and energy. If you have got some of each to spare you can dig your well yourself by hand.

In earth or soft rock

Sinking a well in earth or soft rock is very easy if laborious. You just dig in, keeping the diameter as small as you can, just leaving yourself room to use a shovel. As you get deeper, you send the spoil (dug earth) up to the surface in a bucket hauled up by a friend with a windlass, and you go up the same way. It is almost always necessary to line the well as you dig to stop the earth from falling in. The easiest way to do this is with concrete rings sent down from the top. As you dig down you dig under the lowest concrete ring which causes it to fall and all the other concrete rings on top fall with it. From time to time you put another concrete ring on top. Where timber is cheap you can use a timber lining on the same principle.

In soft sand

Sinking a well in soft sand is very difficult, and can only be done using the process of "spiling", which is hammering sharpened planks down below you where you are working so as to form a lining which is already there when you dig all the sand out.

In rock

Sinking a well through rock is harder in that you have to blast it, but easier in that you probably don't have to line it. In days gone by the rock was shattered by building a fire on it and then quenching this with water. The rapid contraction shattered the surface of the rock. Nowadays we are more likely to use explosives.

Gunpowder will do, although you need a lot and it is a slow job. Gelignite, or any of the modern detonating explosives, are much better. To use either you have to drill holes in the rock. If you haven't got a compressor and pneumatic rock drill you can do this by hand with a hand drill, which is a hardened steel bit, like a long cold chisel. Hold it in your left hand, wallop it with a four pound hammer, and turn it in the hole after every wallop. If you don't turn it, it will jam. To get the powdered rock out of the hole you must pour water down, which turns the powder into a paste which spurts out with every blow. To stop it getting in your face wrap a cloth round the bit at the collar of the hole.

Drill four holes near the middle of your well floor to form a pyramid pointing down into the rock. These are your "cut holes". Drill, say, eight more holes around these, this time vertically. These are your "easers". Then drill holes all round the edge of your face. These are your "slipers".

Fill all the holes with "powder", which is the generic term miners and well-sinkers use for all explosives, light your fuses, and hope that your friend up top who winds you up with the windlass is a real friend and doesn't decide to go away and have a smoke instead.

Gunpowder is set off simply by lighting it, and if you can't buy a safety fuse, which does this job, you can make one yourself by sticking hollow goose feathers into each other, end to end, to form tubes and filling these tubes with gunpowder. In fact any kind of plastic or rubber tube filled with powder will do just as well. Poke one end of the fuse into the gunpowder in the hole and light the other end. Presumably common sense will have told you to test and time a few fuses before you trust your life to them. And remember with gunpowder any spark will light it. A spark struck from a rock with a steel is all it needs, and, if it is in a confined space, it will explode.

Gelignite, plastic H.E. (high explosive), and all the modern detonants are quite different. If you light them they will only burn and make a stink. They have to be detonated, and to do this you need a cap full of fulminite of mercury, called a detonator. Take a measured length of safety fuse, cut one end off straight and clean, put a detonator over this, and crimp the detonator's metal case so it doesn't come off (not with your teeth, with pliers). Then cut the other end off at an angle to expose the powder inside the safety fuse, lay a match head on this powder and strike the match with the box. Light all the fuses thus and shout to your friend to start winding up the bucket. The cut holes must have the shortest fuses because they go off first, then the easers and then the slipers which go off last.

Whichever way you sink a well, when you come to water go on sinking. Even if you have to spend half of each day winding up water in the bucket, go on sinking until the water beats you, because if you don't, when there is a drought and the water table sinks, your well will go dry. When you have got your water the best thing you can do is install a steel pumping windmill (see p. 216). It will pump water from a thousand feet (304 m) and go on doing it for years, free, and will need very little attention.

MAKING A POND

If you are going to keep ducks (see p. 128), or if you want to try the highly rewarding process of fish farming you will need a pond. You can just dig a hole, but if the bottom or sides are porous it will probably be necessary to puddle clay and tamp it in so as to form an impervious sheet, or else bury a large sheet of thick plastic.

Simply piling earth up in a bank to form a dam to impound water seldom works. The fill material may be too porous and "piping" will occur, meaning water will seep through and erode a hole. Or the material may contain too much clay and there will be great drying, shrinkage and cracking. If the soil is just right, and well compacted, and an adequate spillway to take off the surplus caused by rainwater is constructed, a simple earth dam may work, but where there is doubt the dam should be made of porous soil with puddled and tamped clay embedded in it. Nowadays plastic sheeting is sometimes used instead. If your pond is for fish farming then good topsoil should be placed in the bottom for plants to grow on.

FISH FARMING

Fish are marvellously efficient producers of high protein human food: far better in fact than other livestock. This is because they don't have to build a massive bone structure to support their weight (the water supports it), and they don't have to use energy to maintain their body heat (they are cold blooded). In the tropics, particularly in paddy-growing areas, they are a major crop. Modern commercial fish farming, in which only one species of fish is fed on expensive high protein in water which is kept weed-free with herbicides, is ecologically unsound and requires absurd inputs of expensive feed or fertilizer. We should all start experimenting with water ecosystems which achieve a proper balance of nature, and in which a variety of fish species can coexist with a cross-section of other marine life, both animal and vegetable.

Strangely enough in the sixteenth century the matter was far better understood – even in England. At that time a writer called John Taverner wrote that you should make large shallow ponds, four feet deep and more, and keep them dry one year and full of water the next. When dry graze them with cattle, and when wet fill them with carp. The ponds grow lush grass because of the sediments left by the water, and the carp benefit from the fertility left by the cattle. This is the true organic approach to husbandry. You should have at least two ponds so that there is always one full of fish and one dry. Drain the wet pond dry in late autumn, and take the best fish out then to put in your stewpond near the house, where they are ready for eating. Put a lot of young fish in your newly-flooded big pond.

Carp

Carnivorous fish, such as trout, are poor converters of food into flesh. Vegetarian fish are far better. This is why Taverner and the monks of old in Europe had carp in their stewponds.

Carp will give you a ton of fish per acre per year without any feeding if they are in a suitable pond. The way the monks farmed them was to let them breed in large ponds, but then to catch them and confine them to small stewponds near the house in the autumn. The stewponds were deep enough to keep ice-free and the carp were therefore easy to net. As well as being vegetarian, carp are healthy, quick growing, and they can live in non-flowing water. They need half their food from natural provenance, and can be encouraged by a certain amount of muck or rotting vegetation dumped in the water. This is transformed into the sort of food carp eat by bacterial action, but they will also eat oatmeal, barley, spent malt and other similar food.

The Hungarian strain of the Chinese Grass Carp has been tried in England, with success. In China these fish grow up to 100 lbs (45 kg) in weight: in England 30 lbs (13.6 kg) is a good

fish, but they are fine converters of vegetable food. Unfortunately they need 122°F (51°C) to breed, and so are propagated in heated tanks and released out of doors, where they flourish.

Tilapia

The best fish of all for fish-farming are the African *Tilapia*, but because they are tropical fish they need warm water. Nevertheless, putting yourself out for them may well be worthwhile. Research has shown that the average family could provide all its animal protein requirements in a 3,000 gallon (13,640 litre) covered and heated pool full of *Tilapia*. The water should be about 80°F (27°C): less than 55°F (13°C) will kill them.

Tilapia mossambica, which is one of the best of the many species, can be bought from pet shops. The hen fish produce about twenty five to thirty young, which live in their mothers' mouths for the first period of their lives, and the hens bring off several broods a year. Much of their food can be supplied free with a little labour by incubating pond water, slightly fertilized with organic manure, in tanks. After three weeks or a month carefully pump this water into the tilapia pond with the organisms that it contains. The incubation tanks should be partially roofed with glass, but access for mosquitoes and other flying insects should be provided.

In temperate climates *Tilapia mossambica* can be kept in heated pools, and they don't require constantly running water. A combination of solar heating and wind/electric heating has proved successful for growing them in America. They will produce two tons of good meat per acre per year. When adult they will feed on algae or any vegetation you like to put into the water (within reason) or they will eat oatmeal. When young they need protein, which can be supplied in such forms as mosquito larvae, maggots, worms, or as fish meat, or blood meal. They are probably the most delicious of all fish to eat.

Trout

In Berlin most of the city's sewage is discharged into huge lakes, where rainbow trout are reared to provide a colossal tonnage of fish per acre. Brown trout will not stand up to this treatment. The sewage is not eaten by the trout, which are carnivores, but by phytoplankton, which in turn are eaten by zooplankton, on which the fish feeds.

If you want to farm rainbow trout you must give them some kind of meat protein. You can buy proprietary trout food but it is very expensive. If you have a source of very cheap sea fish you can use it for trout food. Salt any of the oily pelagic fish, pile them in stacks six foot high and put boards and weights on them. This will expel the oil from them. You can then dry them in a kiln, powder them, and use them for trout food.

Several breeds of fish lend themselves to farming. A lot of success is had with American bluegills and catfish.

Household Items

SOAP

The first lion I ever shot had been eating a friend of mine's donkeys in Africa. It had a thick layer of fat on it, and my friend's mother turned this into soap. She did it by the simple method of boiling the fat with caustic soda. It worked, but was pretty rough stuff.

The chemistry of soap making is to boil an alkaline with fat, which is an acid. The alkaline, or lye as soap-boilers call it, can be practically any alkali, and caustic soda will do. But there is a simple way of making your own lye. Knock some holes in the bottom of a barrel, lay some straw in the bottom, fill the barrel with wood-ash, and pour a bucketful of cold water on top of the ash. Pour on a bucketful every three or four hours on the first, third and fifth day. The water that drips out of the bottom of the barrel will be lye.

Now, to make soap take your fat and clarify it by melting it in a slow oven, straining it into cold water, and then skimming it off the water. If you haven't shot a lion practically any fat will do: dripping, lard, chicken fat, goose fat and so on. Melt the fat again, let it cool to luke-warm, and warm your lye to luke-warm at the same time. Then very slowly pour the lye into the fat (if you pour it too fast it will not mix) and stir it very gently with a wooden spoon. When the mixture begins to drip from your spoon like honey, stop pouring. Then if you want to make your soap stronger pour in a solution of borax and water (eight tablespoonfuls of borax to a pint (0.6 litres) of water) and a dash of ammonia. To half a gallon (2.2 litres) of soap mixture add a pint (0.6 litres) of the borax solution and half a cup of ammonia. Put a board over the mixture, cover it with a carpet, leave until the next day and cut it.

If you want a soap which will make you and your friends smell good, take: 1 lb (0.5 kg) good fat or tallow; 1 cup olive oil; 1 cup peanut oil; $\frac{1}{2}$ cup water with 2 tablespoons lye in it; 1 cup water with perfume in it.

If the perfume is essential oil bought from the chemist, use about three tablespoons of it, but you can make your own perfume out of lavender, rosemary, lemon balm, or a score of other flowers or herbs, in which case you would probably add more. Melt the fat, add the oils and the scent to it, and warm to 90°F (32°C) stirring all the while of course. Meanwhile mix the lye and the water and pour it into the fat and oil mixture and don't stop stirring. When the mixture thickens pour it into moulds of any fancy shape you like.

Saddle soap

To make saddle soap take: 6 cups tallow; 1 cup lye; $2\frac{1}{2}$ cups water. Heat the tallow to 130°F (54°C). Dissolve the lye in the water, cool it to 95°F (35°C) and pour it slowly into the tallow, stirring the while. Just before it is ready for moulding pour in one cup of glycerine and stir.

SUGAR
From sugar beet

Cut the tops off your sugar beet and press the juice out of them any way you can: with a cider press, a car jack, or an old fashioned mangle. Boil the juice until all the liquid has evaporated and you will be left with unrefined sugar. Refining it is a complicated process involving lime and carbon dioxide. Anyway it would be madness to refine this further, for unrefined sugar is nourishing and meet for all the purposes of sugar, while refined sugar contains 99.9 per cent sucrose, absolutely no vitamins, nor anything else that is of any use to body and soul at all.

From sugar cane

Sugar cane must be thoroughly crushed so as to produce syrup. Cane is tough stuff full of fibres, so you either need a lot of strength and a mortar and pestle, or a steel crushing mill. Put the syrup into a copper boiler, over a fire which you can fuel with the spent cane. Boiling turns the syrup into what in India is called "gor", which is unrefined sugar. As I have said above it is a waste of time to refine sugar any further and it is much better for you like this.

Maple sugar

To make this you must tap the sugar maple, in the chilly month of March, by drilling the trunk and driving in a "spile", a short tube which you can buy or make yourself out of bamboo, willow, sumac, elder or anything you can hollow. Hang a container under the spile (an old can will do, or a bucket, or a plastic bag) and cover it to keep insects out.

As soon as the sap runs carry it to the "arch": to leave it too long is to spoil it. The "arch" is a boiler placed over a wood fire that needs to be kept blazing by a strong draught. The arch must be out of doors for a great deal of moisture is given off. Don't let the sap get more than a couple of inches deep. Keep the level by pouring in more sap. It is an advantage to have two boilers, and use one for the fresh sap and keep ladling the partially boiled sap into the other from which you "syrup off", meaning take the syrup.

Skim the scum off from time to time and watch constantly to see that the sap doesn't boil over. If it starts climbing up the pan add some fresh sap, or drop some creamy milk on the climbing froth, or draw a piece of fat across the bubbles. Test the sap's temperature with a thermometer. When it is boiling at 219°F (104°C) it has turned into syrup. Strain it off into jars, cover while hot and put away to cool. This is maple syrup.

If you want sugar go on boiling until the temperature is 242°F (117°C), but if you pull a spoon out and the drip forms a thin spidery thread, that is boiling enough. Remove from the fire, leave to cool for a few minutes, then stir with a wooden spoon. When the syrup begins to crystallize pour it into moulds and you have sugar.

SALT

If you live near the sea you can make salt by simply boiling and evaporating sea-water. You can use driftwood for fuel and nowadays the oil spillage that coats most driftwood means it gives even more heat. A mobile iron boiler, such as you boil pig-swill in is ideal. Never use a copper boiler. The copper and salty sea-water will react against one another.

PAINT

Very good paints can be made from a mixture of sour milk, hydrated (slaked) lime, and any coloured earth pigment that you can find. The lime and the sour milk must have neutralized each other, and this can be tested with litmus paper: if the paper turns red add more lime, if it turns blue add more sour milk.

The pigment that you add to this is any strongly coloured earth, sediment or clay. Dig it out and boil it in water several times, each time in new water. Strain off the water and dry the sediment in a warm place. Pulverize it as finely as you can and store. Mix this powder with the milk-lime mixture until you get the colour you want. Keen paint-makers keep an eye out as they travel about the countryside for any colourful-looking earth or clay, and grab it when they see it.

PAPER

It is possible to make paper of any fibrous plant, or of wood, or of cotton or linen rags. Nettles, flax, hemp, rushes, coarse grass, and tall fibrous plants like *Tagetes minuta* all make very good paper.

Ret the plants first by soaking them in stagnant water. Then chop them up as small as you can into, say, half-inch lengths. Put the chopped material into a vat and cover with a caustic soda solution made up of two dessert spoonfuls of caustic soda per quart of water. Boil until the material is soft and flabby. Then put it in a coarse sieve and drain. Hold the sieve under the tap, or plunge it up and down in a bath of water. This will clear the pulp away. If you want white paper soak the fibre you now have left in a bleach solution overnight. Otherwise the paper will be the colour of the material you are using. Drain the bleach off through a fine-meshed sieve (you don't want to lose fibres).

Next you must beat the material. You can do this with a mallet, or with any kind of pounding engine your ingenuity can devise. When you have beaten it thoroughly dry add some water and continue beating the pulp. A large food-mixer or a large pestle and mortar will do very well for this stage. During this process put some pulp in a glass of water occasionally and hold it up to the light. If there are still lumps in it go on beating. If you want to make interesting papers don't beat too long and your paper will have fragments of vegetation showing in it.

You make the paper on moulds, which can be simple wooden frames covered with cloth. Cover the moulds with a thin layer of pulp by dipping them into it and scooping. As you lift the mould out of the pulp give it a couple of shakes at right angles to each other. This helps the fibres to "felt", or matt together. If you find the "waterleaf", which is what your sheet is called, is too thin, turn the mould upside down, place it in the vat, and shake the pulp off back in the water. Then add more fibre to your vat.

Now, turn the mould upside down on a piece of wet felt and press the back of the cloth to make the watersheet adhere to the felt. Take the mould away, and lay another piece of wet felt on top of the watersheet. Repeat the operations with another watersheet. Finally you need a press. Any kind of press will do. Make a "post" which is a pile of alternate felts and watersheets and put the post in your press. Press for a day or so, then remove the paper from the felts and press just the paper sheets. Handle the paper very carefully at this juncture. Then lay it out on racks to dry.

RESIN, ROSIN and WOOD TAR

Long-leaf pine, maritime pine, Corsican pine, American balm or gilead, cedars, cypresses and larches can all be tapped for their resin.

The best way of tapping is to clear a strip of bark, about four inches (10 cm) wide and four feet (1.2 m) high, off a large tree. This is called a "blaze". Then, with a very sharp axe, take a very thin shaving of true wood off at the base of the blaze. Drive a small metal gutter into the tree at the base of this cut and lead the sap, or resin, into a tin. Every five days or so freshen the cut by taking off another shaving. When you can get no more out of the first cut make another just above it. Keep on doing this until you have incised the whole blaze, which may take several years. Don't tap between November and February. If you grow conifers for tapping, clean the side branches off the young trees so that the trunks are clean for tapping.

If you distill resin – in other words, if you heat it and condense the first vapour that comes off it – you will get turpentine. "Rosin" is the sticky stuff that remains behind and it is good for many things including violin strings, paints and varnishes.

If you heat coniferous wood in a retort, or even just burn it in a hole in a bank, a black liquor will run out of the bottom. This is wood tar, and it is the best thing in the world for painting boats and buildings.

CHARCOAL

Charcoal is made, quite simply, by burning wood in the presence of too little oxygen. In other words you set some wood alight, get it blazing well and right throughout its mass, and then cut off the air. I have tried many ways of doing it and I have come to the conclusion that the simplest and best is to dig a large trench, fill it up with wood and set light to it. Then when it is blazing fiercely throw sheets of old corrugated iron on to start smothering the fire and then very quickly, and you will need perhaps half a dozen helpers, shovel earth on top of the corrugated iron so as to bury it completely. Leave for several days to cool, then open up and shovel the charcoal into bags. You can use the charcoal for cooking fuel, for making bricks (as I described on p. 232), or anywhere else you need a slow-burning fire.

The All-Purpose Furnace

Firewood is a renewable resource, and the best solar energy collector in the world is a stretch of woodland. Woodland cut for firewood should be coppiced (see p. 35). In other words the trees should be cut right down every ten to fifteen years, depending on how fast they grow, and the stumps left to coppice, or shoot again. Cut over systematically in this way two or three acres of woodland will yield a constant supply of good firewood and other timber.

To burn wood effectively and economically requires several things. The wood must be burned on the floor of the furnace: not on a grid. The fire must be enclosed and there must be a means of carefully regulating the draught. A huge open fire is a romantic thing, but all it does is cheer the heart, freeze the back and heat the sky. Where wood is in limitless supply it may be justified, but not otherwise.

It is an advantage to burn wood in a dead end, admitting air from the front only. A tunnel with the back walled off is ideal. Logs can be fed into the dead end tunnel and lit at the end nearest the door, and the fire then slowly smoulders backwards into the tunnel. The draught control should be such that you can load the tunnel right up with dry logs, get a roaring fire going, and then actually put it out by cutting off the air. If you can feed your furnace from outside your house you will avoid a lot of mess inside. And if you can organize things so that your furnace can take long logs, you save an awful lot of work sawing.

Now any decent economical furnace should be capable of doing at least four things: space heating, oven baking, hot-plate cooking, and water heating, and if it can smoke meat and fish as well so much the better. We have built a furnace that will do all these things on my farm, and as the farm is called Fachongle I call it the Fachongle Furnace. But don't try to build one the same unless you know you can get, for not too much money: firebricks, a cast iron plate big enough to cover the whole furnace, and a massive cast iron fire door.

Building a furnace

We built a firebrick tunnel, four feet (1.2 m) long inside the house. It is bricked off at the back, but the front falls four inches (10 cm) short of the exterior house wall. The house wall there is lined with firebricks. On either side of the tunnel we built a brick wall slightly higher than the top of the tunnel. The bases of these need not be of firebrick, but the tops must be to withstand the heat. On top of the two outer walls we laid a steel plate. (This has since warped slightly which is why I advise you to get a cast iron plate.) This goes from the back of the furnace right to the wall of the building. On top of the steel plate away from the wall of the building we built an oven, and at the very furthest end from the wall we built a chimney. We knocked a hole in the outer wall and in that set a furnace door with firebricks. The furnace is fed through this door, and the heat and smoke has to come back to the front end, curl up through the four inch (10 cm) gap, hit the iron plate, curve back and go under the oven and on up the chimney.

Now we built a back boiler into the back wall of the tunnel, and the pipes from it come back between the tunnel wall and the outer wall, and then come out through two holes in the latter. We partially filled the cavity between tunnel and outer walls with sand to insulate and store heat.

The boiler of this particular furnace has to supply: kitchen, dairy, brewery, laundry and bathrooms, and this it does provided a good fire is kept up. To provide that much hot water with an electric immersion heater would cost a fortune. We are intending to preheat the water with a solar roof in due course so that in the summer, when we don't need so much heat indoors, we won't have to keep such a large fire.

A refinement, which is not completely necessary, is that some of the smoke and heat comes through a slit cut in the iron plate and so travels up the back of the oven, which is hollow, and over a steel plate which forms the top of the oven. The oven bakes magnificent bread providing there is a hot enough fire in the furnace.

Making charcoal in a furnace

One advantage of a Fachongle Furnace is that it will make charcoal. If you get a big fire going in it and then close the draught right down, the fire goes out and the wood turns to charcoal. A final attraction is the smoke chamber which we have built over the oven. It is too hot in there for ham or bacon but marvellous for "cook smoking" fish or meat.

The Fachongle Furnace is a good example, I think, of the new attitude that we people who call ourselves self-sufficient have to adopt. We must learn again to trust our own intuition and judgment, and not always run to the "experts" or specialists. We must learn to improvise and make do with the resources we can get for nothing if we use our eyes, hands and brains. A commercially-produced furnace on the scale of the Fachongle Furnace would cost a thousand pounds. Our furnace is not perfect, but we are improving on it. You can only really succeed as a self-supporter if you are prepared to adapt, experiment and try your own ideas. As you go on you gain confidence in your own ability to do things for yourself, and this is one of the most satisfying aspects of the self-supporting way of life.

Many of the things that we look upon as far too difficult to be done by anybody but a specialist are not difficult at all once we actually come to do them. I think of an old friend of mine who was living in the remote outback in Southern Africa, and who suddenly found himself unable to buy petrol because of the Depression. He invented, and built himself, a "producer gas" plant to go on the back of his old lorry, which he was then able to drive on charcoal.

It worked. It was an apparently impossible task he set himself to do and he did it. We should profit by his example.

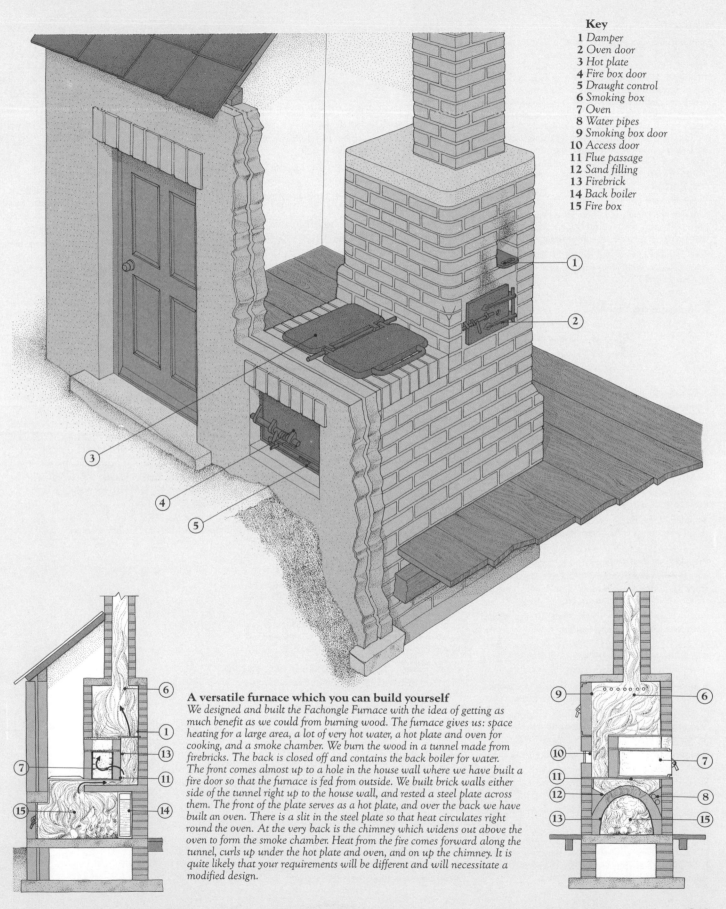

Key
1 *Damper*
2 *Oven door*
3 *Hot plate*
4 *Fire box door*
5 *Draught control*
6 *Smoking box*
7 *Oven*
8 *Water pipes*
9 *Smoking box door*
10 *Access door*
11 *Flue passage*
12 *Sand filling*
13 *Firebrick*
14 *Back boiler*
15 *Fire box*

A versatile furnace which you can build yourself

We designed and built the Fachongle Furnace with the idea of getting as much benefit as we could from burning wood. The furnace gives us: space heating for a large area, a lot of very hot water, a hot plate and oven for cooking, and a smoke chamber. We burn the wood in a tunnel made from firebricks. The back is closed off and contains the back boiler for water. The front comes almost up to a hole in the house wall where we have built a fire door so that the furnace is fed from outside. We built brick walls either side of the tunnel right up to the house wall, and rested a steel plate across them. The front of the plate serves as a hot plate, and over the back we have built an oven. There is a slit in the steel plate so that heat circulates right round the oven. At the very back is the chimney which widens out above the oven to form the smoke chamber. Heat from the fire comes forward along the tunnel, curls up under the hot plate and oven, and on up the chimney. It is quite likely that your requirements will be different and will necessitate a modified design.

249

Useful Addresses

General

Agricultural Development and Advisory Service (agricultural and science), Great Westminster House, Horseferry Road, London SW1P 2AE. Probably the best place for the would-be self-supporter to begin. As well as the London headquarters, regional offices all over the United Kingdom provide advice and pamphlets on every agricultural subject. If you are thinking of buying, clearing or draining land, of suitable equipment and balanced livestock, start by getting advice and help from this Government department. Pamphlets from: Ministry of Agriculture, Fisheries and Food (Publications), Tolcarne Drive, Pinner, Middlesex HA5 2DT. (Single copies free.)

Ministry of Agriculture, Fisheries and Food, Whitehall Place, London SW1A 2HH (for advice and information on all general aspects of farming)

The Self-Sufficiency and Small Holding Supplies, Priory Road, Wells, Somerset (for a large variety of useful items)

Food from the Fields

Wright Rain Ltd, Crow Arch Lane, Ringwood, Hampshire BH24 1PA (for irrigation equipment)

Forestry Commission, 25 Savile Row, London W1X 2AY (for advice and pamphlets on woodland)

John Scott, Royal Nurseries, Merriot, Somerset (for young trees, as well as a variety of garden shrubs)

J.H.B. Implements Ltd, Ickburgh, nr. Mundford, Thetford, Norfolk (for ploughs and tractors)

Russells Ltd, Agric. Engs., Engineering Works, Railway Bldgs, Kirkbymoorside, Yorkshire (for the "Exel" precision seed drill)

R. Hunt and Co Ltd, Atlas Works, Earls Colne, Colchester, Essex (for the "Atlas" hand mill)

Semplex Home Brews Ltd, Old Hall Works, Stuart Road, Birkenhead (for beermaking equipment)

Food from Animals

The British Goat Society, c/o Secretary, Rougham, Bury St Edmunds, Suffolk (for butter churns, milking buckets, milk cartons etc)

Clares Carlton Ltd, Town Hall Bldgs, Wells, Somerset (for all dairying equipment)

Hansen's Laboratory Ltd, Rennet Manufacturers, 476 Basingstoke Road, Reading (for starters and pure cultures for cheesemaking)

Fred Ritson, Goat Appliance Works, Longtown, Carlisle (for goats and information on goats)

C. N. Flack & Co Ltd, Home Farm, Culford, Bury St Edmunds, Suffolk (for large white pigs)

Pig Breeders Supply Co Ltd, Checkendon, Reading, Berkshire (for housing, equipment, etc to do with pigs)

Stanley Brown and Son, Poultry Farm, Chearsley, nr. Aylesbury, Bucks (for poultry)

Mayfield Chicks Ltd, Bunkers Hill, Colne, Lancashire (for young poultry)

John Inkster Ltd, The Chippings, Chigwell Row, Essex (for chicken litter)

E. H. Thorne Ltd, Beehive Works, Wragby, Lincolnshire (for bee equipment)

Food from the Garden

Henry Doubleday Association, Bocking, Braintree, Essex (for general information on soil and organic gardening)

Humus Products Ltd, Brunel House, St Georges Road, Bristol 1 (for soil analysis and composts)

J. Gibbs Ltd, Starwell Road, Bedfont, Middlesex (for a large range of market garden tools)

Jiffy Pot (UK) Ltd, Trulls Hatch, Rotherfield, Crowborough, Sussex (for peat pots)

Stoke Lacy Herb Farm, Bromyard, Herefordshire (for seeds)

The Old Rectory Herb Garden, Ightham, Kent (for seeds and young plants)

The Amateur Winemaker, North Croye, The Avenue, Andover, Hampshire (for winemaking equipment and advice)

Food from the Wild

ASI, Importers and Wholesale Distributors, Alliance House, Snape Maltings, Saxmundham, Suffolk (for a wide range of guns, although to purchase any gun you must have a licence and go through a dealer)

Bridport Gundry Ltd, Net, Line, Twine Mfrs, The Court, West St, Bridport, Dorset (for fishing nets)

Natural Energy

University of Cambridge, Department of Architecture, 1 Scrope Terrace, Cambridge (for bulletins on all forms of alternative technology)

Intermediate Technology Development, Parnell House, 25 Wilton Road, London SW1 (for general information on alternative technology)

The National Centre for Intermediate Technology, Corwen, Machynlleth, Wales (for general information on alternative technology)

Gilbert Gilkes and Gordon Ltd, Turbine Mfrs, Kendal, Cumbria (for water power machinery)

Kent Solartraps Ltd, 10 Albion Place, Maidstone, Kent (for information on solar heating and a wide range of panels)

Conservation Tools and Technology, 143 Maple Road, Surbiton, Surrey (for a range of electricity generating windmills)

Wind Energy Supply Co, Bolney Avenue, Peacehaven, Sussex (for oil pumping and electric windmills)

Whyatt Brothers Ltd, Wayland Works, Whitechurch, Salop (for a variety of windmills)

Crafts & Skills

W. Gadsby and Son (Burrowbridge) Ltd, Burrowbridge Basket Works, Burrowbridge, Bridgwater, Somerset (for willow as well as cane)

Catterson-Smith Ltd, Furnace Mfrs, Woodrolfe Road, Tollesbury, Maldon, Essex (for electric kilns)

Cromartie Kilns Ltd, Dividy Road, Longton, Staffs (for electric kilns)

Wengers Ltd, Garner Street, Etruria, Stoke-on-Trent (for all pottery equipment and supplies)

Harris Looms, Northgrove Road, Hawkhurst, Kent (for looms)

Jacobs, Young and Westbury Ltd, J.Y.W. House, Bridge Road, Haywards Heath, Sussex (for rushes and loom cord)

The Weaver's Journal, c/o Federation of British Crafts Societies, 80A Southampton Row, London WC1B 4BA (for information and suppliers)

T. J. Willcocks, Wheatcroft, Itchingfield, Horsham, Sussex (for wool carders and spinning machines)

Frank Herring and Sons, 27 High West Street, Dorchester, Dorset (for spinning wheels)

Eliza Leadbeater, Rookery Cottage, Dalefords Lane, Whitegate, Near Northwich, Cheshire (for mordants and dyeing equipment as well as dyes)

Moordown Leather and Crafts, 923 Wimborne Road, Moordown, Bournemouth, Hampshire BH9 2BJ (for leather and leather-working tools)

John P. Milner Ltd, 67 Queen Street, Hitchin, Hertfordshire (for leather and tools)

Tiranti, Sculptors' Tools & Materials, 21 Goodge Place, London W1 (for all stone masonry tools, as well as clay)

Macready's Metal Co Ltd, Usaspead Corner, 131 Pentonville Road, London N1 (for steel)

Buck and Ryan Ltd, 101 Tottenham Court Road, London W1 (for metal-working tools)

General Woodworking Supplies, 76/80 Stoke Newington High Street, London N16 (for wide range of British and imported woods)

World of Wood, Industrial Estate, Mildenhall, Suffolk (for wood and all things to do with wood)

Wood Components Ltd, Newburn Bridge Road, Ryton Industrial Estate, Blaydon-on-Tyne, Co. Durham NE21 4TB (suppliers of wood for turning)

R. J. Woodley, The Falls, Exeter Road, Newton Poppleford, Devon (for kick-wheels)

Useful Reading

General

Self-Sufficiency
John and Sally Seymour/Faber

The Fat of the Land
John Seymour/Faber

Food from the Fields

Elements of Agriculture
W. Fream/John Murray

Organic Farming
Hugh Chorley/Faber

Fertility without Fertilisers
Lawrence D. Hills/Henry Doubleday
Association, Bocking, Braintree, Essex

The Horse in the Furrow
George Ewart Evans/Faber

Old Farm Implements
Philip A. Wright/David & Charles

Breadmaking: its Principles and Practice
Edmund B. Bennian/OUP

*Tritton's Guide to Better Wine and Beer Making
for Beginners*
S. M. Tritton/Faber

Food from Animals

The Backyard Dairy Book
Len Street and Andrew Singer/Whole Earth
Tools, Mill Cottage, Swaffham Road,
Cambridge

The Story of Cheese-making in Britain
Val Cheke/Routledge & Kegan Paul

Goat Husbandry
David Mackenzie/Faber

Keeping Pigs
C. Chappell/Hart-Davis

Butchering, Processing and Preservation of Meat
Frank Ashbrook/Van Nostrand Reinhold

Natural Poultry Keeping
Jim Worthington/Crosby Lockwood

The World of Bees
Murray Hoyt/Bodley Head

Food from the Garden

The Complete Vegetable Grower
W. E. Shewell-Cooper/Faber

Grow your own Fruit and Vegetables
Lawrence D. Hills/Faber

Pictorial Gardening
Collingridge Books

The Vegetable Garden Displayed
Royal Horticultural Society

The Fruit Garden Displayed
Royal Horticultural Society

The Living Soil
Lady Eve Balfour/Faber

Compost: for Garden Plot or 1,000 acre Farm
F. H. Billington & Ben Casey/Faber

Grow it!
Richard Langer/Equinox Books

The Herbalist
Joseph E. Meyer/The Oak Tree Press

Herb Gardening
Clare Loewenfeld/Faber

The Complete Book of the Greenhouse
Ian G. Walls/Ward Lock

Putting Food By
Stephen Greene Press, Battleboro,
Vermont, USA

Amateur Wine Making
S. M. Tritton/Faber

Food from the Wild

Food for Free
Richard Mabey/Collins

Pocket Guide to the Sea Shore
John Barrett & C. M. Yonge/Collins

Seaweeds and their Use
V. J. Chapman/Methuen

Edible Wild Plants
Oliver Perry Medsger/Macmillan

How to Enjoy your Weeds
Audrey Wynne Hatfield/Muller

Natural Energy

Energy Primer: Solar, Water, Wind and Bio-Fuels
Portola Institute, 540 Santa Cruz Avenue,
Menlo Park, Ca. 94025, USA

*Radical Technology: Food, Shelter, Tools,
Materials, Energy, Communication,
Autonomy, Community*
ed. Godfrey Boyle and Peter Harper/
Wildwood House

Keeping Warm at Half the Cost
Colesby and Townsend/Prism Press and CTT
Series, Stable Court, Chalmington, Dorchester,
Dorset

*Low Cost Development of Small Water
Power Sites*
Hans W. Hamm/Volunteers in Technical
Assistance, 3706 Rhode Island Avenue, Mt
Rainier, Maryland 20822, USA

Direct Use of the Sun's Energy
Farrington Daniels/Ballantine Books

*Simplified Wind Power Systems for
Experimenters*
Jack Park/Helion, Box 4301, Sylamar,
Ca. 91342 USA

The Generation of Electricity by Windpower
E. W. Golding/E. & F. N. Spon Ltd (out of
print, but the classic work on the subject)

The Dutch Windmill
Frederich Stokhuysen/Merlin Press

*Practical Building of Methane Power Plants for
Rural Energy Independence*
L. John Fry, D. A. Knox, Andover, Hants.

Methane: Planning a Digester
Peter-John Meynell/Prism Press and CTT
Series, Stable Court, Chalmington,
Dorchester, Dorset

Crafts & Skills

Country Crafts Today
J. E. Manners/David & Charles

Studio Vista Guide to Craft Supplies
Judy Allen/Studio Vista

The Craft Business
Rosemary Pettit/Pitman

Country Bazaar
A. Pittaway and B. Scofield/Collins

Baskets and Basketry
Dorothy Wright/Batsford

A Potter's Book
Bernard Leach/Faber

Spin your own Wool, Dye it and Weave it
Molly Duncan/Bell

Index

Index

Index

Acknowledgments

I would like to thank the many people who have helped me with information and advice, particularly Sally Seymour without whom this book would never have been written. The students on my farm, Fachongle Isaf, also assisted in many ways, especially Oliver Harding and David Lee who helped with drawings and diagrams.
John Seymour

Dorling Kindersley Limited would also like to express their gratitude to Sally Seymour and the many people associated with Fachongle Isaf. In addition they would like to thank the following for their special contributions to the book:
Susan Campbell
Peter Fraenkel
John Walters
Mr Woodsford of W. Fenn Ltd.
Cleals of Fishguard
Peter Minter of Bulmer Brick & Tile Co.
Mr Fred Patton of Cummins Farm, Aldham
Rachel Scott
Fred'k Ford
Ramona Ann Gale

John Norris Wood
Richard Kindersley
Barbara Fraser
Michael Thompson and the staff of Photoprint Plates
Barry Steggle, John Rule, Murray Wallis and the staff of Diagraphic

Artists
Dorling Kindersley Limited would especially like to thank Eric Thomas, Jim Robins, Robert Micklewright and David Ashby for their major contributions to the illustrations in this book.
David Ashby
Norman Barber
Helen Cowcher
Michael Craig
Brian Craker

Roy Grubb
Richard Jacobs
Ivan Lapper
Richard Lewis
Robert Micklewright
Dave Nash
Richard Orr
Osborne/Marks
QED
Christine Robins
Jim Robins
Rodney Shackell
Kathleen Smith
Eric Thomas
Harry Titcombe
Justin Todd
Roger Twinn
Ann Winterbotham
Elsie Wrigley